UNDERSTANDING PAUL'S ETHICS

Understanding Paul's Ethics

TWENTIETH CENTURY APPROACHES

Edited by

Brian S. Rosner

WILLIAM B. EERDMANS PUBLISHING COMPANY
GRAND RAPIDS, MICHIGAN

THE PATERNOSTER PRESS
CARLISLE

© 1995 Wm. B. Eerdmans Publishing Co.
255 Jefferson Ave. S.E., Grand Rapids, Michigan 49503

First published 1995 jointly
in the United States by
Wm. B. Eerdmans Publishing Company
and in the U. K. by
The Paternoster Press,
P.O. Box 300, Carlisle, Cumbria CA3 0QS

Printed in the United States of America

00 99 98 97 96 95   7 6 5 4 3 2 1

Library of Congress Cataloging-in-Publication Data

Understanding Paul's ethics: twentieth century approaches /
edited by Brian S. Rosner.
p.   cm.
Collection of 14 articles, previously published, 1903-1992.
Includes bibliographical references and indexes.
ISBN 0-8028-0749-6 (pbk. : alk. paper)
1. Paul, the Apostle, Saint—Ethics.   2. Bible. N.T. Epistles of Paul—Theology.
3. Christian ethics—Biblical teaching.   I. Rosner, Brian S.
BS2655.E8U53   1995
241'.0412'092—dc20   95-4623
                                                CIP

British Library Cataloguing in Publication Data

Understanding Paul's Ethics:
Twentieth-century Approaches
I. Rosner, Brian S.
227.06
ISBN 0-85364-618-X

Contents

III. THE SOCIAL DIMENSION OF PAULINE ETHICS
The Contribution of the Social Sciences

IV. THE SHAPE OF PAULINE ETHICS
Catechisms, Catalogues and Codes

V. THE LOGIC OF PAULINE ETHICS
Indicative and Imperative

VI. THE FOUNDATIONS OF PAULINE ETHICS
Motivations, Norms and Criteria

VII. The Relevance of Pauline Ethics
All You Need is Love?

CONCLUSION

Contributors

1. ADOLF VON HARNACK (1851-1930) taught at Leipzig, Giessen, Marburg and Berlin. He was a prolific author, most notably in the field of early church history and the development of doctrine.

2. TRAUGOTT HOLTZ was Professor of New Testament at Griefswald (1964-70) and Halle (1971-93), and is currently Professor in Mainz. His major essays on Paul are collected in *Geschichte und Theologie des Urchristentums: Gesammelte Aufsätze* (1991). In 1986 his commentary on 1 Thessalonians in the *EKK* series appeared.

3. EDWIN A. JUDGE is Emeritus Professor of Ancient History at Macquarie University, having held the chair from 1969. His monograph, *The Social Pattern of Christian Groups in the First Century*, appeared in 1960. As Director of the Ancient History Documentary Research Centre he fostered the series *New Documents Illustrating Early Christianity*.

4. BRUCE W. WINTER is the Warden of Tyndale House, Cambridge and the Director of the Institute for Early Christianity in the Graeco-Roman world. He is the series editor of the six volume work, *The Book of Acts in its First Century Setting*. His monograph *Seek the Welfare of the City: Early Christians as Benefactors and Citizens* appeared in 1994.

5. GERD THEISSEN is Professor of New Testament at Heidelberg. Among his publications in English are *The Social Setting of Pauline Christianity* (1982), *Psychological Aspects of Pauline Theology* (1987) and *Social Reality and the Early Christians* (1993).

6. GERALD HARRIS is Professor of Theological Studies and Ministry at Lexington Theological Seminary, Kentucky, USA.

7. ALFRED SEEBERG (1863-1915) taught at Dorpat, Rostock and Kiel. His major publications with relevance to Paul's ethics included *Der Katechismus der Urchristenheit* (1903), *Die beiden Wege und das Aposteldekret* (1906) and *Die Didache des Judentums und der Urchristenheit* (1908).

8. LARS HARTMAN is Professor of New Testament and taught at Uppsala University. Currently he is Director of the Research Institute of the Swedish State Church. Among his publications is a commentary on Colossians in the *KNT* series (1985).

9. RUDOLF BULTMANN (1884-1976) was Professor at Marburg from 1921 until his retirement in 1951. His many publications include *Theology of the New Testament*, which has a major section on Paul.

10. MICHAEL PARSONS taught at London Bible College and is currently a PhD student at the University of Wales.

11. EDUARD LOHSE is a bishop who formerly taught at the University of Göttingen. Among his works in English are *Colossians and Philemon* (1968), *The New Testament Environment* (1976) and *Theological Ethics of the New Testament* (1991).

12. ECKHARD J. SCHNABEL is Lecturer in New Testament, at the Freie theologische Akademie, Giessen. He is the author of *Law and Wisdom from Ben Sira to Paul: A Tradition Historical Enquiry into the Relation of Law, Wisdom and Ethics* (1985).

13. WOLFGANG SCHRAGE has been Professor of New Testament at the University of Bonn since 1964. Among his many publications are a commentary on 1 Corinthians (*EKK*, 1991) and *The Ethics of the New Testament* (1982).

14. RICHARD N. LONGENECKER is Ramsay Armitage Professor of New Testament at Wycliffe College, University of Toronto. His works on Paul include *Paul: Apostle of Liberty* (1964), *The Ministry and Message of Paul* (1971) and the *Word* commentary on Galatians (1990).

Acknowledgements

The following chapters originally appeared in the publications indicated:

1. "Das Alte Testament in den paulinischen Briefen und in den paulinischen Gemeinden", by Adolf von Harnack, *Sitzungsberichte der Preußischen Akademie der Wissenschaften*, Berlin (1928): 124-41 (= *Kleine Schriften zur alten Kirche*, Vol. 2, Leipzig 1980. pp. 823-41).

2. "Zur Frage der inhaltlichen Weisungen bei Paulus", by Traugott Holtz, *Theologische Literaturzeitung* 106 (1981): 385-400 (= chapter 14 in *Geschichte und Theologie des Urchristentums: Gesammelte Aufsätze*. Edited by Eckart Reinmuth and Christian Wolff. Tübingen: J.C.B. Mohr [Paul Siebeck], 1991. pp. 205-22).

3. "Interpreting New Testament Ideas", by Edwin A. Judge. In *The Social Pattern of Christian Groups in the First Century: Some Prolegomena to the Study of New Testament Ideas of Social Obligation*. London: The Tyndale Press, 1960. Pp. 7-17.

4. "Civil Litigation in Secular Corinth and the Church: The Forensic Background to 1 Corinthians 6.1-8", by Bruce W. Winter, *New Testament Studies* 37/4 (1991): 559-72 (with a concluding response to A.J. Mitchell, *NTS* 39 [1993]: 562-68).

5. "The Strong and the Weak in Corinth: A Sociological Analysis of a Theological Quarrel", by Gerd Theissen. In *The Social Setting of Pauline Christianity: Essays on Corinth* (Trans. John H. Schütz. Edinburgh: T. & T. Clark, 1982. pp. 121-43). Originally "Die Starken und Schwachen in Korinth: Soziologische Analyse eines theologischen Streites", *Evangelische Theologie* 35 (1975): 155-72.

6. "The Beginnings of Church Discipline: 1 Corinthians 5", by Gerald Harris, *New Testament Studies* 37/1 (1991): 1-21.

7. "Die Sittenlehre: Die Existenz und der Inhalt 'der Wege'", by Alfred Seeberg, Part One, chapters one and two, in *Der Katechismus der Urchristenheit*. München: Chr. Kaiser Verlag, 1966. pp. 1-22 (orig. 1903).

8. "Code and Context: A Few Reflections on the Parenesis of Col 3:6-4:1", by Lars Hartman. In *Tradition and Interpretation in the New Testament: Essays in Honor of E. Earle Ellis for His 60th Birthday*. Edited by G. F. Hawthorne with O. Betz. Tübingen: J.C.B. Mohr [Paul Siebeck] / Grand Rapids: Eerdmans, 1987. pp. 237-47.

9. "Das Problem der Ethik bei Paulus", by Rudolf Bultmann, *Zeitschrift für die Neutestamentliche Wissenschaft und die Kunde der älteren Kirche* 23 (1924): 123-40 (Reprinted in *Exegetica*. Tübingen: J.C.B. Mohr [Paul Siebeck], 1967. pp. 36-54).

10. "Being Precedes Act: Indicative and Imperative in Paul's Writing", by Michael Parsons, *The Evangelical Quarterly* 88/2 (1988): 99-127.

11. "Kirche im Alltag: Erwägungen zur theologischen Begründung der Ethik im Neuen Testament", by Eduard Lohse. In *Kirche: Festschrift für Günther Bornkamm zum 75. Geburtstag*. Edited by Dieter Lührmann and Georg Strecker. Tübingen: J.C.B. Mohr [Paul Siebeck], 1980. pp. 401-14 (= *Die Vielfalt des Neuen Testaments: Exegetische Studien zur Theologie des Neuen Testaments* [Göttingen: Vandenhoeck & Ruprecht, 1982], pp. 187-200).

12. "Wie hat Paulus seine Ethik entwickelt? Motivationen, Normen und Kriterien paulinischer Ethik", by E.J. Schnabel, *The European Journal of Theology* 1/1 (1992): 63-81.

13. "Zur formalethischen Deutung der paulinischen Paränese", by Wolfgang Schrage, *Zeitschrift für evangelische Ethik* 4 (1960): 207-33.

14. *New Testament Social Ethics for Today*, by Richard N. Longenecker, Grand Rapids, Michigan: Eerdmans, 1984. pp. 1-15.

Preface

In a project such as this one many people have played a part. Thanks are due to the living authors and to the original publishers of the essays for their permission to re-publish and where necessary translate their contributions to the volume. On the subject of translation, Dr. Eckhard Schnabel kindly agreed to translate his own essay. Christoph Stenschke, a German post-graduate student at Aberdeen University, translated the chapters by Seeberg and Bultmann with characteristic enthusiasm and care. My father and I undertook the other four translations. It is 57 years since he left Austria, yet the only German words he needed to look up in a dictionary were those that did not find an entry there. Professor Howard Marshall made perceptive comments on my introductory and concluding essays. Dr. Randal Massot bravely took on the onerous task of producing camera-ready copy. Dr. Bruce Winter and Dr. Andrew Clarke of Tyndale House gave helpful advice on aspects of the book's production. Anthony Myrick and Andrew Warren produced the indexes. My wife Leanne provided invaluable assistance at virtually every stage. I am grateful to all of these people. The book is dedicated to my Cambridge PhD supervisor Dr. William Horbury, who, among other things, taught me the value of the history of scholarship. It has been produced in the hope that it will make a small contribution to the understanding of Paul's ethics and with the conviction that beyond understanding Paul's ethics calls for obedience. Concerning his instructions to the churches Paul could say: "what I am writing to you is a command of the Lord."

BRIAN S. ROSNER

INTRODUCTION

"That Pattern of Teaching"
Issues and Essays in Pauline Ethics

Brian S. Rosner

The subject of Paul's ethics is of vital importance to understanding Paul and his letters. On any count practical teaching takes up a large proportion of every one of Paul's letters. After all, the central concern of Paul was not just to affect the thinking of the first Christian churches, but to transform their behaviour. Yet by comparison with some other subjects Paul's ethics has been somewhat neglected by New Testament scholarship. For example, Hans Hübner's wide ranging review of books and articles in Pauline studies, which runs to over 160 pages,[1] and accurately presents the field, devotes only a six page excursus to it. By this indication Paul's ethics is something worth touching upon, but it is hardly of central interest. By contrast, the research on one phrase from Paul's doctrine ("the righteousness of God") takes fully 15 pages to report. The histories of research of

---

[1] Hübner, "Paulusforschung seit 1945. Ein kritischer Literaturbericht", *ANRW* II 25.4 (Berlin/New York: Walter de Gruyter, 1987): 2649-2840.

Neill and Wright and of Kümmel likewise give Paul's ethics little attention.[2]

We can only speculate as to the reasons for this neglect. Perhaps the battles surrounding Paul's doctrine have been more intense and thus work has been concentrated on such fundamentals as the doctrine of God, Christology, Scripture and justification, rather than ethics. One could argue that questions of conduct have enjoyed a broad consensus in the past, though, of course, this could not be said in today's world. Certainly it would be true to say that biblical scholarship and theology in general are more interested in orthodoxy than in orthopraxy.

Nonetheless this book intends to show that Paul's ethics is one of the most fascinating and challenging areas in Biblical studies and one which goes to the very heart of Christian faith and practice. To introduce the study of Paul's ethics we shall ask seven questions which correspond to the seven parts of the book. These concern the *origin, context, social dimension, shape, logic, foundations,* and *relevance* of Paul's ethics. The seven questions are seven angles, seven ways into the subject, seven tasks to perform on any given paragraph or topic, seven ways of research. Our concern is to get the tasks of the study of Paul's ethics into proper relation to one another in order to aid better understanding and more incisive enquiry into the subject.

Paul's ethics is too vast a subject to be covered comprehensively in fourteen essays. Our goal is more modest. This collection of essays aims to present a balanced overview of major problems and various approaches to them. Some of the essays may truly be described as classic. Others were chosen because of their representative or seminal quality or due to their broad coverage or the cogency of their argument. In parts one and six the essays present opposing views. Most of the other parts contain an early ground-breaking contribution which is followed by a more specific investigation or a survey which brings the discussion up to date. The

---

2 Stephen Neill and Tom Wright, *The Interpretation of the New Testament 1861-1986.* 2nd Edn. (Oxford: University Press, 1988); Werner Georg Kümmel, *Das Neue Testament: Geschichte der Erforschung seiner Probleme* (Freiburg/München: Karl Alber, 1958). Watson E. Mills, *An Index to Periodical Literature in the Apostle Paul* (Leiden: E.J. Brill, 1993), includes a specific entry on ethics which covers 5 pages in a volume of over 300 pages (admittedly other literature may turn up under the entries for individual epistles). English speaking scholars have been more a party to this relative neglect than their German speaking colleagues. Full-scale studies of New Testament and Pauline ethics are far more common in German than in English.

fourteen essays cover the study of Paul's ethics in this century. Harnack (1928), Seeberg (1903) and Bultmann (1924) represent ground breaking studies in three of the subject areas. Judge (1960) and Theissen (1975) are two of the earliest examples of their respective approaches, and the essays in parts six and seven report and reflect work from across the century. We shall endeavour to clarify, reinforce and supplement the essays where appropriate in this introductory essay. To sum up, a concluding essay asks the seven questions of a case study in Paul's ethics, 1 Thessalonians 4:1-12.

It is hoped that the book will be of value not only to scholars of Pauline ethics, but also to students in courses on New Testament ethics and anyone interested in investigating the subject. *Suggestions for Further Study* are included to enhance its usefulness as a text book. These could be used for lecture/seminar topics or as assignments. It is not a book of quick and easy answers. Rather, it is as an introduction which celebrates the richness and importance of its subject matter, is concerned to sketch some of the history of scholarship, ask the main questions and point in the right direction for the answers. It aims to stimulate further enquiry and, indeed, more informed application of Paul's moral teaching.

Several of the essays cover the same passages in Paul's letters but with different questions in mind (in the case of chapters 1 and 2 similar questions are asked but different answers given). Readers will soon note the prominence of passages from 1 Corinthians 5-7, Romans 12 and 13, and Galatians 5 and 6, for instance. Certainly a mastery of Paul's ethics depends largely upon a close familiarity with such texts. Ideally, readers would do well to have studied these texts prior to reading the essays.

Two terms call for some definition: Paul and ethics. The dispute over Paul does not concern his identity but the identification of his letters. The authorship of certain letters in the New Testament which bear Paul's name continues to be debated. Thus it is common for studies of Paul's theology or ethics to include only the seven virtually undisputed letters (Rom, 1 and 2 Cor, Gal, Phil, 1 Thess, Philemon) or to exclude the Pastoral Epistles. The present volume takes no account of the ethics of 1 and 2 Timothy and Titus[3] not because the editor considers them not to have been written by Paul, but because

---

3 On the ethics of the Pastorals see *inter alia* Philip H. Towner, *The Goal of Our Instruction: The Structure of Theology and Ethics in the Pastoral Epistles*. JSNT 34 (Sheffield: JSOT Press, 1989).

the other Pauline letters provide sufficient material with which to work and in order to engage a wide audience. A thorough study of Paul's ethics, to which this collection of essays is really just prolegomena, would obviously take full account of all of Paul's letters.

To speak of "ethics" in the case of Paul is to invite the objection that such a focus is arbitrary, artificial and anachronistic. What do we mean by "ethics" in such a context? We do not have in mind Paul's opinions about in vitro fertilisation, organ transplantation, animal rights and the nuclear debate, the way the term is sometimes understood in moral theology and philosophy.[4] Rather, we are simply thinking of the dogmatic distinction between doctrine, what Christians believe, and ethics, how Christians behave. It is true that no Greek word from the New Testament captures this sense of ethics = moral teaching, as we are using it. There are words that denote basic instruction,[5] but these incorporate not only piety and practice but also the content of the faith. But while a sharp distinction between doctrine and ethics cannot be based on lexical grounds, several factors suggest that is not entirely illegitimate to concentrate our attention on the question of conduct in Paul's thought. Some of Paul's letters exhibit a basically two fold structure (eg., Rom and Gal), the first predominantly pertaining to matters of belief, the second primarily to Christian conduct. Though related for Paul, doctrine and ethics are not inseparable. Furthermore, in the first century there was a widespread Jewish concern with the interpretation of the Pentateuch, including legal decisions on conduct according to the Law. This points to an interest in the broad category of moral teaching in Paul's day as a distinct concern.

When we speak of Paul's ethics we simply have in mind "his ways which are in Christ" (1 Cor 4:17); his "instruction as to how one ought to walk and please God" (1 Thess 4:1); "that pattern of teaching"[6] to which he committed the early Christians (Rom 6:17).

---

[4] For introductions to Christian ethics in historical and systematic perspective respectively see Robin Gill, *A Textbook of Christian Ethics* (Edinburgh: T. & T. Clark, 1985); and Arthur F. Holmes, *Ethics: Approaching Moral Decisions* (Downers Grove/Leicester: IVP, 1984).

[5] On these terms see James I.H. McDonald, *Kerygma and Didache: The Articulation and Structure of the Earliest Christian Message* (Cambridge: CUP, 1980).

[6] There is some doubt as to the interpretation of this phrase, particularly whether Paul has his "practical teaching" in mind. See the opening pages of Seeberg's essay (ch. 7) for a discussion of its exegesis, which supports the view assumed here.

I. THE ORIGIN OF PAULINE ETHICS

What is the **origin** of Paul's ethics? In other words, in what tradition does Paul stand when he regulates conduct in the churches? To what extent does he depend upon the Jewish Scriptures (the Old Testament[7])? Does his counsel bear a close resemblance to early Jewish moral teaching which built upon the exhortations of Scripture? Or did Paul simply jettison his Jewish inheritance when he became a Christian apostle? These questions have far-reaching implications, not least of which concerns the ethical use of the Old Testament today. If Paul did not consult Scripture on practical matters, why should we? Many ethical issues are today decided by Christians on purely Old Testament grounds. However, these questions have received markedly different answers.

Representing the view which contends that Paul's Scriptural inheritance did not play an important role in the formation of his ethics is the 1928 essay of *Adolf von Harnack* (chapter one), "The Old Testament in the Pauline Letters and in the Pauline Churches". Harnack is adamant that "from the beginning Paul did not give the Old Testament to the young churches as the book of Christian sources for edification." Finding an article to state this position

---

7 Although scholars are divided on the question of whether the "Jewish Scriptures" in New Testament times comprised those books currently printed in the Hebrew Bible, ie., the Old Testament, there is good evidence that the Old Testament canon was effectively closed before the New Testament was written. (Some argue for a three-stage canonization theory [the Law, c. 400 B.C.; the Prophets, c. 200 B.C.; and the hagiographa, c. 90 A.D. at Jabneh {Jamnia}]; see *inter alia* A.C. Sundberg, *The Old Testament and the Early Church* [London, 1964]; and J. Barton, *The Oracles of God* [London: Darton, Longman and Todd, 1986] who believes that the Prophets were also unsettled in NT times.) The notion of a certain number of books forming a fixed collection at an early date is supported, in particular, by Josephus' *Against Apion* 1:38-42 and 2 Esdras (= 4 Ezra) 14:44-46. See E. Earle Ellis, "The Old Testament Canon in the Early Church", *Mikra: Text, Translation, Reading and Interpretation of the Hebrew Bible in Ancient Judaism and Early Christianity*, ed. M. Mulder (Assen: Van Gorcum, 1988), pp. 653-90 = Ch. One of *The Old Testament in Early Christianity: Canon and Interpretation in the Light of Modern Research*, WUNT 54 (Tübingen: J.C.B. Mohr [Paul Siebeck], 1991); and especially R.T. Beckwith, *The Old Testament Canon of the New Testament Church and its Background in Early Judaism* (Reading: SPCK, 1985) for a full and convincing treatment. Barton reviews Beckwith in *Theology* 90 (1987), pp. 63-65, labelling it an "apologetic for fundamentalism." Beckwith returns the compliment in *VT* 41/4 (1991), pp. 385-95. His criticisms are more substantive, concluding that Barton "misrepresents part of the evidence and fails to do justice to the rest of it" (p. 395).

presents no difficulty. Up to the present day scholars express the same opinion. In recent years two essays did much the same job as Harnack in surveying Paul's practical teaching and concluded as follows:

> Paul understands the Old Testament, his Bible, no longer as Torah in the proper sense; it is no longer the source of the instruction of God for the conduct of people in so far as they are Christians. (Andreas Lindemann, 1986).[8]

> The Mosaic Law played no constructive role in his [ie., Paul's] ethics. (R.G. Hamerton-Kelly, 1990).[9]

Although this is a broad and diverse tradition of Pauline interpretation, and no single figure or movement represents its root, Adolf von Harnack probably exercised the greatest single influence upon it through his forcibly written essay. Harnack's case contains few subtleties and is easily summarised. With an impressive survey of Paul's letters he looks for indications that Paul has based his practical teaching on the Old Testament, but finds none. Out of the ten letters he investigates six are virtually clear of Old Testament quotations, and special circumstances explain the appearance of such quotations in the other four letters. On the other hand, he finds ample evidence that the gospel and the Spirit form the true basis for Paul's ethics.

Two factors help explain Harnack's position. The first is the influence of Marcion, who is sympathetically referred to on several occasions in the essay. Marcion, whose name is synonymous with an outright rejection of the Old Testament, was a second century figure who argued that the God of the Old Testament is in fact a different God from the God of the New Testament. Harnack had written the definitive work on Marcion in his day.[10] In that volume he wrote:

> To reject the Old Testament in the second century was a mistake which the church rightly repudiated; to retain it in the sixteenth century was a fate which the Reformation could not

---

[8] Lindemann, "Die biblischen Toragebote und die Paulinischen Ethik", in *Studien zum Text und der Ethik des Neuen Testaments: Festschrift zum 80. Geburtstag von Heinrich Greeven*. Edited by Wolfgang Schrage (Berlin: Walter de Gruyter, 1986), p. 263.

[9] Hamerton-Kelly, "Sacred violence and 'works of the law'. Is Christ then an Agent of Sin? (Galatians 2:17)", *CBQ* 52/1 (1990): 74.

[10] *Marcion* (Leipzig: J.C. Hinrichs, 1921).

yet avoid; but to continue to keep it in Protestantism as a canonical document after the nineteenth century is the consequence of religious and ecclesiastical paralysis.[11]

That Marcion influenced Harnack is clear, not in terms of his overall scheme, but certainly in his general attitude to the irrelevence of the Old Testament to Paul's gospel in its truest form.

The second factor is a phrase that occurs frequently in the essay, namely, the Lutheran theological construction, law and gospel. This category expresses the heart of the issue for Harnack. Paul, he reasons, bases his moral exhortation on the gracious acts of God, the gospel, not on the works which humanity performs, the law. The law for Harnack is virtually synonymous with the Old Testament. For Harnack the many "Christian" motives Paul employs ("your bodies are members of Christ"; "you were bought with a price"; etc) demonstrate Paul's reliance on the gospel. As is often the case, a theological perspective seems to have played a part in the interpretation of the evidence.

On the other hand there are those, including the author of this essay and the author of chapter two, "The Question of the Content of Paul's Instructions", *Traugott Holtz*, who would argue that the Scriptures continue to exercise pragmatic/practical/halakhic authority for Paul the Christian apostle. The Pauline law/gospel conflict concerns the issue of salvation and really has nothing to do with ethics. It is simply a misapplication of the category to see it implying a negative verdict on the Old Testament as a whole. When Paul says hard things about the Law of Moses he does not discount the continuing value of its ethical precepts.[12] Christian motives are prominent in Paul, but to interpret these as in opposition to the Scriptures is unwarranted. Many times these motives exhibit the same structure of thought, the movement from the identity of the people of God to their obligations as the people of God, as we find throughout the Old Testament, except with a new, but nevertheless

---

11 Ibid, p. 127; cf. Hemchand Gossai, "The Old Testament among Christian Theologians", 22-25 *Bible Review* Feb (1990): 122-25, 36. It is not entirely clear whether Harnack was aware of the possible impact of his words in a time of growing anti-semitism. Regrettably several remarks in the essay could easily have been seized upon by those seeking to persecute Jews. Harnack's views were, if not anti-Jewish, anti-Old Testament, at the very least in the sense that he saw the Old Testament as representing an inferior faith to Christianity.

12 See 1 Cor 4:6; 9:10; 10:6,11; 14:34; Rom 7:12; 15:4, where Paul confesses his profound dependence upon the Scriptures for ethics.

analogous, content in the light of the coming of Jesus Christ (see part five on the logic of Paul's ethics).

Harnack forces us to consider this question: if Paul depends upon the Scriptures for ethics why does he not quote Scripture more often in parænetic contexts? It is of course a matter of judgement as to how often is often. Koch, Ellis and Verhey claim that the occasions where Paul does quote Scripture to express or support a moral admonition represent a major element in his use of Scripture and are not easily ignored.[13] Either way, it is a fallacy to consider that simply by counting quotations one can gauge the influence of Scripture upon Paul's teaching. Quotations are only the most explicit measure of dependence. The genre of ethical instruction does not in fact encourage explicit citation of Scripture. In fact it was common in Paul's day for such texts to use Scripture broadly without employing many quotations. Most Jewish moral teaching of the first century or earlier fits this pattern. Paul quotes Scripture most often when in argument with his opponents over the meaning of Scripture, on issues such as the inclusion of the Gentiles, the place and purpose of the Law, the election of Israel and Christology,[14] not, it is true, in ethical contexts.

To answer Harnack on a specific example, the major lines of Paul's ethics in 1 Corinthians 5-7, a passage he describes as having hardly any links with the Old Testament (presumably because there is only one explicit citation), can be reliably traced back into the Scriptures, in many cases by way of Jewish sources.[15] In 1 Corinthians 5 a case of incest is condemned and discipline employed because of the teaching of pentateuchal covenant and temple exclusion.[16] In 6:1-11 going to court before unbelievers is prohibited with the Scriptures' teaching on judges in mind.[17] In 6:12-20 going to

---

[13] Dietrich-Alex Koch, *Die Schrift als Zeuge des Evangeliums: Untersuchungen zur Verwendung und zum Verständnis der Schrift bei Paulus.* BHT 69. (Tübingen: J.C.B. Mohr [Paul Siebeck], 1986), pp. 296-98; E. Earle Ellis, *Paul's Use of the Old Testament* (Grand Rapids: Eerdmans, 1957), p. 125; Allen Verhey, *The Great Reversal: Ethics and the New Testament* (Grand Rapids: Eerdmans, 1984), p. 110. Examples in 1 Cor alone include Jer 9:23-24 in 1:31; Deut 17:7, etc in 5:13; Gen 2:24 in 6:16; Deut 25:4 in 9:9 and Psalm 24:1 in 10:26.

[14] See Koch, *Die Schrift*, pp. 257ff.

[15] See Brian S. Rosner, *Paul, Scripture and Ethics: A Study of 1 Corinthians 5-7,* AGAJU (Leiden: E.J. Brill, 1994).

[16] See Brian S. Rosner, "Temple and Holiness in 1 Corinthians 5", *Tyndale Bulletin* 42.1 (1991): 137-45; and "Corporate Responsibility in 1 Corinthians 5", *NTS* 38/3 (1992): 470-73.

[17] Brian S. Rosner, "Moses Appointing Judges: An Antecedent to 1 Cor 6:1-6?", *ZNW* 82.3/4 (1991): 275-78.

prostitutes is opposed using the Scriptural doctrine of the Lord as the believer's husband and master, and with advice which recalls early Jewish interpretation of the Genesis 39 story of Joseph fleeing Potiphar's wife.[18] And in 7:1-40 several key texts from the Torah (as understood by much early Jewish interpretation) inform what is said about marriage.

The importance of Jewish interpretation of the Torah for understanding Paul's ethics is a major point of Traugott Holtz's essay. Holtz surveys much of the same material from Paul's letters as Harnack does but reaches the opposite conclusion, finding significant indebtedness to Scripture. A key plank in Holtz's argument is the close connection he posits between Jewish moral teaching of Paul's day and the Torah.[19] We see this most clearly when the instruction concerning head covering in 1 Corinthians 11:3-16 is discussed. Holtz contends that Paul fights for compliance with this Jewish custom because "to him this observance was, naturally, the same as all prescriptions of Judaism, *in accordance with Torah*" (emphasis added). With this perfectly plausible supposition (that Paul knew such Jewish teaching is beyond doubt[20]) in place Holtz is able to recognise the Biblical/Jewish nature of much of Paul's practical teaching.[21]

The other crucial feature of Holtz's discussion is his contention that the arguments Paul advances in favour of a particular moral admonition do not necessarily reveal its ultimate source. Holtz asks: "Where the content of a firmly delineated material instruction of the apostle is not necessarily derived from the arguments which are quoted, from what source does this material derive?" His answer is that most often it comes from Torah as understood by early Jewish interpretation.

We may illustrate the point that Paul's failure to cite a Biblical command does not necessarily indicate the irrelevance of the Bible to

---

18 Brian S. Rosner, "A Possible Quotation of Test. Reuben 5:5 in 1 Corinthians 6:18a", *The Journal of Theological Studies* 43/1 (1992): 123-27.

19 Karl-Wilhelm Niebuhr, *Gesetz und Paränese: Katechismusartige Weisungsreihen in der früjüdischen Literatur.* WUNT 28 (Tübingen: J.C.B. Mohr [Paul Siebeck], 1987), originally a dissertation completed under Holtz's supervision, has shown that the traditional stereotypical form of early hellenistic Jewish paraenesis was shaped largely by the Torah. Niebuhr traces the formative influence of Exod 20-23, Lev 18-20 and Deut 27 upon texts from Josephus, Philo, the Apocrypha and the Old Testament Pseudepigrapha.

20 See M. Hengel, *The Pre-Christian Paul* (London: SCM, 1991).

21 For further explanation see Rosner, *Paul, Scripture and Ethics*, ch 2: "Indirect Dependence: Scriptural Influence Through Jewish Moral Teaching".

the matters at hand. A passenger who wants to convince the driver of a car that he or she is going too fast may summon various proofs: safety, road conditions, expensive fines, no need to hurry, and so on. However, the use of such proofs does not necessarily betray a lack of interest in or allegiance to the law against speeding. In similar fashion many of Paul's proofs stress the severity and weight of a particular action and presuppose that it is sin. A clear example is 1 Corinthians 6:12-20, which Holtz discusses at some length.[22]

Are the Scriptures and Jewish sources then the proper place to look for the origin of Paul's ethics? Harnack and Holtz provide a way into this debate. We will see that one's answer to this question has implications for other aspects of the study of Paul's ethics. For my part, the Biblical/Jewish origin of Paul's ethics is crucial to assessing its shape, logic and foundations and to recognising its continuing relevance.

II. THE CONTEXT OF PAULINE ETHICS

A second question to ask of Paul's ethics concerns its **context**, specifically, *Social Conditions in the Græco-Roman World*. Just as Biblical/Jewish background is vital to understanding Paul, so also is an acquaintance with Græco-Roman background to understanding the situations into which Paul directed his instructions. So we move from, we might say, background to foreground; from the derivation to the direction of Paul's teaching.

The title of part two shares the word "social" with the title of part three, *The Social Dimension of Pauline Ethics - The Contribution of the Social Sciences*. There is indeed some overlap between the concerns of parts two and three. They are both interested in the question, "what are the social facts of life characteristic of the world to which the New Testament belongs?"[23] They are both committed to the study of Paul's ethics not just as a history of ideas, but as a history of communities.[24] Nonetheless, they may be distinguished as the social

---

[22] A complementary point is that some of Paul's points which are not related to Scripture appear in direct response to arguments which had been used by those to whom he was writing.

[23] E.A. Judge, "The Social Identity of the First Christians: A Question of Method in Religious History", *Journal of Religious History* (1980): 210.

[24] The latter phrase is the words of Wayne A. Meeks, "Understanding Early Christian Ethics", *JBL* 105/1 (1986): p. 3.

history and sociological approaches to the study of early Christianity respectively. The former involves historical-descriptive work; the latter consists of analytical study, utilising sociological models and tools.[25]

A pioneer of the social history approach to New Testament study is ancient historian *Edwin A. Judge*. His 1960 monograph, *The Social Pattern of Christian Groups in the First Century: Some Prolegomena to the Study of New Testament Ideas of Social Obligation*, deserves, according to Gerd Theissen, "a place of honor in the history of modern sociological exegesis."[26] The opening chapter, "Interpreting New Testament Ideas" appears as chapter three in this book. It sets the agenda not only for the subject of the principles of social obligation, but also for a host of other topics relevant to Paul's ethics. As Judge states in the preface (p. iii), his work attempts "to clarify certain early Christian ideas about society by defining the particular social institutions that are presupposed, and showing how the behaviour of the Christians was related to them." He describes his work as "an ancient historian's trespassing on New Testament ground." Whether or not this was a fair assessment in 1960, the social history approach is today widely recognised as having a secure abode in New Testament study. Work which places Paul, his letters and their readers in their literary, cultural and social environment is a growing industry.[27] Judge states elsewhere concerning the presupposition of this work: New Testament scholars ought not to "incestuously concentrate all their time on their few texts, when there is a magnificent array of contextual material all around their texts, increasing rapidly every year."[28] A rich and accessible resource

---

[25] On these distinctions see Andrew D. Clarke, *Secular and Christian Leadership in Corinth: A Socio-Historical and Exegetical Study of 1 Corinthians* 1-6, AGAJU 18 (Leiden: E.J. Brill, 1993), pp. 3-7.

[26] Gerd Theissen, *Social Reality and the Early Christians* (Edinburgh: T. & T. Clark, 1992), p. 19.

[27] For surveys of such work, see E.A. Judge, "St. Paul and Classical Society", JbAC 15 (1972): 19-36; "Antike und Christentum. Towards a Definition of the Field: A Bibliographic Survey", in *Aufstieg und Niedergang der römischen Welt*, vol 2, 23.1. Edited by H. Temporini and W. Haase (Berlin, 1979), pp. 3-58; "Gesellschaft und Christentum; Alte Kirche", in *Theologische Realenzyklopädie* (Berlin and New York, 1984), pp. 764-69; and "Gesellschaft: Neues Testament", in idem, pp. 769-73. Cf. also A.J. Malherbe, *Social Aspects of Early Christianity* (Baton Rouge and London, 1977), pp. 1-59.

[28] A comment published in B.J. Malina, "The Gospel of John in Sociolinguistic Perspective", *Protocol of the Forty-Eighth Colloquy*, Centre for Hermeneutical Studies in Hellenistic and Modern Culture (11 March, 1984), 51 (cited in Clarke,

discussing some of the inscriptions and papyri to which Judge is referring, which originates from the Ancient History Documentary Research Centre at Macquarie University, is the series (presently 6 vols) *New Documents Illustrating Early Christianity*.[29]

Three recent studies on texts in 1 and 2 Corinthians illustrate the importance and potential of this approach. First, Peter Marshall, *Enmity in Corinth: Social Conventions in Paul's Relations with the Corinthians* (WUNT 2.23; Tübingen: J.C.B. Mohr [Paul Siebeck], 1987), seeks to explain various aspects of Paul's relations with the Corinthians in terms of Greek social and cultural conventions of friendship and enmity. Secondly, Andrew D. Clarke, *Secular and Christian Leadership in Corinth: A Socio-Historical and Exegetical Study of 1 Corinthians,* compares secular leadership in first century Corinthian society with leadership in the Corinthian church and concludes that one of Paul's major concerns with the church in Corinth is the extent to which significant members were employing secular categories and perceptions of leadership in the Christian community. Thirdly, *Bruce Winter*'s article, "Civil Litigation in Secular Corinth and the Church: The Forensic Background to 1 Corinthian 6.1-8", which appears as chapter four of this volume, contends that to comprehend fully Paul's instructions to the Corinthian Christians who were fighting lawsuits against one another, it is enlightening, even necessary, to study jury-court practice in ancient Corinth. In each case, Marshall, Clarke and Winter shed considerable light on the social setting of Paul's instructions and churches.

Some knowledge of Græco-Roman ethics contemporary with Paul also sheds light on his instructions.[30] Sometimes Greek and Roman ethics stands in contrast to Paul's ethics. That Paul saw humility as a virtue would have been revolutionary in the world of many of his converts. The Greek words "to abase", "to humble oneself", "humility", and so on are never viewed positively in Greek ethics.[31] Paul valued humility because he served Jesus Christ who humbled himself and took the form of a servant and became obedient

---

5-6).

[29] G.H.R. Horsley, *New Documents* (Sydney: The Ancient History Documentary Research Centre, Macquarie University, 1981-92).

[30] For a handy survey see A. Malherbe, *Moral Exhortations: A Greco-Roman Source Book* (Philadelphia: The Westminster Press, 1986).

[31] Eg. Aristotle argues that what whatever prevents the development of virtue makes the spirit "humble." For Epictetus "humility" is a negative term denoting pettiness and baseness (cf. W. Grundmann, *TDNT*, VIII 1ff).

unto death, and because the God of the Jewish Scriptures humbles the proud and raises the humble. Some aspects of Paul's teaching which appear bland and familiar to us stand out in sharp relief in their original setting.

Sometimes the virtues Paul recommends are consonant with those put forward by the moral philosophers of his day, as in the list in Philippians 4:8-9. Five of the six items in this list are rare in Paul's letters and are not uncommon in Græco-Roman ethics. That Paul says whatever is "worthy of praise," ἔπαινος, may reflect the ethical use of the word and refer to the society's approval of human conduct.[32] Some see Paul appealing here to the Philippians' cultural background, their familiarity with current morality. Paul may be saying, live up to the ideals of your fellow men and women, be a good citizen.[33] The context of Paul's ethics, that is, its setting in the Græco-Roman world, is sometimes critical to accurate interpretation.

III. THE SOCIAL DIMENSION OF PAULINE ETHICS

A third question to ask of Paul's ethics concerns its **social dimension**, which brings into focus the contribution of the social sciences. Much in vogue, this interdisciplinary approach has advocates in every quarter of New Testament studies. When seen as complementing rather than substituting the historical, exegetical and theological methods, the sociological approach has a definite contribution to make.[34]

A chief advocate of the study of the social matrix of the New Testament is *Gerd Theissen*. John H. Schutz, the translator of Theissen's essay on 1 Corinthians 8-10 which appears as chapter five in this volume, "The Strong and the Weak in Corinth: A Sociological Analysis of a Theological Quarrel", accurately describes Theissen's

---

32 Cf. Moises Silva, *Philippians*, WEC (Chicago: Moody Press, 1988), pp. 228ff.

33 Cf. 1:27, which literally says: "live as a citizen"; and 1 Thess 4:12: "Behave decently in the view of outsiders."

34 For discussion and evaluation from a practitioner's viewpoint see Bengt Holmberg, *Sociology and the New Testament* (Minneapolis: Fortress Press, 1990) or Howard Clark Kee, *Knowing the Truth: A Sociological Approach to New Testament Interpretation* (Minneapolis: Fortress Press, 1989). Daniel J. Harrington has provided a helpful bibliography covering approximately twenty years of books and articles in "Sociological Concepts and the Early Church: A Decade of Research", *Theological Studies* 41 (1980): 181-90; and "Second Testament Exegesis and the Social Sciences: A Bibliography", *Biblical Theology Bulletin* 18 (1988): 77-85.

work as "marked by bold hypothesis balanced with exegetical insight
and patience for detail."[35] The main task of "The Strong and the
Weak in Corinth" is to discover the reasons for the opposing
attitudes of Christians in Corinth towards meat sacrificed to idols.
Theissen asks: "Which social factors are responsible for the conflict,
religious traditions (whether of Jewish or gentile groups) which have
shaped behaviour, or class-specific customs and attitudes?"
Theissen's answer, which draws on information from across 1
Corinthians and is well-informed about relevant practices in ancient
Corinth, is a model of sociological enquiry which does not play down
the importance of theological factors.

The essay by *Gerald Harris*, "The Beginnings of Church
Discipline: 1 Corinthians 5" (chapter six), offers a sociological perspective on church disicipline in an early Pauline church, considering
the subjects of deviance, norms and sanctions. Harris is right to point
out that the problem in 1 Corinthians 5 is "not just an incident of
individual misconduct, although the case of incest may have been
singular; rather it was a social problem." Paul addresses the whole
church and expects them to act as a group. One of the benefits of this
approach is the new questions it brings to familiar texts. In this case
Harris asks: What does a developing community usually do when its
basic beliefs and patterns of conduct are threatened? What was the
degree of the church's complicity in the incestuous affair? How
cohesive was the church? How did the structure of membership of
the group and the actual or perceived threat from outside the
membership affect their behaviour? Did integration with the larger
community play a role? How significant was the tension between
Paul and the congregation? How did the congregation arrive at its
view of incest? What was to be the congregation's part in disciplining
the man? What was the structure of the sanction?

It must be said that some sociological studies of the New
Testament have been excessive and less useful. The challenge for the
sociological approach is to avoid uncontrolled and overly speculative
projections, take careful note of clues to the answers to their
questions that the epistles themselves contain,[36] try not to explain too

---

35 *The Social Setting of Pauline Christianity*, p. 2.

36 Holmberg, for example, criticises Francis Watson, *Paul, Judaism and the
Gentiles: A Sociological Approach* (Cambridge: CUP, 1986), for "discounting the
information from Paul himself . . . The data have to give way for the model." He
concludes that "this may account for the somewhat unpersuasive picture of the
Pauline sect" that Watson presents (*Sociology and the New Testament*, p. 106).

much in terms of social factors (the New Testament documents are primarily religious/theological documents), somehow be aware of the dangers of imposing social models which were developed to explain cultures far removed from the first century Græco-Roman world[37] and build upon the hard work of historical description (see Part II).

IV. THE SHAPE OF PAULINE ETHICS

Any serious study of Paul's ethics gives attention to the texture of his instructions, to the various forms that appear in his letters, such as the frequent lists of virtues and vices. This brings us to a fourth question which concerns the **shape** of Paul's ethics.

The study of the forms of Paul's ethics has a long history. In 1903 *Alfred Seeberg's Der Katechismus der Urchristenheit* initiated the serious study of the Jewish background to Paul's ethics with a grand and sweeping theory.[38] The first two chapters of this work, "Moral Teaching: The Existence and Contents of 'the Ways'", appear as chapter seven in this volume. Seeberg argues that much of Paul's ethical material consists of the modification of a Jewish catechism. This source, he argued, had been formulated for the instruction of proselytes and was known to John the Baptist and Jesus. In its modified form the Christian catechism consisted of a formula of belief and ethical teaching. The latter supposedly included catalogues of virtues and vices and a household code.[39] The Christian catechism hypothesis posed the problems and asked the questions with which

---

[37] Cf. Harris: "There are serious dangers in applying a model derived from twentieth century social movements to first century Christianity."

[38] See F. Hahn's survey and evaluation of Seeberg's works in the introduction to the 1966 reprint of Seeberg's book. The Jewish systematic theologian, Kaufmann Kohler, who wrote about the same time as Seeberg, also deserves mention as a scholar who was interested in the influence of early Judaism upon Christianity, especially in the ethical writings; see eg., "Didache, or The Teaching of the Twelve Apostles", *The Jewish Encyclopedia* 4 (1903): 585-88.

[39] A household code is a unit as in Col 3 and Eph 5 where admonitions are addressed to Christians according to their station in life—wives and husbands, children and fathers, slaves and masters.

later studies of the Jewish background to Paul's ethics were to grapple.[40]

Seeberg builds his case upon a few, tantalisingly incomplete traces of evidence. Though not implausible, and as fascinating as it is, most scholars have not been persuaded by Seeberg's reconstruction. Nonetheless, his painstaking work on the contents of the Pauline lists is valuable in and of itself, whether or not his overall construction is valid.

The task of research has been taken in several different directions. Some recognised the limitations of concentrating on the larger shape of the ethical material and instead focussed upon individual units such as Pauline household codes and ethical lists. The discovery of the Dead Sea Scrolls and the revival of scholarly interest in the documents of the Old Testament Pseudepigrapha occasioned more specialised investigations in certain quarters of the Jewish background. The function, distinctiveness, and interpretation of Paul's catalogues and codes continues to be debated. *Lars Hartman*'s essay (chapter eight), "Code and Context: A Few Reflections on the Parenesis of Col 3:6-4:1", includes a brief survey of some of the developments in research as they relate to the household codes.

A definite contribution to the study of Pauline ethical forms has been made by focusing upon their Old Testament background and their New Testament context. Hartman demonstrates this in his study of Colossians 3:6-4:1. He points, for example, to the likely influence of the Decalogue, which was so influential in much early Jewish moral teaching, on the choice of vices in Colossians 3:5-9. Such Old Testament influence, as Holtz observes, may not have been direct. Scripturally-based ethical material may have reached Paul through the exposition of the Scriptures in the synagogues. Through

---

[40] For example, in their major studies of the Jewish background to Paul's ethics the following authors feel the need to come to terms with Seeberg's ground-breaking work. K. Weidinger, *Die Haustafeln: Ein Stück urchristlicher Paränese*. UNT (Leipzig: J.C. Hinrichs, 1928), pp. 4ff.; A. Vögtle, *Die Tugend- und Lasterkataloge im Neuen Testament: exegetisch, religions- und formgeschichtlich untersucht* NTAbh 16 (Münster: Aschendorff, 1936), pp. 3ff.; S. Wibbing, *Die Tugend- und Lasterkataloge im Neuen Testament und ihre Traditionsgeschichte unter besonderer Berücksichtigung der Qumran Texte*. BZNW 25 (Berlin: Töpelmann, 1959), pp. 4ff.; E. Kamlah, *Die Form der Katalogischen Paränese im Neuen Testament*. WUNT 7. (Tübingen: J.C.B. Mohr [Paul Siebeck], 1964), p. 7; J.E. Crouch, *The Origin and Intention of the Colossian Haustafel* (Göttingen: Vandenhoeck & Ruprecht, 1972), pp. 13ff.; and K.-W. Niebuhr, op cit (see fn. 19), pp. 1ff.

such activity certain Biblical scruples would have been emphasised and certain exegeses and expositions of prominent passages would have been promulgated.

New Testament ethical forms, since Martin Dibelius have often been regarded as largely unrelated to the letters in which they appear.[41] Such material is supposedly not conditioned by the particular circumstances of the letter. It is in a different style and is relatively self-contained—you could remove some of the ethical sections without too much damage to the flow of the letter. Dibelius argued that such material is simply stock advice to close the letters. However, there is good evidence that this view is mistaken. The moral codes usually have a function in Paul's letters that relates to his overall argument, as Hartman demonstrates in the case of Colossians. The same has been rightly said of Paul's exhortations in Galatians 5:13-6:10 and Ephesians 5:21-33. John M. G. Barclay has shown that the paraenetic material in Galatians "develops out of and concludes his earlier arguments",[42] and concerning the passage in Ephesians, J. Paul Sampley observed that "it reflects in microcosmic fashion several of the concerns of the entire epistle."[43]

V. THE LOGIC OF PAULINE ETHICS

The study of the isolated forms of Paul ethics, the "bits and pieces", though legitimate and enlightening, is prone to create a false impression. The close connection of the doctrinal parts of Colossians, Ephesians and Galatians to the paraenetic, practical parts was Paul's usual pattern. The question of the **logic** of Paul's ethics brings this into focus.

Paul customarily rests his moral imperatives on the basis of God's prior action on behalf of believers in Christ. The ethical injunctions and prohibitions are rooted in the redemptive acts of God. As well as being the overall orientation of Paul's ethics, the close relation of the indicative (what God has done) to the imperative

---

[41] Cf. M. Dibelius, *A Fresh Approach to the New Testament and Early Christian Literature* (London: Nicholson & Watson, 1936), pp. 217-37.

[42] Barclay, *Obeying the Truth: A Study of Paul's Ethics in Galatians* (Edinburgh: T. & T. Clark, 1988), p. 216.

[43] Sampley, *'And the Two Shall Become One Flesh': A Study of Traditions in Ephesians 5:21-33* (Cambridge: CUP, 1971), p. 162.

(what believers must do) can even be seen within the compass of a single verse in three cases:

1) 1 Corinthians 5:7 - "Cleanse out the old leaven (imperative), as you already are unleavened (indicative)";

2) Galatians 5:1 - "It is for freedom that Christ has set us free (indicative). Stand firm then and do not let yourselves be burdened by a yoke of slavery again (imperative)";

3) Galatians 5:25 - "Since we live by the Spirit (indicative) let us also walk by the Spirit (imperative)".

In each of these verses the identity of believers is to inform their behaviour. They are to become what they already are by the grace and in the eyes of God.

The relation of the indicative to the imperative in Paul's thought is a vital subject with a long history of debate. Is it a contradiction to be resolved? Should one mood be given priority over the other? How are the two related? Is the concept central or merely incidental for Paul?

In 1924 *Rudolf Bultmann* in his essay, "The Problem of Ethics in Paul" (chapter nine), drew attention to the indicative and the imperative in such a way as to identify it as the basic structure of Paul's ethics. Up until the time of this essay the indicative and the imperative had been seen as just one aspect of Paul's ethics. Bultmann's essay is widely recognised as a turning-point in the history of interpretation.[44] Sampley is correct when he states that "scholars since Rudolf Bultmann agree that Paul's moral reflections cannot be separated from his theological understandings."[45]

Bultmann's essay contains much with which I disagree. His basic existentialist interpretation of Paul (the Christ event has significance only in the decision of faith) is unacceptable. He stresses Paul's debt to hellenistic mystery religions, which is now largely discounted in favour of a Jewish matrix for Paul's thought.

---

[44] See P.J. Gräbe, "Die Verhouding tussen Indikatief en Imperatief in die Pauliniese Etiek: Enkele Aksente uit die Diskussie sedert 1924", *Scriptura* 32 (1970): 54-66; William D. Dennison, "Indicative and Imperative: The Basic Structure of Pauline Ethics", *Calvin Theological Journal* 14 (1979): 55-78; Michael Parsons, chapter ten of this book; J.T. Sanders, *Ethics in the New Testament: Change and Development* (Philadelphia: Fortress Press, 1975), p. 48.

[45] J. Paul Sampley, *Walking Between the Times: Paul's Moral Reasoning* (Minneapolis: Fortress Press, 1991), p. 3

Anthropology seems to occupy too central a place, to the exclusion of theology proper. Finally, Bultmann gives to baptism a significance which is reserved in Paul for conversion of which faith, repentance and baptism are constituent parts.[46] Nonetheless, Bultmann is correct to insist on the centrality of the indicative and the imperative, that what God has done is the basis of what justified believers must do. The essay brings this out forcefully. The interrelation of the indicative and the imperative is indeed closely linked to the central themes of Pauline theology, including justification, faith, eschatology, Christology and especially the Spirit.

Michael Parsons' essay, "Being Precedes Act: Indicative and Imperative in Paul's Writing" (chapter ten), sketches the history of the research since Bultmann and also offers a careful exegesis of key passages (Rom 12:1-2; Phil 2:12-13; Gal 5:25 and 1 Cor 6:12-20) to support his conclusion that the indicative and the imperative are "certainly and closely related yet distinct."[47]

A few supplementary thoughts on the subject may be given. It ought to be recognized that the logic of the indicative and the imperative is a distinguishing mark not only of Paul's ethics but of biblical ethics in general. The origin of Paul's ethics is here most evident. Throughout the Bible human behaviour is always considered in the context of the underlying and overarching relationship with God. What God's people have become is the basis for what they must do. Examples come to mind easily. The first verses of the Decalogue indicate that the people to whom God gives the laws are those whom He has liberated from Egypt (Exod 20:2). Throughout the Pentateuch, a chief motivation to obedience is, as Numbers 15:41 puts it, "I am the Lord your God, who brought you out of Egypt to be your God." The book of Deuteronomy is basically a call to God's people to reflect upon their past history of salvation, while calling them to present obedience. Deuteronomy 7:5-6; 14:1-2; 27:9-10, for instance, clearly state that God's people should obey Him because of who they have become. In Samuel's farewell speech to Israel (1 Sam 12:20-25) the command to serve the Lord wholeheartedly and not to turn away after idols (the imperative) is reinforced with the reminder

---

46 For an introduction and survey of Bultmann's life and work see D.A.S. Fergusson, *Bultmann* (London: Geoffrey Chapman, 1992).

47 An excellent treatment of the subject can also be found in G.M. Styler, "The Basis of Obligation in Paul's Christology and Ethics", in *Christ and Spirit in the New Testament: In Honour of C.F.D. Moule* (CUP, 1973), ed. by B. Lindars and S.S. Smalley, pp. 175-88.

that the Lord was pleased to make Israel his own and the encouragement to "consider what great things he has done for you" (the indicative). In the Prophets, misconduct is uniformly conceived as unfaithfulness to the God of the covenant who chose and redeemed His people. Even the same balance and reciprocity of the moods that we saw in 1 Corinthians 5:7, Galatians 5:1 and 5:25 can be observed in the Old Testament, in Leviticus 20:7-8:

> Consecrate yourselves therefore, and be holy (imperative); for I am the Lord your God. Keep my statutes and do them. I am the Lord, who makes you holy (indicative).[48]

We may also note the considerable practical benefits of the compelling logic of Paul's ethics. The indicatives show that the imperatives of progressive sanctification are not optional. That believers have been truly set free from sin's power negates despair and insecurity in our experience. The imperatives show that the indicatives do not make progressive sanctification authomatic. That believers have been actively enlisted in spiritual warfare negates pride and overconfidence in our position.[49]

The identity of believers is meant not just to inform but to motivate behaviour. Christian conduct for Paul is appropriate, becoming, seemly conduct. Paul states, to paraphrase Colossians 3:5-14, take off your old clothes, put on something more suitable to your status as those chosen and loved by God. Just as certain nationalities, families and social classes display typical behaviour, so there is for Paul "Christian" behaviour.

Just as Paul links theology and ethics so there is a connection in his thought between orthodoxy and orthopraxy, such that good doctrine leads to good behaviour. The converse also follows: doctrinal departure leads to moral decay and decline. The two are inextricably bound together. To miss this vital point is to embrace a heartless and fruitless orthodoxy or an empty and impotent moralism.

VI. THE FOUNDATIONS OF PAULINE ETHICS

A sixth question to ask of Paul's ethics has to do with its **foundations**. In what way or ways does Paul arrive at his counsels

---

48 Mr Thor Madsen pointed this verse out to me.
49 Here I am indebted to John Grassmick's unpublished lectures on Romans.

and convictions concerning proper conduct for believers? How does he come to ethical decisions? This is again a subject of vast proportions and keen relevance.

The essay of *Eduard Lohse*, "The Church in Everyday Life", is a fine exposition of the love commandment as an answer to our question (chapter eleven). The command to love has "central meaning for the ethical orientation of the church." Or to put it another way: "decision and action influenced by love determines the conduct of Christians." Lohse focusses on two key texts in Romans, 13:9 and 12:1-2, to elucidate his point. Along the way he brings in the teaching of Jesus[50] and Jewish teaching in a helpful manner to show the broad agreement which existed on this point.

Eckhard Schnabel's essay (chapter twelve), "How Paul developed his Ethics", offers a different perspective. Schnabel believes that the foundations of Paul's ethics cannot be "boiled down" to love. In another tour through Paul's letters, this time observing Paul's exhortations to overcome conflict in the church and to strive for unity, Schnabel seeks to answer our question with a concrete example in mind. The result is remarkably comprehensive. Schnabel distinguishes motivations, norms and criteria. Motivations to obedience include christological, salvation-historical, pneumato-logical, ecclesiological and eschatological bases. Valid norms for behaviour, guides to being and doing, consist of Old Testament teaching, the words of Jesus and apostolic teaching. Finally, the realisation of Christian living is governed and led by certain criteria: the Holy Spirit, the governing powers and authorities instituted by God, love, reason, conscience and missionary effectiveness.

VII. THE RELEVANCE OF PAULINE ETHICS

The final question we wish to ask of Paul's ethics is the "so what" question—what **relevance** does Paul's ethics have for us today? This section would be entitled *The Irrelevance of Pauline Ethics* if we wished to reflect the majority scholarly opinion. For one reason or another many authors reduce the contemporary significance of Paul's moral teaching to a bare minimum. Some say that Paul's chief, if not sole,

---

[50] For a balanced assessment of the impact of the teaching and example of Jesus upon Paul's ethics see Michael B. Thompson, *Clothed With Christ: The Example and Teaching of Jesus in Romans 12.1-15.13*. JSNTSS 59 (Sheffield: JSOT Press, 1991).

contribution is his stress on the commandment to love. The totality and fulness of Paul's teaching can be reduced to love God and your neighbour. Others contend that Paul's moral teaching is to be ignored because it is only the result of a de-eschatologising process, formulated due to Paul's facing up to the delay of the second coming of Christ; or it is a compromise between the ideal and the actual; or it is a *provisorium* eventually to be abandoned; or it is merely individual commandments for specific circumstances which are unrepeatable. The reasons for avoiding Paul are numerous, it seems. *Wolfgang Schrage's* essay, "The Formal Ethical Interpretation of Pauline Paraenesis" (chapter thirteen), however, argues convincingly against all of these objections to acknowledging the ongoing relevance of Paul's ethics. The character of Paul's practical teaching, set as it is into the core of his theology, offers a firm rebuttal to such pessimism.

An especially prevalent objection is the emphasis on the adequacy of the Spirit for discerning God's will in the concrete situation. It is sometimes said that whereas the Bible leads you to Christ, it is the Spirit who leads you to right behaviour. The problem with this reasoning is the fact that such a Word/Spirit dichotomy is foreign to Biblical thought. To pit the Spirit against the Word as if they represent alternative approaches to ethics does not ring true for Paul. The Spirit does not replace but cooperates with the Word, as was the case from the very beginning (cf. Gen 1:2-3; cf. Neh 9:20,30; Psalm 33:6; 147:18; Isa 59:21). This can be seen by comparing Ephesians 5:18 with Colossians 3:16, texts written about the same time by Paul. In Ephesians 5:18 an individual being filled with the Spirit results in or is associated with addressing one another in psalms, hymns and spiritual songs, singing to the Lord and giving thanks. In Colossians 3:16 an individual being filled with the Word (in this case "of Christ") occasions a very similar effect: people teach and admonish one another, sing psalms, hymns and spiritual songs and give thanks. The rich indwelling of the Spirit and the Word amount to the same thing. Revival (by the Spirit) and reform (by the Word) go hand in hand.

Whereas in his essay Schrage is on the defensive, *Richard N. Longenecker's* piece (chapter fourteen), "New Testament Social Ethics for Today", is a positive and practical contribution to the full recognition of the value and importance of Paul's (and New Testament) ethics for Christian conduct today. Longenecker looks at the various ways the New Testament has been understood as a guide to Christian morality and suggests that each sets forth a necessary aspect of truth for Christian ethics.[51] His essay is in fact only the first chapter of a book on the subject. In this book, it is the penultimate chapter, reminding us that at best what is achieved here is only to provide an introduction to the subject of Paul's ethics.

Two considerations, in spite of the hermeneutical challenge of relating our world and Paul's world, urge us to recognise the relevance of Paul's ethics for Christian conduct. The first point relates to the origin of Paul's ethics, namely, Scripture (see Part I). Paul considered Scripture to be the word of God, which not only spoke to His people but continues to speak; hence his dependence upon it for moral teaching. If Paul's ethics derives from such revelation, this suggests that his instruction is not some good idea to be considered, but is itself the commandment of God to be obeyed (cf. 1 Cor 14:37). Secondly, that Paul's ethics is firmly set into the core of his theology (see Part V) means that we cannot take Paul's theology and ignore his ethics, nor vice versa. The two are part of the same package for Paul. Founded upon revelation and theology, Paul's ethics are built to last.

The essays on the relevance of Paul's ethics remind us that the ultimate goal is not to master "that pattern of teaching," but to be mastered by it. In Romans 6:17 Paul does not say that he handed his moral teaching over to Christians; the verb is passive. The reverse is actually true. Paul personifies his ethics and states that he handed Christians over to his moral teaching:

> Thanks be to God, that you who were once slaves of sin have become obedient from the heart to that pattern of teaching to which you were handed over.

---

[51] For a recent survey and assessment of work on the question of how Christians ought to use the New Testament in ethics see I. Howard Marshall, "The Use of the New Testament in Christian Ethics", *Expository Times* 105/5 (1994): 131-36. On hermeneutics and the use of the Bible in general see Anthony C. Thiselton, *New Horizons in Hermeneutics* (London: Harper Collins, 1992).

PART I

THE ORIGIN OF PAULINE ETHICS
The Scriptures and Jewish Sources?

CHAPTER ONE

The Old Testament in the Pauline Letters and in the Pauline Churches[*]

Adolf von Harnack
(1928)

In the following essay I develop an observation which I made in my monograph about Marcion (2nd edn., p. 442), but which I have only briefly explained previously. It concerns links with the Old Testament which are found in Paul's letters, or rather not found where one expects them.

Even though the churches founded by Paul are composed of members who are 'believers' and 'saints', these churches need to be constantly edified. This is beyond doubt to their founder. From what sources should they derive growth and edification and did they derive them? These questions have until now not been properly evaluated and answered, perhaps because they appeared settled in answering the logically prior question of the sources of the apostle's own edification. The answer to this question is certainly in no doubt: Paul derived his inner life and growth from faith in the crucified and

---

[*] Translated by George S. Rosner and Brian S. Rosner.

risen Christ, from the Spirit whom he has sent and from prayer to God the Father. It is equally certain that he derived these powers from the holy Scripture, the Old Testament Scripture of God which he now read with reference to Christ and understood in this fashion. Although for him the old was gone and everything had become new, and although he felt himself to be a new creature in Christ, the Old Testament did not lose its edifying power for Paul. On the contrary, it was made stronger for him, since the "veil" which had obscured the sense of the Old Testament had been removed. Thus he now lives in a quite different manner with respect to Scripture than he did in that bygone time when he read it as a Pharisee and as a persecutor of Christ's church.

Has Paul simply transferred this evaluation of the Old Testament, which was inseparable from his being a Christian, directly to his churches? Did he as a missionary, pedagogue and teacher hand the Old Testament to them, order the constant reading of it and feed his children right from the start and again and again out of the Old Testament? Or is this a useless question, because the answer is evident from the apostle's own position regarding Scripture? In any case an examination will not be superfluous. Such an examination must not proceed from the four so-called main letters (*Hauptbriefe*) because those who received those letters still disputed the great question of faith, 'law and gospel'. Rather, one must start with the six letters[1] whose recipients were not made uneasy by this question or at least did not consider it to be a question of serious disputation.[2]

I.

When one considers the six letters, 1 and 2 Thessalonians, Colossians, Philemon, Ephesians, and Philippians, and one poses the question, what do they contain with respect to the Old Testament, the following observations may be made (Philemon need not be considered because one cannot expect in this small letter a relationship to the Old Testament and because there is no relationship):

1) References to the Old Testament under the title of "ἡ γραφή"

---

[1] I also consider II Thessalonians and Ephesians to be genuine letters of Paul.

[2] I leave aside the question of the textual form of the quotations from the Old Testament.

(Scripture) or "γέγραπται" (it is written) do not exist at all in them. This fundamental observation is a paradox: Paul deals in these letters very fully with the most varied themes—theoretical, admonitory, pedagogical, speculative—yet none of these themes has made him refer expressly to the Scripture as such, even if such a reference was suggested by many passages.

2) Literal quotations without the introduction "γέγραπται" (it is written) are found in these letters in only two places, both in Ephesians (4:8; 5:14), and both with the simple formula: διὸ λέγει (therefore it says/is said). This formula does not show where these words of God come from. Indeed, only the first one is found in the Old Testament (Psalm 68:19). The second is a Christian or pre-Christian prophetic word from an unknown source. Apparently, what matters for the apostle, even in the case of the first quotation, is not its origin in the Old Testament, but its divine source. The authority of the Old Testament is therefore referred to neither directly nor indirectly in these letters.

3) When one further considers these letters one by one, the following results emerge:

1 *Thessalonians*: Only once in the letter (2:15) does one see that the people addressed know anything at all about Jewish history ("the Jews have killed their own prophets") and here we are dealing with apocryphal historical knowledge. The Old Testament does not exist for this letter. When the apostle speaks of the "word" (1:6,8; 2:13) or of the "gospel" (2:2,8,9; 3:2) as being the central factor, he always means the specifically Christian proclamation, without even glancing at the Old Testament. When he appeals to the Christian knowledge of his readers (1:4; 4:2; 5:2), it is the same thing. When he deals with brotherly love and the renunciation of revenge (4:9; 5:15), he does not refer to the Old Testament commandment of love, but tells the readers that they themselves are θεοδίδακτοι (taught by God) and are not in need of instruction. When, in longer passages, he speaks of the events of the End Times and mentions the resurrection as a consolation and admonition, he does not refer to Old Testament prophesies, but to words of the Lord (4:15; 5:1f) and to Christian prophesy. When he acknowledges the height of the spiritual state of his addressees, he does not call them children of Abraham or imitators of the prophets, but imitators of himself and of the Lord (1:6). One cannot gain the impression from the letters that there is anything valuable for the readers in the period of time before Jesus Christ. Rather he is the one who begins and fulfills, and Paul is his

apostle ... but not in the sense of being the only one (see "the churches of God in Judea", 2:14). All this shows from what source the church should feed its life of faith: it is the "word of God" or "the gospel" which should define them and which should strengthen them.

2 Thessalonians: This letter is identical to the first letter in its relationship to the Old Testament. It is true that the topics of the first two chapters are coloured more by the Old Testament·than in the first letter. But all the eschatology, which constitutes the main topic of the letter, is proclaimed by the apostle himself as his spiritual property backed by his authority or as Christian knowledge. The formal and central idea is even here only the "gospel" (2:14) or the Christian "tradition" in which the readers stand (2:15; 3:6). When the "word of the Lord" is referred to and glorified (3:1), he is speaking of the proclamation of Christ. It cannot be seen from the letter that there is for the readers an Old Testament at all, even if the eschatology offered sufficient inducement to refer to the authority of Scripture.

Colossians: One might expect a strong reference to the Old Testament in this letter, because here is a warning against gnostic-judaistic teachers of errors and Paul's refutation. Therefore, to deal with the Old Testament, both negatively and positively, seems to be inevitable, but nothing of the kind is found. Furthermore, all the discussions in the letter are offered without any consideration of the Old Testament. Christology is strongly expressed without reference to Scripture in opposition to a teaching about angels which attempts to destroy the central position of Christ. Ceremonial and cultic commandments are rejected under the contemptuous title of "human commandments and human teachings," even if some are, at least partially, Old Testament commandments, and a Christian circumcision which is not done by hands is proclaimed, without even mentioning the Law. But two things are even more important: 1:26 says that "the mystery, which had been hidden for ages and generations, is now revealed to the saints."[3] It is therefore something quite new. And 2:13f proclaims that the new life (rebirth) which occurs through the forgiveness of sin has come to pass through the fact the "written code, which was against us and consisted of commandments, has been erased by being nailed to the cross," and therefore it has lost its validity. How can this be understood in any way other than that the "saints" (thanks to Christ, the world's

---

[3] Nothing is said regarding it having been prophesied beforehand.

saviour) have nothing more to do with the realm which is formed by the Law, that is, by the Old Testament?[4] This liberating message is confirmed by the second part of the letter, the practical part. In these admonitions the apostle rises to a height which stands high above the ethic which was valid up to now with its commandments. The fundamental outlines of the new life are treated out of the experience of salvation. Even the less important themes of communal life are treated without any reference to similar matters in the Old Testament. Finally, 3:16 states quite clearly how and from what sources the new life should be nourished. It is "the word of Christ" and nothing else which should richly dwell in the church, by teaching and mutual admonition in the form of "psalms and hymns and spiritual songs." Paul does not point the church to the reading of the Old Testament, nor to the practising of the old Psalms, but he assumes that the "word of Christ" will furnish ever new and rich means of edification. Here things are the same as in the letters to the Thessalonians: the Old Testament is never mentioned and plays practically no role in the church. In 2 Thessalonians this becomes even more clear, because where one would expect the admonition to read the Old Testament, such an admonition is missing, and because the Law is presumed to be and treated as something that has been done away with. "The word of Christ" ("the word of the truth of the gospel") is the only foundation for the existence of the church and the only source of its life ἐν πνεύματι (in the Spirit).

Philippians: The readers of this letter are well acquainted with the great antithesis "justification through the Law and through faith" (3:9). These Gentile Christians also know that they are now the people of the (true) circumcision (3:3). The terrible characteristics of the Jewish people and the accusations against the Jews would have been nothing new to them. It was also nothing new to them that it had once been an advantage to be blameless "according to the Law" (3:2ff; 3:18ff). There is no passage in this letter which places the synthesis of the old covenant with the new alongside the well-known antithesis of gospel and law, although, in this letter also, the language of the apostle is influenced by reminiscenses of the Old Testament. Nonetheless, here the apostle writes as if no Old Testament existed.

---

4 A synthesis between the gospel and the whole complex of the Law in contrast to the rugged antithesis is only given in a brief hint (2:17) that this is "the shadow of future things," and therefore is not part of its reality, but only a certain depiction in advance.

Even the great christological hymn (2:5ff) is not composed using the sayings of the prophets of the Old Testament, but obtains its building blocks from other quarries. Finally, here it is no different from the letter to the Colossians: Where one expects that the apostle would now recommend the reading of the Old Testament as a source of edification, such an admonition is missing. Rather, his direction (4:8) is: "Whatever is true, whatever is noble, whatever is just, whatever is pure, whatever is lovely, whatever is gracious . . . if anything is excellent or praiseworthy. . . think about such things." In place of the Old Testament, which is not mentioned, which apparently does not serve as a book of edification, everything which gives life a higher quality appears. The new life should achieve its development and action in connection with the "word of Christ."

Ephesians: At first glance this letter, probably addressed to Laodicea, appears to be in a different position as regards the Old Testament, but only at *first* glance: The letter is filled with clear reminiscences of the Old Testament (esp. 4:25f; 2:3.17; 5:18-6:17), but except for two passages they are silent borrowings, that is, the character of quotation is not marked, and in regard to those two passages it has already been observed above that they are not introduced as quotations from the holy Scripture, but simply as words of God. The second passage is not found in Scripture, but is a Christian or pre-Christian prophecy (4:8; 5:14). The letter is a joyous thanksgiving for the fact that God has now brought together the Jews and the Gentiles, who formerly were so far from the πολιτεία τοῦ Ἰσραήλ (the commonwealth of Israel; 2:12) and has made one entity out of two (2:12-18). Here one expects references to numerous Old Testament prophetic statements. Instead, the Law is mentioned only once in an *antithetical* manner (2:15) next to the formula "οὐκ ἐξ ἔργων" (not because of works; 2:9), in the same manner as in Colossians (τὸ μεσότειχον τοῦ φραγμοῦ [the dividing wall of hostility] is torn down and ὁ νόμος τῶν ἐντολῶν ἐν δόγμασιν [the law of commandments consisting of decrees] is done away with). The new appears only as an antithesis of the old, the Israelite. In accordance with this view it follows logically that the prophets to whom the apostle refers in this letter (2:20; 3:5; 4:11) are not those of the Old Testament, but are in all passages Christians. It also follows that, as in Colossians, the mystery is spoken of, namely, that these things were until now hidden in God and only now have been revealed through Christ (3:4f,9). Therefore, even here the Old Testament is not recommended for edification, but rather the reception of the Spirit is exclusively put forward, the one who works through new psalms, hymns and spiritual songs (5:18f). One only learns in passing from the letter (2:12) that the gospel has in prophecy a holy preceding history, which appears as διαθῆκαι τῆς ἐπαγγελίας (the covenants of promise) in Israel and that Gentile Christians were formerly ἄθεοι ἐν τῷ κόσμῳ (without God in the world; 2:12) and φύσει τέκνα ὀργῆς (by nature children of wrath; 2:3). But in the light of the mystery which has now been revealed all differences between Jews and Gentiles have disappeared. The preference for Jews, which consisted in the promises, is set aside, and therefore the new church does not live with Moses and the old prophets, but with the apostles and the new prophets.

Therefore, the six letters of Paul viewed here offer a unanimous and clear finding with regard to Scripture. This finding is quite definitely negative. The question which appears in the introduction is therefore to be negated: The apostle has not given the Old Testament simply as the book of edification to the churches and the Gentiles; he has not fed them out of Scripture from the beginning, nor later on; he has been very reticent to pass on the meaning which the Old Testament held for himself and concerning any appreciation of the history of salvation one might gain from it. When one considers, however, that 1 Thessalonians and 2 Thessalonians are the earliest letters of the apostle, that Colossians, Philemon, Ephesians, and Philippians on the other hand are after Galatians, 1 and 2 Corinthians and Romans, it follows that in those early letters there is not the expression of a factual situation in the churches and a method of the apostle which later changed, but that we are dealing with a procedure which the apostle has not altered.[5] But do not the so called four main letters present a contradiction? In the light of the *Hauptbriefe* is it not necessary to assume that it is only an accident in the six letters that the apostle has not quoted the Old Testament and has paid so little attention to it? This question must be researched.

---

5 In this context the bold attempt of Marcion to consider the "two testaments" as sharply antithetical in the same sense as the apostle did, to reject the Old Testament and to separate the God of salvation from the God of creation, even if this notion is not tenable, is easy to understand and surprisingly easy to carry out. Only a few, superficial, quite insignificant corrections of a few verses would be necessary in order to make all six letters into sure witnesses of Marcion's Christianity. With regard to one main issue, however, namely, that the Old Testament is not the book of edification for the Christians, no correction whatever is needed.

II.

With reference to the Old Testament the four main letters, which were written about the same time, share something important in contrast to the other six letters. The basic character of them does not appear plainly in the letters to the Corinthians, especially in the second letter, because these letters deal with numerous, colourful, personal matters and other themes. But a common character is nevertheless apparent.[6] It can be derived from the fact that the Galatian churches were subjected to the heaviest judaizing temptation, the Roman church, personally unknown to the apostle, had been founded by more or less strict Jewish Christians and was probably under the influence of the spirit of the Old Testament, and in the Corinthian church there was also a strong Jewish Christian element. In all four letters the gospel had to be directly or indirectly separated from Judaism.[7] The main qualities of the four letters with regard to the problem before us are the following:

1) In all four letters there are express γραφή (Scripture) or rather γέγραπται (it is written) quotations. There are nearly fifty, whilst in the six letters there is not one.

2) In these letters the antithesis as well as the synthesis regarding the Old Testament is spelt out (but in 2 Cor this remains in the background). This renders to the four letters, apart from other matters, a special character compared to the six letters. This character would be described one-sidedly, if one emphasised only the antithesis regarding the Law. Rather, it is equally important that in contrast to the six letters the synthesis between the Old Testament and the gospel is just as plainly expressed as the matter of the antithesis.

This state of affairs allows two interpretations: Either it is just by 'chance' that in the six letters the Old Testament is hardly mentioned, or Paul's position in the four letters regarding the Old Testament has come about because of special circumstances in which the people addressed found themselves. It cannot be thought, however, that Paul derived his teaching on law and gospel from

---

[6] This explains why Baur and the Tübingen school considered only these four letters to be genuine. This was clearly a mistake.

[7] We cannot here consider the differences between Judaism in Galatia, Rome and Corinth. It may be assumed that the Old Testament was more familiar to the Corinthians than in other Pauline churches because the apostle laboured there for 18 months.

Scripture. Nor is it true that its validity (or rather non validity) for Gentile Christians came about only in an *ad hoc* fashion and, as it were, was a passing phase in the fight against Judaism. Only rarely and on special occasions did he bring the Scripture near to them in addition to the great facts (creation, sin, prophecy, the giving of the law) which he proclaimed orally. Such a supposition is excluded because of its central meaning for the apostle. But we may well assume that he explained to the Christians, which he won from the Gentile world, the complicated judgement and validity of the Old Testament only when they were in danger of falling into the judaizing error. An examination of the Γραφή (Scripture) quotations in the four main letters should reveal whether their absence in the six letters is only by chance or whether it should be explained through the special circumstances which brought them into being.

Galatians: In this letter there are references to Scripture, with the exception of one passage, only in the two sections 3:6-29 and 4:22-31, which serve as the foundation of both the antithesis 'law and gospel,' and the synthesis (the Law as a teacher). Here, however, they are numerous. They serve solely as the proof that Christians are the true sons of Abraham and the heirs of the promise, being justified through faith and not through works. This proof, even if it should also in the forum of the Old Testament be "valid according to the Law" and sure,[8] could only be furnished out of Scripture. The apostle does just that in 3:6ff. and 4:22ff. with the help of the allegorical method. Beyond that he does not use the Old Testament in the description of living in the Spirit and by faith (chs. 5 and 6),[9] because his statement (5:14): "The whole law is fulfilled in one word, You shall love your neighbour as yourself" neutralises in a certain way the antithesis of 'law and gospel.' But even the allegorical Old Testament proof does not complete the theoretical proof. Rather, a second proof (4:1ff) stemming from natural law is more important to the apostle. The person who gains an impression from the whole letter must feel that its character is not formed by the two Old Testament scholarly proofs, but in the aim of these proofs and in the rest of the content.

Finally, one must ask if the apostle supplies these scholarly

---

8   But this forum exists even for the apostle.

9   Even though he himself as a Jewish Christian personifies Scripture, completely identifying ἡ γραφή (the Scripture) and ὁ θεός (God), so that he can write (3:8): Προϊδοῦσα ἡ γραφή (the Scripture foreseeing); and in 3:22: Συνέκλεισεν ἡ γραφὴ τὰ πάντα ὑπὸ ἁμαρτίαν (the Scripture consigned all things under sin)!

proofs as something new to the Galatians or as a reminder of something already known. I have no doubt that the first is the case and that therefore even the two final formulas (3:29: "You are the seed of Abraham and the heirs according to the promise"; and 4:31: "We are not the children of the slave woman but of the free") are in this formulation new to the readers. They do not belong to the missionary sermons, which he had given orally in Galatia. Certainly he assumes two things, that they know where righteousness comes from and that they have a certain knowledge of Scripture (4:21 in connection with Genesis 16 and 21: τὸν νόμον οὐκ ἀκούετε; [do you not hear the Law?]). But, he delivers his proofs from Scripture not as well known by them, but as a new foundation for the main theme of the gospel. Therefore, Galatians has the same relationship to the Old Testament as the six letters: Scripture is not used as the book of edification, but rather, the Spirit edifies by faith. The special situation suggested the appeal to Scripture as an instrument of proof.

1 and 2 Corinthians: When evaluating these letters several things must always be kept in mind. Paul knows the Corinthian church through long labour in their midst as well as through letters and reports. The church consisted of a majority of Gentiles, but did not form a spiritual unity, being complicated in its makeup. Belief in the authority or the cult of the person as well as a spiritually inspired arrogance and pride of knowledge played an important role. Judaistic controversy played a strong part in the life of the church. Finally, Christian life was lagging behind quite definitely, behind an arrogant consciousness and odd religious speculations.

In no other letter did Paul have to make use of his whole apostolic wisdom regarding conversion and teaching as in 1 Corinthians. In no other letter did he have to explain the foundation of what he had to say quite so clearly as in this letter. In the great theoretical part of the letter to the Romans we deal only with the spelling out of a single main thought to unknown and wary readers. Romans, therefore, is written clearly and carefully, more than any other letter of Paul. Only the fifteenth chapter of 1 Corinthians is written with such extravagant care. But no theme in this letter is dealt with lightly; rather, one admires in all chapters the apostle's success in combining pedagogic force, clear completeness and precision.

Why and how is Scripture referred to so richly in this letter? An examination yields the following results: In the first main section (chs. 1-4) Paul deals with schisms and the lack of virtue shown thereby by the Corinthians, namely, worldliness, a false sense of knowledge and arrogance. To combat them the apostle explains that their supposedly deep wisdom is not God's wisdom but empty worldly wisdom and that God's Spirit, which truly leads into the depths of knowledge, is lacking among the Corinthians. Nothing else could serve as a surer foundation for these rules than the expressed sayings of God which reveal the abyss between God's wisdom revealed in the foolishness of preaching the cross and worldly wisdom. Nothing else could condemn worldly wisdom and declare that in each case the glory of the knowledge of God belongs to the Creator. In fact the six quotations from Scripture contain nothing other than the foundations for this: Isaiah 29:14 (1 Cor 1:19): Ἀπολῶ τὴν σοφίαν τῶν σοφῶν καὶ τὴν σύνεσιν τῶν συνετῶν ἀθετήσω (I will destroy the wisdom of the wise, and the cleverness of the clever I will thwart); Jeremiah 9:23f (1 Cor 1:31): Ὁ καυχώμενος ἐν κυρίῳ καυχάσθω (Let the one who boasts, boast in the Lord); the apocryphal citation (1 Cor 2:9): Ἃ ὀφθαλμὸς οὐκ εἶδε, καὶ οὖς οὐκ ἤκουσε καὶ ἐπὶ καρδίαν ἀνθρώπου οὐκ ἀνέβη, ἃ ἡτοίμασιν ὁ θεὸς τοῖς ἀγαπῶσιν αὐτόν (What no eye has seen, nor ear heard, nor the heart of man conceived, what God has prepared for those who love him), in contrast to the ἄρχοντες τοῦ αἰῶνος τούτου (the rulers of this age), who have not understood any of this. Furthermore, Scripture has ascertained (2:14f) in Isaiah 40:13 that unspiritual persons are unable to understand the Spirit and his sphere and that they cannot know God (Τίς γὰρ ἔγνω νοῦν κυρίου; [For who has known the mind of the Lord?]). Scripture has revealed God's conduct in relationship to them in Job 5:13 and Psalm 54:11 (3:19f): Ὁ δρασσόμενος τοὺς σοφοὺς ἐν τῇ πανουργίᾳ αὐτῶν (He catches the wise in their craftiness) and Κύριος γινώσκει τοὺς διαλογισμοὺς τῶν σοφῶν, ὅτι εἰσὶ μάταιοι (The Lord knows that the thoughts of the wise are futile). In a certain sense these six quotations are a single witness, because they come wholly from the motive to contrast God's expressed judgement over against the proud conduct of the Corinthians. Such an important witness cannot be derived directly from the gospel. Furthermore, probably the Corinthians (the students of Apollos) enjoyed the 'involved' exposition of Scripture and now were forced to hear from the apostle how this letter judged such speculations.[10]

The second section has hardly any links with the Old Testament (chs. 5-7). Scripture is not quoted at all as Scripture but

---

10   The Old Testament is not employed with reference to the *essential* character of divine wisdom. This is not unimportant.

only once as God's Word (Gen 2:24 in 6:16), as the reasoning for the paradoxical and shattering claim: Ὁ κολλώμενος τῇ πόρνῃ ἓν σῶμά ἐστιν (the one who joins himself to a prostitute becomes one body [with her]).[11] Apart from that the discussion of various matters including marriage takes place without reference to the Old Testament. It is based exclusively on the authority of the Lord and the apostle's enlightened judgement itself. In chapter 6 there is an appeal to the Christian knowledge of the readers six times with the formula: οὐκ οἴδατε (do you not know; vss. 2,3,9,15,16,19). The readers do not have this postulated knowledge from Scripture but from Christian, or rather the intertestamental eschatology, from Christian common sense and from Paul's preaching.

The third section (chs. 8-10) brings us closer to Scripture because it contains a principal statement of what the Old Testament means to believers and how it should therefore be understood. The apostle saw the need (9:3-18) to find a reason for the right of apostles and teachers to be kept by their students, a right which he himself never used. However, this matter must have been very important for him, for he supplies many proofs. Before he cites the arguments from the natural right of the priests to support (9:13)[12] and from a clear word of the Lord (9:14), he quotes Scripture (Deut 25:4; 1 Cor 9:9), for which, however, he needs a very daring allegorical explanation ("you shall not muzzle the ox which is threshing"). He also employs a second apocryphal word (9:10: "the plowman should plow in hope and the thresher should thresh in hope of a share in the crop"), which likewise can serve here only under a certain stress. Therefore, it must have meant much to him to be able to refer in this matter to Scripture. Probably the Corinthians argued about the right of missionaries from Scripture and demanded proofs. In this context the apostle had already mentioned the important word in relation to Scripture (9:10): δι᾽ ἡμᾶς ἐγράφη (it was written for us). Now he wishes to show the intelligent and superficial Corinthians how one should read and understand the stories of the Old Testament, namely as τύποι (types; 10:6,11) and as a νουθεσία (warning; 10:11)—because they have been written for that purpose, that is, as a future depiction of Christian history and of the coming judgement (πρὸς νουθεσίαν ἡμῶν, εἰς οὓς τὰ τέλη τῶν αἰώνων κατήντησεν [for our instruction, upon whom the end

---

[11] Christ (5:7) is incidentally allegorically called "our Passover lamb."

[12] He had already referred to the analogous right of the soldier and peasant in 9:7 ("who serves as a soldier at his own expense?", etc).

of the ages has come]). Until now we have never in Paul's letters heard anything of this hermeneutical key.[13] The solemn introduction in 10:1 (Οὐ θέλω ὑμᾶς ἀγνοεῖν [I do not want you to be ignorant]) indicates that the apostle is saying something new to his readers.[14] That means that during the eighteen months in which he preached to them he did not give them this concept. Only now do they learn that the crossing of the Red Sea by the old children of the covenant (πατέρες ἡμῶν [our fathers]) and the travelling under the 'cloud' meant baptism for the fathers, that the manna and the drink out of the rock was already spiritual food (= the Lord's Supper), and that Christ himself led the people as their accompanying rock. But all these blessings which all of them shared only helped some of them. The others were subjected to one exemplary punishment after another (10:1-10), so that the faithful of the present time should know what will happen to them if they soil themselves by lasciviousness, idolatry, whoring, tempting God or complaining. That is all the apostle says here. The Holy Scripture appears as the great book of types and examples for believers in Christ. But even here it is in the final analysis only a document of proof because the material content with which we are dealing is not derived from it but from Christian and eschatological history. What is called in modern times 'Old Testament' *Heilsgeschichte* has hardly anything in common with the concept of Scripture as a history of types concerning judgement depicted before it happened.

Chapters 11-14 assume in 11:9 knowledge of the story of paradise and render in 14:21 a surprising quotation. Isaiah 28:11 is quoted as νόμος (law) in order to prove that speaking in tongues and its disappointing success have already been proclaimed in the old covenant. But apart from that any reference to Scripture is missing in these four chapters. It is also missing where one certainly expects it. In 14:26 the apostle recounts what is heard in the gatherings for edification of the churches: ψαλμός ... διδαχή ... γλῶσσα ... ἀποκάλυψις ... ἑρμηνεία (a hymn, a lesson, a revelation, a tongue or an interpretation [of revelation]), but the reading of Scripture is missing as in Colossians and Ephesians.

Finally, at the start of the last main section (ch. 15) the apostle

---

[13] It is used in the two great passages of Galatians and is also mentioned in Romans 4:24 and 15:4.

[14] This is different from 10:18 (which is presumed as being known): "Consider the people of Israel; are not those who eat the sacrifices partners in the altar?" Here we are dealing with empirical Israel.

reminds his readers of the fundamental kerygma of Christ and within it of the fact that he has proclaimed to them the death and resurrection of Christ as a fulfillment of scriptural prophecy (15:3-4), that is, as facts proven by Scripture. The great eschatological arguments which follow were not derived from the Old Testament, but are the spiritual property of the apostle on the basis of late-Jewish apocalyptic traditions (Adam-Christ speculations, etc.) with a silent connection to several Old Testament passages. Just as in the start of the powerful argument there stands the double κατὰ τὰς γραφάς (according to the Scriptures), the argument concludes with (v. 54) the fact that the triumph of life over death has been predicted by Scripture (Isa 25:8; Hos 13:14) and is therefore proven.

In 2 Corinthians 3 Paul assumes the knowledge of the process of lawgiving and of the tables of the Law by the people addressed and gives them (vss. 2-18) a specific midrash on Exodus 34. This was certainly new to them. Its relationship to the Law and the Old Testament is once more just as clear for the synthesis as for the antithesis, which still exists in the present: If even the letter of the Law had δόξα (glory), how much more the διακονία τοῦ πνεύματος (the dispensation of the Spirit)!; then and now the people of the Old Testament cannot suffer the lesser δόξα (glory) of the Law with their eyes: but we, however, see the uncovered δόξα (glory) of the Lord! In 4:6 the apostle refers to Genesis 1:3. In 11:3 he refers to Genesis 3:4 (the apostle fears that the Corinthians will behave like Eve, who was seduced). The readers naturally knew these stories. In 4:13 he refers incidentally to Psalm 116:10 to show that with him, too, it is faith which forces him to speak. In 6:2 he says that now is the time in which the word of Isaiah (49:8) of the καιρὸς δεκτός (acceptable time) and the ἡμέρα σωτηρίας (day of salvation) is fulfilled. And in 6:16-18 several Old Testament passages are assembled for the proof that the believers are the temple of God and that they may regard themselves as sons and daughters of God, provided they sharply renounce the world and paganism. From here on there are in the second half of the letter only two more quotations from the Old Testament (within the admonitions regarding the collection; chs. 8 and 9). They do not mean a great deal. The first, 8:15 ("he who gathered much had nothing over, and he who gathered little had no lack"; Exod 16:18), is to show that the present rule was already valid before; and the second, 9:9 ("He scatters abroad, he gives to the poor; his righteousness endures forever"; Psalm 112:9), is to strengthen faith in the promise of God, that He blesses the giver for the gift. It is remarkable that the whole great discourse (or final reckoning) in the last part of the letter against the judaizing opponents and the false apostles takes place without any recourse to Scripture.

When reading the letters to the Corinthians in comparison with the other letters of Paul one gains the certain impression that the apostle reveals in them his own lively and manifold relation to Scripture. This happens because he has worked in this church for so long (therefore he may assume more than in other churches), because many questions and errors suggested referring to the authority of Scripture and because the spiritual and unspiritual speculations of the church could be refuted by a truly spiritual consideration of the Scriptures. The single word of Scripture can be considered as an authority and individual stories as types and words of wisdom. But one is surprised that the church has not long ago discovered what the apostle tells it from Scripture. Furthermore, he does not use Scripture in these letters directly as a book of edification. Even in 1 and 2 Corinthians that which is important derives exclusively from the gospel and the 'Spirit'.

Romans: When one surveys the practical-ethical second part of this letter (chs. 12-14), one receives the same impression as in the other letters: the Old Testament is not the source for the rich edifying admonitions of the apostle, but he forms them freely out of the Spirit of Christ, who carries him and works through him. Here, too (as in Gal 5:14), the tension between the Law and the gospel appears to be done away with, since in love all commandments find their fulfillment (13:8f). Quotations from the Old Testament are only found in two passages. In 12:19 the Scriptures are referred to in order to give a most secure foundation to the prohibition against taking revenge oneself by pointing to the fact that God has expressly reserved revenge for himself (Deut 32:35). In the same way in 14:11 judging one's brother is forbidden by the quotation of Isaiah 45:23, because God has reserved judgement for himself. Such striking and convincing arguments cannot be derived from the gospel.

Romans 1-11 and 15 make quite a different impression. These chapters are in the frame of an exhaustive discussion with Scripture as a law, and with the problems which are behind the Law and the gospel, judgement and grace. In all the writings of the apostle they only have a parallel in Galatians 3:6-29 and in 4:2-31 (see above), but even here the parallel is only a limited one. Because these chapters are so weighty their author consistently presents himself in a one-sided fashion. But one's position (or disposition) even regarding the greatest problems of religion and the history of religion must not by itself be decisive for judging the character of a theologian, who in life was confronted by great practical tasks and left behind him many witnesses of his labour, his piety and his theology.

Posterity received the letter to the Romans (that is, chs. 1-11 and 15) because of a quite particular situation in which the apostle of the Roman Christian church found himself, a church personally unknown to him. His missionary zeal, which he experienced as God's commission, drove him to the capital of the world, but what he knew of the local church did not make him confident of a good reception or of favourable soil (for his work). According to the reports, which he had received, it appeared that there was in that place a Jewish Christianity which was inimical to his gospel and to him personally or, at the least, suspicious. It was a church still imbedded in Judaism. But he did not possess a sure image of the Christianity of the church and of the kind and strength of the impression made by him or of their judgment of him as a person. He therefore did not know how they would react to his coming or his not coming. The fact that he had not already come was because at the time he could not come, partly because he himself was unsure of when he should come. Also, he had decided that he would bring the collection personally to Jerusalem, which he had collected in his churches, before he travelled to Rome, in order to make an earnest attempt to overcome the increasing distrust of that church and of those leading it. Even in all the independence which he allowed himself as a called apostle of Jesus Christ, the thought of being separated from the mother church in Jerusalem was for him an unbearable, perhaps one can say, an impossible one. But what will happen in Jerusalem? Will he achieve peace and fellowship with the church there? Or will it come to a break, thereby endangering his person and shattering (or violently shaking) his life's work? And how would that affect the church of the capital of the world and his coming? Will he be allowed to come at all? And if he comes, will he be allowed to remain and to teach? Must he not right now take precautions and announce his trip to Rome only as a short visit, as a stage of the missionary journey to the far West, which had also been planned?

The letter to the Romans is born out of these considerations, worries and doubts. The most weighty writing of the apostle is to a much greater degree a personal, occasional writing than all the other letters to the churches! This is usually not understood in judging this letter. This misjudgement is forgiveable. After all, how has the apostle saved himself in this situation? By placing himself at the highest watchtower (or at the highest level) and by demonstrating to the Romans his gospel of the free grace of God in Christ, which can be received only by faith. He demonstrates this on the foundation of scriptural proofs. Only thus could he hope to make an impression on the Roman Christians, who were prejudiced and probably more strongly influenced by Scripture than by the gospel. In this definition of the gospel the apostle has achieved the highest level which mattered to him as a Christian and as a Christian thinker, and the highest thoughts which a Christian has ever been able to express. This definition will be at all times felt and judged to be the summit of knowledge of the gospel. But he who does not from the start acknowledge this definition as being totally and in every word canonical, cannot overlook the fact that the scriptural proof is scholastic and illusionary and that the alleged synthesis next to the antithesis between the Law and the gospel ("we establish the law") leads to serious doubts. More than that: the apostle did not succeed completely, on his high level, to overcome the doubts and worries about how things would go in Jerusalem and in Rome and how he should behave. Next to the unsatisfactory scriptural proof one feels in the letter a certain unsure policy, which is shown in the characterisation of the readers and in several formulations—in "earthen vessels", not only in silver or gold ones, are the treasures offered which the apostle reveals here. But is there a more difficult task than the one of presenting himself and his concerns before a half-unknown suspicious public and of having to defend himself and his position?

This state of affairs forbids one to use the letter at all with its unusually rich use of Scripture in answering the question how the apostle in the instruction of *his* churches refers to the Scriptures and how he utilises them. In its theoretical part the letter is an apologetic monologue with a few short fictitious dialogues. It is in no sense typical of the usual procedure of the apostle with respect to the churches, but rather it stands by itself and forms a great exception. Just as the reference to the Old Testament foundation of the gospel at the start of the letter is quite unusual ("the gospel which he promised beforehand through his prophets in the holy Scriptures, concerning his son, who was descended from David according to the flesh"), so also are many other features. In particular, we may note the large number of quotations from Scripture (addressed to Jewish Christians, not to Gentile Christians), the endeavour in carrying through the main thought (the working out [or explanation] of the nature of the gospel as it concerns grace and judgement, the cross, the Spirit and faith) to prove that everything has happened according to Scripture. The Law has not been abolished, but has been erected in a new way. Israel's privileges remain in force without being diminished. By chapter 8 and 11:32-36 all which torments and separates is abolished and a splendid universality has been achieved. But that does not alter the fact that in Romans we find a writing of the apostle which is useless for answering the question how the apostle as a missionary, teacher and writer has in his churches positioned himself regarding the Old Testament and how he has used it. I shall therefore dispense with discussing the use of Scripture and scriptural quotations in Romans here.[15]

III.

It is now possible to conclude and to answer the question originally asked: the text relating to the Old Testament, as it is found in the earliest and the latest letters of the apostle, is no coincidence, but rather the frequent Γραφή—quotations in the so called main letters (missing completely in the six letters) have been called forth by special conditions. From this it follows that from the beginning Paul did not give the Old Testament to the young churches as the book of Christian sources for edification. Rather, he based his mission and teaching wholly and completely on the gospel and expects edification to come exclusively from it and from the Spirit accompanying the gospel. The assumption that in the services of the Gentile churches there was from the beginning a 'reading of Scripture' is highly doubtful—not only because one may rightly ask how and from where it would have been possible to obtain the expensive volumes of Scripture,[16] but also because in the letters there is nowhere the mention of a reading of Scripture even where one may expect it. Certainly one has to assume that the apostle together with the proclamation of the gospel also reported the story of creation, the fall into sin, prophecy and the Law in outline and that he pointed to the old covenant. But all that could be mentioned in the first part of a

---

[15] Marcion had to decimate this letter; in the case of all other letters he could limit himself to several small excisions.

[16] A private reading of the Scriptures was at first virtually ruled out. The cost of a complete Old Testament would have come to several hundred marks.

single missionary sermon, because what matters were not the details but only the great facts as such. From the letters one does not get the impression that the churches knew more: because not only does the silence of the six letters speak for itself, but also, as we have seen, the content of Galatians and 1 and 2 Corinthians agrees. In Galatians the use of Scripture is limited to defending the Galatians from the severe and threatening danger of judaizers. What the apostle quotes from Scripture is new to the readers. But in the letters to the Corinthians he is addressing a church in which he has worked for eighteen months, which also received teaching and instruction from other Christian teachers, from Apollos and Peter, and which had members who tried to make their own way into theological secrets. So it is not surprising that he may assume more regarding their knowledge of Scripture and may offer more than in the other letters. Nevertheless even here the most important clarifications concerning Scripture are given by the apostle as new things. And even the whole viewing of Scripture from the point of view of the typological νουθεσία (warning) and the words δι᾽ ἡμᾶς ἐγράφη (it was written for us) appears not to have been heard by the apostle's readers before in such a definite way. At least they were not yet competent to absorb this knowledge.

With the words δι᾽ ἡμᾶς ἐγράφη (it was written for us) the story of the Old Testament begins as a book of edification in the Gentile church (a fact which should not be overstressed). Paul thereby stated this, but, as it were, only in passing.[17] The edification of his churches in outline and in detail should come through the Spirit from the gospel. The letters, rightly interpreted, bear witness to this.[18]

IV.

The bishop of Antioch, Ignatius, almost two generations after Paul, maintains virtually the same position as the apostle in his letters to the churches of Asia Minor and to Rome with regard to teaching the gospel and the Old Testament.[19] Everything is measured in relation

---

[17] Scripture cited as proof for the gospel is the other route which would result in an overvaluation of the Old Testament.

[18] It must be pointed out again how much more understandable Marcion's radicalism is regarding the Old Testament and his endeavour to free Paul's letters from supposed interpolations if one has gained the correct insight how Paul acted in his churches with regard to the Old Testament.

[19] Refer to von der Goltz in the 'Texts and enquiry of the ancient Christian history of literature', vol. XII, 3 (1894): 80ff.

to the gospel which is Jesus Christ. Any edification apart from it is denied. Nothing is allowed to stand alongside of the gospel. Of course the Old Testament is for him the Holy Scripture. He recognises the Law, honours the Prophets, who witnessed to Christ, and he affirms repeatedly that Jesus is the son of David against the docetics. But in the seven letters there are only two express quotations from Scripture (γέγραπται [it is written]) of colourless content (from the Proverbs, To the Ephesians 5:3 and To the Magnesians 12) and a few implicit references. Because Ignatius fully and completely lives in the new proclamation (χριστομαθία [teaching of Christ]) he says to those people who deliberately prefer the Old Testament and do not want to believe the gospel if it is not in the Old Testament text (To the Philadelphians 8:2): "for me the archives [ie. the Scriptures] are Jesus Christ, the inviolable archives are his cross and death and his resurrection and the faith which comes through him." Von der Goltz remarks correctly (page 82f): "Ignatius refers only to the story of Jesus, never to the Old Testament . . . ; he himself obviously did not place a high value on the evidence of the Old Testament . . . he believes in Jesus not because of the prophecy, but rather for Christ's sake he believes in those prophecies . . . in any case, Ignatius appears to stand far from the Law and has arrived at faith in Christ without it." It is surprising that the bishop of a main church, like that of Antioch, around the year 115 stood at such a distance from the Old Testament as a preacher and teacher and did not use it as a book of edification and warning in his letters.

But even another outstanding Christian writer, twenty years after Ignatius and, paradoxically, in Rome, shows a similar, even greater distance from the Old Testament: a man called Hermas, who wrote the book called "The Shepherd." This Christian prophet shows no knowledge of the Old Testament whatsoever, and if one would ascribe to him such knowledge based on vague references, it is in any case certain that he never quoted Scripture or referred to its authority. For him it is neither a book of edification, nor an instrument of proof or prophecy. It is not even a book of typological history. This is all the more evident in that he quoted (Vision 2:3-4) an obscure Jewish apocalyptic book ('Eldad and Modat') as an authority. He also used late Jewish traditions. He is a world apart from Paul's gospel. Naturally, one must not doubt that he used the Old Testament—otherwise he could not stand in the midst of the Roman church. But for him it was not an enlivening power which formed his piety. It is strange that such an attitude was possible at that time in

Rome! This is a strange state of affairs because we possess from that church a large official correspondence sometime before Hermas, the so called first letter of Clement, which in relation to the Old Testament shows a contrary attitude.[20]

According to 1 Clement Christianity is what it is not with Paul. It is rather what Paul refuses indirectly (πνεύματος, οὐ γράμματος [spirit not letter]), a religion of the book, that is, of the Old Testament. One may not choose a weaker expression here because every detail in the letter of Clement, including teaching, admonition, and even those details which concern the organisation of the cult are given on the basis of Old Testament sayings which have validity as a direct authority for giving the church rules. More than one hundred long and short quotations from Holy Scripture (about thirty printed pages!) are cited—the letter is really an elaboration of Old Testament sayings. Only two quotations from the gospel (chs. 13 and 46) are found and these take up a very small space. They concern the specifically evangelical facts and thoughts derived from them and stand next to the spiritualised, allegorised or directly used Old Testament thoughts and commandments. A few sparse thoughts of Paul (chs. 32, 37, 47, 49 etc) appear alongside. Yet this letter is strictly universal and has no relation to national and specifically Jewish Christianity. With regard to its derivation the church is apparently now for the greater part Gentile Christian, and the nation of Israel does not enjoy the slightest preference. It is not even mentioned. Nevertheless Christianity is the religion of the Law and of the Book, and Paul's thinking, with which the author tries to agree, almost appears to be a foreign body in it. Therefore, I have no doubt that one may from this letter make a verdict regarding the spiritual condition of the Roman church at the time when Paul wrote the letter to the Romans. Even then (apart from the superficially received Paulinism) the church had a 'Christianity of the book', which according to the letter characterises it. Even though it sounds therefore paradoxical— he who undertakes to write an introduction to Paul's letter to the Romans should above all stick critically and carefully to the first letter of Clement in order to gain a fundamental outline for the Christianity of the Roman church in Paul's time.[21] He will soon see

---

20   Refer to my paper regarding this letter in the conference report of 1909, pp. 38ff.

21   Although the first letter of Clement has been studied extensively by and since Lightfoot, this letter has even now not been valued as highly as it ought (except by Sohm). As an historical, dogmatic and literary document from the first

why, strikingly, this letter makes hardly any use of Paul's letter to the Romans: because the antithesis and the synthesis, determined by the apostle in Romans between the Law and the gospel, old people and new people, including the prerogative of the latter, is in a disparate position to the thoughts of the Roman church and would have embarrassed them.

Whilst Paul worked for a Christianity which had its centre and its driving power in the gospel and which regarded the Old Testament as the subordinate part, right from the beginning in Palestine and in the Diaspora a Christianity grew up which, as a matter of course, had a second focus next to the gospel, the Holy Book. This focus was very strong compared to the first and threatened to push it into the background. In the so called Letter of Barnabas, with one hundred Old Testament quotations, probably written in Alexandria, the situation is no different, even if its author understood a little bit more of Paul's gospel than Clement did. The public reading of the Old Testament which appeared in the last decades of the first century in the Gentile Christian churches (1 Tim 4:13: "Attend to the public reading of Scripture, to preaching . . .") and which was found in the church services fixed the Old Testament as a foundation of Christian faith. The admonition, "All Scripture is inspired by God and is profitable for teaching, for reproof, for correction and for training in righteousness" (2 Tim 3:16), has with its absolute claim of Old Testament *littera scripta* (written documents) to take preference over the proclamation which had not yet any *littera scripta* (written documents). Thus out of the religious presuppositions of the Greek world the Old Testament was pushed alongside the gospel and the vulgar Christianity of the Book and Law came about, because Paulinism as propaganda teaching was not powerful enough[22] and Marcion tried to dynamite the Old Testament in vain.

Paul did not want the religion of the Book of the Old Testament for Christianity and he did not create it. But since he, next to his fundamental concept of law and gospel, works and faith, slavery and freedom, not only allowed the typological view of the Old Testament to stand, but himself practised it, and in some cases with regard to

---

century and as an official letter of the main Christian church it is absolutely unique and should be treated in exegetical lectures as thoroughly as the New Testament scriptures.

[22] It is astonishing and a proof of the spiritual power and importance of one man that he so strongly modified it, as is taught by the development from the first letter of Clement right up to the ancient Catholic fathers.

the gospel he simply appealed to the authority of the Old Testament, he is partly guilty of the dubious developments which appeared in the churches. But through the mightiest creation of church history (one might say: prepared by Paul), the New Testament, all this could have been completely reformed and nullified if the church had possessed the courage to draw out all the consequences of its own creation. In any case, since the fight against Marcion and against gnosticism and since the creation of the New Testament, the Old Testament was pushed into the second position. But since it was a rule-giving, *but at the same time partially superceded Word of God*, it averted the position that the churches' Christianity became the religion of the book based on the New Testament. Because the Old Testament, which stood next to the New, was in part only relatively valid, this did not allow absolute 'grammatolatry' with regard to the Bible generally. Biblicism received its wholesome corrective from the authority of apostolic teaching, which appeared side by side with the authority of Scripture, organising and limiting it.

CHAPTER TWO

The Question of the Content of Paul's Instructions*

Traugott Holtz
(1981)

The question before us is this: how far does the binding force of the ethical passages of the New Testament reach?[1] Does it consist only in a universal instruction for unspecified moral action, which in its historical outworking must be applied in accordance with the new situation, and therefore cannot be firmly defined in advance of and apart from a given historical situation? In other words, can it be made binding according to its content? Or does it extend also to concrete action, which—whatever the historical situation may have been—is to be carried out in a firm way according to the content? There are therefore two alternative possibilities to consider. We must naturally assume that both may contain some truth.

---

* Translated by George S. Rosner and Brian S. Rosner.
[1] This essay is based on a lecture given in the autumn of 1979 in Halle and Greifswald (during a theological workshop), which addressed the question of the specifics and obligation of Christian ethics.

Since it is impossible, at any rate not rational because of the limits of an article, to address this question to the whole New Testament, we shall refer in the following essay only to Paul. It is from him that the tradition of the New Testament supplies the richest material for an answer to our question.

W. Schrage has already covered an important area of our theme in his monograph.[2] The decisive insight of this book is that Paul's paraenesis is by necessity unfolded in concrete single commandments, which have more than merely paradigmatic character and are not only valid for an interim period (until the Christian has matured to the free and elementary unfolding action of love). This is an accurate assessment of the evidence. Schrage contends that his research:

> has led again and again to the conclusion that Paul's answer
> to the question of how a Christian should behave is not only
> the paradoxical answer: 'like a Christian!' With regard to the
> question, 'what shall I do as a loving person?' Paul has not
> only answered: 'to love as you love yourself', but Paul has
> also clearly and unmistakeably shown what love forbids and
> what love commands, . . . that even the most concrete
> obedience of a concrete commandment can fall short of
> obedience and love does not negate the fact that there are
> normative, concrete commandments. In Paul's ethics we do
> not find only a colourless and formless imperative, bare of all
> shape and concreteness. It is true that as an immortal demand
> love goes *beyond* the single commandments but it does not
> simply *pass them by*.[3]

Despite such fundamentally correct insights into the character of Paul's paraenesis, the last word on the problem has not been spoken. It certainly pays to refocus our attention upon it. Establishing the "that" of concrete single instructions does not answer the question regarding their "why." Only an answer to the "why" can make the binding force of this kind of ethics theologically transparent. The question remains open whether only the concreteness of paraenesis as such, such as we have it in single commandments, is binding according to Paul's theology or whether single commandments claim lasting validity. The last sentence of the

---

2 *Die konkreten Einzelgebote in der paulinischen Paränese: Ein Beitrag zur neutestamentlichen Ethik*, Gütersloh, 1961.

3 *Ibid*, pp. 270f.

quotation from Schrage appears to me to signal the uncertainty in which he leaves the reader in this respect: love transcends single commandments but it does not pass them by. Thus love remains for Schrage a principle which in regard to single commandments is of a higher order, which can at the same time by itself demand real obligation.

Schrage already posed the question of the fundamental norms of content underlying the apostolic demands in the final part of his monograph (Section VIII).[4] O. Merk has also fully addressed this question.[5] Both authors reach the same conclusion regarding this fundamental concern. They say that Paul knows no coherent norm for moral action as far as it is concrete action, but rather that he presents his concrete paraenesis with a large number of different reasons and arguments. This is also the case when Merk rightly states, with reference to his analysis of several paraenetic paragraphs, that they are founded on only one or at least a few basic arguments, with auxiliary arguments playing only a secondary role. In each case Merk shows (in his 'summary') that Paul uses manifold arguments in his paraenesis.[6] Here we may notice that a glance at the concordance regarding *agapaō* (I love) and *agapē* (love) teaches us that though Paul knows love as the substance of paraenesis, he uses the two named terms in surprisingly small measure as the reason for his instructions.

An example will make this clear. In 1 Corinthians 6:12-20 Paul deals with the question of whether one may have sexual intercourse with a harlot. It is true that this theme does not immediately appear at the start of verse 12. It appears at first quite generally in verse 13b with the word *porneia* (which may include several things[7]). Only at the end of verse 15 is it stated openly with the word *pornē*. This fact does not force us to assume that Paul's line of thought was not quite clear and did not take true aim from the beginning. It rather means that the apostle is dealing very concretely with a situation in the church, a church which knew what was at stake. Paul is from the

---

[4] *Ibid*, pp. 187-271.

[5] *Handeln aus Glauben: Die Motivierungen der paulinischen Ethik* (= Marburger Theol. Stud., 5) Marburg, 1968; cf. also the 'Vorstudien zu einer Ethik des Neuen Testaments' by G. Strecker, *Handlungsorientierter Glaube*, Stuttgart-Berlin 1972, as well as the instructive essay by the same author: 'Autonome Sittlichkeit und das Proprium der christlichen Ethik bei Paulus', *ThLZ* 104, 1979, pp. 865-872.

[6] *Ibid*, pp. 231-248.

[7] Cf. Hauck-Schulz, *TDNT* 6:579-595; summarised by Test Sim 5:3; similarly Test Reub 4:6; Jub 25:1.

start dealing with arguments which concern the matter in question in this particular church.

Paul uses a slogan in verse 12 which appears to legalise every behaviour: "Everything is permissible for me." He does not even limit this when he further states "but not everything is useful." If a thing is not useful, it is not necessarily harmful. At least it is not forbidden. And even in the repetition of the sentence it is by no means made invalid by the addition of "but I will not allow anything to dominate me." This qualification does not touch upon the "everything" but rather it only shows the limitation of all principally free action. Paul obviously does not wish to speak against the words "everything is permissible for me." However, he wants to take away their significance in the present context. This explanation of the text brings about the supposition, expressed by H. Lietzmann, that this slogan is in fact Paul's own words, which he had used in an anti-judaistic sense.[8] We find it again in a similar repetition and limitation of its meaning in 10:23. But there the strongly individual "to me" is missing. This allows the supposition that Paul used the words (in the form of 10:23) in the dispute which concerned pure and impure, in the discussion regarding the question of forbidden or permitted food (cf. Rom 14:14-23; 1 Cor 8:8; 10:27). Corinthian theologians, however, have by analogy transferred these words to the realm of sexuality, which from their point of view was obvious. Paul's first thought refutes this analogy and refers to the fornication committed by a man who is in relationship to the Lord, in contrast to food which is in a relationship to the belly. The person of a man, however, unlike his stomach, does not belong to the sphere of mortality and apparent unimportance. The person, by contrast, is in the realm of God's resurrection. It seems that behind this is the unspoken thought, a thought which is a matter of course for Paul, that the body must be kept from fornication. The body's link with fornication is against the future action of God. Verse 15 introduces a new thought. Since Christians are members of Christ they must not make themselves members of a harlot, which happens by sexual union. Paul stresses this with reference to Scripture (Gen 2:24). Finally, verse 18 introduces a still different thought. The argument here is that only fornication is a sin against one's own body. This is difficult to

---

[8]   *An die Korinther* I.II,4., by W.G. Kümmel (Hdbch NT 9), Tübingen 1949, p. 27.

understand.[9] Nevertheless, the exact interpretation of this thought does not have to occupy us here, when we recognise that it does not prove, but rather assumes that "to fornicate" = "to sin." It does not actually argue for the warning against the sin of fornication, but rather argues for its degree of importance, since it is truly a sacrilege against the temple of the Holy Spirit.

When one looks at the type of proofs used in this passage, a three-fold type of proof which employs thoughts that are not entirely unconnected, but are rather independent, this shows that Paul does not produce a single, powerful argument for the material content of the instruction: "flee immorality" (vs. 18a). This becomes even more apparent when one looks closely at the content of the first two proofs. The third one, however, as we saw, already presupposes the position that is being argued, that fornication is sin. Thought through properly, the two first lines of thought are against every sexual union, not only with a harlot. It has therefore been thought—up to a point rightly—that such a method of proof shows that for Paul sexual intercourse as such is sinful. Since that is obviously not the case, as the following chapter (1 Cor 7) shows, one must conclude that the reasons for the conduct to which Paul in 1 Corinthians 6:12-20 refers, namely, not to have relations with a harlot, do not actually furnish a really binding argument for that assumption. They only have force if beforehand it is established that intercourse with the harlot is sinful action. In any case, the instruction which Paul gives cannot possibly have grown out of the content of the argument. Rather, it builds upon traditional instruction. This instruction is found clearly in the area of Jewish thought from which Paul is descended.[10]

Going to a harlot did not appear as a matter of course to be forbidden to the Corinthians who defended such conduct. A. Schlatter formulated several possible questions which may have justified intercourse with a harlot: "Did not intercourse with the whore fall within the conduct of Christian freedom? After all nothing happened to her, except what she herself wanted and what furnished her means of existence."[11]

The fact that the content of the instruction given by Paul cannot

---

[9] The assumption by H. Conzelmann, *1 Corinthians*, Philadelphia, 1975, p. 112, that it is "of course formulated in an ad hoc fashion" is in any case unsatisfactory.

[10] Cf. eg. CD 7:1f. "To keep away from whores in accordance with the law"; Test Rub 5:5: "flee from fornication, my children."

[11] *Paulus der Bote Jesu*, 2nd Edition, Stuttgart 1956, p. 198.

have grown from his argument has already been observed in another example, namely, 1 Corinthians 11:3-16. Even here Paul advances several reasons for his instruction to the women to cover their heads when praying or prophesying. Yet none of the reasons advanced shows that such conduct is required. E. Käsemann remarks correctly with reference to this:

> The use of several arguments proves to the sober listener and reader only that none of the reasons advanced out of several independent arguments are valid on their own. Thus one [i.e., Paul] is arguing on the defensive."[12]

This demonstrates to Käsemann, "that the concrete reasoning of Paul's paraenesis can be problematical. It may be neither truly theologically based nor enlightening without further information."[13]

In view of 6:12ff one may ask if this reasoning has general validity and significance. The situation which Käsemann observes in 1 Corinthians 11:3ff. only emerges so clearly there because the content of Paul's instruction appears to us to be so strange and unacceptable. It does not appear in itself reasonable without all reasons being given. In the interest of the question just mentioned we shall quickly look at the content and reasoning of other norms of conduct which Paul advances or recommends to the church. For a start we shall stay with the first letter to the Corinthians. In chapter 5 Paul turns to the questions of the concrete way of life in the church, after he has dealt with a fundamental theological argument against false developments at Corinth (chs. 1-4). To begin with there is the discussion of an especially gross case. A member of the church is living with his father's wife in sexual union. Even the way in which Paul describes this case in the introduction, "fornication of such type, which is not even found among the heathen", verse 1, shows the negative verdict which he gives in this case. Thus his following instruction is not aimed to undo this conduct and to advance a reason to forbid it, but it aims to remove the culprit from the church (with, however, the aim of final salvation for him, which one ought after all to consider). For Paul it is of course certain that we are here dealing with fornication and fornication of such a severe kind cannot co-exist with membership of the church.

Even though this may appear to us to be self-evident, it is not

---

12   *Exegetisch Versuche und Besinnungen*, Vol. 2, Göttingen 1964, p. 217.
13   *Ibid*.

so without certain quite firm presuppositions, which really are assumed, but not spelt out in the passage. The Corinthians show that it is indeed in no way self-evident. Apparently in their church such a case is not considered a severe fault which makes membership in the church impossible. "And you are arrogant! Ought you not rather to mourn? Therefore remove such a one from your midst?!"; 5:2. It must be considered possible, even when the text does not clearly say so that the deed had been established as 'Christian' and that such reasoning was accepted at least by part of the church.[14]

The 'assumption' with which Paul approaches this case is evidently of a Jewish nature. This is shown by the use of the term "fornication" for its description[15] and even more from the close characterisation of this "fornication" as being one, "which is not even found among the heathen." When speaking of the ethnē Paul evidently is thinking precisely of the "heathen."[16] It is a special accusation consisting of the fact that such a shameful deed was condemned even by the heathen. This "even," however, implies that the condemnation was naturally pronounced by the Jews and that this clearly should be sufficient. Finally, naming the female partner of the sinner "wife of the father" shows that this case is considered with Jewish eyes. This is so because "wife of the father" ('eschaet-'ab) is a technical term in Old Testament Jewish law which is differentiated from "mother" ('em) and which signifies the step-mother.[17] Sexual union with her was according to Leviticus 18:8 (as well as the text from the Mishnah in note 17[18]) considered a crime worthy of death. We may assume that Paul's assumption stems from this.[19]

---

14 Cf. A. Schlatter, fn. 11, pp. 171f.

15 Cf. concerning NT-Jewish linguistic style Hauck-Schulz, *TDNT* 6:583f., 587-590; this extended meaning does not correspond to the pagan Greek linguistic style, cf. also p. 583 fn. 25: "it appears in the pure catalogues of vices not as *porneia* but as *akolasia*"; in Liddell-Scott, *A Greek-English Lexicon*, Oxford 1940, s.v. *porneia* only passages of the New Testament are quoted to support the translation of *porneia* as "fornication, unchastity."

16 Otherwise he could have said (as in vs. 12f) *en tois exō* (those who are outside); concerning the *ethnē* "heathen" cf. Schmidt, *TDNT* 2:369-72.

17 Lev 18:7-8 *'em* and *'eschaet-'ab* next to each other; similarly mSanh 7:4 (4a "these are to be stoned: he who has intercourse with his mother or his father's wife": 4b and c clearly show the difference).

18 Cf. also eg. Ps-Phocylides 179f; see P. van der Horst, *The Sentences of Pseudo-Phocylides* (= SVTP 4), Leiden 1978, p. 230 ("frequently discussed in Jewish literature," with quoted proofs).

19 In Ps-Phoc 179 there is, remarkably, the Greek word for "stepmother," namely *mētryiē*.

The next concrete case which is dealt with in our letter, 6:1ff, concerns the conduct of lawsuits at heathen courts of law. For Paul this is a severe derailment: "someone among you has the audacity!" (6:1). Again the reasoning for the condemnation of such conduct is very strange: "Do you not know that the saints will judge the world?" (vs. 2); "Do you not know that we will judge angels?" (vs. 3). These are statements which are only understandable within the framework of the eschatological expectation of Judaism,[20] which has been accepted by the early church. On closer view such arguments do not relate directly to the matter under discussion. It is true that from the verbal analogy of "the saints" and "to judge", verse 3, the thought emerges which has a bearing on the matter, that of worthiness. But the instruction to avoid heathen courts of law does not emerge from this in any clearly convincing way. As a matter of fact Paul advances further in his argumentation and depicts lawsuits as wrong in principle in the life of the church.[21]

However, this last step does not obliterate the fact that Paul, with regard to the conditions in Corinth, in the first place condemns going to heathen judges instead of those in the church. Even here the real reason for such a decision is found in the the fact that Judaism, with reason, acted like this. And again such derivation from Judaism shows itself linguistically with great probability. The heathen judges are in verse 1 called *adikoi*, the unrighteous. This is not a verdict regarding their subjective character: of course there were enough "just" judges in the heathen world (a fact known to the Corinthians, who came from this world). In verse 9 Paul uses this word in a quite different manner. It would already go too far to consider that the heathen judges who are called *adikoi* are "despisers of divine law."[22] They simply do not know it, just as they do not know God. They are in an objective sense "unrighteous." Even the change in verse 6 to the proper 'Christian' word *apistoi*, unbelievers, as well as the different use of language of *adikoi* in verse 9, merely shows that Paul in verse 1 does not formulate the instruction himself, but relies in this way of speaking on the synagogue, which ordered its members to use their own justice system.[23] Taking over linguistic terms signals the taking

---

[20] Cf. 1 QpHab V 4f; P. Volz, *Die Eschatologie der jüdischen Gemeinde*, Tübingen 1934, 275f.

[21] Cf. the important essay of E. Dinkler, 'Zum Problem der Ethik bei Paulus', in: *Signum Crucis*, Tübingen 1967, pp. 204-240.

[22] Thus Schrenk, *TDNT* 1:151.

[23] Cf. Jos., Ant 14,235 (10,17); Schürer III, pp. 113f; Billb. III, pp. 362f.

over of the decision in this matter.

In 1 Corinthians 7 the situation is considerably more complicated than in the three cases we have discussed so far. The
fundamental decisions, however, clearly show Jewish assumptions.
F.M. Cross comments with a view to the consideration of marriage in
Qumran: "Paul's opinion of marriage derives from the same
theological idea, namely, that he who marries does a good thing and
he who remains single, an even better thing, for 'the time is short.'"[24]
In allowing or recommending marriage as being better than
fornication (7:2) Paul is probably "dependent on Judaism, for there
too we find the view that marriage protects from fornication."[25]

Whether the fundamental instruction in verse 1, "a man does
well not to touch a woman" represents Paul's position or is the
quotation of the words of Corinthian 'gnostics,' whom Paul refutes
with verse 2, is debated.[26] To me the first is the more probable.
However, even without a plain decision on this question it is
revealed that Paul truly tends to counsel celibacy (7:6f,26,32).[27] This,
however, seems to be strongly against the law of Judaism because
"the overwhelming opinion of rabbinic scholars indicates that for a
man marriage was an unconditional commandment of duty".[28]
However, the community at Qumran showed that there were Jewish
groups which at least in part lived the celibate life. The conduct of the
Essenes (to which we relate the community at Qumran) with
reference to marriage is not completely transparent. There were
certainly Essene groups which lived in marriage.[29] But certainly there
were also celibate groups and there is much that suggests that they
were in the majority.[30] Equally important as the fact that a strictly

---

24 *Die antike Bibliothek von Qumran und die moderne biblische Wissenschaft*,
Neukirchen 1967, p. 104.

25 W. Schrage, 'Zur Frontstellung der paulinischen Ehebewertung in 1 Kor 7,1-
7', *ZNW* 67, 1976, p. 228.

26 Cf. Schrage, fn. 25, pp. 214-234.

27 Even Schrage finally admits this, see fn. 25, 233, "abstention from marriage,
which Paul according to vs. 7a undoubtedly prefers."

28 Billb. III, pp. 367f.

29 Cf. Jos., Bell 2, 160f as well as CD 7:6-8 (= 19:3-5); cf. 1 QSa 1,4.9f ("Rules for
the whole community of Israel in the last days").

30 Jos., Ant 18:21; Jewish War 2:120f; Pliny, Hist. Nat. 5:17; Philo, Hypothetica
14. "In any case the great main cemetery of Qumran with about 1,000 graves
appears to consist only of men's graves" (F.M. Cross, fn. 24, p. 101)—a strong
witness for the fact that the main group at Qumran lived in celibacy. H. Hübner,
'Zölibat in Qumran?', *NTS* 17, 1971, pp. 153-167, denies the state of celibacy at
Qumran. In his view there was a limited cultic abstention (limited in time) for the

legal Jewish group did not feel bound to obey Genesis 1:28 regarding
the strict commandment to marry is the argument that seemingly
justified such conduct:

> The refusal of marriage corresponds to the radicalisation of
> priestly prescriptions for purity caused by the great
> eschatological expectation, that is, the conviction that one was
> living in the holy camp of God's hosts.[31]

It is decisive for us that Paul's recommendation of celibacy
cannot be considered impossible for a Jew, but rather may grow out
of the spirit of the Judaism of his time. Paul does not tell his church
that celibacy is unconditionally demanded. The reasoning which he
gives for his own disposition (7:28,32-35) is one which he did not add
to traditional teaching, but which in fact contains the content of the
recommendation (one may ask whether the assumptions of the
reasoning are correct, but this belongs to a different subject).

Of course the individual instructions in 1 Corinthians 7 are also
influenced by other motives and conditions. Thus, above all the
reference to the instruction of the "Lord" regarding the question of
divorce must be considered (vs. 10), which invalidated the
permission of the Law or at least strongly limited it. We shall have to
merely refer to the importance of Jesus for Paul's understanding of
the Law in passing. Here we note only that this is not an instruction
against the Law.

With regard to the next chapters, 1 Corinthians 8-10, we
proceed on the assumption that it is not necessary to dissect them in a
literary critical manner (and therefore we must not do so). They deal
entirely with one limited theme: the question of the use of "meat
offered to idols." Paul immediately describes it with a purely Jewish-
Greek term, *eidōlothyton* (8:1; presumably in answering a question by
the church, which—as taught by Paul—already used this term). For
Judaism the issue was absolutely clear. Food, which had been

Sabbath period. It may be considered that some members of the *yahad* widened
this sexual abstention, which was limited to a period of time, into a continual
abstention," p. 167.

[31] Michel/Bauernfeind, *Flavius Josephus, De bello Judaico*, I, Munich, 1959, pp.
431f; cf. also Cross, fn. 24, pp. 100-104 ("The New Testament as well as Qumran
advise not to marry in this time of crisis, since this world is about to pass away");
similarly H. Braun, *Qumran und das Neue Testament I*, Tübingen 1966, 192f;
Schrage, fn. 25, pp. 225f; both authors emphasise a dualistic ascetic motive more
strongly.

brought into contact with pagan cults, was strictly forbidden as being unclean.[32] In Corinth, however, quite a different decision was established theologically. If our supposition, which we have already mentioned, is correct that the slogan "everything is permissible (for me)" goes back to Paul himself, at least in substance (cf. above), then he has certainly initiated this development. Romans 14 clearly shows that, not only in reaction to the Corinthian dicussion, but in any case, this has validity for Paul: "I know and am convinced in the Lord Jesus that nothing is unclean in itself" (vs. 14). This sentence cannot be compared in meaning to the famous words of Rabbi Johanan b. Zakkai:

> Neither does a dead person create an unclean state nor does the water clean, but rather it is the decision of the King of Kings. The Holy One . . . has said: I have decreed a statute, I have made a decision; no one shall transgress my decision (Pes 74/40b).

Paul's words are strictly contrary to this. Paul indicates in Romans 14:14, quoted above, upon what his judgment regarding this matter is founded, namely, on the *Kyrios* Jesus.

If we now return to 1 Corinthians 8-10, we must establish that the reasoning which is based upon the profession of Christ speaks for the content of the decision made by the Corinthian partners in the discussion. Even Paul cannot get away from that. All the same, he clearly resists the consequences of this insight. The limitation of liberty in the use of all food, which is asserted in 8:7, is still theologically convincing: the consideration of the weaker brother, which Paul so expressly (and certainly not without an additional special cause) bases on his personal example in chapter 9. However, 10:1-22, which despite the gap between verses 13 and 14 is a unity, looks in quite a different direction. Whatever one may say theologically regarding meat offered to idols, nevertheless in this sphere great dangers lie in ambush. This is shown first of all in the fate of "our fathers" in the desert, who gave in to their greed for food,

---

32 Dan 1:8ff: Daniel, together with his companions, did not eat any of the king's food and only ate vegetables and water (and nevertheless were in splendid health). Regarding the food Joseph ate in the house of the priest of Pentephres Joseph and Asenath 7:1 states: "And he had a separate table, for this [eating with Egyptians] was considered by him to be an abomination" (in contrast to Gen 34:32: the Egyptians do not eat together with the Hebrews, "because it was an abomination for the Egyptians" [also similarly LXX]!).

drink and play and were thereby ruined. The one who takes part in the community meal, in the Lord's Supper, cannot take part in ceremonial meals which aim at communion with other superhuman powers, no matter what their "objective" reality may be. The Lord your God is a jealous God (cf. 10:22). It cannot be overlooked that Paul is here speaking out of the "hypothesis" of Judaism, and that is what advises him in this regard. The admonition "flee idolatry" (vs. 14) is the main comment on this matter for Paul.

We shall not consider 11:3-16 more closely here. That the reasoning for the content of the decision, that women had to cover their heads when praying or prophesying, cannot convince, has already been shown above. Why then is Paul insisting so forcefully on this regulation? It does not appear to me to be very probable that he has adopted this fashion out of the Christian church before his time and therefore established it with apostolic authority.[33] But also, it is not convincing to think that Paul wishes to stand against the emancipation from the relationship to the creation of Christian service in the world.[34] After all, the refusal to assume this "custom only introduced for the first time by him, and in any case completely foreign to the Greek woman"[35] cannot in any way be understood as an emancipation or as the expression of 'enthusiasm.' Rather, the order of Judaism provides the explanation here: "The Jewish custom . . . is in accordance with Paul's direction: the Jewish woman may appear in public only with her head covered."[36] Paul fights for the introduction or the observance of the Jewish custom, even if he can only find a reason for it with great difficulty.[37] To him this observance was, naturally, the same as all prescriptions of Judaism, in accordance with the Torah.

In 1 Corinthians 11:17ff. Paul considers matters which concern specific areas of Christian church life which have to be arranged according to its needs and with attention to the suppositions of such institutions. There is no direct gain to be made here regarding our chosen theme.

It is not possible in this essay to go through all of Paul's letters with the question which alone is important for us. That question is:

---

[33] So Merk, fn. 5, p. 135.
[34] So Käsemann, fn 12, p. 217.
[35] Käsemann, fn. 12, p. 216.
[36] Conzelmann, fn. 9, p. 217; cf. A. Schlatter, *Die Theologie des Judentums nach dem Bericht des Josefus* (= BFchTh 2,26), Gütersloh 1932, 169; Billb. III, 427ff.
[37] Cf. Kümmel in Lietzmann/Kümmel, fn. 8, p. 184.

where the content of a firmly delineated, material instruction of the apostle is not necessarily derived from the arguments which are quoted, from what source does this material content derive? This question has naturally and especially to be posed where an argument is completely missing. This is the case in 1 Thessalonians 4:1-8. In this paragraph Paul simply reminds the church of the instructions which it received regarding "how one ought to walk and please God" (vs. 1). However, from the phrase "I have given you instructions through the Lord Jesus" (vs. 2) it does not follow that Paul argued the content of the instruction christologically, but only that he founded the instructions in their relevance for the members of the church in *Kyrios* Jesus. The content, the "will of God" (vs. 3), with its double substance, namely, refraining from fornication and from greedily cheating one's brother, corresponds exactly with a basic Jewish catechism of behaviour, which can be shown as the basic argument of a great many parts of the *Corpus Paulinum*.[38]

An exact analysis of the content of the individual directions, which Paul introduces after pointing to the "reasonable worship of God" in Romans 12:1 and 12:9ff, shows us that where the instructions are concrete there is concord with Jewish demands. This also applies where one may assume a word of the Lord in the background. It is rather characteristic that the two circumstances are not exclusive; and this applies with reference to this subject both for Paul's understanding as well as for the understanding of Jesus.[39]

It has recently again been supposed that Romans 13:1-7 was not originally part of the letter to the Romans, but that it was rather a traditional passage coming from the synagogue.[40] In this view the agreement of these instructions with Judaism is clearly delineated, which is something that has otherwise been clearly established, even if, as I assume, 13:1-7 originally belonged to Romans.[41]

---

[38] [The editor: A student of Holtz has developed these thoughts in a monograph: Eckardt Reinmuth, *Geist und Gesetz: Studien zu Voraussetzungen und Inhalt der paulinischen Paränese* (Berlin: Evangelische Verlagsanstalt, 1985)].

[39] Cf. the interesting essay by Ch. H. Talbert, 'Tradition and Redaction in Romans 12:9-21', *NTS* 16, 1969/70, pp. 83-93 ("There does seem to be a Semitic ethical tradition behind Rom XII, 9b-21 but it has been subjected to redaction in Hellenistic Christianity," p. 93). On the other hand he does not ask the question of the thematic relationship to Judaism.

[40] W. Schmithals, *Der Römerbrief als historisches Problem*, Gütersloh 1975.

[41] Cf. eg. U. Wilkens, in *Dimensions de la Vie Chrétienne*, ed. L. De Lorenzi (= Monogr. "Benedictina," Sect. Bib.-Oecum. 4), Rome 1979, pp. 107-110 (= *Rechtfertigung als Freiheit*, Neukirchen-Vluyn 1974, pp. 223-226).

In addition to this passage, the apostle summarises the exhortations at the end of the general paraenetic part of Romans.[42] This summary consists of: "love one another" (13:8). By doing this one thing the Law is completely fulfilled. The word "completely" in this saying carries special weight! All demands of the Torah are summarised, for Paul recounts commandments of the second part of the Ten Commandments and this list is expressly rounded off with the words "and whatever commandment there is in addition" (vs. 9). The whole (Law) is summarised in the commandment of Leviticus 19:18: "you shall love your neighbour as yourself". "Therefore, the fulfillment of the law is love" (vs. 10).[43] The text clearly shows that "love" does not only mean the attitude, but the deed of love, which cannot present itself in any way apart from fulfilling the demands of the Law. That the commandment to love "does not tolerate in its character the formulating of any positive conditions,"[44] does not really apply for Paul. Neither does the reference to Romans 13:10a, "love does not do evil to your neighbour",[45] make this clear.

Galatians 5:14 shows how fundamental the thought is for Paul that the Christian's action of expressing love is nothing other than the fullfillment of the Law. "The entire *nomos*" is fulfilled in one commandment, Leviticus 19:18. Verse 22f once more shows that the love mentioned presents itself in concrete, positive and provable demonstration. When Paul finishes recounting such a fruit of love with a sentence, which is formed as a litotes, 5:23b,[46] then he wishes to say, in a slightly ironical way according to the situation of the letter, that it is quite in accordance with the Law![47]

Finally, the definition of what really matters in the life of the Christian according to Paul is given in 1 Corinthians 7:19 and

---

[42] E. Käsemann, *An die Römer* (= HNT 8a), Tübingen 1974, p. 347: Title to 13:8-14, "Summary of the General Paraenesis."

[43] *pleroma = plerosis*, cf. Delling, *TDNT* 6:305.

[44] R. Bultmann, *Theologie des Neuen Testaments*, Tübingen 1968, p. 570.

[45] So Bultmann, also fn. 44; on the other hand also Schrage, fn. 2, p. 269.

[46] Cf. this with BDF; F. Rehkopf, 'Grammatisches zum Neuen Testament', in: *Der Ruf Jesu und die Antwort der Gemeinde*, FS J. Jeremias, ed. E. Lohse, Göttingen 1970, pp. 220-222 (Grammatik parag. 495,2: "Paraphrase of an increase out of restraint by the negation of the contrary"); on the other hand he does not consider our passage in that regard.

[47] *nomos* is the subject of the sentence; with regard to *einai kata tinos* refer to Bauer, *Wörterbuch*, s.v. *kata* I 2b *g*: "to be against someone"; the translation "against such there is no law" (eg. F. Mussner, *Der Galaterbrief* [= HThK IX] Freiburg 1974, p. 384) is therefore incorrect.

Galatians 5:6. Galatians 5:6: "Faith, which works through love"; 1
Corinthians 7:19: "keeping God's commandments." In mentioning
these items side by side the fact that the deed of love and the
fulfillment of God's commandment are identical is made clear. The
two statements refer to each other because of the statement which in
each case precedes the word "rather." At the same time the words
which introduce the sayings pose a fundamental problem for the
entire complex with which we are dealing. It is in both cases
identical: circumcision or uncircumcision is irrelevant (rather what is
relevant is what is shown in each case in the following sentences). If
the words "keeping God's commandments" (1 Cor 7:19), as well as
the deed of love which is motivated by faith (Gal 5:6), are related to
the fulfillment of the Law (Rom 13:10), this appears to speak against
the prior sentence, which declares the fulfillment of the claim of the
law regarding circumcision to be meaningless.

Indeed, we are here confronted by one of the central problems
of the theology of the Law not only for Paul, but for the New
Testament generally, and furthermore for early Judaism, which
requires more thorough thematic research.[48] In any case, Bultmann
states: "As far as the *nomos* in the Old Testament Law with all its
cultic and ritual commandments confronts Paul . . . it is self evident
that the *nomos* cannot in its entirety be valid."[49] With the last part of
this statement Bultmann passes too quickly over the matter, which
indeed can hardly be termed "self evident." The Law "as far as it
contains God's demand . . . , maintains its validity."[50] But this must in
fact be valid for Paul even regarding the cultic and ritual laws
because, according to Bultmann, "he does not in the Jewish sense
value the cultic-ritual commandments according to their content, but
only looks upon them in the sense that they are demands like the
ethical commandments."[51] A solution to this problem, which appears
if the various statements of Bultmann should be valid next to one
another, can only arise in the assumption, "that the identical sense of
the cultic-ritual and of the ethical demands are only valid for man
before *pistis*, and that there is in faith an unreflected effective

---

48 [The editor: The problem was addressed by one of Holtz's students: Karl-
Wilhelm Niebuhr, *Gesetz und Paränese: Katechismusartige Weisungsreihen in der
frühjüdischen Literatur* (Tübingen: J.C.B. Mohr [Paul Siebeck], 1987).]

49 Bultmann, fn. 44, p. 342.

50 *Ibid.*

51 Bultmann, fn. 44, p. 261.

principle of criticism."[52]

Such an explanation of Paul's position with respect to the Law, which is sharply delineated, does not do justice to the historic position of the cultic-ritual commandments in Paul's world. Even the earliest church, which formed in Jerusalem and which manifestly lived according to the order of the Torah, and which stayed close to the temple, did not live according to the cult of the temple even though it was a demand of the Torah. The so called "hellenists" went decisively further by getting away from the temple and the holy city,[53] but they maintained, at least at first, the rite of circumcision.[54]

Tradition shows that such an attitude, at least at its foundation, goes back to Jesus himself. Even the Gospel of Matthew, which strictly observes the Law, and has such a decisive passage as 5:18, shows at important points the word of Hosea quoted by Jesus, "I desire compassion, not sacrifices" (9:13; 12:7; Hosea 6:6). Even if these were only the words of Matthew, the witness is quite meaningful. It is certain in any case that Jesus interpreted the Law in a sovereign way according to its foundation and has therefore declared it to be partly invalid in its historic form. But he did it in the claim: "Do not think that I came to annul the Law or the Prophets; I came not to annul them but to fulfill them!" (Matt 5:17).

It is particularly significant that in hellenistic-Jewish literature like Joseph and Asenath, Pseudo-Phocylides and the Testaments of the Twelve Patriarchs, the cultic-ritual commandments, especially that of circumcision,[55] play no role at all.[56] The cult of the temple was indeed not a living reality for Judaism outside of Jerusalem and Judea, especially in the diaspora. According to the experience of that part of Judaism the practise of the cult was not a necessary part of life according to the order of the Law. This part of the Law was not of course thereby made invalid. Whether there are connections between this conduct and the attitude of Jesus and the early church is still not completely decided. That the two things should have nothing to do

---

[52] Ibid.

[53] Cf. this fundamentally with M. Hengel, 'Zwischen Jesus und Paulus', ZThK 72, 1975, pp. 151-206; also Zur urchristlichen Geschichtsschreibung, Stuttgart 1979, p. 64.

[54] Cf. T. Holtz, 'Die Bedeutung des Apostelkonzils für Paulus', NovTest 16, 1974, pp. 133ff.

[55] In the Test of the Twelve Patr circumcision is only mentioned in Test Lev 6 in connection with the punishment of Shechem.

[56] Cf. also Ps-Menander (-Philemon): "Make a sacrifice to God by being pious at all times!"

one with another does not of course appear probable.

Jesus did not want to abolish the Torah; he wished to fulfill it (Matt 5:17). The early church, and Paul with it, understands the Torah from the point of view of such fulfillment. But it remains the Torah which is thus understood and fulfilled. Paul believes that the Torah is summarised in the commandment of love, which is in line with the words of Jesus (Mark 12:28-34; par.). And whereas in the question of divorce (1 Cor 7:10) an instruction of the Lord is known it is valid; not against the Torah, but rather as its fulfillment. Historically there has never been the Torah as such, but rather always the interpreted Torah. Although, of course, everybody who followed his own valid interpretation of the Torah did this in the certainty of following the Torah. This process of ever new understanding and interpretation of the Law is already visible for us in the Old Testament. It continues in the history of early Judaism, despite the progressive canonisation of the Old Testament, and naturally does not come to a full stop due to the limitation by the rabbinic interpretation of the Torah through the Mishnah and Talmud. Thus the Law exists for the early church and for Paul only as an interpreted Law, but nevertheless as the Law. The valid interpretation of the Law was that of Jesus. Of course this interpetation is at the same time the fulfilment of the Law, up to the point when he by fulfilling it suspends it, as in his sacrifice which fulfilled and made unnecessary the sacrifices in the temple.[57] Nevertheless, his claim remains the claim of the Law, which according to God's original will was fulfilled through Jesus.

In order to avoid any misunderstanding of these thoughts it must be stated categorically that through the gospel, God's deed in the story of Christ, the function of the *nomos* in relation to God has been completely altered. Here we are only considering the Law as an order of life, not the function of the Law as a foundation or consequence of salvation. But now, in order to focus again on the question of our theme, we must ask why it is that for Paul the Torah has such an unmoveable position as an order of life, and what significance this has theologically. For Paul the Torah is plainly not accidental or changeable or a historically caused and maintained order which can be overturned by another nationally and historically

---

[57] This appears to be the earliest point in time when the early church separated itself from the order of the Jewish community. The fact that this happened in the temple in Jerusalem gave the process its *importance*.

caused and maintained order, without causing any damage. Even the heathen Christian church at Corinth ought to conform to the order of the *nomos*, including the veiling of women during divine worship.

It is decisive that this unalterable validity of the Torah comes from its relationship to creation, which it has according to the Jewish faith and which we have to presuppose for Paul. H.F. Weiss[58] summarises the result of his research of the idea of the Torah as a cosmic principle in Judaism as follows:

> The idea of the Torah as a cosmic principle, that is as the 'tool' with which God created the world, belongs to a very old rabbinic tradition, which reaches far back in time, and which had already been arrived at at the time of early Christianity.[59]

Of course we do not know to what extent Paul shared these thoughts. It was hardly the case that he assumed that a real pre-existing Torah was the tool or the building plan of God at the creation of the world. On the other hand, one cannot refute this thought for Paul by merely quoting Galatians 3:17 and the related passages Galatians 3:19; Romans 5:13,20. The "historic" facts reflected there were of course also known to Jewish theologians who knew their Bible, for whom nevertheless the Torah was the pre-existing ground of the world.[60] Even when a person bases his thought from the time of the revelation

---

[58] *Untersuchungen zur Kosmologie des hellenistischen und palästinischen Judentums* (TU 97), Berlin 1966.

[59] p. 300; Philo shows in his own way that even the hellenistic Judaism of the New Testament era knew this notion and shared it; for him "the cosmic law is the Mosaic Law," "first of all this Law is . . . the cosmic principle, according to which the world has been created and which also determines the 'natural' course of world events" (Weiss, fn. 58, p. 278; same passage, also p. 6, On the Creation of the World 3: "And thus the man who is faithful to the Law is always at the same time a citizen of the world, because he determines his actions according to the will of nature, according to which the entire cosmos is also managed").

[60] With regard to the question of how few dogmatic statements are understood as being historicising, how little the historic description can fight against the dogmatic statement, cf. the famous Midrash bMen 29b: "When Moses rises to heaven in order to fetch the Torah God shows him the house where Rabbi Akiba teaches so that he can listen: He [Moses] did not understand their conversation and was therefore dismayed. When Akiba expressed a view regarding a certain problem his students asked him, how do you know this? Akiba answered them: This is a teaching of Moses from Sinai! Then Moses was reassured" (according to P Schäfer, 'Die Thora der messianischen Zeit', ZNW 65, 1974, p. 29; also A. Nissen, *Gott und der Nächste im antiken Judentum* [= WUNT 15] Tübingen 1974, p. 352).

of the Torah to Israel, then it is still certainly the ground of creation. This signifies for instance "the rabbinic idea that the world is really only firmly established since the acceptance of the Torah by Israel and can only be maintained by the Torah and its fulfillment (eg. Aboth 1:2)."[61] "If God had not found a place for his revelation, creation would have lost its meaning and would have been changed back into chaos."[62]

Even for Paul the Torah represents the only norm of life and its order represents the order of the wholesome life. This is revealed by the meaning of a verse like Romans 5:15: "where there is no law there is also no transgression." *Parabasis* (transgression) is only the transgression of the order of the Torah. This fact is made perfectly clear in Romans 5:13f. The reality of sin, since the Torah was not yet given, can only be discerned for the generations between Adam and Moses by the fact of the presence of death in the world. Only since the Torah does sin exist which is accountable and verifiable. But not because the Torah and the keeping of it is sin, but rather, on the contrary, sin is exclusively its non-keeping. The one who remains within the order of the Torah, remains within the realm of salvation. The order of the Torah is the God-given order of the wholesome life.

This order is indeed formulated by God but it is not equal to a product of a cosmic necessity. The world in which we live is not the best of all imaginable worlds. It is not the only possible of all imaginable worlds. But it is as it is according to the sovereign action of God, who thus reveals Himself as its real Creator. Jewish thought has clearly seen this set of circumstances. We have already mentioned the words of Rabbi Johanan b. Zakkai:[63]

> Neither does the dead man make unclean, nor does the water make clean, but it is the decision of the King of all Kings. The holy one has said: I have pronounced a statement, I have made a decision; no human being shall transgress my decision.[64]

---

61 Nissen, fn. 60, p. 50.
62 Nissen, fn. 60, p. 49.
63 Pes 74/40b; cf. Nissen, fn. 60, p. 172.
64 Cf. also NumR 19:1 with 19:2 (78a) and Pesiq 54f/29b-30a (Nissen, fn. 60, p. 338) concerning the contradictions of several prescriptions of purity: "Who did that? Who ordered that? Who prescribed that? Not the Unique One of the world?"; and finally: "I have formulated a text, prescribed an order; you do not have the right to transgress my orders."

The belief in the identity of God and the conviction about the identity of the created world in which God acts in the Christ event make it necessary that the order of the world which God has established, which is the order of the Torah, remains valid and must remain valid. Furthermore, for the same reason we have certainty regarding the eschatological validity of the order of the Torah.[65] For Paul this certainty also results from the belief that salvation is already at work in the present time and from the fact that this salvation does not remove one from this world. Here is the decisive difference from the 'enthusiastic' theology of the Corinthians and from every gnosis, which logically can neither hold on to a unified concept of creation nor to the Old Testament.

The consequences of all this for each consideration of the structure, foundation and binding nature of Christian ethics, and also its decisive specific quality, are quite plain. Christian ethics cannot only proclaim the motive for fundamentally free and definite action which relates only to history, especially history freely made by men and having a definite aim. Rather it is bound to norms of content, which cannot be transgressed, to the order which God gave to his world, the creation. The world is not without order. It is not up to the will of humans to make it. There are firm limits to the world and therefore to humans, which can only be transgressed at the price of the world itself, at the price of one's own life. Order has been firmly imprinted on the world, in which alone it functions, if it wishes to remain itself. According to Jewish belief, a belief shared by Paul, this order has been revealed to humanity in the *nomos*. Therefore, every order, according to which we live and which we have to proclaim to the world for the ordering of its life, has to be identical with the order of the *nomos*. Of course this does not mean that we simply have to repeat any laws which at any particular time had once been formulated. As we already said, there is no such thing as the Torah as such, but always and only the interpreted, the historically applied Torah. The world is always the historical world. The same applies for the gospel. It has to be this way if the *nomos* as well as the gospel are the revelation of the same God to the same world. Jesus, and following him Paul, is able to summarise the whole Torah in the commandment of love. But this love commandment does not unfold itself merely as a motive but rather as a concrete commandment

---

65 P. Schäfer has proved this faith of Judaism, fn. 60, pp. 27-42; cf. also 1QS 4:19ff. ("And then the truth of the world will emerge forever. . .").

which by being made concrete in love proves itself to be identical with the Torah. But each commandment must firmly know that it cannot serve to create the world itself. It only serves to comprehend and explicate the structure of a world that has already been created.

The interpretation of this order, which is only real order when it is interpreted, is the task given to mankind. Nobody takes this task away from mankind. It is not enough for mankind to reproduce a bygone interpretation, nor to wait for a new revelation. Nevertheless, this task holds the promise of truth. This matter has been depicted in a rabbinic tradition in a way which is fascinating yet very strange. Rabbi Eliezer and the majority of rabbis differed on a certain issue. Rabbi Eliezer (around the year 90) tried to legitimate his view using miracles. However, the miracles were not recognised as proof.

> So Eliezer said: "If my view is in accordance with the right laws, then heaven will now prove it." A voice sounded from heaven and said: Why do you dispute with Rabbi Eliezer? The interpretation of the Law is always according to his view! Then Rabbi Joshua arose and said: "The Torah is not in heaven" (Deut 30:12). What does it mean, it is not in heaven? Rabbi Jeremiah answered: "The Torah has already been given from Mount Sinai. Therefore we need not listen to a voice from heaven, because you [God] have written on Mount Sinai in the Torah: it should be decided according to the majority" (Exod 23:2). Rabbi Nathan met the prophet Elijah and asked him: "What did the Holy One, blessed be he, do in that hour?" Elijah replied: He smiled and called out: "My children have defeated me, my children have defeated me!".[66]

---

[66] bBMes 59b.

PART II

THE CONTEXT OF PAULINE ETHICS
Social Conditions in the Græco-Roman World

CHAPTER THREE

Interpreting New Testament Ideas

Edwin A. Judge
(1960)

A generation ago the attempt to discover the principles of social obligation held by the early Christians was still common. Since then interest has largely petered out. This need not necessarily mean that there were no such principles to be found; it may simply have been that the enquiry itself was misdirected. It is the object of this study to support a revival of the issue by opening up some new lines of interpretation.

Earlier writers, failing to define adequately the social institutions assumed in the New Testament, often formulated the problems in anachronistic terms. Indeed one is still confronted with discussions of 'Church' and 'State' in the New Testament,[1] or with tirades against slavery and the enormities of Imperial Rome.[2] We are still the victims of Tacitean cynicism, it seems. But the New Testament writers would have found much of this puzzling. They

---

[1] E.g. T. M. Parker, *Christianity and the State in the Light of History*, 1955; and O. Cullmann, *Der Staat im Neuen Testament*, 1956 (English version, 1957).

[2] E.g. E. F. Scott, *Man and Society in the New Testament*, 1947.

were not thinking in such terms. Modern students have thus created
for themselves the problems of New Testament acquiescence and
inconsistency, through neglecting to identify the situation to which
the New Testament writings were actually addressed. This lack will
perhaps justify an ancient historian's trespassing on New Testament
ground. For while the religious background to the New Testament
has been thoroughly searched, the political and social material
summed up here does not seem to be familiar enough to students of
theology.[3] Ancient historians, too, it is hoped, will not find the
reassessment useless.

Although interest in the social ideas of the New Testament
writers has waned, the new appreciation of their eschatological views
will inevitably reopen the question. We already have new treatments
of their idea of history,[4] but more needs to be done in applying the
recovered eschatology to government and society.[5] Obviously if the
New Testament groups saw themselves standing at the climax of the
ages, and anticipated an imminent end, this must have profoundly
affected their view of their obligation to society. The old search has
thus been unexpectedly provided with a new and revolutionary
starting-point. There still remains however the lack of definition that
partly stultified earlier efforts.

It may be asserted that ideas are never satisfactorily explained
merely by discovering their philosophical connections. They must be
pinned down in relation to the particular circumstances in which
they were expressed. The meaning is fixed at this point, and cannot
be certainly ascertained until it is identified. This view has
presumably been axiomatic in earlier New Testament criticism, but it
seems to be implicitly called in question by certain modern methods
of interpretation. Demythologizing may result in looking for the
meaning not primarily in terms of the situation in which the ideas
were originally expressed, but in the existential realization of the
truth concerned.[6] The eliciting of patterns of symbolism may also

---

[3] Two newly translated collections should help to fill the gap: E. Barker, *From
Alexander to Constantine, Passages Illustrating the History of Social and Political Ideas*,
1956; C. K. Barrett, *The New Testament Background, Selected Documents*, 1956.

[4] E.g. C. H. Dodd, *History and the Gospel*, 1938; O. Cullmann, *Christus und die
Zeit*, 2 Aufl. 1948 (English version, 1951); E. Dinkler, *The Idea of History in the
Ancient Near East*, ed. R. C. Dentan, 1955; R. Bultmann, *History and Eschatology*,
1957.

[5] Cf. A. N. Wilder, *The Background of the New Testament and its Eschatology*,
Studies in honour of C. H. Dodd, ed. W. D. Davies and D. Daube, 1956.

[6] Cf. R. P. C. Hanson, 'History and Revelation', *Theology*, 1957.

lead to a neglect of the historical situation.[7] However illuminating these approaches may seem to be, they are misleading if they attract attention away from the original situation. At the very least this ought to be properly explored before it is abandoned in favour of other modes of interpreting the meaning.

In accepting this as its method, however, New Testament criticism encounters a notorious difficulty. While Christianity originated in Galilee, it flourished in the great cosmopolitan cities of the eastern Mediterranean. The New Testament is itself the product of this shift. Its writers are mainly Jews of Palestinian associations; their readers the Greek-speaking members of Hellenistic communities. It interprets the religious significance of certain events in Judaea to a public unfamiliar with that situation. It applies ideas derived from it to their own situation.

This tension between Hebraic origins and Hellenic application can be resolved in strikingly different ways. The tendency in recent years has been to stress the Hebraic as primary, and to regard the Hellenic as incidental.[8] But the material is also being reassembled for a detailed review of the Hellenic affinities of early Christianity.[9] The greatest progress towards a balanced appraisal of this duality has been in lexicography.[10] Here the most painstaking classification of word usage in the New Testament and related literatures has demonstrated what ought in any case to be obvious, that the meaning of a word is not ultimately determined by antecedent, parallel, or derived instances, but by its situation in its own context. A word means whatever its writer meant it to mean.

In the interpretation of the ideas the same standard should be applied. They must not be treated simply as stages in a system of thought. The New Testament is not an orderly statement of dogma, but a heterogeneous collection of writings addressed to various occasions. While the affiliation of the ideas will generally govern their content, there will normally be a particular construction to be

---

7 Cf. H. Gardner, *The Limits of Literary Criticism, Reflections on the Interpretation of Poetry and Scripture*, 1956.

8 E.g. the works of A. Schlatter, inadequately appreciated.

9 E.g. C. Schneider, *Geistesgeschichte des antiken Christentums*, 1954; T. Klauser, hrsg., *Reallexikon für Antike u. Christentum usw.*, 1950 (in progress).

10 E.g. G. Kittel, *Theologisches Wörterbuch zum Neuen Testament*, 1933 (in progress) (English extracts appearing); W. Bauer, *Griechisch-Deutsches Worterbuch zu den Schriften des N. Testaments usw.*, 4 Aufl. 1952 (English adaptation, W. F. Arndt and F. W. Gingrich, 1957).

placed on them in relation to the particular situation. Neglect of this may result in imprecision or even error.

Thus the present study concentrates not on the writers, but on the readers. We must know who they were and what they thought if we are to understand completely what was being said to them. The teaching of Jesus is therefore not the starting-point. We do not possess the teaching of Jesus, *tout court*. We possess the teaching of Jesus, an itinerant Aramaic Preacher, as collated and formulated in Greek for the information of religious societies in Hellenistic cities. If it is to be understood properly, it must be understood from their point of view. The only meaning that can be certainly recovered from the Gospels in their present form is the meaning they were intended to convey to their original readers. We must therefore begin with the readers, and explain their social situation as it is shown in the Acts and Epistles. It was very different from that of Jesus, which may now be summed up in order to clear the ground for this central enquiry.

The region to which Jesus belonged was notoriously backward by the standards of contemporary civilization. Its population was economically rural, and resident in villages or small towns. Jesus Himself thought in terms of this circumscribed manner of life-witness the parables. His followers, if not He Himself, were thoroughly out of sympathy with the sophisticated classes of the cities. Financial, legal, and religious professionals (the publicans, scribes, and Pharisees) were mistrusted by them, and retorted with open contempt. It was the same with intellectuals (the Sadducees) and the administration (the rulers and chief priests).

The form of government the disciples most readily understood was monarchy. The sayings of Jesus make this plain. The social distinctions involved are accepted. 'Behold, they which are gorgeously apparelled, and live delicately, are in kings' courts' (Lk. vii. 25). International affairs can still be talked of in terms of rival kingdoms. 'What king, going to make war against another king, sitteth not down first, and consulteth whether he be able with ten thousand to meet him that cometh against him with twenty thousand? Or else, while the other is yet a great way off, he sendeth an ambassage, and desireth conditions of peace' (Lk. xiv. 31, 32). Royal methods of internal administration are sufficiently familiar to be used in depicting the character of the kingdom of God. A nobleman 'went into a far country to receive for himself a kingdom, and to return' (cf. the dependence of the Herods on Roman approval for legitimacy). He was hated by his subjects, and took reprisals on them for their insubordination, selecting governors of tested loyalty for the administration of groups of cities (Lk. xix. 11-27).

Now the evangelist himself shows by his careful dating (Lk. iii. 1) that the old royal government of Judaea was in commission at the beginning of the ministry of Jesus, though the Galilæan tetrarch still lived in sufficient state to impress the popular mind and keep tongues wagging (Mk. vi. 21-28). The disciples of course belonged to this principality, but their political interests ran beyond it. Their thinking was still dominated by the idea of a national monarchy established in Judaea proper, which had now been administered for a generation by the priestly authorities under Roman supervision. One of the things that appealed to them most about Jesus was that He promised the inauguration of a new kingdom which looked like fulfilling their wildest dreams. 'I appoint unto you a kingdom, as my Father hath appointed unto me; that ye may eat and drink at my table in my kingdom, and sit on thrones judging the twelve tribes of Israel' (Lk. xxii. 29, 30). They clung persistently to their ambition. 'Lord, wilt thou at this time restore again the kingdom to Israel?' (Acts i. 6). They thought of themselves then in nationalistic terms, and the rest of the world was similarly lumped together as 'the nations'.

The eschatological fervour that motivated the disciples was of course not unparalleled among the non-Hellenized Palestinians of the day, as the discovery of the Qumran community has emphasized.[11] A similar mood of expectation governed most of the early Christian groups. But while the fundamental conviction that the end is being realized is common to all three cases, its expression took remarkably different forms. The covenanters of Qumran, withdrawn and fastidious, must have abhorred the vulgarity and opportunism of the disciples. But a narrow provincial outlook distinguishes both of them from the first Christian societies. The peculiar orientation of Palestinian political thought ('councils', 'synagogues', 'rulers', 'kings', 'nations', Mk. xiii. 9, 10) was thoroughly alien to the Hellenized peoples of the rest of the eastern Mediterranean.

Even the original Christian group at Jerusalem, though certainly not typical of early Christianity, is to be sharply marked off from other Palestinian religious movements. It was drawn from a

---

11 Cf. J. M. Allegro, *The Dead Sea Scrolls*, 1956; F. F. Bruce, *Second Thoughts on the Dead Sea Scrolls*, 1956; M. Burrows, *The Dead Sea Scrolls*, 1956; T. Gaster, trans., *The Scriptures of the Dead Sea Sect*, 1957.

population with broad international links, imposing social conditions on it that were very different from those governing either the Galilæan peasantry or the secluded community in the Dead Sea hills. Qumran is only a few miles away from Jerusalem as the crow flies, but from a social point of view its inhabitants lived in another world. Much the same could be said of Galilee.

Nevertheless Jerusalem must also be distinguished from the Hellenistic cities abroad. Sophisticated and cosmopolitan though its population was, it remained Jewish in faith and was administered under peculiar local arrangements.[12] Apart from the Jerusalem group, however, the Christians known from the New Testament were practically all drawn from communities living under civil institutions of the republican kind. The thirty or more places from Caesarea to Rome for which such groups are specifically attested are all republican. Moreover since they are widely distributed across areas where this was regarded as the normal constitution of society, such other groups as are implied for these parts by a number of general references in the Acts and Epistles may safely be placed in the same category. Other forms of public organization were only retained in backward areas where penetration by Christianity is likely for that very reason to have been delayed.

The only clear exceptions to this occur in certain parts of Palestine itself where, as in Jerusalem, republican institutions had not yet been introduced. For Judaea proper neither the topographical references nor the evidences for Christianity are very explicit. The early apostolic activities attracted 'a multitude out of the cities round about unto Jerusalem' (Acts v. 16), and refugees were later 'scattered abroad throughout the regions of Judaea and Samaria' (Acts viii. 1). It is not at all certain what places are meant,[13] and in the first instance it cannot be asserted that they became Christians, nor in the second that they remained in these parts. General references, such as that to Judaea in Acts ix. 31, need imply no more than Jerusalem itself. We do know however that the coastal towns were visited by Christian preachers (e.g. Acts viii. 40), and there were certainly Christians at Lydda and Joppa (Acts ix. 32, 36), which did not enjoy republican constitutions at this period.[14] The Christians in Galilee and Samaria (Acts ix. 31) could have been members of the republics of Tiberias

---

12 Cf A. H. M. Jones, *The Herods of Judaea*, 1938.
13 Cf. F. F. Bruce, *The Acts of the Apostles*, 1951, *ad loc*.
14 Cf. A. H. M. Jones, *Cities of the Eastern Roman Provinces*, 1937.

and Sebaste respectively, but in so far as they were the former adherents of Jesus this is unlikely. Although He frequented the region around the sea of Tiberias, it is not recorded that He visited the city itself. Its peculiarly heterogeneous population (Josephus, *Ant.*, xviii, 2. 3) was perhaps uncongenial. Sebaste may have been the place where Philip preached (Acts viii. 5), but the text is uncertain,[15] and the rest of the terminology (Acts viii. 9, 25) does not support the idea. Both cities in any case controlled only small territories.[16] The Galilæan and Samaritan Christians may therefore safely be left in the non-republican category.

But the situation that was to become characteristic is already found in the case of Caesarea, which appears in the Acts as the most important Palestinian centre of Christianity after Jerusalem. It is not surprising that the first conversion of a non-Jew, an event to which the writer pays great attention, should take place here. Caesarea was a republic, and the seat of the Roman administration. Cornelius himself was an officer of the occupation forces (Acts x. 1). Even earlier than this (Acts xi. 19) the new cult had spread northwards up the Phoenician coast, and a series of seaport republics each had its group of Christians, Ptolemais (Acts xxi. 7), Tyre (Acts xxi. 3, 4), and Sidon (Acts xxvii. 3). They were drawn however from the Jewish population (Acts xi. 19); it was not till the Syrian metropolis of Antioch was reached that there was a mass conversion of non-Jews sufficient to excite the alarm of the original group in Jerusalem (Acts xi. 20-22), and the curiosity of the local public (Acts xi. 26). Success in Antioch established Christianity socially on a new footing. From here the lines of communication run westwards to the other great cities of the Mediterranean. 'Syrus in Tiberim defluxit Orontes' (Juvenal, *Sat.*, 3. 62). What is heard today on the Orontes, is repeated tomorrow on the Tiber.

Thus once the sect is established beyond the homeland of its parent religion, at least within the Roman area, which is as far as our records go, it belongs inevitably, as a social phenomenon, to the Hellenistic republics. Its thinking and behaviour naturally reflect the social institutions of these states. In political terminology it is not now so much a matter of rulers, kings, and nations, as of republics, assemblies, and magistrates.

---

[15] Cf. F. F. Bruce, *The Acts of the Apostles*, 1951, *ad loc.*

[16] Cf. A. H. M. Jones, 'The Urbanisation of Palestine', *Journal of Roman Studies*, 1938.

The word *polis* is of course regularly used in the New Testament as a general term for a town or city. That this is sometimes inconsistent with its republican connotation reflects the fact that parts of the New Testament, as already pointed out, deal with an area that was peculiar, in that its population was not yet incorporated on a republican basis. It only emphasizes the extent to which republican government was taken for granted in the Hellenistic area, that when writing in Greek the standard terms should have been applied indiscriminately. Where the Hellenistic cities proper are referred to, the technical sense is naturally apparent in constitutional connections (e.g. Acts xiii. 50, xvi. 12, 20, xix. 35, xxi. 39, xxvi. 11; Rom. xvi. 23; Tit. i. 5). It will be noticed that the one blanket term covers Roman colonies, too; the distinction did not affect their basically republican character. Contrary to what has usually been thought, the word *demos* is not used except in its technical sense of the assembly of a citizen body (cf. Acts xii. 22 [at Caesarea, as is stated in Josephus xix, 8. 2], xvii. 5, xix. 30, 33). The various magistrates referred to[17] need not be enumerated here; the terminology reflects the variety of local traditions; but it ought not to obscure the fact that the communities concerned had long been assimilated to a broadly uniform pattern of society.

How narrow a backwater, on the other hand, Galilee and the other unincorporated regions were may be seen from the fact that even the itinerary of Jesus frequently took Him into the territories of neighbouring republican centres. But it is obviously in the Aramaic-speaking rural communities dependent on them, and not in the Hellenized urban centres themselves that His interests lie. He passes through 'the coasts (*sc.* territory) of Tyre and Sidon', and 'the midst of the coasts of Decapolis' (Mk. vii. 31). He visits 'the towns (*sc.* villages) of Caesarea Philippi' (Mk. viii. 27). To these villagers republicanism was presumably as foreign as it was to Jesus Himself. They were after all the subjects of the republic, not its citizens.

This distinction is also implied in the Gospels. Jesus performed a sensational exorcism across the sea of Tiberias, in 'the country (*sc.* the region of administration) of the Gadarenes' (Mk. v. 1). The variant reading 'Gerasenes' is geographically improbable, but does not affect the present point in any case: both communities were constituted as republics, and grouped together with a number of others as the Decapolis (Mk. v. 20). The exorcist was not welcomed

---

17   Cf. H. J. Cadbury, *The Book of Acts in History*, 1955.

for His feat. 'The whole city came out to meet Jesus: and when they saw him, they besought him that he would depart out of their coasts' (Mt. viii. 34). The reaction was mutual. To the plea of a woman who was 'a Greek, a Syrophenician by nation' (*sc.* a member of the Hellenized citizen class of one of the Phoenician republics, Tyre or Sidon), the retort was 'it is not meet to take the children's bread, and to cast it unto the dogs' (Mk. vii. 27).

Thus though the non-republican area was geographically very limited, emotionally the gulf between it and the civilized world was profound. The real division was of course cultural. When a community was incorporated its population was usually augmented from abroad to stimulate its Hellenization, and distinguish it from the peasantry newly subjected to it. Cultural gap and political boundaries were kept artificially in alignment. Thus while within the republican area the innumerable boundaries were culturally meaningless, the borders of the Jewish territories symbolized their alienation. When Jesus cryptically threatened to put Himself beyond the reach of the authorities, His opponents replied in scorn, 'Whither will he go, that we shall not find him? Will he go unto the dispersed among the Gentiles (lit. Greeks), and teach the Gentiles?' (Jn. vii. 35). The original Jerusalem Christians, though assiduously propagating their faith in the other coastal towns, automatically avoided the neighbouring republic of Caesarea, and were scandalized at the idea of admitting even a very respectable and pro-Jewish resident of it to their circle (Acts x, xi). Even Paul, himself dually qualified as a member of the Hellenistic citizen class, conforms to the isolationist terminology when addressing a Jewish ruler. His 'strange (*sc.* foreign) cities' (Acts xxvi. 11) need refer only to Damascus, but as a republic Damascus belongs irrevocably to the undifferentiated heathendom beyond the shrinking frontiers of the chosen land.

It was nevertheless among communities living in this alien world that the New Testament writings circulated. That many of the readers practised the Jewish religion does not make their situation irrelevant to their thinking. They still lived under the Hellenistic social institutions and largely shared in the common tradition of civilization. It is the pattern of society in the Hellenistic republics that must be determined if New Testament social precepts are to be understood.

If there is a risk of distortion in approaching the subject from the Palestinian end, there is at least an equal danger in working from the non-biblical literary material. Practically all that survives was produced in circles patronized by the Roman administration or by the members of that government itself. It consequently has a pronounced Roman slant. The concentration on the affairs of the Roman capital leads to the facile view that the Mediterranean was run by a centralized, totalitarian administration for the benefit of a vicious imperial house. Many popular accounts of the situation of the New Testament Christians are falsified by this assumption. Many problems of New Testament interpretation are created by it. But the New Testament itself shows it up as absurd. These writings, limited though they are, offer one of the few accounts we have of the general life of the eastern Mediterranean that does not reflect the Roman outlook.

CHAPTER FOUR

Civil Litigation in Secular Corinth and the Church
The Forensic Background to 1 Corinthians 6.1–8

Bruce W. Winter
(1991)

Paul's teaching about the attitude of the Christian towards the state is well known in Romans 13. There the rulers are God's vicegerents, God's deacons for the praising of those who do good and for the punishing of evil-doers.[1] All are to be subject to them in order to avoid God's wrath and to maintain a good conscience. They are deserving of financial support as God's servants (λειτουργοί) and are to be shown honour and respect. Does Paul espouse a contradictory view of the state in 1 Corinthians 6?[2] Here they are not God's

---

[1] For a discussion of the former function see the author's 'The Public Praising of Christian Benefactors: Romans 13.3-4 and 1 Peter 2.14-15', *JSNT* 34 (1988) 87-103.

[2] E. Käsemann, *An die Römer* (Tübingen: J.C.B. Mohr [Paul Siebeck], 1973), ET *Commentary on Romans* (London: SCM, 1980) 345/357: 'From an apocalyptic standpoint secular courts, thus political authorities, are disparaged and rejected when it is a matter of settling disputes within the community.'

servants, but 'the unrighteous' (οἱ ἄδικοι), v. 1. They are those least esteemed in the church, v. 4, and appearing before them is plainly wrong for Christians, v. 6.[3] The Corinthians were not called upon to honour them by Paul in 1 Corinthians 6, if they are indeed the same persons mentioned in Romans 13.

It can be assumed that while Romans 13.1-7 deals with aspects of the role of the ruler, including jurisdiction over criminal cases, 1 Corinthians 6 discusses the nature of civil litigation in Corinth with brother taking brother to court on the 'smallest causes'.[4] The purpose of this discussion is to seek to explain the statements which Paul makes about the character of civil litigation and the courts in Corinth by drawing from both literary and non-literary sources.[5] As much of

---

[3] For the most recent discussion of 1 Cor. 6:1-8 see E. Dinkler, 'Zum Problem der Ethik bei Paulus: Rechtsnahme und Rechtsversicht, I Kor. 6,1-11', *ZThK* (1952) 167-200, reprinted in *Signum Crucis: Aufsätze zum Neuen Testament und zur christlichen Archäologie* (Tübingen: J.C.B. Mohr [Paul Siebeck], 1967) 204-240; L. Vischer, *Die Auslegungsgeschichte von 1 Kor. 6.1-11* (Tübingen: J.C.B. Mohr [Paul Siebeck], 1955); D.W.B. Robinson, 'To Submit to the Judgement of the Saints' *TynB* 10 (April 1962) 1-8; A. Stein, 'Wo trugen die korinthischen Christen ihre Rechtshandel aus?' *ZNW* 59 (1968) 86-90; M. Delcor, 'The Courts of the Church of Corinth and the Courts of Qumran' in J. Murphy-O'Connor (ed.), *Paul and Qumran: Studies in New Testament Exegesis* (London: Geoffrey Chapman, 1968) ch. 4; S. Meurer, *Das Recht im Dienst der Versöhnung und des Friedens: Studien zur Frage der Rechts nach dem Neuen Testament* (Zürich: Theologischer Verlag, 1972) 141-56; R.H. Fuller, 'First Corinthians 6:1-11—An Exegetical Paper', *Ex Auditu* 2 (1986) 96-104; J.D.M. Derrett, 'Judgement and I Corinthians 6', *NTS* 37 (1991) 22-36; and A.J. Mitchell, 'Rich and Poor in the Courts of Corinth: Litigiousness and Status in 1 Corinthians 6.1-11' *NTS* 39 (1993) 562-586. It is not proposed to discuss the OT and inter-testamental background to the eschatological judgement by the saints, but there will be an examination of the implications of civil litigation for an understanding of 1 Cor. 6:1-11. I am grateful to Professor J.A. Crook, Emeritus Professor of Ancient History, University of Cambridge who discussed aspects of an early draft of this chapter with me and also drew my attention to the importance of the *Lex Irnitana*.

[4] κριτήριον='a legal cause': ἐλάχιστος = 'smallest'. See n. 7.

[5] It has been argued that the Corinthian Christians were submitting their cases to Jewish judges, A. Stein, *op. cit.*, 87-88 but in the words of H. Conzelmann, *A Commentary on the First Epistle to the Corinthians* (ET Philadelphia: Fortress, 1975) 105, n. 23 that conclusion is 'misguided'. See also G.D. Fee, *The First Epistle to the Corinthians* (Grand Rapids: Eerdmans, 1987) 236 who notes that Stein's major difficulties arose out of the use of the verb καθίζειν in v. 4, which can mean 'to appoint a judge'. Fee cites Josephus, *Ant.* 13.75 where the verb is used of plaintiffs asking that a court be convened to hear their arguments. See also Dio Cassius *Roman Histories* 37.27.1 where one group in a disagreement demanded that their rights be exercised and the court be convened to hear the case (ἵνα καθιζήση); cf. *LS* 'to cause an assembly or court' i.e. to institute

1 Corinthians records only one part of the conversation, it is important that the student of the NT recognises that any interpretation of this passage requires illumination from the reader's knowledge of forensic litigation. In the absence of a correct perception of its first century legal context this situation will be reconstructed from a twentieth century understanding of legal processes.[6]

There are six issues which clarify Paul's discussion in 1 Corinthians 6.1-11, *viz.* (I) the nature of civil litigation in Roman Corinth, (II) judges and 'the unrighteous', (III) the powerful and 'the unrighteous', (IV) enmity and civil litigation, (V) the *arbiter* and litigation, and (VI) those least esteemed in the church.

I. Civil Litigation in Roman Corinth

In the first century there were specific offences covered by civil as against criminal actions. The former related to claims concerning legal possession, breach of contract, damages, fraud and injury.[7] As the breach of the law in 1 Corinthians 6:2 is described as 'the smallest cause', it is right to regard the actions initiated by a Christian against his fellow believer as coming within the scope of civil and not criminal law.

---

proceedings. Furthermore, in Acts 18:12ff. the Jews had already dragged Paul before Gallio. The animosity engendered by that unsuccessful attempt, in addition to normal divisions created with the arrival of the Christian message among Jews, made for a lasting break with the synagogue. That makes it extremely unlikely Christians would have gone for arbitration to a Jewish court which operated under the aegis of the synagogue and was presided over by a Jewish *ḥākām*, an official one step below a rabbi in status. See E. Dinkler, 'Zum Problem der Ethik bei Paulus: Rechtsnahme und Rechtsversicht, I Kor. 6,1-11', 171-208 on the Jewish official. On the legal problems raised by Stein, 'Wo trugen die korinthischen Christen ihre Rechtshandel aus?' 88-89 see the most recent treatment by P. Garnsey, 'The Civil Suit', *Social Status and Legal Privilege in the Roman Empire* (Oxford: Clarendon Press, 1970) Part III.

6 On the influence of status and the accepted function of witnesses as partisans in Greece compared with today's perceived role see S. Todd, 'The Purpose of Evidence in Athenian Courts', *Nomos: Essays in Athenian Law, Politics and Society* (ed. P. Cartledge, P. Millett and S. Todd [Cambridge: CUP, 1990]) 27ff.

7 P. Garnsey, *Social Status and Legal Privilege* 181. Criminal cases included high treason, embezzlement of state property, bribery at elections, extortion in the provinces, murder by violence or poisoning, endangering of public security, forgery of wills or coins, violent offences, adultery and seduction of reputable unmarried women. See W. Kunkel, *An Introduction to Roman Legal and Constitutional History* (Oxford: Clarendon Press, 1973[2]) 66.

The right to prosecute was not granted to all. If the defendant was a parent, patron, magistrate, or a person of high rank, then charges could not be brought by children, freedmen, private citizens and men of low rank respectively.[8] Generally, lawsuits were conducted between social equals who were from the powerful (οἱ δυνατοί) of the city, or by a plaintiff of superior social status and power against an inferior.[9] The reason for these proscriptions was to avoid insult being given to the good name of the person concerned or concern for the lack of respect being accorded to one's patron or one's betters. 'Discriminatory rule or discriminatory practices, then, protected members of the higher orders from being taken to law in some circumstances' and 'the evidence shows that a humble prosecutor might be rejected merely because of the quality of his opponent'.[10]

Augustus declared of the provincial governor that 'he must himself act and judge or appoint a panel of jurors (αὐτὸς διαγεινώσκειν καὶ ἱστάναι ἢ συμβούλιον κριτῶν) [in capital cases] but with the rest of such affairs it is my wish that Greek jurors be appointed'.[11] 'In Cyrene, a "province of the Roman people", under Augustus, juries (iudices) were normal for all civil suits'.[12] A great deal of minor litigation was left by the governor of a province to local municipal courts, for his concern was with matters which related to public order.[13] This would have been no less true in the Roman colony of Corinth. Certainly in the early years of the empire, minor civil actions were left to the local courts and not provincial courts as Mitchell wrongly supposes.[14] They could be tried by judges or juries.[15]

---

[8]   P. Garnsey, *Social Status and Legal Privilege* 182.

[9]   J.M. Kelly, *Roman Litigation* (Oxford: Clarendon Press, 1966) 62ff. Exceptionally, there were cases where a patron took up the cause of his client: see P. Garnsey, *Social Status and Legal Privilege* 216 n. 4.

[10]   P. Garnsey, *Social Status and Legal Privilege* 187.

[11]   SEG IX. 8, IV *ll.* 67-69 cited by V. Ehrenberg and A.H.M. Jones, *Documents Illustrating the Reigns of Augustus and Tiberius* (Oxford: Clarendon Press, 1976) No. 311, IV *ll.* 66-68; D.C. Braund, *Augustus to Nero: A Sourcebook on Roman History 31 BC - AD 68* (London and Sydney: Croom Helm, 1985) No. 543, D; and for discussion see A.H.M. Jones, *The Criminal Courts of the Roman Republic and Principate* (Oxford: Blackwells, 1972) 98-100.

[12]   J.A. Crook, *Law and Life in Rome* (London: Thames and Hudson, 1967) 86.

[13]   A.N. Sherwin-White, *Roman Society and Roman Law in the New Testament* (Oxford: Clarendon Press, 1963) 14.

[14]   Mitchell, 'Rich and Poor in the Courts of Corinth' 566, 567.

[15]   J.A. Crook, *Law and Life in Rome* 79. See the *Lex Irnitana* chs. 86-89 on the *iudex, arbiter* and *recuperatores*.

The civil case began in the court of the law officer. In Corinth he was one of two honorary magistrates (*duoviri*) who were chosen from among leading citizens.[16] The office was undertaken for the year, and among the duties to be performed was the administration of justice.

The plaintiff, when petitioning the magistrate, explained the grounds for the charge, and if there was a case to answer, a private summons was issued requiring the other party to appear in court.[17] When the parties came to court, the preliminary pleadings were entered into, and the official declared the parameters within which the case was to be heard. It could then be tried by a single judge or argued before a jury which was chosen from among well-to-do citizens.[18] The task of the magistrate hearing a case in court in Corinth was to preside, to inform the court of the verdict and to decide the penalties.

II. Judges and 'the Unrighteous' of 1 Corinthians 6.1

Who were 'the unrighteous' (οἱ ἄδικοι) in v. 1? One solution has been to equate them with 'the unbelievers' (ἄπιστοι) in v. 6 and not to regard the comment in v. 1 as 'a moral judgement'. Paul is not said to be implying that 'the Corinthian courts were corrupt', nor did he 'intend to demean the Roman courts, to which he himself had recourse more than once, as if they were corrupt'.[19] Is that judgement correct or does it refer to 'judges whose judgement is unjust'?[20]

---

16   Mitchell, 'Rich and Poor in the Courts of Corinth' 564 wrongly designates them as 'provincial' magistrates as no such office existed.

17   At times, compelling an opponent to appear in court could be an extremely difficult task and it was not until the Principate of Trajan that penalties were used to ensure that the accused appeared, P. Garnsey, *Social Status and Legal Privilege* 170-1, 193. See *P.Oxy.* 2852 (AD 104/5) for a summons and the initiating of a civil action and 726 (AD 135) *ll.* 17-20 where a representative was appointed to make the journey to the assize centre 'because of illness'. The substitute was to represent him whether the case was heard before the prefect, the *epistrategus,* or 'other judges' (ἕτεροι κριταί).

18   P. Garnsey, *Social Status and Legal Privilege* 6 and J.A. Crook, *Law and Life in Rome* 78-79. Dio Cassius, *Roman Histories* 52.7.5, notes that 'when one is accused of committing a private wrong, one is made a defendant in a private suit before a jury of one's equals . . . they shall sit in judgement of one'.

19   H. Conzelmann, *A Commentary on the First Epistle to the Corinthians* 104 n. 12 and G.D. Fee, *The First Epistle to the Corinthians* 232. See also H.H.B. Ayles, 'I Corinthians VI.1', *ET* 27 (1915-16) 334, 'the prevailing idea of ἄδικος is not of one

I suggest that 'the unrighteous' (ἄδικοι) is a reference to the character of judges or the juries who pronounced verdicts in civil cases and not to non-Christians involved in secular judicial processes *per se*. There are two reasons for this. The first arises from the text itself and the other from what is known about civil litigation. In v. 6 we are told that a brother goes to court against a brother and that before 'unbelievers' (ἄπιστοι). The use of the plural, 'the unbelievers' in v. 6 and 'the unrighteous' in v. 1 allows that the civil action may be adjudicated by a 'judge' (ὁ κριτής) with 'jurors' (οἱ κριταί). If this is so, then Paul may well be passing a moral judgement on Corinthian judges, arbitrators or juries, for it is at this level of litigation that Christians were involved against Christians.

But is there evidence that would warrant such an adverse evaluation of those engaged in resolving civil actions in the empire? The edict of Augustus of 7-6 BC clearly shows that injustices were being perpetrated by the jury-courts in Cyrene. Augustus refers to Roman jurors (οἱ κριταί) who have formed certain 'cliques' (συνωμοσία) and who act oppressively against Greeks on capital charges with the same people (*i.e.* the cliques) taking it in turn to act as prosecutors and witnesses. The emperor states, 'I have learnt that innocent individuals have been oppressed in this way and have been consigned to the ultimate penalty'. The personal knowledge of Augustus suggests the problem of corruption was not confined to Cyrene.[21]

There is other non-literary evidence which confirms that juries could not be relied upon to administer justice impartially. In Egypt a former magistrate of the city of Arsinoïtes was taken to court by a money lender who was charging 48% (double the current rate) on a debt. A petition had originally been sent to the prefect of Egypt, who passed the case on to a judicial adviser so that it would be heard before a jury. The plaintiff then sent a further petition arguing that

---

who acts unfairly to others, but of one who breaks the law of God'; C.K. Barrett, *The First Epistle to the Corinthians* (London: A. & C. Black, 1971) 135 ἄδικος = 'non-Christians' and ἄγιος='Christians'; L. Vischer, *Die Auslegungsgeschichte von 1 Kor. 6.1-11*, 9, 'Das Wort ist nicht im moralischen Sinne gemeint'; R.H. Fuller, 'First Corinthians 6:1-11' 98, 'Neither word ἄδικος nor ἄγιος is intended in a moralising sense.' Paul's use of ἀδικέω in conjunction with ἀποστερέω in vv. 7-8 would suggest that the cognate has a moral sense. Certainly in v. 9 the ἄδικοι are connected with moral conduct.

20   D.W.B. Robinson, 'To Submit to the Judgement of the Saints' 3.

21   *SEG* IX. 8, A *ll.* 11-12. V.B. Ehrenberg and A.H.M. Jones, *Documents Illustrating the Reigns of Augustus and Tiberius* 99.

the jury would be open to the influence of a person of more senior status and therefore could not act impartially.[22]

An edict of AD 111 from the prefect of Egypt, dealing with judicial procedures of a court in session, adds further support for the view that there was substantial corruption in the judicial processes. He 'absolutely prohibits the receiving of bribes, not now for the first time forbidding this evil'.[23]

Corinth differs little from elsewhere. Dio Chrysostom records c. AD 100 that there were in Corinth 'lawyers innumerable perverting justice'.[24] A decade later Favorinus refers to the unjust treatment which he has received at the hands of the leading Corinthian citizens. He contrasts that with the actions of their forefathers who were in pre-Roman days 'pre-eminent among the Greeks for cultivating justice' and showed themselves to be 'lovers of justice' (φιλοδίκαιοι).[25] Those in Roman Corinth were obviously not. Later in the second century, Apuleius inveighs against the Corinthians alleging that 'nowadays all juries sell their judgements for money'.[26]

III. The Powerful and the 'Unrighteous'

The powerful in the city exercised a number of unfair advantages in the judicial system of the first century. These included financial qualifications for jury service, influence on honorary magistrates and judges, and the importance given to social status in weighing judgements.

Jurors were selected from the highest census group of men, whether Romans or Greeks, 'none having a census rating and property (if there is a sufficient number of men) of less than 7,500

---

22 *P.Fouad.* 26 (AD 157-159).

23 *P.Oxy.* 2745 *ll.* 7-8. It is of interest that many of the cases were referred to the 'friends' (φίλοι) of the prefect, *i.e.* his legal advisers who could act as judges.

24 *Or.* 8.9. στρέφειν was used of a wrestler trying to avoid an adversary and metaphorically of arguments. On the use of the wrestling image for demonstration pieces or declamations see also Philo, *Det.* 41 'they will be exhibiting the prowess of men sparring for practice [declamations], not that of men engaged in real combat [actual debates]'. The young men were declaiming forensic pieces in the courtyard of Poseidon's temple during the Isthmian Games in the hope of securing a case from a plaintiff. For the dating see C.P. Jones, *The Roman World of Dio Chrysostom* (Cambridge, Mass. and London: Harvard University Press, 1978) 136.

25 *Or.* 37.16-17. The contrast is between Greek Corinth and Roman Corinth.

26 *Metamorphoses* or *Golden Ass* IX.33.

denarii'.[27] They also had to be over the age of twenty-five. In the time
of Claudius one could be exempted if one had a large number of
children. In Rome the list of jurors was revised by the emperor and it
was said of Claudius that he struck from the list a man of high birth
who was a leading citizen of Greece.[28]

In Nero's reign there was a complaint about the influence of a
local power. 'We have therefore been robbed on every side by this
man, against whom we made petitions and presented reports many
in number, which he scorned in virtue of this superior local power'.[29]
A prosecutor believes that his case cannot succeed because the
defendant 'possesses great local influence through his insolence and
violence' and 'he will be unable to oppose him before a jury of this
kind (*i.e.* local), for he is very influential'. In the original petition the
prosecutor refers to the fact that the defendant, a former civic office
holder, is a man 'relying on the prestige of his position and [is]
possessing great local influence'. He is able to cite a previous case
heard against the same defendant before a magistrate in which the
son of a gymnasiarch instigated proceedings against the same
defendant who 'behaved insolently, and the magistrate made an
entry about him in his memorandum-book'. The fact that the
defendant cites a person of status, the son of a gymnasiarch, in a
former case demonstrated that the jury could not be trusted to be
impartial in the face of the powerful. This accounts for the attempt of
the prosecutor to have the case heard by the prefect and not a jury.[30]

Seneca's case of a rich and powerful man threatening a poor
man to dare to institute proceedings provides an apt illustration of
the problem which the powerful created in the judicial processes.
'Why don't you accuse me, why don't you take me to court?' was his
taunt, and Seneca comments, 'This rich man was powerful and
influential, as not even he denies, and thought he never had anything
to fear, even as a defendant'. The poor man's response epitomises the
reality, 'Am I, a poor man, to accuse a rich man?' The rich man all but
exclaimed, 'What would I not be ready to do to you if you impeached
me, I who saw to the death of a man who merely engaged in
litigation with me?'[31]

---

[27] *SEG* IX. 8, A *l.* 18. See also the *Lex Irnitana* ch. 86 where 5,000 *sesterces* was
specified.

[28] Suetonius, *Claudius*, 15.16.2.

[29] *P.Ryl.* 119 (AD 54-67).

[30] *P.Fouad.* 26 *ll.* 21-24.

[31] Seneca, *Contr.* 10.1. 2 and 7.

Even the veracity of a witness was determined by his status and wealth. Juvenal was to complain:

> At Rome you may produce a witness as unimpeachable as the host of the Isaean goddess . . . the first question asked will be about his wealth, the last about his character: 'how many slaves does he keep? how many acres does he own?' . . . A man's word is believed to be in exact proportion to the amount of cash he keeps in his strong-box'.[32]

Another unjust influence on the outcome of judicial decisions was the payment of bribes. The edict of AD 111 adds further support to the view that there was substantial corruption in the judicial processes. The prefect 'absolutely prohibits the receiving of bribes, not now for the first time forbidding this evil'.[33] The jury in civil litigation could be persuaded to return a 'guilty' or a 'not guilty' verdict because of bribery.[34] It may have been for this reason that some were said to have had a passion for jury service.[35]

Finally, the relative importance of the social status of the prosecutor and the defendant was a consideration for the magistrate whose function it was to see that the law was administered.[36] He decided whether or not to carry out the sentence and fixed the fine. Social status and legal privilege were clearly connected in the Roman empire.[37]

There were, of course, exceptions and the very recording of one such case in an unknown town near Spinx, Egypt proves the rule. The city fathers expressed their gratitude for having been blessed with an honest magistrate and specifically mention that 'in his judgements he always dispenses justice fairly, correctly and without bribery' (δίκαιος καθαρῶς καὶ ἀδωροδοκήτως).[38]

Cicero's observation of his own day also sums up the problems with litigation in the secular courts in the East. He declared that there were three major hindrances in civil litigation: 'excessive favour'

---

[32] Juvenal, *Satire* III. 136-44.

[33] *P.Oxy.* 2745 *ll.* 7-8. On the similar problem of the bribery of juries in Greece, see E.S. Staveley, *Greek and Roman Voting and Elections* (London: Thames and Hudson, 1972) 108ff.

[34] P. Garnsey, *Social Status and Legal Privilege* 4 and 199ff.

[35] Suetonius, *Claudius* 15.1.

[36] J.A. Crook, *Law and Life in Rome* 74.

[37] P. Garnsey, *Social Status and Legal Privilege* 4.

[38] *SEG* ix 527 (AD 22-23) *ll.* 9-10.

(*gratia*), 'possession of resources' (*potentia*) and 'bribery' (*pecunia*).[39] Those who were 'the righteous' were highly susceptible to these financial and social pressures.

IV. Enmity and Civil Litigation

Litigation caused personal enmity and was used to aggravate personal enmity.[40] The proceedings were not conducted dispassionately by the parties but with great acrimony.

> What the Romans called *reprehensio vitae* or *vituperatio*—a personal attack on the character of one's opponents—was taken as absolutely normal; and manuals of rhetoric dealt in great detail with the most effective ways to construct a *vituperatio* . . . [it] was the rule also in ordinary civil cases.[41]

What has been observed of Roman Greece litigation had been no less true in the Hellenistic period.[42]

The prosecutor, with his hostile speeches and the damaging evidence of his witnesses, caused great personal resentment with loss of dignity for the defendant. No areas were immune from ferocious attacks. 'The advocate . . . was permitted to use the most unbridled language about his client's adversary, or even his friends or relations or witnesses.'[43] There were no rules of evidence which guarded against this. Defendants could be subject to muck-raking and fabrication and this lack of legal restraint helps to explain why prosecutor and defendant could so rarely avoid lasting animosity.[44] It is there-

---

[39]   Cicero, *Pro Caecina* 73.

[40]   'Litigation as a Source of *inimicitia*' and 'Litigation as a Manifestation of *inimicitia*', D.F. Epstein, *Personal Enmity in Roman Politics 218-43 BC* (London: Croom Helm, 1987) 90-100. *Cf.* Dio Chrysostom in his Alexandrian oration where he portrays the character of the first-century judicial scene in the East with 'a multitude of quarrels and lawsuits, harsh cries, tongues that are mischievous and unrestrained, accusers, calumnies, writs, a hoard of professional pleaders [forensic orators]', *Or.* 32.19.

[41]   J.M. Kelly, *Studies in the Civil Judicature of the Roman Republic* (Oxford: Clarendon Press, 1976) 98-9.

[42]   J.W. Jones, *The Law and Legal Theory of the Greeks* (Oxford: OUP, 1956) 151, comments on 'bitter wrangling rather than calm judicial inquiry'.

[43]   J.W. Jones, *The Law and Legal Theory of the Greeks* 98.

[44]   D.F. Epstein, *Personal Enmity in Roman Politics* 91. See also J.M. Kelly, *Studies in the Civil Judicature of the Roman Republic* 102. 'In Quintilian's manual on rhetoric . . . we are expressly told that the beginning of a court speech should

fore plain to see why litigation was the cause of long-standing enmity. It could also be the motivation for instituting legal proceedings.[45]

Furthermore, young men were keen to display their talents as orators by taking well-known citizens to court.[46] They were greatly admired when they successfully undertook such prosecutions because they were undeterred by the enduring enmity which that created. Such enmity was not restricted to the prosecutor, but included the presiding honorary magistrate, the witnesses and even jury members. All could be the objects of the defendant's fury.[47] Cicero notes that jurors 'consider the man they have condemned to be their enemy'.[48]

Was the enmity evident in the Corinthian church caused by civil litigation or was litigation used publicly to express personal or household enmity in 1 Corinthians 6?[49] It is clear that it had developed in the church because of personal loyalty to Christian teachers in the church. This 'strife and jealousy' arising from the issue of Christian leadership also found expression in litigation with one of the leading Christians taking another leading Christian to court. If in 1 Corinthians 3:1-4 'strife' (ἔρις) and 'jealousy' (ζῆλος) were signs of an 'immature person' (σάρκικος) and walking in a secular fashion, as sophists and their 'disciples' did in Corinth,[50] then the litigation of 1

---

contain a consideration of the persons involved: and this must involve blackening (*infamandam*) the person on the other side'.

45 In Roman society, enmity 'could be the major impetus of a trial', D.F. Epstein, *Personal Enmity in Roman Politics* 102 -103.

46 D.F. Epstein, *Personal Enmity in Roman Politics* 90.

47 D.F. Epstein, *Personal Enmity in Roman Politics* 90.

48 Cicero, *pro Cluentio* 116; D.F. Epstein, *Personal Enmity in Roman Politics* 95.

49 P. Marshall's important work *Enmity in Corinth: Social Conventions in Paul's Relations with the Corinthians*, WUNT 2.23 (Tübingen: J.C.B. Mohr [Paul Siebeck] 1987) ignores 1 Corinthians 6 in his discussion of enmity in Corinth, although that passage fits well into his *hubristic* thesis and shows that the attitudes and actions of those who were 'wise in this world' were not only reserved for the apostle. L.L. Welborn, 'On the Discord in Corinth: 1 Corinthians 1-4 and Ancient Politics', *JBL* 106/1 (1987) 85-111, whose starting point is politics rather than the model of sophistic leadership as it related to μαθηταί in παιδεία, also ignores 1 Corinthians 6 where his suggestion has most relevance.

50 For evidence see my *Philo and Paul among the Sophists: a Hellenistic Jewish and a Christian Response* (forthcoming CUP).

Corinthians 6 was a reflection of the same problem, but manifested this time in the courts rather than the congregation.[51]

It needs to be remembered that if some had already successfully prosecuted fellow Christians, they would have been awarded financial compensation. This would only have aggravated the problem of strife. Whether one won or lost a court case, the effect could only be deleterious to relationships in the congregation.

V. The *Arbiter* and Litigation

'Is there no wise man among you who is able to judge?' (v. 5). Is Paul's question full of irony?[52] There were wise men 'according to this age' who were members of the congregation, 1 Corinthians 1:20, 26; 3.18. Their secular education consisted not only of intensive instruction in literature but also of training in oratory, including forensic skills. They engaged in declamation pieces before their fellow pupils and were also taught to evaluate court cases.[53] Reference has already been made to the desire of young men—those under twenty-five years of age who were not eligible to enter into debates in the official gathering of citizens (ἐκκλησία)—to practice their forensic abilities after completing their formal training by initiating a court action. Is Paul making a reference to them?

Provision existed in Greek, Roman and Jewish legal systems for the use of arbitrators who acted in a legal capacity with the agreement of the defendant and the plaintiff.[54] Why had some in the

---

[51] The basis for this argument is the established nexus between the various branches of oratory, in particular declamation and forensic oratory, at the highest level of παιδεία and therefore in the life of secular Corinth. For a general discussion see M.L. Clarke, *Higher Education in the Ancient World* (London: Routledge & Kegan Paul, 1971) 39ff.

[52] It is 'biting sarcasm' according to G.D. Fee, *The First Epistle to the Corinthians* 237, where he argues for Paul's use of irony which is seen in the series of questions in this passage.

[53] For a good example of a handbook of legal cases prepared for pupils by Quintilian, see A. Winterbottom, *Declamationes pseudo-Quintilianeae: Declamationes minores* (Berlin and New York: de Gruyter, 1984). English pupils of the seventeenth century used *The Minor Declamations of Quintilian: Being an Excitation or Praxis upon his XII Books, Concerning the Institution of the Orator* (London, 1686).

[54] See P.J. Rhodes, 'Political Activity in Classical Athens', *JHS* cvi (1986) 137 and J.A. Crook, *Law and Life in Rome* 78-79, for the Roman period. For Judaism, see R.H. Fuller, 'Judicial Practices in Judaism', 103-4 and M. Delcor, 'The Courts of the Church of Corinth and the Courts of Qumran', J. Murphy-O'Connor (ed.)

church not used their gifts and training in a profitable way by acting in an extra-judicial capacity as an arbitrator, *i.e. arbiter ex compromisso*?[55] Christians who were wise were 'capable' (δύνασθαι) of actually applying the fruits of their secular education in disputes which could normally be settled by a civil action. Paul's question in v. 2, 'Are you not competent to judge a minor case?' may be a reference to such people. Those who boasted of their secular wisdom and who had clearly been the source of disaffection particularly against Paul, had dissipated their energies in the wrong direction creating havoc and disunity within the church.[56] They could have helped settle minor legal disputes. Paul's preference is that they do not engage in such disputes among themselves,[57] but rather be prepared to suffer wrong even from other Christians (v. 7).

VI. Those Least Esteemed 'in the Church'

Is the comment concerning those 'least esteemed' another case of Paul's use of irony or does it refer to Christian Jews as 'competent judges in the church who have been ignored and despised by those whom Paul is addressing'?[58] In 1 Corinthians 1:26ff. Paul has dealt with the way in which those 'least esteemed' in society (v. 28), had been chosen by God.[59] In the on-going discussion in 4:6ff. Paul uses with great irony the technique of 'covert allusion', deliberately

---

Paul and Qumran: Studies in New Testament Exegesis (London: G. Chapman, 1968) ch. 4.

55 J.A. Crook, *Law and Life in Rome* 78-79 cites as an example the Herculaneum Tablets where a person was to be 'arbitrator by agreement' between X and Y and was 'to give a decision'. See also the *Lex Irnitana* ch. 86 where the parties by agreement could also have access to an *arbiter* who was appointed on an annual basis.

56 *Contra* D.W.B. Robinson, 'To Submit to the Judgement of the Saints' 4ff., where he suggests that the Jewish Christians had the right to act as judges in the congregation because they were 'the saints', *i.e.* the faithful Jews who had the scriptures.

57 His instructions cannot be construed to mean that he was setting up a quasi-permanent court parallel to the Jewish ones. *Contra* M. Delcor, 'The Courts of the Church of Corinth and the Courts of Qumran' 71, although he is careful to argue that similarity does not imply dependence.

58 D.W.B. Robinson, 'To Submit to the Judgement of the Saints' 6.

59 Paul uses the same verb, ἐξουθενεῖν, in 1:28 and 6:4. For comments of the sophists using a similar *syncrisis* see Philo, *Det.* 32-34 and my discussion *Philo and Paul among the Sophists*.

applying the high-status terms to the Corinthian Christians.[60] The low-status term of a person who is 'least esteemed' is then applied to himself as an apostle of the crucified and humiliated Messiah who has been called to follow in his steps. He summoned the Corinthians not to imitate their teachers in the way secular followers of their sophist did, but to follow him in his non-status ministry. The comment in 1 Corinthians 6 about those least esteemed in the church should be seen as a continuation of Paul's use of irony, and not as a reference to Jewish Christian teachers.

Is Paul's question concerning those 'least esteemed' a reflection of the Corinthians' attitude or his own? At least some, if not all the Corinthian Christians were only too conscious of the importance of secular status. This status expressed itself in the activities of the official gathering of citizens (ἐκκλησία) of Corinth, and was epitomised by facility in rhetoric. The boasting which Paul confronts in 1 Corinthians 1-5 appears also to have spilt over into the issue of the successful litigant scoring a victory. It does not appear that the Corinthian Christians felt a sense of disgust at the way in which the local legal system operated. On the contrary, they endorsed it by taking cases to it. The question is to be taken as a reflection of Paul's concept of status in the Christian 'meeting' (ἐκκλησία), as against the city's official gathering (ἐκκλησία). For him, those who had status by reason of their birth, wealth and position in the latter context did not thereby have any special status in the Christian meeting. He had already stressed that it is what men are in Christ which gives them status (1:30). Paul indicates that the social class from which secular Corinthian judges and juries were drawn had no status *per se* within the actual meeting of the assembly (6:4). Christians needed to be reminded of that reality, hence his description of the judges and juries as non-status people. They have no status in the Christian meeting.[61]

The issue of status also lies behind the comment 'To have lawsuits at all is a defeat for you . . . You do wrong, you defraud and

---

[60] B. Fiori, ' "Covert Allusion" in 1 Corinthians 1-4' *CBQ* 47 (1985) 85-102. See further the discussion in *Philo and Paul among the Sophists*, which shows how Paul deliberately negates the covertness of that rhetorical device.

[61] In this passage Paul uses the term ἐκκλησία to mean the actual gathering of Christians in the same way as it was used to refer to a recognised gathering in the secular world, *cf.* Acts 19:39.

that [action against] brothers (τοῦτο ἀδελφούς)', vv. 7-8.[62] The action of taking a brother to court which may have resulted in successful prosecution was seen by Paul as a defeat. Why is this? The decision to institute proceedings was determined by the social status of the one against whom the initiator of litigation proposed to proceed. The plaintiff had to take into account the enmity arising from the actual court proceedings, or he might wish to express his existing personal enmity by means of civil litigation. The awarding of financial damages as an additional penalty may well have been what Paul had in mind when he wrote of 'defrauding' a brother. The very initiating of legal proceedings against a brother was thus seen as a sign of defeat in relationships long before the verdict was pronounced in court.[63]

VII. Conclusions

The foregoing study has shown how the interpretation of 1 Corinthians 6:1-8 is modified when the text is read in light of the difficulties of civil litigation in the first century. Paul's condemnation of Christians appearing before judges (κριταί) who were patently unjust in the way they arrived at judicial decisions is explicable.

It also becomes clear that the strife and jealousy over teachers in 1 Corinthians 1:11ff had spilt over into the area of seemingly minor disputes which were being settled by civil action. The power struggle in the church was not restricted to 1 Corinthians 1-4. Enmity in the public arena (πολιτεία) characterised those relationships in the citizens' official gatherings in Corinth which were not based on 'the politics of friendship'. Those in the church of God (ἐκκλησία τοῦ θεοῦ) who belonged to the class of the wise, the powerful and the

---

62 The place of τοῦτο ἀδελφούς in the whole sentence lays stress on the Christian status of the defendant. G.D. Fee, *The First Epistle to the Corinthians* 239, n. 4 believes that the use of τοῦτο combines the wronging and cheating together. The continuative use of the single neuter demonstrative pronoun which points to a previous action would suggest that the reference is to cheating.

63 For an interesting example of Christians resolving a claim and counter-claim involving a large sum of money and garments in AD 481, see H.B. Dewing, 'A Dialysis of the Fifth Century AD in the Princeton Collection of Papyri', *AJP* liii (1922) 113-127. They signed a *dialysis*, which was a legal contract recording the settlement between a bishop and two presbyters and a deacon.

well-born allowed that secular phenomenon to surface in their dealings with one another especially in the area of civil law.[64]

In presenting his argument, Paul not only referred to the important issue of the future role of the saints in judging the world. He also asked ironically about 'the wise man in your midst' and 'those least esteemed'. The former group was clearly represented in the Christian community by the 'wise among you in this age', 3:18. The latter group was readily recognised in the city of Corinth in stark contrast to those 'most esteemed' in the secular Council (βουλή) and the citizens' gathering (ἐκκλησία). Those most esteemed in Corinthian society had no special standing in the Pauline doctrine of the church by reason of that secular status, cf. 1 Corinthians 1:26 ff.

Paradoxically, on the one hand the Corinthian church had judged the outsider when they had no right to do so (5:12) but failed dismally to judge the insider when they should have done so (5:13). On the other hand, they had allowed the unrighteous outsiders to judge the insiders (6:1) when they should have resorted to the use of a fellow Christian from their number who, by reason of his legal training,[65] would have had the requisite qualifications to act as a private arbitrator.

The difference between 1 Corinthians 6:1-8 and Romans 13:1-7 has now become clearer. In Romans 13 Paul discusses the attitude of the Christian citizen with his obedience to the law. It included a recognition of the right to administer criminal law which arose from the divine *imperium* held by government. Civil litigation in Corinth came within the purview of the local honorary magistrates who appointed judges or juries comprised of the well-to-do in that city and were known for their partiality.[66]

The exclusive commitment to various Christian teachers was a usual secular response by 'followers' in Corinth.[67] The working out of enmity between the élite members of the community in the public

---

[64] Cf. 1 Cor 3. 4 κατὰ ἄνθρωπον περιπατεῖν.

[65] *Philo and Paul among the Sophists,* 209.

[66] *Contra* A. Robertson and A. Plummer, *A Critical and Exegetical Commentary of the First Epistle of St Paul to the Corinthians* (Edinburgh: T. & T. Clark, 1914) 110 who suggested that a 'fair, if rough summary' of Paul's teaching in the two passages was 'obey the criminal courts, but do not go out of your way to invoke the civil courts'. However, Paul proscribes the use of the latter.

[67] See my *Philo and Paul among the Sophists.*

place in this Roman colony was also perfectly acceptable in society.[68] Epstein observes of the peculiar role played by enmity.

> Roman society was unusual in allowing *inimicitiae* to compete along with other more conventional values such as patriotism and humanity in guiding a public figure's conduct. A reputation for successfully pursuing *inimicitiae* was a vital asset to a Roman politician seeking to establish and maintain an influential voice.[69]

1 Corinthians 6:1-8 then reflects a typical, first century stage on which the struggle for power among the élite was often played out. This time it was not one arising out of dispute between citizens taking an active role in the city's gathering (ἐκκλησία) or problems within some local association but it came from within the Christian gathering (ἐκκλησία). What they did have in common with the public arena in which such clashes occurred was that the struggle was also between élite who were social equals or near equals. The contest which had surfaced in jealousy and rivalry between factions in the Christian meeting which Paul refers to earlier in the letter also spilt over into in the secular courts of Corinth in a civil action.

This conclusion runs counter to a recent and important study, 'Rich and Poor in the Courts of Corinth' which argued that in 1 Corinthians 6 rich Christians took their poor brethren to court.[70] The actual title of the essay introduces an unhelpful dichotomy which colours our perception of Corinthian society. The concept of 'rich' and 'poor' is an imprecise and misleading description of the social composition of any Roman colony or any Greek city in the first century. It is better not to use such categories but rather resort to a term current in the ancient world which Paul also chose *viz.* 'the have nots' (τοὺς μὴ ἔχοντας) (1 Cor. 11:22) and its antonym 'the haves'.[71] That classification, if correctly understood, avoids the error of ideo–

---

68 For a discussion of this group in the church see A.D. Clarke, *Secular and Christian Leadership in Corinth: a Socio-historical and Exegetical Study of 1 Corinthians 1-6* (Leiden: E.J. Brill, 1993) ch. 5 and D.W.J. Gill, 'Acts and Urban Élites' in edd. D.W.J. Gill and C. Gempf, The *Book of Acts in its Graeco-Roman Setting*, The Book of Acts in its First Century Setting (Grand Rapids and Carlisle: Eerdmans and Paternoster, 1994) ch. 5.

69 D.F. Epstein, *Personal Enmity in Roman Politics* 127.

70 Mitchell, 'Rich and Poor in the Courts of Corinth'.

71 For a discussion see my 'The Lord's Supper in Corinth: An Alternative Reconstruction', *Reformed Theological Review*, xxxvii (1978) 80-1.

logical attachments of the twentieth and the last century and can be a helpful aid in explaining the social character of this Roman colony.

The 'have nots' did not belong to a household. They were not close or extended members of the family, clients, servants or freedmen i.e. they did not 'have' households. They could have been artisans and may even have held property,[72] but they were among the 'insecure'. They lacked the safety net which a master or a patron afforded in times of uncertainty or adversity such as famines or strife caused by political machinations. On the other hand, the secure or 'the haves' may not have been materially wealthy. Indeed they may have possessed very little, but they did have a household which guaranteed them protection. There perhaps needs to be moratorium on the use of such terminology as 'rich' and 'poor' and even 'middle class' when discussing the social fabric of first century Corinth or other cities in the East by New Testament scholars.[73]

By following Meeks' classification, the essay sees 'Chloe's people' as slaves or former slaves and therefore among 'the poor' i.e. lower status persons.[74] It is believed that it was such as these who were prosecuted through the civil courts by rich Christians. But 'Chloe's people' belong to a household and these were those whom the head of the house trusted to undertake an unspecified journey across the sea to Ephesus where they met Paul. It is inappropriate to designate slaves or freedmen as 'the poor' in view of their place among 'the haves' in Roman Corinth. It is also wrong to assume that freedmen were 'poor', because some of the leading citizens of Corinth were wealthy freedmen.

It has also been suggested that Corinth was 'a society where money was tight', and this added to the burden of litigation costs for the poor who had to hire a lawyer to defend their cause.[75] However, in the Claudian era and subsequent periods Corinth experienced a greater prosperity than it had known before.[76] Furthermore,

---

[72] A.R. Hands, *Charities and Social Aid in Greece and Rome* (London: Thames and Hudson, 1968) 62-5.

[73] 'There is no genuine "middle class" in the sense of an intermediate group with independent economic resources or social standing' P. Garnsey and R. Saller, *Roman Empire: Economy, Society and Culture* (London: Duckworth, 1990) 116.

[74] W.A. Meeks, *The First Urban Christians: The Social World of the Apostle Paul* (New Haven: Yale University Press, 1983) 59.

[75] Mitchell, 'Rich and Poor in the Courts of Corinth' 579.

[76] In Corinth magistrates had authority to issue coins, M. Amandry, *Le monnayage des douvirs corinthiens*, Bulletin de correspondance Hellénique,

plaintiffs and defendants did not have to be represented by a hired lawyer, for there was a long tradition in the ancient world which allowed them to present their own case. The essay speculates that the reason for the disputes at law between the upper class and the lower class was connected with 'services provided'. Engels' thesis that Corinth was 'a service city' is the basis for this conclusion.[77] However, Engels' 'alternative model' has been rightly rejected by ancient historians on the basis of archaeological, literary and methodological considerations.[78] The model has been shown to be incorrect, and the precise nature of the 'smallest matters' that gave rise to civil litigation has not been given (6:2).[79]

The foregoing study has demonstrated that the interpretation of 1 Corinthians 6:1-8 needs to have adequate controls based on the available data of the social fabric of first century Corinth. What Paul designates as 'the smallest causes' must not be read as a reference to the socially 'smallest' litigants. Reconstruction of the background can be hindered by the retrojection of an ideological class conflict drawn from social categories which are either misleading or inadequate descriptions of those who lived in first century Corinth. Understanding the role of vexatious litigation in civil actions among society's élite as a way to secure power in associations and public life in the first century is also crucial for an appreciation of Paul's judgement on the ethical issues involved in litigation against 'brothers'.

Supplément xv (1988). The issue of coins in this period together with archaeological evidence of trade indicate a prosperity which grew even greater in the Claudian era, see C.K. Williams, 'Roman Corinth as a Commercial Center' ed. T.E. Gregory *The Corinthia in the Roman Period*, Journal of Roman Archaeology Supp. 8 (Ann Arbor, 1994) 31–46 esp. 46.

[77] Mitchell, 'Rich and Poor in the Courts of Corinth' 583 citing D. Engels, *Roman Corinth: An Alternative Model for the Classical City* (Chicago and London: University of Chicago Press, 1990). Engels sees 'a service city' as one whose commerce was based on rents and fees, and whose trade involved imports, rural exchange and east-west trade through its ports, but not exports.

[78] C.K. Williams who is the Director of Corinth Excavations, American School of Classical Studies in Athens in his 'Roman Corinth as a Commercial Center' 31-46 discusses in detail the evidence of Corinth's prosperity and calls for a reassessment of Engels' model. For other critiques of Engels' thesis see for example D.P. Thompkins, *Bryn Mawr Classical Review* 1.1 (1990) 20-33, R. Saller, *Class. Phil.* 86.4 (1991) 351-7, A.J.S. Spawforth, *Cl. Rev.* 42.1 (1992) 119-20 and D.W.J. Gill, 'In Search of the Social Élites in the Corinthian Church', *Tyn.B.* 44.2 (1993) 326.

[79]For evidence as to how the seeking for primacy in an association or a city gave rise to civil litigation see 'Civic Responsibilities' in my *Seek the Welfare of the City: Early Christians as Benefactors and Citizens*, Early Christians in the Graeco–Roman World (Grand Rapids: Eerdmans, 1994) Vol. 1, ch. 5.

PART III

THE SOCIAL DIMENSION OF PAULINE ETHICS
The Contribution of the Social Sciences

CHAPTER FIVE

The Strong and the Weak in Corinth
A Sociological Analysis of a Theological Quarrel*

Gerd Theissen
(1975)

Sociological analysis investigates human social behavior with an eye to those characteristics which are typical and those conditions which transcend individuals. It is interested in what is usual and normal, in what applies to many individuals and many situations. By contrast, what has come down from the past focuses primarily on the unusual or unique. For that reason, evaluating such materials sociologically is often difficult if not impossible. Among the unusual and singular events about which we have some knowledge, however, conflicts play a special role. Here the various customs of social groups collide with one another. In such circumstances the unusual actually sheds light on the ordinary, the dramatic conflict reveals the banal. If ever we can derive information about the social background of our historical traditions, it is through the analysis of such conflicts.

---

* Translated by John H. Schütz.

The quarrel between "the strong" and "the weak" in the Corinthian congregation is a matter of just such different customs. The weak avoid all meat sacrificed to idols since it could never be known with certainty that ritual actions had not accompanied the slaughter of the meat. The strong, on the other hand, appeal to their "knowledge": there is only one God; there are no idols and hence "no meat sacrificed to idols" (1 Cor. 8:4ff.).

Paul argues differently. He distinguishes cultic meals in an official setting (8:10) from meals in private houses (10:25ff.). To be sure, his opinion about official cultic meals in a temple is not quite uniform, but the intention is clear. Thus in 8:10ff. he urges the general waiver of a right which he himself would not contest, the right to participate in temple meals with the appropriate mental reservations. In 10:1-22 he goes further and regards such meals as fundamentally incompatible with the Christian Lord's Supper. This shift in accent could be explained by a situation such as this: anyone who only passively participated in such pagan cultic meals, that is, did so as an invited guest, would eventually face the problem of whether or not he was obliged to extend a reciprocal invitation for the same kind of meal. To do so would make him the initiator of "idol worship." Whether this is the problem cannot be settled here.

What is in any event unmistakable in our text is the fact that from 10:23ff. Paul deals with the problem of private meals. These may be meals eaten at home but involving meat bought in the market—a wholly unproblematic case (10:25-26)—or meals by invitation to others' houses where one is served meat (10:27ff.). Paul has reservations about such meat only if its "sacred" character has been specifically pointed out. Since it would be understood that in a temple only consecrated meat would be offered, he must be referring to a meal in a private setting. It could be said that Paul is inconsistent in distinguishing between public and private behavior and that his position is dependent on the social context of the behavior. He is inclined to go along with the weak where the eating of meat takes on an official character (because of the location, or because of the formula "this is sacred meat") and to go along with the strong when the problem is one of a private setting.

Our task is to analyze the reasons for the opposing attitudes of the weak and the strong. It is doubtless proper to look for theological reasons, on the assumption that at the root of different behavior are to be found different convictions about humanity, the world, and God. Yet the truth of that does not preclude a sociological analysis as well. Convictions and concepts are usually effective only if social groups have invested them with the power to shape behavior. In the case of this conflict it is particularly true that social relationships represent a major theme. Since meals are an important form of social communication and the customs surrounding them are often socially determined there can be no argument, in my opinion, about whether one can or ought to interpret this conflict sociologically. The only argument is about how to do so. Which social factors are responsible for the conflict, religious traditions (whether of Jewish or gentile groups) which have shaped behavior, or class-specific customs and attitudes? It goes without saying that apart from all of this there can be divergent opinions about the significance of sociological analysis for throwing light on the meaning of theological texts. The sociological analysis of a theological quarrel does not, in my opinion, mean reducing it to social factors.

SOCIO-CULTURAL FACTORS

To a great extent exegesis has confined itself to these alternatives: either the weak are Jewish Christians or they are gentile Christians.[1] Paul himself, however, seems to have regarded the problem as somewhat more general. He refers to his own behavior as an example of that respect which it is necessary to show the weak, but does so without limiting his behavior to a particular ethnic group: to the Jews he became a Jew, to those outside the Law as one outside the Law, and so forth (9:19-22). This could be a generalization which deliberately goes beyond the concrete context. But at the end of his instructions about meat sacrificed to idols Paul again addresses the strong with these words: "Give no offense to Jews or to Greeks or to

---

1 For an overview of opinions cf. M. Rauer, *Die "Schwachen" in Korinth und Rom nach den Paulusbriefen*, Bst(F) 21, 2-3 (Freiburg, 1923), 36ff.; K. Maly, *Mündige Gemeinde* (Stuttgart, 1967), 96-99. On the basis of 1 Cor. 8:7 the weak are most often identified with gentile Christians. Among those championing an identification with Jewish Christians, however, are L. Batelaan, *De Sterken en Zwakken in de Kerk van Korinthe* (Wageningen, 1942), 21-26; M. Coune, "Le problème des idolothytes et l'éducation de la syneidêsis," *RSR* 51 (1963): 497-534; W. T. Sawyer, "The Problem of Meat Sacrificed to Idols in the Corinthian Church" (diss., Southern Baptist Theological Seminary, 1968, according to *Dissertation Abstracts* 29, 1968/69, no. 1285A). H. Conzelmann, *1 Corinthians* (Philadelphia, 1975), 138, is among the few exegetes who have freed themselves from the alternative Jewish *or* Gentile.

the church of God" (10:32). If both Jews and pagans can take offense, then the weak Christians who take offense could themselves have once been either Jews or pagans. Nor do other clues suggest that the weak were an ethnically or socio-culturally homogeneous group. Some of the weak were certainly gentile Christians. It makes no difference whether in 8:7 we read συνηθείᾳ or συνειδήσει, for in either case it is assumed that some eat meat sacrificed to idols "even now." On the other hand, the opposite conclusion follows from 8:10: if there is a danger that the behavior of one of the strong will mislead someone into eating meat sacrificed to idols, then presumably at the moment this person does not eat such meat but is only tempted to do so. In 8:10 it is a matter of being seduced into eating, while in 8:7 the eating is presupposed as taking place. Naturally, there are possible ways of harmonizing these texts. But it is quite possible that there were two different types of weak Corinthians: a gentile Christian type who always used to eat such consecrated meat but developed a guilty conscience after conversion to Christianity, and a Jewish Christian type who had always avoided such ritually slaughtered meat and who, after conversion, could exercise his unaccustomed freedom from restrictive ritual rules only with a bad conscience.

Finally, it should be pointed out that some of the Corinthian Christians cannot be sorted into these alternatives of Jewish or gentile Christians. These are the former "God-fearers," Gentiles who were sympathetic to Judaism well before their conversion to Christianity but never made a complete commitment to Judaism, possibly because of restrictive ritual rules such as the ban on consecrated meat. For these God-fearers Pauline Christianity offered an "accommodated Judaism."[2] In Corinth these people will have been of particular significance for the Christian congregation. The house of one "God-fearer" provides Paul with the base for his successful missionary work (Acts 18:7-8). Perhaps just such people now find themselves among the strong.

Socio-cultural customs, traditions and attitudes of various ethnic groups certainly will have been significant in influencing behavior regarding consecrated meat. At the same time, however, it is also conceivable that divergent cultural traditions led to similar

---

[2] The idea comes from A. von Harnack, *The Mission and Expansion of Christianity in the First Three Centuries* (New York, 1908), 1ff. On the God-fearers cf. K. G. Kuhn and H. Stegemann, "Proselyten," P.R.E. Suppl. IX, cols. 1248-83. A fair number were of high social status, and this may also be supposed for the strong (see below).

rather than divergent behavior. Therefore, we should look for other factors as well.[3]

SOCIO-ECONOMIC FACTORS

Paul himself suggests that we look for the weak among the lower strata. It is hardly an accident that the first chapters of the Corinthian letter already give voice to the distinction between strong and weak, connecting this with the social structure of the Corinthian congregation. In 1:26ff. Paul states that among the Corinthians are not many who are "wise, influential, of noble birth" (author's trans.)—δυνατοί is the term he uses for the influential, the same term he uses for the strong in Rom. 15:1—and he continues: "God chose what is weak in the world to shame the strong." It appears that already here Paul wants to say that it is precisely the weak, people who admittedly lack wisdom, whom God has chosen. And when in 4:10 he draws the contrast with the Corinthians, "We are weak, but you are strong," we may be hearing reverberations of Paul's solidarity with the weak people of Corinth; for in connection with the question of meat sacrificed to idols he expressly repeats the idea that to the weak he himself became weak (9:22). The first Corinthian letter itself, therefore, suggests the hypothesis that the socially weak of 1:26-27 are identical with those who are weak in the face of consecrated meat. This hypothesis can be tested only by looking for class-specific characteristics in what can still be discerned of the behavior of the weak and the strong, that is, behavioral traits which can be correlated with wealth, occupation, and education and thus to a higher or lower social status.

---

[3] It is frequently held that the weak were members of the party of Cephas who wished to make the apostolic decree obligatory in Corinth. So T. W. Manson, "The Corinthian Correspondence I," in *Studies in the Gospels and Epistles* (Manchester, 1962), 190-209, esp. 200; C. K. Barrett, "Things Sacrificed to Idols," *NTS* 11 (1964/65): 138-53, esp. 146; idem, "Cephas and Corinth," in *Abraham unser Vater, Festschrift für O. Michel* (Leiden, 1963), 1-12, esp. 7-8. The reference to Peter in 1 Cor. 9:5 and the fact that he did not renounce his rights cannot be cited in support of this view. In fact, the strong could well be the very people who have cited his example. If 1 Cor. 8-10 is addressed to the same people in Corinth, then perhaps those circles most closely associated with the strong were playing Peter and other apostles off against Paul. But it is idle to identify the weak with one of the parties named in 1:12. Their anxiety does not fit the self-consciousness of any "party." So also Rauer, "*Schwachen*," 67, and Conzelmann, *1 Corinthians*, 175.

Class-specific Characteristics in Eating Habits

We can begin with the commonplace assumption that then, as today, wealthy people could eat meat more often than others. We cannot base our judgment of eating habits in the ancient world on the literary depictions of great banquets (Petronius, *Satyricon* 52ff.; Juvenal, *Satura* 5; Martial, *Epigrammata* III, 60), as if these revels were typical for ordinary people.[4] It must be borne in mind that most such testimonies are produced by a narrow upper stratum and its followers, and that even so, meat was not necessarily a part of such festive meals. When his friend Septicius fails to show up at a meal which the younger Pliny had prepared for him, Pliny writes a letter of reproach (*Epistulae* I, 15) cataloguing the delights which his friend has missed, including lettuce, snails, and eggs. Nothing is said about meat. Pliny, as it happens, lived quite modestly, and perhaps that is why he was left in the lurch at his own table, for he discreetly hints that his friend had preferred to dine where he could get better food than this.

From other sources we learn something about the ordinary person's meal habits. Greek cities, like Rome, had a system of public food distribution.[5] This provisioning included grain, but not meat. Such is the case both for the public distribution of foodstuffs in Samos and for the Roman grain distribution which was regulated by law from the time of Gaius Gracchus. Septimius Severus (193-211 C.E.) was the first to add to the grain a daily ration of oil, and Aurelian (270-275 C.E.) subsequently expanded the provisions by allowing the sale of pork and wine at reduced prices. A Roman citizen of lower social status probably had little more available than what he was allowed from the state.

In Greece the great mass of the people were nourished by food made from flour, such as porridge made of barley flour (ἄλφιτα) or bread baked from wheat flour (ἄρτος). That the terms σῖτος and ἄλφιτα could mean simply "sustenance" speaks for itself. In addition,

---

4 M. Rostovtzeff, *The Social and Economic History of the Hellenistic World* (Oxford, 1941), II: 1177: "Bread and fish, with the addition of olive-oil and wine, formed in ancient times the most substantial parts of the diet of the people, rich and poor." But see H. Blümer, "Die römischen Privataltertümer," in HAW VI, 2, 2 (1911): 173.

5 Cf. on that H. Bolkestein, *Wohltätigkeit und Armenpflege im vorchristlichen Altertum* (Utrecht, 1939 = Gröningen, 1967), 251-67, 364-78; F. Millar, *The Roman Empire and Its Neighbours* (New York, 1967), 26.

we know from Delos that three stonemasons spent nineteen drachmas and four oboli, or almost two-thirds of their monthly income of thirty drachmas, just for barley flour.[6] Not much was left over for other kinds of food.

The same is true for the Roman situation. From reports that soldiers ate meat only in exceptional circumstances (when no grain was available) it can be concluded that meat did not normally belong to their diet: *ipse exercitusque . . . ita per inopiam et labores fatiscebant, carne pecudum propulsare famem adacti* ("He himself and his army . . . were yet beginning to feel the strain of short rations and hardship—they had been reduced to keeping starvation at bay by a fish diet," Tacitus, *Annales* 14, 24); *usque eo ut complures dies frumento milites caruerint et pecore ex longinquioribus vicis adacto, extremam famem sustentarent* ("...so much so that for several days the troops were without corn, and staved off the extremity of famine by driving cattle from the more distant hamlets," Caesar, *Bellum Gallicum* 7:17). H. Bolkestein is of the opinion that "the mass of people, in Italy as in Greece, lived primarily on a diet of flour, in earlier times made into porridge (*puls*) and later baked into bread."[7]

On the relationship between social status and meal habits *b. Hullin* 84a is also instructive: "A man having one *maneh* may buy a *litra* of vegetables for his bowl; if ten a *litra* of fish; if fifty *maneh* a *litra* of meat. If someone has a hundred *maneh* he may have a pot cooked for him every day. And how often for the others? From Sabbath eve to Sabbath eve" (that is, once a week).

If in the Corinthian Christian congregation the problem of eating meat became a central point of strife between different groups, that was hardly because of the behavior of Christians of lower social status. Those who scarcely ever eat meat can hardly give offense by eating consecrated meat.[8] For those who lack sufficient money to procure meat in the market, it is a purely theoretical question

---

6   *BCH* (1890) 481, cited according to Bolkestein, *Wohltätigkeit*, 251-52. On the price of food at Delos cf. J. A. O. Larsen, "Roman Greece," in T. Frank, ed., *An Economic Survey of Ancient Rome* (Baltimore, 1938), IV: 259-498, esp. 379ff.

7   Bolkestein, *Wohltätigkeit*, 365. Barrett, "Things Sacrificed," 145, refers to Caesar, *Bellum Civile* III, 47, according to which meat was much in demand among soldiers.

8   The class-specific nature of the problem of meat in the Corinthian congregation is also seen by Barrett, "Things Sacrificed," 146, and A. Ehrhardt, "Social Problems in the Early Church," in *The Framework of the New Testament Stories* (Manchester, 1964), 275-312, esp. 280-81. To be sure, both presume that the Corinthian community was socially homogeneous.

whether all such meat bought there should be avoided (10:25). To the extent that the conflict originates in the area of private meals it can be explained by the eating habits of various classes. Such instances (10:25ff.), however, do not constitute the real problem. There can be no doubt that Paul is primarily concerned with the problem of cultic meals which take place in an official setting, which means that the matter is more complicated.

From 8:7 it can be inferred that the weak certainly did eat meat, even if they did so with a bad conscience. According to 8:10ff., doing so in a cultic setting is a genuine temptation. In fact, the consumption of meat in a cultic setting is a problem for all citizens and residents of a city, regardless of their social status, since at a celebration open to the public all might participate. Even the lower classes had their chance to eat meat under such circumstances. We can sketch briefly the various kinds of opportunities which might arise.

1. In Greece and Rome meat was publicly distributed to all citizens in connection with extraordinary events[9] such as the celebration of a victory (Plutarch, *Demetrius* 11; Suetonius, *De vita Caesarum* 38) or at a funeral (Livy, VIII, 22, 2, 4; XXXIX 46, 2; XLI 28, 11). More generally, Cicero includes the distribution of meat among the public *beneficientia* by which private individuals seek to win the public's good will (Cicero, *De officiis* II, 52ff.), for example when competing for a municipal office.

2. In addition to such irregular occasions, public sacrificial meals were instituted for particular days. These were sometimes intended for only a limited circle of people, but often they were intended for all the citizens and residents of a city. Xenophon, for example, who instituted a feast at Scillum, expressly states that "all the citizens and men and women of the neighborhood took part in the festival" (πάντες οἱ πολῖται καὶ πρόσχωροι ἄνδρες καὶ γύναικες μετεῖχον τῆς ἑορτῆς, *Anabasis* V, 3, 7ff.). Everyone received flour, bread, wine, and meat. A document for a banquet at Amorgos from the second century C.E. provides that not only all the citizens are to be treated to meat but also all sojourners, strangers, Romans, and women (*IG* XII, 515).[10]

---

9 Cf. W. Eisenhut, s. v. "visceratio," *PRE* II, 17, cols. 351-53; P. Stengel, "Die griechischen Kultusaltertümer," in HAW V, 3 (1920³), 106ff. On *beneficientia* in Cicero cf. Bolkestein, *Wohltätigkeit*, 314ff.

10 Cf. B. Laum, *Stiftungen in der griechischen und römischen Antike*, 2 vols. (Aalen, 1964). The document from Amorgos is found in vol. II, no. 50. Its detailed account of the course of a feast is very instructive. On charitable endowments cf. further Bolkestein, *Wohltätigkeit*, 233-34.

3. More permanent than these bequests were the great religious feasts, frequently involving a distribution of meat to the general populace paid for either by the state or by the contribution of wealthy individual citizens. For example, meat was served in Athens at the Dionysia and Panathenaea. Was there, perhaps, a public sacrificial meal at the international Isthmian games?[11]

4. Further possibilities for the ceremonial or cultic consumption of meat were provided by the many associations whose bylaws provided for specific feasts. It may be questioned whether in these cases the lower classes always got to eat meat, since the *collegium* of Lanuvium (136 C.E.), for example, provided no meat for its feasts, which were celebrated six times a year (*CIL* XIV 2112 = Dessau, 7212), but only wine, bread, and sardines.[12] This *collegium* included slaves.

5. Finally, there were private invitations to a temple. Those found in Oxyrhynchus are well known, as, for example, "Charemon invites you to a meal at the table of the Lord Serapis in the Serapeum tomorrow, the fifteenth, beginning at 9 o'clock" (*P. Oxy.* I, 110). Whether such invitations could be found among the poor may be questionable, however.

To sum up: Members of the lower classes seldom ate meat in their everyday lives.[13] For that they were largely dependent on public distributions of meat which were always organized around a ceremonial occasion. The community meals of the *collegia* were also religious feasts. As a result, those from the lower classes knew meat almost exclusively as an ingredient in pagan religious celebrations, and the acts of eating meat and worshiping idols must have been

---

[11] Cf. O. Broneer, "The Apostle Paul and the Isthmian Games," *BA* 25 (1962): 1-31; idem, "Paul and the Pagan Cults at Isthmia," *HThR* 64 (1971): 169-84. Unfortunately, no distribution of meat can be documented.

[12] The association laws are reprinted in H. Lietzmann, *An die Korinther I/II*, HNT 9 (Tübingen, 1949⁴), 91-93. Cf. also J. Carcopino, *Daily Life in Ancient Rome* (New Haven, 1940), 275.

[13] From Pliny (*Epistulae* X, 96, 10) it could be concluded that Christians from the lower classes also bought meat, for he says that with the spread of Christianity there was no market for sacrificial meat. But it is to be observed that (1) Pliny explicitly states that Christians embraced all social classes (*Epistulae* X, 96, 9), and only those Christians with purchasing power could possibly have endangered the market for meat; (2) the native priestly aristocracy will have exaggerated the problems of the market, in accordance with their own personal interests. Pliny himself can no longer determine that this is a problem. Ehrhardt's assumption ("Social Problems," 282ff.) that the Christians seriously endangered the meat market of the ancient world is improbable.

much more closely connected for them than for members of the higher strata who were more accustomed to consuming meat routinely. For the poorer classes meat was truly something "special." It belonged to a sacred time segregated from the everyday world. It had a "numinous" character.

Conversion to Christianity brought similar difficulties to both Jewish Christians and gentile Christians of the lower classes. Those who had been pagans must have found it difficult to view meat as something perfectly natural and independent of its ritual setting, while at the same time they were sorely tempted not to miss out on what little bit of meat was offered to them by pagan feasts and institutions. Hence they would eat meat, but with a guilty conscience (8:7). Former Jews who had converted to Christianity had been liberated from Judaism's restrictions. Must it not have been tempting finally to be able to participate in public ceremonies involving meat (8:10)? Yet if they had but little opportunity, now as before, to buy meat which had not been ritually slaughtered, they would not have found it easy to break down the old negative taboos surrounding such meat. On the other hand, we can look for the "less biased" position of the strong among members of the higher classes. Someone accustomed to getting around the positive as well as negative taboos of eating meat could shed any anxiety over demonic infection to the very extent that he has survived eating meat without coming to harm.

Signs of Stratification Within Patterns of Sociability

Invitations to sacrificial meals served basically as a means of communication. Families, associations, and cities came together on such occasions and in so doing expressed ceremonially their common membership. This social aspect emerges particularly clearly in Aelius Aristides:

> Moreover, in sacrifices men maintain an especially close fellowship with this god alone. They call him to the sanctuary and install him as both guest of honor and host, so that while some divinities provide portions of their common meals, he is the sole provider of all common meals, holding the rank of symposiarch for those who at any time are gathered about him. Just as Homer said (*Odyssey* iii, 62) that Athena both poured a libation and completed each request, so he is at one and the same time both participant in libations and the one

who receives them, both coming himself to the revelry and inviting to himself the revellers, who because of him dance their dance free from the fear of evil and carry homeward with their crowns a feeling of true well-being, offering a return invitation (*Orationes* 45, 27).

Here we clearly have harmless forms of sociability, the "parties" of the ancient world. The hint about reciprocal invitations at the close marks a connection with the usual obligations of social, and sociable, life.

Restrictions on meat sacrificed to idols were barriers to communication which raised the problem of the relationship of Christians to the society of the ancient world. Originally the debate began over the general problem and only later shifted to the question of eating meat. In 5:9 Paul mentions a lost letter to the Corinthians[14] in which he warned them against contact with the πόρνοις, the greedy, robbers, and idolaters. That must have been interpreted as his wishing to check every contact with non-Christians. In any event, he corrects himself: He is not referring to contact with non-Christians outside the congregation, but to contact with sinners within it. The relationship of Christians to those outside the community is not to be limited. These relationships, however, cannot have been restricted to casual contact. To the prohibition against contact with Christian sinners Paul specifically adds that one should not even eat with them. From this it follows indirectly that common meals are included among the kinds of contact allowed with non-Christians. Thus even here we encounter the problem raised in 1 Cor. 8-10, but in a somewhat different light. The religious aspect of common meals is touched on, certainly, but contact with idolaters is only mentioned fourth in a list as a special instance of social contact with the world in general. If this social aspect has faded in 1 Cor. 8-10 that is because the debate has there been focused on one issue most accessible to theological argument, the problem of meat sacrificed to idols.

It is perfectly clear, I think, on which side of this conflict the wealthier Christians must have stood. Erastus, the "city treasurer" (Rom. 16:23), could have jeopardized his public position had he rejected all invitations where "consecrated meat" might have been expected. If he is identical with the aedile Erastus known from an

---

14 On that cf. N. A. Dahl, "Der Epheserbrief und der verlorene erste Brief des Paulus an die Korinther," in *Abraham unser Vater*, 65-77; J. C. Hurd, *The Origin of I Corinthians* (London, 1965), 213-39.

inscription,[15] and thus somebody who at one time or another wished to be chosen as overseer for those public places and buildings where such meat was sold, he scarcely could have demonstrated an attitude of reserve about "consecrated meat." Such an attitude would have been wholly inappropriate for his office.

The relationship between high social status and "idolatry" is not ignored by early Christian paraenesis. It is not accidental that the specific vice of the rich, πλεονεξία "wanting to have more," is closely linked with idolatry and even identified with it (Col. 3:6; Eph. 5:5; cf. 1 Cor. 5:10-11). There are also social reasons for this close association of wealth and idolatry. Those who are wealthy, or want to be, must seek and cultivate contact with pagans. That is clearly stated in Polycarp's letter: "Unless one steers clear of greed he will be tainted by idolatry and judged, as it were, with the pagans" (*Phil.* XI, 2). A greedy person belongs with the pagans. He has numerous social contacts with the pagan world. The Shepherd of Hermas says reproachfully of the wealthy that they live together with the pagans (*Similitudines* VIII, 9, 1). There may have been only a few powerful and well-born in Corinth (1:26), but it is among them that we ought to look for those "gnostics" who, in their contacts with the pagan world, neither could nor did take much notice of their poorer Christian brother's scruples.

It could be objected that according to 10:27ff., both the weak and the strong Christians alike appear in social contact with pagan hosts. The information that this is consecrated meat, however, cannot have come from a Christian. Only a pagan could describe ritually slaughtered meat this way. Respect for this pagan's conscience has a quite different motive from the respect for a Christian brother's conscience in 8:10ff. Thus his conscience is never characterized as "weak," a term which would suggest that it lagged behind the norms appropriate for him. Only "conscience" as such is mentioned. And while in 8:11-13 Christ's death serves as the motive for renouncing a right on the basis of love, this specific Christian motivation is completely missing in 10:27-30. Thus the passage does not

---

[15]   Cf. H. J. Cadbury, "Erastus of Corinth," *JBL* 50 (1931): 42-58. In my opinion, his objections to an identification can be refuted. For the identification see J. H. Kent, *The Inscriptions 1926-1950: Corinth, Results of Excavations Conducted by the American School of Classical Studies at Athens VIII*, 3 (Princeton, 1966), 27, 99-100.

presuppose that weak and strong Christians find themselves together as guests at the same meal.

Public and professional duties dictated that Christians of high social status were probably integrated into pagan society than the Christians of more modest circumstances. We may question whether those who belonged to the lower classes might not now be motivated to remain in their pagan clubs in order to participate in the feasts. Paul certainly assumes that the weak also ate meat sacrificed to idols. But it must be remembered that many of these clubs did not offer much more than did the Christian Lord's Supper—bread and wine— while Christians shared meals together far more frequently than perhaps did the members of the *collegium* of Lanuvium, mentioned above, which sponsored six modest public banquets in a year. The lower strata of society found in the congregation full compensation for what they gave up elsewhere. Indeed, they found even more. For while the ancient clubs were largely socially homogeneous,[16] these people had access in the congregation to the upper classes who could use their wealth to serve the congregation and thus to serve the socially weaker. There is also another reason why we must look for the weak among the lower strata. Those who do not have much to lose in the way of "worldly" relationships are more inclined to free themselves of these. In the process a certain *ressentiment* may color their negative opinions. Those for whom the world is full of demons and taboos show by their views, which are designed to steer clear of these, how much at heart they are nevertheless attracted to that world.

Class-specific Traits in the Forms of Legitimation

The strong base their position on their "gnosis." Paul seems to take up some of their arguments:[17] "All of us possess knowledge" (8:1); "an idol has no real existence . . . there is no God but one" (8:4); "all things are lawful" (10:23). The idea of the "weak conscience" (8:7, 10, 12) may have come from them, as well as the argument that "food is meant for the stomach and the stomach for food" (6:13). Unmistakable in all these arguments is the determination to

---

[16] Cf. E. A. Judge, *The Social Pattern of Christian Groups in the First Century* (London, 1960), 44; F. Bömer, *Untersuchungen über die Religion der Sklaven in Griechenland und Rom. IV*, AAWLM.G 10 (Mainz, 1963), 236-41.

[17] Hurd, *Origin*, 68, offers an overview of the passages which exegetes have supposed are citations from the congregational letter.

surmount obsolete religious restrictions through "knowledge." Even if the speculative fantasies of later Gnostics cannot be imputed to the Corinthian "gnostics," as they certainly cannot, neither can the parallels between the two be ignored. For a comparable "liberal" position on meat sacrificed to idols the only analogies within Christianity come from Gnostic groups, as may be seen in the following:[18]

Justin on Gnostics in general: "But know that there are many who profess their faith in Jesus and are considered Christians, yet claim there is no harm in their eating meat sacrificed to idols" (*Dialogus cum Tryphone* 35, 1). ". . . Of these some are called Marcionites, some Valentinians, some Basilidians and some Saturnilians" (*Dial.* 35, 6).

Irenaeus on the Valentinians: "For this reason the most perfect among them freely practice everything which is forbidden. . . . For they eat food that was offered to idols with indifference, and they are the first to arrive at any festival party of the gentiles that takes place in honor of the idols, while some of them do not even avoid the murderous spectacle of fights with beasts and single combats, which are hateful to God and man. And some, who immoderately indulge the desires of the flesh, say that they are repaying to the flesh what belongs to the flesh and to the spirit what belongs to the spirit" (*Adversus haereses* I, 6, 3).

Irenaeus on the followers of Basilides: "They despise things sacrificed to idols and think nothing of them, but enjoy them without any anxiety at all. They also enjoy the other (pagan) festivals and all that can be called appetite" (*Adv. haer.* I, 24, 5; cf. Eusebius, *History ecclesiastica* IV, 7, 7).

Irenaeus on those descended from Basilides and Carpocrates: "Others . . . taught promiscuous sex and many marriages and claimed that God does not care about their participation in pagan cultic meals" (*Adv. haer.* I, 28, 2).

Irenaeus on the Nicolaitans (cf. Rev. 2:14f.; 2:6; Hippolytus, *Adv. haer.* VII, 36): "They live promiscuously. They teach that it is of no significance if one fornicates or eats food sacrificed to pagan gods . . ." (*Adv. haer.* I, 26, 3).

Origen on the Simonians: "Nowhere in the world are Simonians now to be found, although Simon, in order to win a larger following, freed

---

18 Cf. W. Schmithals, *Gnosticism in Corinth* (Nashville, 1971), 224-29, 372-73. Ehrhardt, "Social Problems," 278-79, cites as evidence *Gospel of Thomas* 14 and a fragment of Mani. *Gospel of Thomas* 14, however, contains no reference to meat.

his disciples from the peril of death, which the Christians are taught to prefer, by instructing them to regard pagan worship as a matter of indifference (*Contra Celsum* VI, 11).

Epiphanius on libertine Gnostics of a much later period: "And whatever we eat, be it meat, vegetables, bread or anything else, we are doing a kindness to created things by collecting the soul from all things and transmitting it with ourselves to the heavenly world. For this reason they eat every kind of meat and say that they do so that we may show mercy to our kind" (*Panarion* XXVI, 9, 2).

It cannot simply be assumed on the basis of these texts that eating meat sacrificed to idols was common to all Gnostic groups. There were also ascetic currents in Gnosticism (cf. Irenaeus, *Adv. haer.* I, 24, 2; Tertullian, *Adv. haer.* I, 14). Eating such meat is not *the* typical, but *one* typical behavior of the Gnostics. Orthodox Christianity rather uniformly forbade eating such consecrated meat.[19] That is confirmed by the one example of doing so which we have from non-Gnostic groups. Lucian reports of Peregrinus that when he was a Christian charismatic he was caught in a lapse from the prohibition: "Then he somehow committed an offense—I believe he was seen eating something which was forbidden . . ." (*De morte Peregrini* 16), following which he lost all influence in the Christian community and became a convert to Cynicism. Thus it seems to be the case that a liberal attitude toward meat sacrificed to idols was to be found only among Gnostic Christians.

The links between the "gnosis" in Corinth and Christian Gnosticism of the second century are a matter of controversy, and with good reason. There is scarcely a direct connection. Yet that simply underlines the problem of how to interpret the obvious analogies. The opinion that in Corinth we are dealing with an incipient Gnosticism is of itself unsatisfactory. Gnosticism's beginnings can be dated much earlier if by that is meant the initial appearance of concepts which play a role in the later Gnostic systems.

What is needed is a sociological-structural perspective to complement the developmental-historical perspective. For example, analogies between Corinthian gnosis and later Gnosticism could be

---

19 Cf. Acts 15:20, 29; 21:25; *Did.* 6:3ff.; Minucius Felix, *Octavius* 30; Tertullian, *Apologeticum* 9; Eusebius, *Hist. eccl.* V, 1, 26; Pseudo-Clementine *Recognitiones* 4:36; *Homiliae* 7:4, 8; *Homiliae* 8:19, 23.

found in the fact that in both instances a typical recasting of Christian faith is evident with its rise into the higher classes. Inferences from Gnosticism to the Corinthian gnosis would then have to be confined to those characteristics which could result from a comparable social situation: intellectual level, soteriology based on knowledge, and elite self-consciousness within the community combined with taking pleasure in contact with the pagan world. Problematic assumptions about the Corinthian gnostics' concepts can thus be left to one side.[20]

a. The Gnostic systems of thought demand a high level of intellect. Their speculations are full of ludicrous systems and logic, and as such were not accessible to simple people. These are set down in numerous books which, in the second century, quite possibly outnumber the writings of orthodox Christians.[21] Basilides will serve as an example of a prolific author. He is said to have written a book of odes (*Muratorian Canon* 83f.), a gospel (Origen, *Homiliae in Lucam 1*), and twenty-four books of gospel commentary (Eusebius, *Hist. eccl.* IV, 7, 7; Clement of Alexandria, *Stromateis* IV; 12, 1). More writings have been preserved from the Valentinians than from all other Gnostic groups. Such an enormous production of books is conceivable only in relatively wealthy circles—and one recalls the wealthy Valentinian Ambrose who could put seven stenographers at Origen's disposal so that his lectures could be copied and published (Eusebius, *Hist. eccl.* VI, 18, 1; 23, 1-2). The Corinthian gnostics, to be sure, did not produce any books, but they did avail themselves of the medium of writing. The community's letter is written entirely from their point of view. Its arguments assume a certain intellectual standard.

b. A soteriology of knowledge, faith in the saving power of discernment, can also be a class-specific factor. Where salvation takes place less through the agency of a deity than through the inner process of "knowledge," the felt need which gives rise to the quest for salvation is also less likely to be rooted in material circumstances. Max Weber has ascribed to the upper classes this kind of hope for salvation: "The success

---

[20] On the problematic nature of Corinthian gnosis, cf. most recently R. McL. Wilson, "How Gnostic were the Corinthians?" *NTS* 19 (1972): 65-74. H. G. Kippenberg, "Versuch einer soziologischen Verortung des antiken Gnostizismus," *Numen* 17 (1970): 211-31, rests on inference from mythical ideas. For criticism see P. Munz, "The Problem of 'Die soziologische Verortung des antiken Gnostizismus,'" *Numen* 19 (1972): 41-51. In any case, Kippenberg is correct in observing that the Gnostics belonged to the upper classes.

[21] Cf. W. Bauer, *Rechtgläubigkeit und Ketzerei im ältesten Christentum*, BHTh 10 (Tübingen, 1964²), 150-97; Eng. trans., *Orthodoxy and Heresy in Earliest Christianity*, ed. R. A. Kraft and G. Krodel (Philadelphia, 1971), 147-94.

of philosophical salvation doctrines and the propaganda of salvation cults among the lay elite during late Hellenic and Roman times parallels these groups' final turning aside from political participation."[22] When the educated classes no longer can or will shape the world, they frequently transcend it all the more radically by means of ideas. The transition from being lost to being saved is then regarded as one of gaining "true knowledge." On this score there are comparable characteristics in the "knowledge" of Gnosticism and that of the Corinthian gnosis. For the latter, knowledge means recognizing that idols do not really exist, that is, stripping this world's mythically intensified appellate agencies of their demands. This might be called demystifying a portion of the world. In later Gnosticism such knowledge becomes radicalized so that even the Old Testament's creator God is unmasked as a mythical being to whom this world traces back its restrictive commands and prohibitions.

c. People who understand themselves to be elevated above the "world" also understand themselves to be superior in a very concrete way to those who are imprisoned by it. The division of humankind into three classes encountered in so many Gnostic writings, and especially the differentiation of Christians as either pistics or gnostics, betrays a sharply elitist consciousness in Gnostic circles: normal Christians are only second-rate people. Such rankings may reflect the internal stratification of Hellenistic Christian communities in which—as for example in Rome[23]—Christians of the upper classes frequently separated themselves as Gnostics from the common Christian people. In Corinth there were the beginnings of such a differentiation within the community. Here too the strong were distinguished from the weak, and we even find the terminology of *pneumatikoi* and *sarkikoi* (3:1). Here too some Christians seek to distinguish themselves from others of a lower rank on the basis of "wisdom" and "knowledge."

d. Finally, there is the matter of the relative openness of Gnostics to the culture of antiquity. An example is the reception of pagan mythology

---

22 M. Weber, *The Sociology of Religion* (Boston, 1963), 124, who also mentions the "Gnostic mysteries."

23 Cf. K. Langerbeck, "Zur Auseinandersetzung von Theologie und Gemeindeglauben in der römischen Gemeinde in den Jahren 135-165," in *Aufsätze zur Gnosis*, AAWG.PH 3, 96 (Göttingen, 1967), 167-79. The Valentinians, who only later separated from the community (Irenaeus, *Adv. haer*. I, 6, 3), testify that sacrificial meat was eaten in the Roman community. The polemic of Hermas against the rich may also refer to them. Thus, for the first half of the second century the problems are like those in Corinth. May not the conflict there between the weak and the strong in the first century also have had a similar background as in Corinth—despite different arguments?

and literature among the Naasenes (Hippolytus, *Adv. haer.* V 6, 3-11, 1). Many of the moral objections raised by the church fathers against Gnostics concern what was but ordinary behavior for that time. Gnostics take part in the pleasures of their day, banquets, theatrical performances, and social life. Many of them were no more strict about sexual morality than was the era itself. They cautioned against seeking martyrdom. In the case of Basilides and Valentinus themselves, however, there can be no denying the earnestness and sympathetic differentiation within their ethical views. C. Andresen is right when he says: "These people belonged to social strata which did not usually find their way into the early catholic communities. The aura of a certain liberality, one that spills over the narrow limits of a community piety anxious for its own traditions, suffuses the testimony to Valentinian and Basilidian Gnosis."[24] It is for just such groups that we have evidence of eating meat sacrificed to idols. This fits with their liberal disposition. It is a mark of broader integration within the society of that day which is at the same time thoroughly comfortable with a radical "theoretical" critique of the world. The world is rejected in a theoretical way in order to profit from it in a practical way—the usual verbal radicalism of the affluent.

The Christian Gnosticism of the second century may have been largely a theology of the upper classes. And even if we may not assume that there were Christians of elevated social status in all Gnostic groups, we may assume that such were to be found in those groups said to eat meat sacrificed to idols, for example, the Valentinian and Basilidian Gnostics. It is permissible to make a connection with the Corinthian gnosis since doing so rests not on an inference from the realm of mythic concepts but on the four criteria listed above. In the case of the Corinthian gnostics we also find a certain level of education, the significance of knowledge and wisdom for ethics and salvation, and an elitist self-consciousness within the community which goes hand in hand with a considerable liberalism about associating with the pagan world. In both instances these characteristics taken together point to an elevated social status.

What thus seems probable on the basis of analogy is also independently plausible. Is it not likely that in class-specific conflicts those of higher social standing will appeal to their superior insight? In other instances they were certainly accustomed to play their better insight off against the common man. On the other hand, it seems

---

24 C. Andresen, *Die Kirchen der alten Christenheit* (Stuttgart, 1971), 103-4.

more reasonable to ascribe superstitious notions of a sort which impede contact with outsiders to the perspective of the lower classes, with their limited experience, than to those whose social status gives them a broader perspective.

Class-specific Traits in the Forms of Communication

First Corinthians is itself a social fact, evidence of communication between Paul and the congregation. From it we learn, first of all, something about the position within the community of those involved in the communication. Indirectly, however, we also get some hints about their general position in society. Three matters are particularly instructive: Paul's informants, those whom he addresses, and his critics.

Paul is told of the problems by a congregational letter which clearly is formulated from the standpoint of the strong. Other opinions are not reflected, the catch phrase "all of us possess knowledge" (8:1) leaving little room for that. The authors write in the conviction that they can represent the community. They comprise the leading circles. Paul is thus informed on the basis of a perspective "from above." It is scarcely an accident that in contrast to this he receives oral information (1:11; 11:18) about problems within the Corinthian community which sees things from below (1:26ff.; 11:20ff.). Might these divergent paths by which information travels have a class-specific character?

Interestingly, Paul also addresses his reply almost exclusively to the strong. Almost all passages in which we find the second person used are directed to them, as for example "Only take care lest this liberty of yours somehow become a stumbling block to the weak" (8:9; cf. 8:10, 11; 10:15, 31). On that basis we can conclude with M. Rauer that the weak have no position of leadership within the congregation.[25]

It is also significant that in his statements addressed to the strong Paul includes a long excursus (9:1-27) in which he appears to have two groups in mind. One group consists of some critics who have attacked him because of his renunciation of support (9:3). The other consists of the strong to whom he represents this posture as a model. Is it not likely that the critics and those whom Paul addresses are partly identical? The critics who reproach Paul because he would

---

25 Rauer, "*Schwachen*," 67.

not accept material support from them are not likely to have belonged to the materially impoverished, since they are at the moment supporting other missionaries. If these critics of Paul are at least in part identical with the strong, that would confirm their sociological orientation, since renunciation of material privileges is a much more effective example in an exhortation directed to those who are materially privileged.

All of our observations, about forms of eating, sociability, legitimation, and communication, point to the fact that the strong probably belong to the few who are "wise . . . powerful . . . and of noble birth" (1:26). Their more liberal attitude belongs primarily in the upper classes. Naturally, this attitude will have been extended beyond those limits. It is just such Christians of higher social status who bring with them a larger household unit. It is just such Christians who have been influential. But they were unable to win all to their position. There were also the weak, for whom pagan or Jewish traditions still had their influence. Such traditions, however, could be effective only because they undergirded a class-specific attitude.

Finally, we must consider Paul's own position in this conflict between the strong and the weak. It has always been something of an offense to modern exegesis that Paul does not consistently champion the enlightened position of the strong, even though he is in basic agreement with it. If we understand his argument—quite possibly in a way which goes beyond the self-understanding inherent in it—as a plea for consideration of the lower strata by the higher strata, then Paul's alleged inconsistency appears to be quite consistent. For the fact is that for Paul the revaluation of all norms of social rank and dominance—including the dominance of a higher "knowledge" and "wisdom"—proceeds directly from the preaching of the cross (1:18ff.). To be sure, seen from today's perspective it must be emphasized that this revaluation has no "revolutionizing" consequences in the social realm. Paul's recommendation, based on love, that the higher classes accommodate their behavior to the lower classes, only mitigates the tension between the two but allows the differing customs to continue to exist. The factual privileges of status enjoyed by the higher strata are preserved. For example, private meals with consecrated meat continue to be allowed in principle (10:23ff.). Nor is participation in cultic meals excluded in principle. All that is prohibited is disturbing a weak person by doing so. In other words, everything must take place in a very "exclusive" circle.

But just those possibilities continue to be available which, as it happens, are more accessible to members of the upper classes. To be sure, the norms for the Christian community are advocated with vigor. But without doubt there is the obvious danger that those who are better off have de facto more possibilities of avoiding the restrictive effects of these norms than do those of the lower classes. The latter come up short—as far as the material side of things is concerned. For it is those very cultic feasts of an official nature, where each can monitor the behavior of the other, but which also would have afforded an opportunity for the lower classes to eat some meat, which are covered by the prohibition against pagan worship. Paul's solution is a compromise. The wishes (or prejudices) of the weak are upheld just as is the knowledge (and social privilege) of the strong. For that very reason it is realistic and practicable. Something comparable is to be found in the solution to a conflict referred to in 1 Cor. 11:17ff. There we find that wealthy Christians can eat their "own" meal privately to their heart's content (11:33-34), but in the congregation they are to be satisfied with the Lord's Supper, with the bread and wine of the fellowship.

These are solutions which are characteristic for the love-patriarchalism of the Pauline letters. This love-patriarchalism[26] allows social inequities to continue but transfuses them with a spirit of concern, of respect, and of personal solicitude. Concern for the conscience of the other person, even when it is a "weak" conscience and obedient to norms now superseded, is certainly one of the congenial characteristics of this love-patriarchalism. This should not be overlooked even if Pauline love-patriarchalism cannot be considered the solution to contemporary social problems. It must be asked critically, however, whether love and knowledge can be joined without restricting knowledge. Was it just cynicism if some of the strong in Corinth believed that under the circumstances they could "edify" the weak by their example (1 Cor. 8:10)? Could they not have believed, with a very clear conscience, that the lower classes should not further curtail their already limited possibilities in life with such religious scruples? For the most part we hear only one side of the argument between Paul and the "gnostics." That should be kept in

---

26 In my opinion, the characterization of this love-patriarchalism by E. Troeltsch, *The Social Teaching of the Christian Churches* (New York, 1931), 69-89, is still pertinent. To be sure, the term "love-patriarchalism" is not found there but is implicit in what is said.

mind by anyone attributing simply unsocial behavior to the "gnostics." We do not know precisely how they argued their case. The gnostic *Gospel of Philip*, which comes from a later time but is close in spirit to these people, proposes a relationship between love and knowledge in which neither is compromised by the other: "Love, however, builds up. But whoever is free because of knowledge is a slave on account of love for those who cannot yet accept the freedom of knowledge. But knowledge makes them suitable by working to make them free" (110). Perhaps in principle Paul felt not much differently. Perhaps the Corinthian gnostics were even his best "pupils." We ought not to blame Paul because he wanders from this principle. It was being played off against the socially weak. In such a context one can insist on one's right in such a way as to wind up in the wrong.

CHAPTER SIX

The Beginnings of Church Discipline
1 Corinthians 5

Gerald Harris
(1991)

INTRODUCTION

Since the rise of the interdisciplinary approach to the study of Christian origins in the 1970s, little attention has been given to the problem of social control within the early church. This is true although control issues arose early in the Christian movement and have continued throughout Christian history. Before 1970 scholars treated the problem historically and theologically under the topic of discipline.[1] Among scholars who utilize the social sciences in their

---

[1] A notable example of the historical approach is the chapter on discipline by M. Goguel in *The Primitive Church* (New York: Macmillan, 1964) 224-46. An example of a theological approach is the essay by G. W. H. Lampe, 'Church Discipline and the Interpretation of the Epistles to the Corinthians', *Christian History and Interpretation: Studies Presented to John Knox* (ed. W. R. Farmer, C. F. D. Moule, R. R. Niebuhr; Cambridge: Cambridge University, 1967) 337-61. For bibliography on earlier studies, see G. Forkman, *The Limits of the Religious Community: Expulsion from the Religious Community within the Qumran Sect, within*

approach to Christian origins, there are some scattered materials on internal social control but little direct, sustained investigation.[2]

This study utilizes some sociological concepts and models in examining one passage of early church discipline – 1 Cor 5, the case of the incestuous man. A sociological perspective on discipline should open up some new questions and contribute to a fuller understanding of the passage and the community in which it arose. The investigation takes account of primary institutionalization and the broad category of social control, but it does not centre on these concepts. Berger and Luckmann indicate the priority of the socially constructed world:

> Institutions . . . control human conduct by setting up pre-defined patterns of conduct, which channel it in one direction as against the many other directions that would theoretically be possible. It is important to stress that this controlling character is inherent in institutionalization as such, prior to or apart from any mechanisms of sanctions specifically set up to support an institution. These mechanisms (the sum of which constitute what is generally called a system of social control) do . . . exist in many institutions . . . Their controlling efficacy, however, is of a secondary or supplementary kind. As we shall see again later, the primary social control is given in the existence of an institution as such.[3]

The issue of discipline within the larger context of social control may be expressed thus: if mechanisms of social control are secondary and supportive of the more basic institutional world, what does a developing movement do when its basic features (beliefs, patterns of conduct, rituals) are threatened? This investigation focuses on one

---

Rabbinic Judaism, and within Primitive Christianity (Lund, Sweden: C.W.K. Gleerup, 1972) 10-11.

[2] See G. Theissen's studies in *The Social Setting of Pauline Christianity: Essays on Corinth* (ed. and trans. J. Schütz; Philadelphia: Fortress, 1982) esp. 182-6; W. Meeks, *The First Urban Christians: The Social World of the Apostle Paul* (New Haven: Yale University, 1983) 111-39, esp. 127-31; also B. J. Malina, *Christian Origins and Cultural Anthropology: Practical Models for Biblical Interpretation* (Atlanta: John Knox Press, 1986) esp. 112-38. Forkman, *Limits*, is the most comprehensive study since 1970. His main emphasis is on expulsion from the community.

[3] P. L. Berger and T. Luckmann, *The Social Construction of Reality: A Treatise in the Sociology of Knowledge* (Garden City, New York: Doubleday and Company, 1967) 55. See further, 47-92.

instance of social control in the early church, the disciplinary action directed against the incestuous man, as it is reflected in 1 Cor 5.

Discipline is the key traditional English term in the investigation of the problem, and a definition will help to frame the problem. *The Oxford English Dictionary* gives a useful ecclesiastical definition. Discipline is:

> The system or method by which order is maintained in a
> . church, and a control exercised over the conduct of its
> members; the procedure whereby this is carried out; the
> exercise of the power of censure, admonition, excommu-
> nication, or other penal measures, by a Christian Church.[4]

This definition assumes an established institution, whereas in the period under investigation the church is not fully separate from Judaism nor distinctly organized, so it is important to allow for the dynamics of an emerging movement.

Implied in the definition given above are norms, deviance, and sanctions. These basic sociological concepts will serve as a conceptual framework for analyzing 1 Cor 5. In addition, some sociological models will be utilized: (1) a model of reaction to deviance developed from an article by H. Himmelweit, (2) a formula of norm development in millenarian sects from K. Burridge, and (3) a theory of legitimation from P. Berger.[5]

The Corinthian correspondence is a good beginning point for a study of discipline in early Christianity, for the church in Corinth was marked by conduct which led to disciplinary action on more than one occasion, and Paul has responded to the problems in his letters.[6] 1 Cor 5 is one of the more detailed texts on discipline in the New Testament.

---

4 *The Oxford English Dictionary* (Oxford: Clarendon, 1933) 3. 416.

5 H. Himmelweit, 'Deviant Behaviour', *A Dictionary of the Social Sciences* (ed. J. Gould and W. L. Kolb; New York: The Free Press, 1964) 1967; K. Burridge, *New Heaven, New Earth: A Study of Millenarian Activities* (Oxford: Basil Blackwell, 1969); P. Berger, *The Sacred Canopy: Elements of a Sociology of Religion* (Garden City, New York: Doubleday, 1987).

6 In addition to 1 Cor 5, see 2 Cor 2. 5-11; 12. 19-13. 10. I accept the widely held view of modern scholarship which does not identify the deviant of 2 Cor 2. 5-11 with the incestuous man of 1 Cor 5. See V. Furnish, *II Corinthians* (Anchor Bible 32A; Garden City, New York: Doubleday, 1984) 159-66.

DEVIANCE

The chapter begins with a reference to πορνεία among the Corinthian Christians. 'Sexual immorality (πορνεία) is actually reported among you, even such sexual immorality as is not tolerated among pagans – someone is living with his stepmother' (5. 1).[7] Πορνεία is translated 'fornication' by KJV, 'immorality' by RSV, and 'sexual immorality' by NEB, TEV, JB, NJB, and NIV. In common English parlance 'immorality' is equated with 'sexual immorality'; however, precision calls for the latter translation, which technically is not a tautology.[8] Sociologists, in general, consider deviance to be rule-breaking and other nonconformity viewed in a negative way and hence reacted to with scorn, hostility, punishment, or an effort to effect change.[9] It is 'behaviour which departs from, or conflicts with, standards which are socially or culturally accepted within a social group or system'.[10]

Do we have here an example of deviant behaviour? The term πορνεία is a general one which covers a range of sexual conduct including prostitution and incest, but is it always disapproved? The term is used in the New Testament only with a negative connotation; hence for the user of the term it designates deviance;[11] however, we must distinguish Paul's labelling of the man's behaviour from the reaction of an approving group within the congregation.

The nature of the reported offence calls for discussion before it can be classified as deviance. What was the offence which Paul condemned? He gives a specific content to the term in v. 1; it is incest: γυναῖκά τινα τοῦ πατρὸς ἔχειν. The present tense of the infinitive, ἔχειν, indicates a continuing relationship.[12] The phrase, γυνὴ τοῦ

---

[7] My translation. Biblical quotations are from the RSV unless otherwise indicated.

[8] Cf. J. C. Hurd, Jr., *The Origin of I Corinthians* (New York: Seabury Press, 1965) 51, n. 2.

[9] See E. Sagarin, 'Positive Deviance: An Oxymoron', *Deviant Behavior* 6 (1985) 169-81. See also D. Black, *Toward a General Theory of Social Control*: Vol. 1, *Fundamentals* (Orlando: Academic Press [Harcourt Brace Jovanovich] 1984) 5, n. 7. The main debate in defining the term concerns whether norms or reactive behaviour is the crucial element.

[10] Himmelweit, 'Deviant Behaviour', 196.

[11] Barrett says, 'In the New Testament however [πορνεία] is regularly used for unchastity and sexual irregularity of almost any kind.' *A Commentary on the First Epistle to the Corinthians* (London: Adam and Charles Black, 1968) 121.

[12] See H. Lietzmann, *An die Korinther I-II* (Tübingen: J. C. B. Mohr [Paul Siebeck], 1949) 23. Also Conzelmann, *I Corinthians: A Commentary on the First Epistle to the Corinthians* (Hermeneia; Philadelphia: Fortress, 1975) 96.

πατρός, refers to 'stepmother' in the LXX.[13] The man may have married his deceased father's widow, although the father could have secured a divorce and have been alive at the time Paul was writing. We cannot tell whether the father was dead or alive; however, the sexual relationship would have been deviant in either case in the eyes of the larger community, for 'marriage between stepmother and stepson is forbidden both by Jewish and by Roman law'.[14] J. C. Hurd, Jr.'s speculation that the marriage may have been spiritual and hence innocent stretches one's imagination beyond the limits of the vocabulary used and of the total context.[15] The man's behaviour was a continuing sexual relationship with his stepmother which was forbidden by Jewish and Roman law.

It is important to distinguish social units in considering deviance, for the larger society may have one set of norms, and a social group within that society may have another. The behaviour of the man and his stepmother could have been deviant in one group (the Christian movement represented by Paul) and not deviant in another (the congregation in Corinth). It is clear that Paul, a leader and representative of an important segment of the Christian movement, considered such sexual behaviour to be deviant. He reacted to the report of incest negatively and sought to effect a change in the situation. This instance of πορνεία represents deviance not only in the Jewish world and Roman society but also in the portion of the emerging church under Paul's leadership, which apparently included some of the Corinthian congregation, perhaps Chloe's people (1 Cor 1. 11) or whoever informed Paul of the situation.

There are two foci to Paul's reaction: there is concern over the man's behaviour and over the attitude of the congregation in condoning the incest. The offence is referred to in 1 Cor 5. 1 as 'sexual immorality *among you*' (ἐν ὑμῖν πορνεία), that is, the Corinthian Christians. Paul's major concern throughout the passage is the practice and acceptance of πορνεία in the congregation. Peter S. Zaas thinks that 'Paul's argument moves from a condemnation of a specific vice to a denunciation of a general one, the vice of "sexual

---

13 E.g., Lev 18. 8, where the term is distinguished from one's mother (18. 7). See further, C. H. Talbert, *Reading Corinthians* (New York: Crossroad, 1987) 12.

14 Conzelmann, *I Corinthians*, 96. Forkman, *Limits*, 141, explains the man's behaviour as 'an established sexual relationship with his stepmother'. See also J. Héring, *The First Epistle of Saint Paul to the Corinthians* (London: The Epworth Press, 1962) 34 n. 1.

15 *Origin*, 278.

immorality".'[16] It would be better to say that Paul is concerned with a general topic throughout the passage, and that the case of incest is an instance of the general topic. The problem was not just an incident of individual misconduct, although the case of incest may have been singular; rather, it was a social problem. The text makes clear that Paul is discussing a common attitude in the congregation and a case of continued behaviour by the individual, which implies a period of time in which the congregation could have disciplined the offender but did not; thus Paul calls on the church, the social unit, to act.

In 1 Cor 5. 2 Paul addresses the church and demands the removal of the man: 'And you are arrogant (πεφυσιωμένοι)! Should you not rather mourn so that the one who has done this may be removed from among you?'[17] The problem is not only the conduct of the incestuous man, but it is the attitude of the congregation in allowing the behaviour to continue in the church. Paul calls on the congregation to change its attitude (to mourn rather than to be arrogant) and to exercise severe discipline.

Keeping the focus on deviance, we move to vv. 6-8 where Paul again takes up the congregation's arrogance in terms of boasting (καύχημα). 'Your boasting is not good' (v. 6), he says, and then admonishes the congregation with a metaphor based on Passover observance. The imagery serves to legitimate the expulsion which Paul is calling for and to confront the congregation with its offence. This section (vv. 6-8) underscores Paul's emphasis on group purity rather than on restoration of the individual.[18]

In vv. 9-11 Paul clarifies an earlier letter in which he had instructed the community not to associate with sexually immoral people. He had meant for them not to associate with sexually immoral members of the congregation; he had not meant outsiders. Paul reminds the church of his previous instructions in which he had apparently used a traditional vice list (v. 10). In v. 11 he reinforces his instruction for members to avoid Christians who deviate from the norms previously set forth. They are not to associate with any brother (τις ἀδελφὸς ὀνομαζόμενος) who is sexually immoral or greedy or idolatrous or a slanderer or a drunkard or a robber, not even to eat with such a person.

---

[16] Cf. P. S. Zaas, '"Cast Out the Evil Man from Your Midst" (1 Cor 5:13b)', *JBL* 103 (1984) 259.

[17] My translation.

[18] See M. Newton, *The Concept of Purity at Qumran and in the Letters of Paul* (SNTSM 53; Cambridge: Cambridge University, 1985) esp. 86-97.

Does the vice list indicate various kinds of deviant behaviour in the Corinthian church, or is it only a traditional list which Paul is using without direct reference to Corinth? What is the relationship of the vice catalogues to the actual situation in Corinth? Conzelmann argues that because the catalogues are traditional forms, they do not give a realistic description of conditions in Corinth. He continues, 'The vices listed are not individual (Corinthian), but typical.'[19] However, a traditional formula may be closely related to an actual situation (as Conzelmann notes in regard to 1 Cor 6. 11). The lists are not inherently specific, but they are related to the addressees' situation by the writer's choice and adaptation. For example, in 6. 9-11 a catalogue of vices appears: 'Neither the sexually immoral, nor idolaters, nor adulterers, nor catamites, nor sodomites, nor thieves, nor the greedy, nor drunkards, nor revilers, nor robbers will inherit the kingdom of God, and such were some of you' (6. 9c-11a) [my translation]. The last clause (v. 11a) is important in showing that Paul has related the traditional list to the Corinthian situation.[20] The types of deviance in the lists of 5. 10-11 seem to reflect conditions in the Corinthian church. So there appears to be a general correspondence between the traditional lists and the situation in Corinth, especially so regarding πορνεία.

What was the degree of the congregation's complicity in the incestuous affair? Was it a simple condoning of behaviour which the community knew to be deviant or was it celebrating a behaviour which they considered normative or wanted to make normative? Paul admonishes the congregation for being arrogant and boastful, and the context of these words suggests that the arrogant, boastful attitude was closely related to the case of incest. At least some in the congregation seem to have embraced the incestuous behaviour as an expression of a new norm.

The significance of utilizing the concept of deviance emerges if we apply a model based on the sociological concept of deviance to the passage. Himmelweit gives an analysis of deviance which can be used as the basis for a model. He says:

> The extent to which such [deviant] behaviour is disapproved
> of has been shown experimentally to vary with the co-

---

19 I Corinthians 101, n. 72. See further, the Excursus on 'The Catalogues of Virtues and Vices', 100-1.

20 See further, Conzelmann, I Corinthians, 107; Barrett, First Epistle, 141; Forkman, Limits, 172, on 2 Cor 12. 20-13. 2.

hesiveness of the group, the structure of the membership of the group (authoritarian v. democratic), and the actual or perceived threat to the group by outside forces. The more cohesive the group, the more authoritarian its structure, and the more threatened it feels, the stronger will be the demand for conforming behaviour and the greater the rejection of deviant members.

It is also important to remember that deviant behaviour is differently evaluated and reacted against depending upon . . . the relevance of the behaviour in question to its social norms [and] the tasks of the group.[21]

Using elements from Himmelweit's analysis of reaction to deviance, we re-examine 1 Cor 5 at four points: (1) cohesiveness of the group; (2) structure of the membership; (3) actual or perceived threat from the wider society; and (4) relevance of the deviance to group norms and tasks.

1) Cohesiveness: 'The more cohesive the group, . . . the stronger will be the demand for conforming behaviour and the greater the rejection of deviant members.' The congregation's reaction to the incest was accepting, and by reverse inference Himmelweit's theory suggests that the congregation was not cohesive; otherwise the reaction would have been one of condemnation and non-acceptance. Data from the Corinthian letters support this inference. In 1 Cor party loyalties and dissensions are mentioned in 1. 10-13 ('I belong to Paul; I belong to Apollos', etc.). There are other tensions, as well, over eating meat offered to idols (chap. 8), over the Lord's Supper (11. 18-19), over spiritual gifts (chaps. 12 and 14). Studies by G. Theissen support the view that the Corinthian congregation was marked by social stratification which led to conflict.[22] The sociological theory helps to explain why the congregation accepted πορνεία within its ranks. Because of the lack of social unity, a *laissez faire* attitude prevailed in regard to sexual morals. There may have been an ideological basis for the attitude in the minds of some, such as antinomianism or proto-gnosticism, but the lack of social unity within the congregation supported the ideology.

---

[21] Himmelweit, 'Deviant Behaviour', 197. See further, Lewis Coser, *The Functions of Social Conflict* (New York: The Free Press, 1956) esp. 95-104.
[22] 'Social Stratification in the Corinthian Community: A Contribution to the Sociology of Early Hellenistic Christianity', *Social Setting*, 69-119.

2) Structure of membership: 'The more authoritarian its structure, . . . the stronger will be the demand for conforming behaviour and the greater the rejection of deviant members.' There is tension not only within the congregation but between what Meeks calls 'local charismatic authority and supralocal, unitive governance through the apostle and his itinerant associates'.[23] There is a wide variety of interpretations of Paul's relationship to the congregation[24] but agreement that the church did not give Paul unquestioning authority. So Himmelweit's theory suggests that the relatively non-authoritarian structure within the community contributed to the acceptance of the deviant behaviour. If Paul's authority had been greater, the deviant would more likely have been disciplined.

3) Outside threat (actual or perceived): 'The more threatened [the group] feels, the stronger will be the demand for conforming behaviour and the greater the rejection of deviant members.' The church's acceptance of incest points to a group which is rather secure in its cultural setting. This is in contrast to Paul's experience of suffering at the hands of the dominant culture.[25] In Corinth Christians were willing to use the secular courts to settle personal differences (6. 16) and to dine with pagans where meat sacrificed to idols was served (1 Cor 8. 10). This manner of living suggests trust in the society and its institutions and helps to explain the congregation's acceptance of the incest. They did not consider themselves to be endangered by the deviance.

4) Relevance of the deviant behaviour to group norms and tasks: 'Deviant behaviour is differently evaluated and reacted against depending upon . . . the relevance of the behaviour in question to its social norms [and] the tasks of the group.' Here we encounter the ideological element in social action, and because of the complexity of this question, a brief glance at group tasks or mission must suffice at this point. Social norms will be examined in the next section of the paper. Talbert notes that Paul is bothered by the incest because it is behaviour that even pagans reject (v. 1b), because he wanted to give 'no offense to Jews or to Greeks . . . that they may be saved' (10. 32),

---

23 *Urban Christians*, 128.

24 See Barrett, *First Epistle*, 21, 124-25. Cf. C. J. Roetzel, *Judgement in the Community: A Study of the Relationship between Eschatology and Ecclesiology in Paul* (Leiden: E. J. Brill, 1972) 118.

25 See 2 Cor 4. 8-9; 6. 45; 11. 23-29; 12. 10; also 1 Cor 15. 32; and 2 Cor 1. 3-11. See also Furnish, *II Corinthians* 122-4; D. Georgi, *Paul's Opponents in Corinth* (Philadelphia: Fortress Press, 1986; repr. Edinburgh: T. and T. Clark, 1987) 16.

and because the behavior might interfere with evangelization of pagans and Jews.[26]

SUMMARY OF DEVIANCE

We have seen the importance of distinguishing the perspective of Paul from that of the church. First, Paul was concerned about continuing (unrepented) sexual immorality within the Christian community of Corinth. He had written his first (non-extant) letter exhorting members not to associate with the sexually immoral (5. 9-10) and had received a report that πορνεία was present in the congregation, and he wrote again in 1 Cor 5 to deal with the general attitude, the apparent misunderstanding of his instructions, and the specific problem of incest. Paul was disturbed about the effect of this behaviour on the whole congregation (5. 6-8), which had become arrogant in condoning it. Thus he saw the need for decisive action toward the incestuous man.

Although our knowledge of the attitudes and actions of the congregation depend upon the apostle, we have accepted his letter, written to the church itself, as yielding substantial information about the group. We have seen a congregation marked by deep party divisions within and doubts about the authority of its founding leader, not of the same mind with him on ethical questions, and immature in its understanding of the gospel, at least from Paul's viewpoint; yet the church was integrated with the wider society and did not feel threatened when one of its members disdained a well-established norm; thus it condoned or even celebrated an instance of continuing incest. We have been able to move backward without serious difficulty from Himmelweit's theory to previously known information about the congregation. Then, turning in the other direction, the theory was used to help explain why the Corinthian church accepted the incestuous relationship. The social bases of the acceptance of πορνεία consisted of internal disunity, lack of clear authority within the congregation, and integration with the larger community. We turn now to examine how the group's social norms are related to the sexual misconduct.

---

[26] *Reading Corinthians*, 19.

NORMS

A brief and quite general definition of social norm is the following: 'A norm is a belief shared to some extent by members of a social unit as to what conduct *ought to be* in particular situations or circumstances.'[27] A more traditional definition includes sanctions: a norm is 'a standard shared by the members of a social group to which the members are expected to conform, and conformity to which is enforced by positive and negative sanctions'.[28] These definitions will serve our purposes in the present study.

What social norms are reflected in 1 Cor 5? G. Theissen has pointed out that there are few legal norms with institutional mechanisms in early Christianity,[29] but norms are expressed in ethical teaching where sanctions are left to God and no institutional procedure is evident. In the traditional vice lists of 5. 10-11 several norms are expressed; however, we confine our focus to πορνεία. Paul's treatment of the case of incest in 1 Cor 5 appears to have elements of both forensic and sacred norms.[30] There are two conflicting norms, the one of Paul and the church under his leadership, which we may designate 'sexual purity', and the one of the opposing element in the Corinthian congregation, which we may call 'sexual freedom'.

Paul urges the congregation to remove the incestuous man from their midst (5. 2, 13). We have a negative sanction to enforce the assumed norm of sexual behaviour. The norm may be inferred from the deviance of πορνεία in chaps. 5 and 6 where the term refers to incest and prostitution. Thus the immediate context shows that the norm, stated negatively, is abstinence from incest and sexual relations with prostitutes. In clarifying his previous letter (5. 9-11) Paul says that he did not mean for the Corinthian Christians to avoid associating with non-Christians who are sexually immoral, or greedy and robbers, or idolaters, for such a life would be impossible in this world (v. 10). In v. 11 he continues, 'But now I write to you not to

---

27 J. P. Gibbs, *Norms, Deviance, and Social Control: Conceptual Matters* (New York: Elsevier, 1981) 7.

28 William L. Kolb, 'Norm', *A Dictionary of the Social Sciences*, ed. J. Gould and W. L. Kolb (New York: The Free Press, 1964) 472. On norms in the Pauline corpus see G. Theissen, *Social Setting*, 182-6; W. Meeks, *Urban Christians*, 138-9; B. J. Malina, *Christian Origins*, 112-38.

29 *Social Setting*, 183. Cf. Matt 18. 15-17, which is an early form with some legal characteristics.

30 See E. Käsemann, *New Testament Questions of Today* (London: SCM, 1969) 70-3.

associate with any brother if he is sexually immoral, or greedy, or an idolater, or a slanderer or a drunkard, or a robber, not even to eat with such a person.'[31] In 6. 18 Paul expresses the norm negatively, φεύγετε τὴν πορνείαν. His stance represents a traditional Jewish and pagan norm which governs sexual relations among family members and forbids a liaison between stepmother and stepson.[32] However, Paul's concern was not so much a sexual ethic as it was the purity of the Christian community.

The tension between Paul and the congregation is significant for understanding the norms. Either the church is simply lax in enforcing the common norm, or it does not share the incest norm with Paul. Paul's strictures against arrogance and boasting within the congregation suggest the latter. A. Y. Collins argues that 'the allusions to the Corinthians' arrogance and boasting in 5. 2, 6 imply that the incestuous alliance was not a deed done secretly out of weakness, but an ideological act done openly with the approval of at least an influential sector of the community.'[33] The congregation's accepting attitude toward the incestuous man seems to reflect the emergence of a new norm competing with the one held by Paul.

What was the basis of the congregation's acceptance of πορνεία? Paul's ambivalent stance toward the Mosaic Law may have contributed to the congregation's attitude. His complex under-standing of the Law can be seen in 1 Cor 9 where he expresses freedom from the Mosaic Law ('to those under the law I became as one under the law – though not being myself under the law – that I might win those under the law' [v. 20]), and yet he cites its authority in support of his right to financial support ('Do I say this on human authority? Does not the law say the same? For it is written in the law of Moses, "You shall not muzzle an ox when it is treading out the grain"' [vv. 8-9]).[34] If this hypothesis is correct, the incestuous man

---

31 My translation.

32 On Jewish and Roman law governing marriage of in-laws, see J. Héring, *First Epistle*, 34; Conzelmann, *I Corinthians*, 96. On sexual norms in the whole culture, see Meeks, *Urban Christians*, 101; C. Talbert, *Reading Corinthians*, 12-14; and A. Y. Collins, 'The Function of "Excommunication" in Paul', *HTR* 73 (1980) 251-63.

33 'Function of "Excommunication"', 253.

34 E. P. Sanders, *Paul, the Law and the Jewish People* (Philadelphia: Fortress, 1983) 105, explains the tension in Paul's position on the law by saying, 'Paul's statement "not by works of law" has to do with entry into the body of Christ. It is not at all inconsistent that he expects correct behaviour on the part of those who

and the people who condoned incest in the community apparently heard and adhered to only one side of Paul's position on the law.

The conflict is mainly an internal matter; however, it has implications for the community's relationships with the wider culture. Meeks has pointed out the ambiguity in the Pauline communities' relationship to the outside world. They have the strong group boundaries of an eschatological sect and, at the same time, an openness to outsiders in order to evangelize them.[35] Paul is not so much concerned that standards of the wider culture differ from those of the Christian movement as he is that the community adhere to its own principles (5. 12-13a; 6. 9-20).

The congregation's attitude toward the case of incest was counter-cultural, not just internal rebellion against the authority of Paul. The sexual norm which has been violated is not peculiar to the Christian community; rather it is a generally accepted cultural norm. Paul says that such conduct 'is not tolerated even among pagans' (5. 1). There is no functional distinction between the rule forbidding incest in the Christian community and in the community under Torah. On this point, Paul and the church he represents are not at odds with Judaism or with pagan society, but the offender's conduct and the congregation's acquiescence reflect a counter-cultural stance which concerned Paul because of his understanding of the gospel and his emphasis on mission.

Besides the likelihood that Paul contributed to the Corinthian attitude toward the incestuous man, what more can we say? Heikki Räisänen believes that '1 Cor 5-6 and 2 Cor 12. 10 f. are serious indicators of what could happen in a congregation which, by and large, lacked the moral basis provided by Judaism.'[36] Was there not also a positive social and ideological basis for the Corinthian church's stance, as well as a lack of grounding in Jewish ethics?

In New Heaven, New Earth Kenelm Burridge presents a theory of social development based on a study of modern millenarian movements which can help to clarify the Corinthian Christians' conflict with Paul and their acceptance of incest. There are serious dangers in applying a model derived from twentieth century social movements to first century Christianity. I do so on the basis that

---

are in Christ, nor that he thinks that transgressions on the part of Christians will be punished.'

[35] See *Urban Christians*, 97-103.

[36] H. Räisänen, *Paul and the Law* (Philadelphia: Fortress Press, 1983) 117, n. 112.

Pauline Christianity can be classified as a millenarian movement.[37] Burridge's model opens up the text to some new questions and insights which must then be tested by careful attention to the literary evidence.

Burridge traces the process of revitalization into the stage of institutional formation and maintenance. When the original impulse of millenarianism, which he defines quite broadly, begins to take form in a sect, 'traditional sources of authority are tapped and rechannelled'.[38] He summarizes the process in a formula: 'The formula, old rules – no rules – new rules, fits our view of the thought and action of a millenarian movement.'[39]

'Old rules' refers to the established life which has been left by those seeking salvation. Paul's background in Pharisaic Judaism represents his 'old rules'. The phrase, 'not even among pagans' (5. 1), suggests the Jewish foundation for his understanding, as do vv. 6-8 with the imagery of leaven and Passover, as well as the quotation from Deuteronomy in v. 13.

Burridge says that in millenarian movements 'redemption itself refers to complete release from obligation'; it is 'a condition of being which is without rules'.[40] This phase of millenarian development fits the Corinthian congregation's attitude toward πορνεία. There are no rules, no obligations. The slogan which Paul quotes in 6. 12 (πάντα μοι ἔξεστιν) 'All things are lawful for me',[41] whether derived from Paul or not, is an explicit formulation of the Corinthian norm. In effect, it held that there are no rules, and it legitimated a deviant sexual relationship between a man and his stepmother.

If a millenarian movement endures and becomes a sect, there must be 'new rules', which are a reinterpretation of the 'old rules'. Paul himself may have passed through a 'no rules' phase of development in regard to the Mosaic Law, but in his relationship with the Corinthian church as reflected in 1 Cor 5, he represents a 'new rules' stage of millenarian development. His 'new rule' is the

---

[37] See R. Jewett, *The Thessalonian Correspondence: Pauline Rhetoric and Millenarian Piety* (Philadelphia: Fortress Press, 1986) 161-78. See also J. Gager's earlier use of Burridge's model, *Kingdom and Community: The Social World of Early Christianity* (Englewood Cliffs, New Jersey: Prentice Hall, 1975) 20-37.

[38] *New Heaven*, 97.

[39] *New Heaven*, 166. See also Gager's use of the formula, *Kingdom and Community*, 35-7.

[40] *New Heaven*, 13, 99. See further R. Jewett, *Thessalonian Correspondence*, 172-3.

[41] See also 1 Cor 10. 23.

'old rule' of sexual purity (6. 13, 18) understood in terms of being in Christ (6. 15, 19-20). He commends a norm of sincerity and truth (5. 8), which he associates with the new unleavened loaf, that is, the new community in Christ. Paul understood the millennium or salvation differently from the Corinthians, not only because of his grounding in Jewish ethics and because of his theology, but because of his social role as community founder and consolidator. For him there were new rules oriented toward building up the community.

But what was the origin of the congregation's norm, which was opposed to that of Paul? Did the Corinthian church's attitude regarding the incestuous man stem from their former pagan life? Some commentators have stressed Corinth's reputation as a place of low morals. Bauer observes that the low morality of Corinth is indicated by the famous proverb from Strabo (8, 6, 20).[42] However, both Barrett and Conzelmann dispute the contention in regard to the refounded Roman city.[43] Pagan culture, no doubt, is part of the answer, but that alone cannot adequately account for the Corinthian congregation's stance in the case of incest. Even if Corinth was a place of exceptionally low morals, it cannot be assumed that the Christian converts represented the lowest moral stratum in the city. Paul's use of the slogan, πάντα μοι ἔξεστιν (6. 12), points to a norm within the Corinthian congregation which he is trying to modify. What we have, then, is not an attempt to bring pagan standards into the church, but an attempt to be freed from any standards. Why did the congregation not accept Paul's instruction on sexual relations and the traditional norm? There appears to be a social foundation like that which Burridge finds in the 'no rules' stage of millenarian sect development as well as an ideological foundation like that which has been investigated under various headings such as antinomianism, gnosticism, proto-gnosticism, and libertinism.

The normative tension was between those who understood the new community to be free from the rules of the old religion (e.g., Lev 18. 8) and from the rules of the established society, indeed free from any rules, and Paul, a leader who was free from the old law but who retains the old sexual norms in the new community but on the basis of the new law of Christ. The conflict seems to fit in the developmen-

---

42 W. Bauer, *A Greek-English Lexicon of the New Testament and Other Early Christian Literature* (2nd ed.; Chicago: University Press, 1979) 444.

43 Barrett, *First Epistle*, 2-3; Conzelmann, *I Corinthians*, 11-12.

tal stage between Burridge's 'no-rules', exemplified by the Corinthians, and 'new-rules', exemplified by Paul's reinterpretation of Torah.

Kolb's definition of norms stressed that conformity is enforced by positive and negative sanctions. We turn now to look at what is reported about sanctions in the case of incest.

SANCTIONS

In a voluntary religious group members commit themselves to certain social obligations of ritual, conduct, belief, and also to the sanctions of the community.[44] Simply put, a sanction is a punishment or reward designed to achieve conformity to group standards.[45] Sanctions are clear indicators of the secondary level of social control which reflect institutional structures. When a movement becomes sufficiently organized, it develops juridical or legal procedures to enforce its sanctions.[46] In the sanction levied against the incestuous man, we have evidence for an early stage of church discipline.

What was the sanction in 1 Cor 5 and what was the congregation's part in the sanctioning? We must distinguish what Paul expressed in the letter from local community action. We do not know whether the congregation carried out the sanction which Paul decided and commanded. Conzelmann rules out the congregation's active part in the sanction, in these words: 'What is plain (in vv. 3-5] is that Paul is resolved upon a judicial act of a sacral and pneumatic kind against the culprit. The community merely constitutes the forum; it does not share in the action.'[47] Conzelmann seems to be separating Paul's judgment from the formal act of expulsion in assembly and from the continuing element of non-association by the congregation. Also, his interpretation does not take adequate account of Paul's integrated relationship with the congregation. Paul does not

---

[44] Cf. B. R. Wilson, ed. *Patterns of Sectarianism: Organisation and Ideology in Social and Religious Movements* (London: Heineman, 1967) 8.

[45] See D. Lockwood, 'Sanction', *A Dictionary of the Social Sciences* (ed. J. Gould and W. L. Kolb; New York: The Free Press, 1964) 616. See further A. R. Radcliffe-Brown, 'Sanction, Social', *Encyclopedia of the Social Sciences* (New York: Macmillan, 1934) 13. 531-4.

[46] Cf. Radcliffe-Brown, 'Sanction', 533.

[47] *I Corinthians*, 97.

consider himself to be acting unilaterally, as though he were separated from the community (vv. 3-5).[48]

The syntax of vv. 3-5 is notoriously difficult; however, the following rough translation gives the basic sense:

> For I, absent in body but present in spirit, have already judged (being present) the one who did such a thing in the name of the Lord Jesus; you and my spirit are to gather with the power of the Lord Jesus to deliver such a one to Satan for destruction of the flesh so that his spirit may be saved on the day of the Lord. (My translation)[49]

It is clear that Paul urges the congregation to remove the man from their midst (vv. 2, 13) and to assemble to deliver him to Satan for destruction of the flesh so that his spirit may be saved on the day of the Lord (vv. 4-5), but what precisely was the sanction which Paul had decided and expected the congregation to carry out? There is no question that the man is to be removed from the church,[50] but is he to be permanently excluded, and is the exclusion total or partial? What was the degree of severity of the punishment? Did the discipline entail physical, material penalties including death? How is 'destruction of the flesh' to be understood in relation to the saving of his spirit on the day of the Lord?

Paul, perhaps thinking of a baptismal formula known to the Corinthians, may be referring to two realms – that of Christ and that of Satan, the spheres of life and of death.[51] The 'delivery to Satan' (v. 5) was a curse or ban which would reverse the effects of baptism and expel the man from the community. The penalty was not limited to a spiritual or psychological realm only, apart from material and social consequences. Forkman thinks that consignment to Satan meant a powerful curse eventuating in 'material losses, personal tragedies, illnesses and finally death (cf. 1 Cor 11. 27-32 and Acts 5. 1-11)'. He concludes that beyond the curse and its effects 'no sanctions

---

48 Cf. R. W. Funk, 'The Apostolic "Parousia": Form and Significance', Farmer, Moule and Niebuhr, *Christian History and Interpretation*, 264; also Meeks, *Urban Christians*, 127.

49 See Conzelmann, *I Corinthians*, 96-7, and Forkman, *Limits*, 141-3, on various construals. A. Y. Collins argues for taking ἐν τῷ ὀνόματι τοῦ κυρίου Ἰησου with τὸν οὕτως τοῦτο κατεργασάμενον. 'The Function of "Excommunication" in Paul', *HTR* 73 (1980) 253. Our study of deviance supports this understanding.

50 See H. von Campenhausen, *Ecclesiastical Authority and Spiritual Power in the Church of the First Three Centuries* (London: Adam and Charles Black, 1969) 133-5, esp. 134, n. 50.

51 So Forkman, *Limits*, 146.

are made. The curse works by itself.'[52] Expulsion is an extremely severe penalty in a voluntary group, and, continuing nonassociation, which is dependent on cooperation of community members as the agency of enforcement, should be given full weight. Also, the social effects of the expulsion should be noted. The Corinthian Christians had only recently taken the risk of joining a movement on the fringes of society. In most cases this would have meant alienation from their former social world. There would have been strain on family relationships in those cases where the *pater familias* was not converted, and even for the 'strong' a significant break with former social moorings would have been necessary. A person expelled from the new community would find himself in a nether world, for it would be difficult if not impossible to return to one's pre-Christian life. Hence expulsion from an urban Christian group would not be as socially punitive as from an isolated sect such as Qumran, but, nevertheless, it would have quite serious social consequences.

Forkman points out a possible logical inconsistency in Paul's instruction not to associate with group members who are guilty of certain vices. If a deviant member were expelled, then association with such a person as an outsider would be allowed. He explains the inconsistency psychologically (as well as theologically): 'The apostate is generally viewed with more suspicion than someone who has never come into the community.'[53]

Strangely, Forkman concludes that the expulsion was not total separation from the community but was only partial. Μὴ συναναμίγνυσθαι, he says, 'presumably does not imply every association but only such a relationship which is of significance from the point of view of purity' – eating with serious transgressors.[54] His interpretation is in conflict with the language of v. 2, 'so that the one who has done this may be removed from among you'; of v. 5, 'give over this person to Satan for the destruction of his flesh'; the closing quotation from Deuteronomy, 'Drive out the evil one from among you', (v. 13); the imagery of contaminating leaven (vv. 6-8); as well as the force of μηδέ (v. 11). On the contrary, the exclusion appears to be total and permanent.

---

52 *Limits*, 144, 146-7; similarly, Conzelmann, *I Corinthians*, 97. See further, Roetzel, *Judgement*, 116-17.

53 *Limits*, 150.

54 *Limits*, 150-1. See further, P. Marshall, *Enmity at Corinth* (WUNT 2/23; Tübingen: J. C. B. Mohr [Paul Siebeck] 1987) esp. 341-95.

What was the structure of the sanction? To what extent was the proposed action formal and organized, a social process, as opposed to unorganized, diffuse actions by individuals? Paul uses the term κέκρικα 'I have judged', in v. 3. The same root term is used three times in vv. 12-13 in connection with the expulsion formula from Deuteronomy ('Drive out the evil one from among you'),[55] where it has a strong technical legal sense. Although Paul makes the decision to expel the man, he calls for an assembly in which he is spiritually present with the power of the Lord Jesus in order to deliver the man to Satan (vv. 4-5). This points to a rather formal ceremony of removal carried out in the assembly. This is not to deny that the effectiveness of the exclusion would depend on individuals.

From his functionalist perspective A. R. Radcliffe-Brown thought that the general effects of social sanctions are more important for the community which applies them than for the individual who receives the sanctions. He says,

> In a consideration of the functions of social sanctions it is not the effects of the sanction upon the person to whom they are applied that are most important but rather the general effects within the community applying the sanction. For the application of any sanction is a direct affirmation of social sentiments by the community and thereby constitutes an important, possibly essential, mechanism for maintaining these sentiments.[56]

The explicit function of the expulsion was to rid the congregation of impurity (vv. 6-8), but a latent function of strengthening commitment to the community and its norms among non-deviant members may well have been an additional result of the disciplinary action.

There is no suggestion that the expulsion was to be temporary or socially restorative. There is hope for the man's spirit on the day of the Lord Jesus, but this does not presume reinstatement in the community. The expressed concern is maintenance of group purity and the offender's eschatological salvation, not reconciliation and restoration into the community as Lampe contends. His argument depends on linking 2 Cor 2. 5-11 with 1 Cor 5, and it will not stand without this old but tenuous connection.[57] He says, 'On balance,

---

[55] Deut 17. 7; 19. 19; 21. 21; 22. 21, 24; 24. 7.

[56] 'Sanction', 532-3.

[57] See Furnish, *II Corinthians*, 163-8.

then, the probability is quite strong that in 2 Cor 2. 5-11 we have evidence that the severe sentence passed in 1 Cor 5. 5 was not only intended to be, but actually was, remedial: an extreme and painful form of pastoral discipline rather than capital punishment.'[58] How Paul thought that the destruction of the flesh was related to the saving of the man's spirit on the day of the Lord is beyond the scope of this study; however, Lampe's use of the term, 'capital punishment', is unfortunate. It is important to keep in mind the pervasive ancient worldview pertaining to ban and curse.[59]

Sociologically, we have a negative sanction which is legitimated by an eschatological hope. In *The Sacred Canopy*, Peter Berger presents a theory of legitimation which sheds light on the disciplinary action and on the sanction in particular. He argues that legitimating formulas must be repeated for the sake of the continuing community and that any explicit social control demands additional legitimation beyond the institutional arrangements. This is so because the given structures and norms are put in question by resisters. Berger says,

> The sharper such resistance, and the sharper the means employed to overcome it, the more important will it be to have additional legitimations. Such legitimations serve both to explain why the resistance cannot be tolerated and to justify the means by which it is to be quelled . . . . The seriousness of the challenge will determine the degree of elaborateness of the answering legitimations.[60]

Applying Berger's legitimation theory to 1 Cor 5, we notice first the sharpness of the resistance. The case of incest openly contradicted Paul's previous instructions, and thus his apostolic authority. The congregation's failure to take action against the man accentuated the conflict. Paul feared contamination of the whole community. The man's continuing relationship with his stepmother could infect the entire congregation, as the leaven imagery implies (vv. 6-8). The sanction against the man was quite sharp, resulting in his total exclusion from the church and his anticipated death. The sanction is legitimated with an elaborate set of religious symbols: there is to be an assembly in the spiritual presence of the apostle with the power of

---

58 'Church Discipline', 354.
59 See Conzelmann, *I Corinthians*, 97.
60 *Sacred Canopy*, 31.

the Lord Jesus and employing a curse formula against the offender. The terrible ban, however, will provide for the ultimate salvation of the man on the day of the Lord. This last eschatological element is a positive reason for the disciplinary action and serves as further legitimation. Finally, an excommunication formula from Deuteronomy gives the authority of Torah to the procedure.

From Paul's perspective there are two kinds of deviance, the case of incest and the congregation's failure to discipline the offender. He treats the two quite differently. Against the incestuous individual, he uses a process which has institutional features – including an assembly of the congregation, a powerful curse (effective in a group with a religious worldview of that time and place), and removal of the offender from the community. There is no mention in the text of warnings to the offender (cf. Matt 18. 15-17), and there is no reference to designated disciplinarians although 1 Cor 6. 5b hints at a specialized function of judgment within the congregation.

In reference to the congregation's arrogant, boastful attitude and its failure to discipline the incestuous man, Paul did not use a formal procedure with definite sanctions, for the deviance was different, and there was no mechanism, such as a bishop, for handling congregational deviance. So Paul uses admonition and 'psychic coercion'. He admonishes the church ('You are arrogant! Should you not rather mourn?' [v. 2]) and employs symbolic threats and promises (the Passover metaphor of vv. 6-8: 'A little leaven leavens the whole lump', and 'Let us celebrate ... with the unleavened bread of sincerity and truth').[61]

In discussing various sanctions, Weber says,

> In any case the means of coercion are irrelevant. Even a 'friendly admonition', such as has been used in various religious sects as a form of gentle pressure on sinners, is to be included if it is carried out according to rules by a specially designated group. Another case is the use of censure as a means of enforcing norms of moral conduct. Psychic coercion

---

[61] On Paul's use of rhetoric, see P. Marshall, *Enmity at Corinth*, esp. 341-95. See also Elisabeth Schüssler Fiorenza, 'Rhetorical Situation and Historical Reconstruction in 1 Corinthians', *NTS* 33 (1987) 386-403, as well as Jewett, *Thessalonian Correspondence*.

has indeed become the specific disciplinary technique of the church.[62]

Finally, the mixture of sacred and forensic law is seen in vv. 12-13. There Paul says that the congregation judges those inside while God judges outsiders. The sanction against the man is an instance of sacred law, for Satan as God's agent does the punishing (v. 5), but it is the congregation who gives him over to Satan, and presumably the flesh would not be destroyed apart from this formal, legal act by the assembly. Yet the congregation acts as a whole in the sanctioning, and Paul's spirit and the name and power of the Lord Jesus are emphasized.

The sanction against the incestuous man shows the undeveloped beginnings of church discipline. A more developed institutional stage of discipline can be seen in the Qumran Community Rule (IQS VI and VII).[63] In a fully developed disciplinary proceeding we might expect more nuanced laws or specific norms coupled with definite sanctions; degrees of severity would be spelled out more fully. There might also be a designated agency of enforcement within the group. In 1 Cor 5 Paul assumes the sexual norms from Torah and Hellenistic Judaism as well as the general culture. The sanction which he imposes has roots in the Law, but Paul couples his concern for the purity of the community, reinterpreted according to the gospel, with concern for the ultimate salvation of the offender.

CONCLUSION

In this study some basic sociological concepts have been used to describe the discipline reflected in 1 Cor 5 in order to emphasize the social dimension of the action. Some selected sociological models were used to give an added dimension to the disciplinary action.

We found, first, that the incest could be classified as deviance and that the congregation's acceptance of the incestuous relationship was also deviant. On the basis of Himmelweit's analysis of deviance, we found that the social features of disunity (lack of internal cohesion), lack of clear, authoritative leadership, and lack of threat

---

[62] See M. Weber, *The Theory of Social and Economic Organization* (Oxford: University Press, 1947) 129; see also 154.
[63] See Furnish, *II Corinthians*, 161.

from the outside world set the stage for acceptance of incest within the congregation.

We found, second, that there were two conflicting norms. Paul advocated a norm of sexual purity which was in harmony with both Jewish and pagan cultural norms. The Corinthian congregation, or at least that portion which accepted the incest, held to a norm of 'sexual freedom' as one aspect of a wider norm expressed in the slogan: πάντα μοι ἔξεστιν. Paul's ambivalent position on the Law probably contributed to the behaviour and attitude which he considered deviant and to the 'no rules' norm within the church, but a social process typical of millenarian movements contributed to and supported both the Corinthian norm and Paul's and may be summed up in two terms from Burridge's formula: 'no rules' and 'new rules'.

Third, we found that the social function of the sanction was negative (punitive) in regard to the individual and positive in regard to protecting group purity. Further, the sanction was legitimated by the religious hope expressed for the man's salvation on the day of the Lord. His exclusion from the church was total and permanent, but Paul understood it to work toward his ultimate salvation. The sanction had elements of sacred law and some adaptation of existing legal forms. Thus we have here in the earliest stages of the Christian movement, the beginnings of church discipline.

PART IV

THE SHAPE OF PAULINE ETHICS
Catechisms, Catalogues and Codes

CHAPTER SEVEN

Moral Teaching
The Existence and Contents of "the Ways"*

Alfred Seeberg
(1903)

I. The Existence of "the Ways"

In his study *Das apostolische Zeitalter der christlichen Kirche*[1] Carl Weizsäcker presented some evidence which should have received more attention than it actually did. Weizsäcker argues that 1 Corinthians 4:17 refers to "a Christian halakha, which Paul calls τύπος

---

* Translated by Christoph W. Stenschke.
[1] 2. ed. (Freiburg im Breisgau: J.C.B. Mohr [P. Siebeck], 1892), p. 594, cf. p. 560 = *The Apostolic Age of the Christian Church II*, J. Millar, Theological Translation Library V (London, Edinburgh, Oxford: Williams and Norgate, 1895). [Material presented in parenthesis is not in the German original and is added for the reader's convenience. In some cases the identification of the exact reference remains doubtful. I usually refer to the latest edition of a work available at the time of Seeberg's writing, according to the catalogues of the Universitäts-bibliothek Gießen, the Fachbereichsbibliothek Evangelische Theologie in Marburg (Alte Aula) and Aberdeen University's Queen Mother Library.]

τῆς διδαχῆς (form of teaching)[2] in Romans 6:17 and παραδόσεις ἃς ἐδιδάχθητε (the teachings we passed on to you) in 2 Thessalonians 2:15, cf. Romans 16:17."

Our task is to substantiate this point of view. The importance of the passages cited above leads us to ascertain their precise sense through careful exegesis.

We commence with Romans 6:17. Paul expresses his thanks to God that the readers, who had been enslaved to sin in the past, have now become obedient in their hearts to εἰς ὃν παρεδόθητε τύπον διδαχῆς (the form of teaching to which you were entrusted). The present construction is more naturally arranged as εἰς τύπον διδαχῆς, ὃν παρεδόθητε. But what do these words mean? It is impossible that εἰς τύπον (form; accusative plus a preposition) means the same as τῷ τύπῳ (form; in the dative), so that τύπος (form) would indicate the object of the reader's obedience. ὑπακούειν εἴς τι (to be obedient to something) can only refer to obedience in relation to something. In other words, the noun dependent upon ὑπηκούσατε (you obeyed) cannot refer to "something demanding something," but only to something demanded. However one might understand ὁ τύπος τῆς διδαχῆς (the form of teaching), these words do not correspond to this postulate. Therefore, εἰς τύπον (to the form) cannot refer to the dimension claiming obedience. But the cause of their obedience could be thus referred to.[3] The same use of εἰς appears in Matthew 12:41; Acts 7:53; Psalm 17:45 (LXX) and 2 Kings 22:45. However, this linguistically justified interpretation is repugnant to the thought of the verse. This verse, according to the first part (ἦτε δοῦλοι τῆς ἁμαρτίας, you used to be slaves to sin), can only define the relationship of the readers to the τύπος τῆς διδαχῆς (form of teaching). Stating the cause of the reader's obedience is not suited as a contrast to their former state as slaves to sin.

Therefore it seems that the present construction has to be broken down otherwise. Indeed, most of the recent interpreters follow Chrysostom's arrangement of the verse: τῷ τύπῳ τῆς διδαχῆς, εἰς ὃν παρεδόθητε (to the form of teaching, to which you were entrusted). The former service of sin is contrasted with obedience to the τύπος τῆς διδαχῆς (form of teaching), to whose authority the

---

2 The English rendering is taken from the NIV and where necessary adapted to the sentence, unless a technical term should require a different translation.

3 J.Chr.K. von Hofmann, [*Der Brief Pauli an die Römer*, Die heilige Schrift neuen Testaments zusammenhängend untersucht III (Nördlingen: C.H. Beck, 1868), pp. 251-52]; Ewald; Goebel.

readers were consigned. This understanding seems to do full justice to the text. However, it only appears to do so. To begin with, the notion of consigning somebody to the power of a certain form of teaching, however one may understand this term, is strange. It becomes unbearable, when the form of teaching appears at the same time as the object, to which the readers became obedient, even (wholeheartedly) obedient ἐκ καρδίας. The one who thanks God that somebody became obedient to a good cause, not through compulsion, but by his own *free choice*, cannot at the same time say that the same person was *consigned* to the power of this good cause. There have been efforts to eliminate the contradiction by interpreting the words εἰς ὅν παρεδόθητε (to which you were consigned) as if they only meant that the readers were thus enabled to make a free-will-decision about the form of teaching.[4] It is obvious that the words to be explained are thereby given a new interpretation. Wherever the words παραδιδόναι εἴς τι (to consign to something) occur in the New Testament, they refer to consigning something to the power of an entity,[5] so that one has lost one's freedom of choice to that entity. This passage requires, if not reinterpreted, the impossible notion of rejoicing over the free will decision of the readers with respect to an entity, to the recognition of which they were actually forced.

Paul can only have thought of ὅν παρεδόθητε, rather than εἰς ὅν παρεδόθητε, words which have the same meaning as ὅς παρεδόθη ὑμῖν (which has been passed on to you; cf. Rom 3:2). As much as the rejected interpretation is impossible, so this second interpretation is very acceptable, since teaching and tradition are very closely related to each other. Traditions are taught (2 Thess 2:15) and teaching is learnt (διδαχή, Rom 16:17) or handed down (cf. 2 Thess 2:15 with 3:6 and also Phil 4:9). Since both words, διδαχή (teaching) and παραδιδόναι (to pass on), are found in Romans 6:17 there can be no question that the usual relationship exists between the words. Every interpretation of this difficult verse must pay due regard to this

---

4 B. Weiß, *Kritisch exegetisches Handbuch über den Brief des Paulus an die Römer*, Kritisch exegetischer Kommentar über das Neue Testament IV, 9. ed. (Göttingen: Vandenhoeck & Ruprecht, 1899).

5 G.B. Winer, *Grammatik [des neutestamentlichen Sprachidioms als sichere Grundlage der neutestamentlichen Exegese*, ed. G. Lünemann], 7. ed. [(Leipzig: F.C.W. Vogel, 1867)], § 31. 5, [pp. 200-01 = *Grammar of the New Testament*. E. Masson from 6. German ed. (Edinburgh: T. & T. Clark, 1859), pp. 226-27 and *A Treatise on the Grammar of New Testament Greek. . .*, W.F. Moulton, 8. ed. (Idem, 1877), pp. 267-68].

postulate. So the present construction must be rearranged by transposing it to εἰς τύπον διδαχῆς, ὅν παρεδόθητε (to the form of teaching, which has been passed on to you). But how are we to understand it? G.A. Deißmann has shown that replacing the dative of advantage with εἰς followed by an accusative is a quite common feature of the language, which the authors of the New Testament were bound to use.[6] This phenomenon is generally acknowledged for Paul in 1 Corinthians 16:1; 2 Corinthians 8:4; 9:1,13 and Romans 15:26. Passages like Romans 15:26 and 2 Corinthians 11:6 also belong to this category.[7] Other passages would need closer investigation. The grammatical construction being established, it seems legitimate to try its application to our passage. This results in the thought that the readers became obedient, to the benefit of the form of teaching which had been passed on to them. The parallel with the preceding phrase is now fully realised: Slavery to sin is contrasted with obedience, to the benefit of the form of teaching.[8]

So what does ὁ τύπος τῆς διδαχῆς now mean? Most interpreters translate it as: a distinctly marked form or character of teaching. If we have Christian teaching in general in mind it is difficult to understand why Paul did not content himself to speak about διδαχή.[9] Considering, however, a particular Pauline form of teaching gives these words the monstrous consequence that Paul must have known of another Christian form of teaching, which allowed for service to sin.[10] But the fact that Paul never uses τύπος (form) in the sense of

---

6 Bibelstudien [: *Beiträge, zumeist aus den Papyri und Inschriften, zur Geschichte der Sprache, des Schrifttums und der Religion des hellenistischen Judentums und des Urchristentums* (Marburg: N.G. Elwert, 1895; repr. Hildesheim, New York: G. Olms, 1977), pp. 113-15 = *Bible Studies*, A. Grieve, 2. ed. (Edinburgh: T. & T. Clark, 1903)].

7 Cf. Weizsäcker and Weiß concerning 2 Cor 11:6.

8 Analogous to our passage is the contrast between dative and the construction of εἰς with accusative in Luke 12:21. Cf. the exposition by B. Weiß, [*Die Evangelien des Markus und Lukas*, KEK I.2, 9. ed. (Göttingen: V. & R., 1901].

9 *Contra* Hofmann and C.E. Luthardt, [*Die Briefe an die Thessalonicher, Galater, Korinther und Römer: Ausgelegt von O. Zöckler, G. Schnedermann, C.E. Luthardt*, Kurzgefaßter Kommentar zu den heiligen Schriften Alten und Neuen Testaments sowie zu den Apokryphen, 2. ed., B.3 (München: C.H. Beck, 1894), p. 467].

10 *Contra* W.M.L. de Wette, [*Kurze Erklärung des Briefes an die Römer*, Kurzgefaßtes exegetisches Handbuch zum Neuen Testament II.1, 4. ed. (Leipzig: Weidmann, 1847), pp. 86-87]; F. Godet, [*Kommentar zu dem Brief an die Römer*, 2. ed. (Hannover: C. Meyer, 1892-93) = *Commentary on St. Paul's Epistle to the Romans I*, trad. A. Cusin, Clark's Foreign Theological Library, N.S. II (Edinburgh: T. & T. Clark, 1880), pp. 434-37]; Weiß and others.

distinctly marked form or character excludes considerations of a certain form of teaching. Τύπος is always used by Paul to mean "pattern" (*Vorbild*), designating something that has characteristic traits and attributes which have the disposition to express themselves in something else. Only in this sense could he have used the word in our passage.[11] We are dealing with *the pattern provided through the Christian teaching* and the norm contained in it. Because a norm claims the right to be followed, conduct according to it can be presented as happening to its benefit. Therefore, taking the preposition εἰς to designate a dative of advantage is fully justified. The slavery to sin of the readers was replaced by an obedience which was to the advantage of the norm of teaching passed on to them. This contrast only allows for *moral prescriptions* to be intended by the norm of teaching. Paul therefore presupposes knowledge and validity of a certain form of teaching of ethical content in the Roman Church, a group which was personally unknown to him. This remarkable result would even be valid if one might translate: you became obedient to the form of teaching to which you were entrusted. Even thus the form of teaching could be nothing else than the norm given in the teaching.

Romans 16:17 also refers to normative teaching for the moral life of the Christians. Paul exhorts the readers to watch those causing division and σκάνδαλα (offenses) against the form of teaching. Meyer understands σκάνδαλα as seduction to deviate from right Christian faith and living. But he writes nothing on how to understand the words παρὰ τὴν διδαχήν (according to the teaching). Weiss answers this question by writing: "Seduction to deviate from right Christian teaching." Adapting his comment to the text would lead to: "seduction to that which deviates from the teaching which you learnt." Σκάνδαλα παρὰ τὴν διδαχήν (offenses against the teaching) can evidently not mean that. Hofmann writes: "Those causing division, inventing and teaching things contradicting common Christian teaching and which can bring to a fall those gathered by them." This

---

11 Cf. Chrysostom, Euthymius Zigabenus, Theodore of Mopsuestia, Oecumenius, Reiche, H. Olshausen, [*Der Brief des Apostels Paulus an die Römer*, Biblischer Commentar über sämtliche Schriften des Neuen Testaments... III.1, 2. ed. (Königsberg: A.W. Unzer, 1840) = *The Epistle of St Paul to the Romans*, Biblical Commentary on the New Testament..., Clark's Foreign Theological Library XIII (Edinburgh: T. & T. Clark, 1849), pp. 222-23]; W. Sanday, A.C. Headlam, *A Critical and Exegetical Commentary on the Epistle to the Romans*, International Critical Commentary, 4. ed. (Edinburgh: T.& T. Clark, 1900).

would lead to the translation: those who create divisions and things (teachings) which cause a fall and are contrary to the teaching you learnt. This corresponds to de Wette's translation, who replaces the things which cause a fall by the things here considered, namely errors. This is a legitimate explanation, for the connection of παρὰ τὴν διδαχήν (according to the teaching) and τὰ σκάνδαλα (the offenses) is less obvious than the connection to τὰς διχοστασίας καὶ τὰ σκάνδαλα ποιοῦντας (those who cause divisions and put obstacles in your way). And this connection is indeed possible. But it presupposes that the two actions of the opponents referred to contradict the received tradition in the same way. The text cannot at one point deal with transgression of a prohibition and at another point with neglect of proper teaching, but the apostle must have had *ethical instructions* in mind as the *content of the διδαχή* (teaching).[12] The opponents cause division and create things (teachings) which lead to moral downfall. In both cases they are in conflict with the teaching received by the readers. When Paul refers to the teaching, which the readers learnt, he does not think of his own specific teaching[13] or the common foundation of Christian doctrine (1 Cor 15:1).[14] Rather, he thinks of the *sum-total of ethical instruction*, which he called the norm of teaching in Romans 6:17.[15]

1 Corinthians 4:17 sheds further important light on the Christian moral teaching known in those days. After Paul admonished the readers to become his imitators, he writes that in order that they become his imitators he has sent them Timothy to them, his beloved and reliable son in the Lord, ὃς ὑμᾶς ἀναμνήσει τὰς

---

[12] Cf. de Wette.

[13] *Contra* R.A. Lipsius, [*Briefe an die Galater, Römer, Philipper*, Hand-Commentar zum Neuen Testament II.2, 2. ed. (Freiburg im B.: J.C.B. Mohr [P. Siebeck], 1892)].

[14] *Contra* Sanday and Headlam.

[15] Our result is not changed by another explanation, which I consider not impossible and therefore have no wish to conceal. Σκάνδαλον (offense) does not only describe that which is able to bring another to fall, but also something annoying, provoking, so in LXX Ps 49 (50):20, Jes Sir 7:6, 1 Jn 2:10, Gal 5:10, 1 Cor 1:23. This meaning of the word would suggest that Paul cautions the readers against those causing the divisions and offensive things known among them, who are thereby contradicting the received teaching. Things bringing about annoyance and irritation would then refer to expressions of sin, known to the readers as caused by the same opponents. We can only suppose the nature of these expressions. It suggests itself to consider sins which often do accompany division, like envy, dissension, slander, bickering and the like. This understanding of the passage proves also that Paul assumes knowledge of teaching of moral content among the Christians.

ὁδούς μου τὰς ἐν Χριστῷ, καθὼς πανταχοῦ ἐν πάσῃ ἐκκλησίᾳ διδάσκω (who will remind you of my way of life in Christ Jesus, which agrees with what I teach everywhere in every church).

If the readers are to become Paul's imitators through Timothy reminding them of the apostle's ways in Christ, it is safe to understand "the ways" as Paul's conduct. Almost all expositors follow this line. But how are we then to understand the sentence beginning with καθώς? The most common explanation[16] may be rendered with the following paraphrase: "Timothy will remind you of my ways according to how I behaved, while teaching." But how can διδάσκειν mean "to behave while teaching"? And why did Paul limit the exemplary character of his conduct to his behaviour shown while teaching? Vss. 10-13 do not speak of his conduct in such limited terms. Neither the construction nor the train of thought allows for this explanation. Others[17] assume therefore that the reminder of Paul's Christian life should be according to the measure of the manner in which he himself taught every church the Christian life. But it is plain nonsense that the standard in the reminder of Paul's conduct should consist of anything else than this very conduct.

The addition starting καθώς (for this reason) remains inexplicable as long as we understand ὁδοί (ways) as a reference to

---

16 Cf. H.A.W. Meyer, [*Kritisch exegetisches Handbuch über den ersten Brief an die Korinther*, KEK V, 4. ed. (Göttingen: V. & R., 1861) = *Critical and Exegetical Handbook to the Epistles to the Corinthians I*, trad. D.D. Bannerman, Critical and Exegetical Commentary on the New Testament V (Edinburgh: T. & T. Clark, 1877), pp. 132-33]; W.M.L. de Wette, [*Kurze Erklärung der Briefe an die Corinther*, ed. H. Messner, Kurzgefaßtes exegetisches Handbuch zum Neuen Testament II.2, 3. ed. (Leipzig: S. Hirzel, 1855), p. 42]; G. Heinrici [*Der erste Brief an die Korinther*, KEK V, 8. ed. (Göttingen: V. & R., 1896) or *Das erste Sendschreiben des Apostel Paulus an die Korinthier* (Berlin: W. Hertz, 1880), pp. 147-48] and P.W. Schmiedel, [*Die Briefe an die Thessalonicher und an die Korinther*, Hand-Commentar zum Neuen Testament II.1, 2. ed. (Freiburg im B., Leipzig: J.B.C. Mohr (P. Siebeck), 1893)].

17 J.Chr.K. von Hofmann, *Der erste Brief Pauli an die Korinther*, Die heilige Schrift neuen Testaments zusammenhängend untersucht II.2, 2. ed. (Nördlingen: C.H. Beck, 1874)]; C. Holsten, [*Das Evangelium des Paulus dargestellt: Die äußere Entwicklungsgeschichte des paulinischen Evangeliums: Abt. 1 Der Brief an die Gemeinden Galatiens und der erste Brief an die Gemeinde in Korinth* (Berlin: G. Reimer, 1880), pp. 283-85]; B. Weiß, [Die Paulinischen Briefe im berichtigten Text mit kurzer Erläuterung zum Handgebrauch bei der Schriftlektüre (Leipzig: J.C. Hinrich, 1896), p. 152]; F. Godet, [*Kommentar zu dem ersten Brief an die Korinther* (Hannover: C. Meyer, 1886-88) = Commentary on St. Paul's First Epistle to the Corinthians I, A. Cusin, Clark's Foreign Theological Library, N.S. XXVII (Edinburgh: T. & T. Clark, 1886), pp. 232-34].

Paul's conduct. And why should Timothy remind them of it, when Paul himself had eloquently done so in the preceding verses (10-13)? Αἱ ὁδοί (the ways) are not Paul's way of life but rather designate the *name of the Christian moral teaching*, which was Paul's moral teaching, insofar as he made use of it in his ministry. Αἱ ὁδοί μου (my ways) should therefore be considered in the same sense as τὸ εὐαγγέλιόν μου (my gospel; Rom 2:16, 2 Tim 2:8). The words ἐν Χριστῷ (in Christ), which designate "the ways" as Christian ways, only serve to remind Gentile Christian readers of the dignity of this teaching, and do not exclude that the same teaching was also in use among Jews. In our explanation the otherwise inexplicable appendix attaches well to αἱ ὁδοί μου (my ways). Καθώς then means, as in Luke 24:24, 1 Corinthians 11:2 and Colossians 3:7, "in the manner, in which" or "of the content, which content." This will be the content of faithful Timothy's reminder in Corinth of "the ways," a content which Paul himself not only taught in Corinth, but teaches everywhere, in every church. The obvious object of διδάσκειν (teaching) are the ways, so that no further words need to be added. If then our passage demonstrates that Paul used a form of teaching called "the ways" and that he used to teach this form in all churches, we may not conclude that this teaching was passed on only to already existing churches, since the apposition ἐν πάσῃ ἐκκλησίᾳ (in every church) to πανταχοῦ (everywhere) refers our understanding back to the Corinthian church. Not only in the Corinthian church but in every church Paul teaches these "ways." If this is the reason why the apostle changes this thought—his teaching the "ways" simply everywhere—to teaching in every church these words obviously do not exclude the teaching being passed on in places where no church yet existed.

Only the present explanation does justice to the text. But is not the context against it? Can a reminder of a certain teaching cause the Corinthians to become imitators of Paul? These reservations seem to have kept commentators from recognising the true state of affairs. However, this objection is unfounded. After all, it is a peculiarity of the apostle that he understands the content of his *teaching* and the content of his *personal conduct* to be in an utterly striking manner closely related to each other and authoritative for his readers. The Philippians (4:9) are to put into practice whatever they have learnt and received or heard from him or seen in him. Paul substantiates the command to the Thessalonians (2 Thess 3:6) to keep away from every brother who is idle and does not live according to the *paradosis* (teaching) they received from him and his co-workers on the assumption that the readers knew themselves of the obligation to imitate him (cf. also 2 Tim 3:10f). The one who could write these words could also aim at the imitation of his person through a reminder of his teaching.

Looking back to the passages we have discussed we see that Paul knew of a *teaching comprising moral instructions*, a teaching called "*the ways*." Those who learnt this teaching received it through oral instruction by their teachers (παραδιδόναι, to pass on). Paul spread this teaching wherever he was working in the fifties of the first century.

II. The Content of "the Ways"

How shall we think of the content of "the ways"? We already know that they must have contained moral instructions. But what kind of moral instruction? The epistles to the Thessalonians offer the best point of departure for answering this question. The apostle presupposes in 2 Thessalonians 3:6 that the young church is living according to the *paradosis*, which they had received from him and his co-workers. In 1 Thessalonians 4:1f he reminds the readers of that which they received from him, namely, instructions as to how they must live and please God. As a foundation for this he points them to their acquaintance with the instructions which he gave them in the Lord Jesus. Since these passages deal with the handing down and the reception of moral instruction there is no question that the apostle refers to the same instructions which belong to the moral teaching, to "the ways."

But 1 Thessalonians 4:3-8 also offers important clues as to the *content of the traditional material of the ways*. According to this passage πορνεία (sexual immorality), perhaps also πάθος ἐπιθυμίας (passionate lust) and definitely πλεονεξία (covetousness) must have been forbidden in the ways and furthermore the fate sinners will have to face must have been presented.

This insight leads us further. Πορνεία (sexual immorality) and πλεονεξία (covetousness) are sins which are often mentioned in the vice catalogues of the New Testament. We find πορνεία in the lists of 1 Corinthians 12:21, Galatians 5:20; 1 Timothy 1:10; Revelation 9:21, 21:8, 22:15. Πλεονεξία is found in Romans 1:29 (cf. φιλάργυροι [lovers of money] in 2 Tim 3:2). Besides that several catalogues mention sexual immorality and covetousness either separated by other sins (1 Cor 6:9f and Mark 7:21f) or directly next to each other (1 Cor 5:10f, Eph 4:19; 5:3,5 and Col 3:5[18]). The close connection between sexual immorality and covetousness also explains why it is that these quite different sins are mentioned directly next to each other in 1 Thessalonians 4:6. Even more conspicuous is the combination ἀκαθαρσία πᾶσα ἐν πλεονεξία (every kind of impurity in covetousness) in Ephesians 4:19. If then the prohibition of these two sins certainly belonged to the ways and if they are very frequently found in the catalogues of sins in the New Testament, often next to each other and in closest combination, we may assume that *the catalogues of sins are based on a pattern*, which belonged to the traditional material of the ways.[19]

This assumption is *supported* strikingly by 1 Thessalonians 4:6. Here the apostle writes about his announcement and testimony to the Thessalonians that the Lord is an avenger in all these matters. Bearing witness of this was therefore connected to the passing on of the instruction (cf. Gal 5:21). The reference to a bad end which sinners face can be found in a large number of catalogues of sin. Paul announces in Colossians 3:6 that God's wrath will come upon evildoers, in Romans 1:32 he speaks of their deserving death and in Galatians 5:21; 1 Corinthians 6:9 and Ephesians 5:5 we read of this group not inheriting the Kingdom. We must also pay attention to the connection in which the catalogues of sin in Revelation 21:8 and 22:15 stand. Furthermore, Hebrews 13:4 has an admonition to honorable conduct within marriage which is substantiated by God's judgement on the adulterer and all the sexually immoral. It appears that the author of Hebrews reckons this to be a widely known truth. If the reference to punishment belonged to the ways and if we often find it in the catalogues of vice, the assumption that the catalogues of vice are based on an underlying pattern, which was part of the ways, receives strong support.

But in what form did the reference to punishment appear in the ways? Only exclusion from the Kingdom can be considered. Not only do we find this form four times, while the two other expressions appear only rarely, but also Paul states explicitly in Galatians 5:21: ἃ

---

[18] Rom 1:29 only omits sexual immorality because the preceding passage dealt with it extensively.

[19] P. Wernle also assumes that the catalogues of vices in the New Testament are based on a fixed tradition (*Der Christ und die Sünde bei Paulus* [Freiburg im B., Leipzig: J.C.B. Mohr, 1897], pp. 129-34).

(referring to the preceding catalogue) προλέγω ὑμῖν καθὼς προεῖπον, ὅτι οἱ τὰ τοιαῦτα πράσσοντες βασιλείαν θεοῦ οὐ κληρονομήσουσιν (I warn you, as I did before, that those who live like this will not inherit the kingdom of God). This is, in addition, Paul's only reference to the phrase κληρονομεῖν βασιλείαν θεοῦ (inherit the kingdom of God). The only other reference in 1 Corinthians 15:50 is not a real exception, since the statement that flesh and blood cannot inherit the kingdom of God obviously only denotes contact with the form of the *paradosis*. It is highly significant then that βασιλεία (kingdom) in our formula is always used without the article, whereas Paul otherwise always uses the article with this word (Rom 14:17; 1 Cor 4:20; Eph 5:5; Col 1:13; 4:11; 1 Thess 2:12; 2 Thess 1:5). The phrase therefore does not follow normal Pauline usage, which proves beyond doubt that it is a formula. Since the formula must have belonged to the basis of the catalogues of sins, in other words, to the ways, and since it cannot be of Pauline origin, the ways cannot have been devised by Paul. Rather, he must have received them in a more or less fixed form.

It now seems certain that a catalogue of sins belonged to the ways. This is further confirmed by the words περὶ πάντων τούτων (for all such) in 1 Thessalonians 4:6. It is striking that "all such (sins)" are spoken of even though only two sins are mentioned. This striking fact becomes explicable if a longer list of sins, including sexual immorality and covetousness, was in Paul's mind. Therefore the moral instruction, that is, the ways, contained a list of sins. A phenomenon similar to 1 Thessalonians 4:6 appears in Colossians 3:8. The Apostle contrasts the reference to the former sinful life of the readers with the admonition that the Colossians should, like all the others hearers of the apostolic word, rid themselves of *all such things* such as anger, etc. Expositors discuss whether τὰ πάντα (all things) refers only to the sins mentioned in v. 5[20] or whether it also includes those of v. 8.[21] The former interpretation is excluded because the connection between ὀργήν (wrath) and τὰ πάντα (all things) can only

---

[20] H.A.W. Meyer, [*Kritisch exegetisches Handbuch über die Briefe Pauli an die Philipper, Kolosser und Philemon*, KEK IX, 4. ed. (Göttingen: V. & R., 1874) = *Critical and Exegetical Handbook to the Epistles to the Philippians and Colossians*, trad. J.C. Moore, Critical and Exegetical Commentary on the New Testament IX (Edinburgh: T. & T. Clark, 1875), pp. 429-30]; J. Chr. K. von Hofmann, [*Die Briefe Pauli an die Kolosser und an Philemon*, Die heilige Schrift neuen Testaments zusammenhängend untersucht IV.2 (Nördlingen: C.H. Beck, 1870), pp. 116-18].

[21] J.E. Huther; A. Klöpper, [*Der Brief an die Colosser kritisch untersucht und in seinem Verhältnisse zum paulinischen Lehrbegriff exegetisch und biblisch-theologisch erörtert* (Berlin: G. Reimer, 1882)].

be understood as an apposition. The latter interpretation is flawed because two things cannot be in view at the same time. Τὰ πάντα can only really be explained if it neither refers to the sins of v. 5 nor to these and those mentioned in v. 8, but only if it refers to a number of sins, of which Paul presupposes that the readers were conscious of their being reprehensible. But this number must have included sins such as mentioned in v. 5 and v. 8. Only then is the linking of ὀργήν κτλ. (wrath etc.) without the use of a particle comprehensible. It cannot be excluded that Paul himself introduced one or the other sin to both verses, but the sins he names must have been in general those of the *paradosis*. Therefore, also the Colossian church, not founded by Paul but by Epaphras, knew of a list of sins and with it knew of the ways. This confirms the perception that the ways were taught by all missionaries of that time.

It will be our task as we proceed to determine so far as it is possible the list of sins that the New Testament vice catalogues presuppose. We have already ascertained that πορνεία (sexual immorality) and πλεονεξία (covetousness) definitely belonged to the *paradosis*. Romans 16:17 suggests that διχοστασία (causing division) is a possibility. This possibility becomes very probable when we observe the same word occurring again in the list of sins in Galatians 5:20. What is true for διχοστασία also holds for πάθος ἐπιθυμίας (passionate lust) in 1 Thessalonians 4:5. Πάθος (lust) is of course only found in Colossians 3:5, thus allowing for some doubt whether the word belonged to the *paradosis*, but ἐπιθυμία (passion) not only occurs in Colossians 3:5 but also in 1 Peter 4:3.[22] The probability that ἐπιθυμία belonged to the *paradosis* is reinforced by the fact that it is found among the sins mentioned in Colossians 3:5, sins which belonged to the *paradosis*.

The passage in Colossians 3:5 and 8 mentions not only πορνεία, πάθος, ἐπιθυμία (sexual immorality, lust, passion) and πλεονεξία (covetousness) but also ἀκαθαρσία, ὀργή, θυμός, κακία, βλασφημία and αἰσχρολογία (impurity, anger, rage, malice, slander, filthy language). We have already noticed that Paul himself could have introduced some of these vices, considering them to be of similar character, even though he attaches them to the known list of sins. Concerning ὀργή (wrath) we must leave it as merely possible since its occurrence in Ephesians (4:26,31), a letter so closely related to Colossians, does not

---

[22] Cf. otherwise also Rom 13:14, Titus 3:3; 2 Peter 2:18.

prove anything.[23] The same is true for αἰσχρολογία (filthy language), which is only paralleled by related expressions in Ephesians 4:29 and 5:4. It is certain, however, that the sins of Colossians 3:5,8, which appear repeatedly in the New Testament catalogues of vice, belong to the *paradosis*. This is true for θυμός (rage; Gal 5:20; 2 Cor 12:20; Eph 4:31); κακία (malice; Rom 1:29; Eph 4:31; 1 Peter 2:1; cf. Tit 3:3); βλασφημία (slander; Eph 4:31; Mk 7:22; Mt 15:19; cf. 2 Peter 2:11; 1 Tim 6:4; 2 Tim 3:2; Tit 3:2) and ἀκαθαρσία (impurity; Gal 5:20; 2 Cor 12:21; Eph 5:3,5). Λοιδορία (slander; 1 Cor 5:11; 6:10; cf. 1 Peter 3:9) is probably just another expression for the sin otherwise named βλασφημία.

In the endeavour to determine the sins belonging to the *paradosis* we have used several fixed points of reference which enabled us to find several sins, which certainly or probably or possibly belonged to the *paradosis*. Now continuing our task would be easy, if the authors of the New Testament had repeatedly quoted longer parts of the *paradosis* exactly. But they do not do that. Among the many catalogues of vice in the New Testament not even two are identical. The results we have gained so far already show that the authors each time picked single sins out of the multitude given in the *paradosis*. These are combined, often without order, to form a new longer or shorter catalogue of vices. The only order which can be established here and there is that related sins are linked together, but in such a way that sequence and choice of words often differ. Only once do we find four sins in exactly the same sequence and form in two catalogues. Galatians 5:20 and 2 Corinthians 12:20 refer to ἔρις, ζῆλος, θυμοί, ἐριθίαι (discord, jealousy, fits of rage, selfish ambition). The repetition of four sins, of which two are in the singular and two in the plural at both occurrences would in itself be enough evidence to prove beyond doubt that Paul's catalogues of vice must be based on a fixed pattern in spite of the liberty usually taken in their construction. We already know that θυμός (rage) belongs to the *paradosis*. But Romans 13:13 also links ἔρις (discord) and ζῆλος (jealousy); ζῆλος and ἐριθία (selfish ambition) are linked by James 3:15. 1 Timothy 6:4 should be compared with regard to ἔρις and Philippians 2:3 concerning ἐριθία.

Since we now have found a large number of sins which certainly belonged to the *paradosis*, namely πορνεία, ἀκαθαρσία, πλεονεξία, κακία, βλασφημία, ἔρις, ζῆλος, θυμοί, ἐριθίαι (sexual

---

[23] Cf. also ὀργίλος (quick-tempered) in Titus 1:7.

immorality, impurity, covetousness, malice, slander, discord, jealousy, fits of rage, selfish ambition), we may further consider it to be certain that other sins in the catalogues of vice were also part of the *paradosis*. But which sins? In continuing our investigation we stand on uncertain ground instead of being able to count on certain factors. If the authors of the New Testament feel completely free in their usage of the *paradosis*, does not then the possibility, with which we already had to reckon, become indisputable that they added some sins themselves? How are we to discern whether a sin is taken over from the *paradosis* or introduced by the author himself? And who is to tell us that the *paradosis*, which Paul, Peter, the apocalyptic and synoptic writers presuppose, is identical? The opposite seems to be probable right from the start. If even the exact words of the Lord's prayer and of the institution of the Last Supper were handed down in different areas and times in varying forms, a difference of form in enumerating sins is even more probable. Our further investigations will of course not lead to assured results for the time being, but this is not sufficient reason to stop at this point. Even results which only claim probability are not without value in a matter of such importance. But the probability of a sin belonging to the *paradosis* may only then be maintained if the sin is found not only in one but in several catalogues of vice. The more often it occurs and the more authors use it, the greater the probability will be that it was to be found in the *paradosis* or at least in a form of the same. It also is not impossible that an author or even several authors repeatedly introduced by chance one and the same sin on their own, but it is not probable if we admit the existence of a fixed *paradosis*. If it is now possible, according to these rules, to prove that a number of sins belonged—with greater or lesser probability—to the *paradosis* or to a certain form of the same, we still must withhold any verdict regarding sins for which such evidence cannot be adduced. It is possible in any case that a sin is only mentioned in one list and belonged nevertheless to the *paradosis* or to a certain form of it. This could be the case for πάθος, ὀργή, αἰσχρολογία (lust, anger, filthy language). In such a case we have to forgo a definite decision whether the word belongs to the paradosis and content ourselves with stating the mere possibility.

Before we begin to classify the various sins according to the principles laid down, we need to point out the peculiarity of several books of the New Testament. The special kinship of the letter to the Ephesians to that to the Colossians is well-known. If then these two letters testify to a sin, this testimony naturally carries less weight than when the letter to the Colossians and another writing of the New Testament stand side by side. Ephesians 4 and 5 , as it turns out, feature only meagre lists of sins. Here we mostly find expressions which betray mere contact with the *paradosis*. This is another reason why the testimony of the letter to the Ephesians must be used cautiously. The catalogues of the *Pastoral Epistles* are also of special character.[24] These epistles are also aware of a fixed moral teaching, the ὑγιαίουσα (sound) or καλή (good) or κατ᾽ εὐσέβειαν διδασκαλία (godly teaching; 1 Tim 1:10; 4:6; 6:3). 1 Timothy 1:10 demonstrates that the moral teaching which Timothy followed (4:6; 2 Tim 3:10) contained the same or a similar list of sins (cf. 1 Tim 6:4). But there is an issue of considerable difference between the catalogues of the Pastoral Epistles and the other New Testament writings. While the latter only comparatively rarely list a sin which does not occur in other catalogues, the Pastoral Epistles do so exceedingly often. Later on we will adduce the evidence for this assertion. However, we must now draw attention to this fact, because it decreases the value of the testimony of these epistles. If we find the sin of a catalogue occurring for example in Romans, and its only other occurrence is in a catalogue of the Pastoral Epistles, the result carries less weight than if its other occurrence were for instance in one of the Corinthian letters. The large number of sins mentioned only in the Pastoral Epistles strongly points to the possibility that a sin only mentioned once in the other catalogues of the New Testament, which reoccurs in the Pastoral Epistles, is only mentioned by chance in the latter. This possibility becomes even more probable if such a sin is only mentioned once in the Pastoral Epistles.

We may claim for the following sins the *highest degree of probability for belonging to the paradosis*: μοιχεία (adultery; Mt 15:19; Mk 7:21; Lk 18:11; 1 Cor 6:9), ἀσέλγεια (lewdness; Mk 7:22; Rom 13:13; 2 Cor 12:21; Gal 5:20, Eph 4:19, 1 Peter 4:3; 2 Peter 2:18); φθόνος (envy; Rom 1:29; Gal 5:20; 1 Peter 2:1; Titus 3:3), which only is another word for ὀφθαλμὸς πονηρός (lit. evil eye, meaning envy; Mk

---

24 I feel obliged to distinguish between Paul and the author of the Pastoral Epistles because the latter display in the question we are dealing with now and in matters investigated in the following sections of this book unmistakeable differences when compared to the Pauline epistles. Nevertheless I am convinced that the Pastoral Epistles go back, in some hitherto unknown sense, to Paul himself.

7:22)²⁵; εἰδωλολατρία (idolatry; 1 Cor 5:10f; 6:9; Gal 5:20; Col 3:5; Eph 5:5; 1 Peter 4:3; Rev 21:8; 22:15); φόνος (murder; Mt 15:19; Mk 7:21; Rom 1:29; Rev 9:21; 21:8; 22:15; also cf. 1 Tim 1:9: ἀνδροφόνος [murderer]); κλοπή (theft; Mt 15:19; Mk 7:21; 1 Cor 6:10; Rev 9:21; also cf. Eph 4:27); δόλος (deceit; Mk 7:22; Rom 1:29; 1 Peter 2:1); ψεῦδος (falsehood; Col 3:9; Eph 4:25; Rev 21:8; 22:15; cf. 1 Tim 1:10); καταλαλία (slander; Rom 1:29; 2 Cor 12:20; 1 Peter 2:1); φαρμακία (witchcraft; Gal 5:20; Rev 9:21; 21:8; 22:15) and μέθαι, κῶμοι (drunkenness, orgies; Gal 5:21; Rom 13:13; similarly 1 Peter 4:4: κῶμοι, πότοι [carousing]; also cf. 1 Cor 5:11: μέθυσος [drunkard] and further Eph 5:18 and 1 Tim 1:7).

The following words *probably* also belonged to the *paradosis*: ἀκαταστασία (disorder; 2 Cor 12:12, James 3:16; both times we find the word in the vicinity of ζῆλος [envy]); ψιθυρισμός (gossip; Rom 1:29; 2 Cor 12:20); ἁρπαγή (robbery, fraud; 1 Cor 5:10f; 6:10; Lk 18:11); ὑπερηφανία (arrogance; Mk 7:22; Rom 1:30; 2 Tim 3:2); πονηρία (sexual immorality; Mk 7:21; Rom 1:29, where this is beyond doubt the correct reading). We award a lesser degree of probability to κενοδοξία (vain conceit), occurring in two passages where undertones of the *paradosis* can be recognised (Gal 5:26 and Phil 2:3). Ἀδικία (wickedness) in Romans 1:29, a passage which is only paralleled by the very short enumeration of Luke 18:11, might be on a similar level.

Furthermore, we have to list a number of sins which can only be classified as *possibly belonging to the paradosis*. We start with four words occurring only once in Pauline catalogues but which occur again in the Pastoral Epistles. They are: ἀλαζονία (boasting; Rom 1:30 and 2 Tim 3:2); γονεῦσιν ἀπειθεῖς (disobedience towards parents; Rom 1:30; 2 Tim 3:2; also cf. Tit 3:3); ἄστοργοι (without love; Rom 1:31; 2 Tim 3:3); ἀρσενοκοῖται (homosexual offenders; 1 Cor 6:9; 1 Tim 1:10).

The following sins are mentioned only once in the New Testament catalogues of vice: διαλογισμοὶ πονηροὶ or οἱ κακοί (evil thoughts; Mt 15:19 = Mk 7:21; also cf. ὑπόνοιαι πονηραί [evil suspicions] in 1 Tim 6:4); ψευδομαρτυρία (false testimony) in Matthew 15:19, which could have been introduced with the decalogue in mind; μαλακοί (male prostitutes) in 1 Corinthians 6:9; φυσιώσεις (arrogance) in 2 Corinthians 12:20; ἔχθραι and αἱρέσεις (hatred, factions) in Galatians 5:20; ὑπόκρισις (hypocrisy) in 1 Peter 2:1; οἰνοφλυγία

---

²⁵ Cf. the association of φθόνος and ἔρις (rivalry) in Phil 1:15 and 1 Tim 6:4.

(drunkenness) in 1 Peter 4:3; κοῖται (sexual immorality) in Romans 13:13; ἀσύνετοι (senseless) in Romans 1:31; ἀφροσύνη (folly; Mark 7:22)[26]; furthermore, several sins which we find in Romans 1:29ff, namely, κακοηθία, ἀνελεήμων, θεοστυγεῖς, ὑβρισταί, ἐφευρεταὶ κακῶν, ἀσύνθετοι (malice, ruthless, God-haters, insolent, inventing ways of doing evil, faithless). It is very plausible to assume that Romans 1:29ff, especially its second part, constitutes a freely composed catalogue of vice with many additions of its own. Δειλοί, ἄπιστοι, ἐβδελυγμένοι (cowards, unbelievers, vile; 21:8) and κύνες (dogs; 22:15) are only mentioned once in the book of Revelation. Apparently these four words are only designations for the heathen and were certainly added by the author himself. I shall not list the individual sins in Ephesians, since it is often hard to determine here whether individual vices are understood as belonging to a catalogue or not. The same applies to 2 Peter, a letter which in any case contains much unique material.

Reviewing now our investigation of the New Testament catalogues of sin we may conclude that *nine sins*, mentioned within them, *definitely belonged to the paradosis* (πορνεία, πλεονεξία, κακία, βλασφημία, ἀκαθαρσία, ἔρις, ζῆλος, θυμοί, ἐριθίαι). *Thirteen sins most probably* were part of the *paradosis* (ἐπιθυμία, μοιχεία, ἀσέλγεια, φθόνος, εἰδωλολατρία, φόνος, κλοπή, δόλος, ψεῦδος, καταλαλία, φαρμακία, μέθαι, κῶμοι) and for *eight sins* it is *more or less probable* (διχοστασία, ἀκαταστασία, ψιθυρισμός, ἁρπαγή, ὑπερηφανία, πονηρία, κενοδοξία, ἀδικία). To these thirty sins we may add *twenty eight which have a mere possibility* of belonging to the *paradosis* (πάθος, ὀργή, αἰσχρολογία, ἀλαζονία, γονεῦσιν ἀπειθεῖς, ἄστοργοι, διαλογισμοὶ πονηροί, ψευδομαρτυρία, μαλακοί, ἀρσενοκοῖται, φυσιώσεις, ἔχθραι, αἱρέσεις, ὑπόκρισις, οἰνοφλυγία, κοῖται, ἀσύνετοι, ἀφροσύνη, κακοηθία, ἀνελεήμων, θεοστυγεῖς, ὑβρισταί, ἐφευρεταὶ κακῶν, ἀσύνθετοι, δειλοί, ἄπιστοι, ἐβδελυγμένοι, κύνες). It seems justified to exclude the four designations of the heathen in the book of Revelation and the eleven sins which are without parallel in Romans 1:29ff. Thus only *thirteen sins* remain as *only possibly* belonging to the *paradosis*.

There is a much greater number of isolated sins in the Pastoral Epistles. These are in 1 Timothy 1:9f: ἄνομοι, ἀνυπότακτοι, ἀσεβεῖς, ἁμαρτωλοί, ἀνόσιοι (cf. 2 Tim 3:2), βέβηλοι, πατρολῷαι, μητρολῷαι, ἀνδραποδισταί, ἐπίορκοι (lawbreakers, rebels, the ungodly, sinful,

---

[26] The last two words might also be different names for the same sin (cf. ἀνόητοι [foolish] in Titus 3:3).

unholy [cf. 2 Tim 3:2], irreligious, those who kill their fathers and mothers, slave traders, prejurers); in 1 Timothy 6:4: ὑπόνοιαι πονηραί (cf. Mt 15:19), διατριβαί (evil suspicions, constant friction); in 2 Timothy 3:2: φίλαυτοι, ἀλαζόνες (lovers of themselves, boastful, cf. Rom 1:30), γονεῦσιν ἀπειθεῖς (disobedient to their parents, cf. Rom 1:30), ἀχάριστοι, ἄστοργοι (ungrateful, without love, cf. Rom 1:31), ἄσπονδοι, διάβολοι, ἀκρατεῖς, ἀνήμεροι, ἀφιλάγαθοι, προδόται, προπεθεῖς, τετυφωμένοι, φιλήδονοι (unforgiving, slanderous, lacking self-control, brutal, not lovers of the good, treacherous, rash, conceited, lovers of pleasure); in Titus 1:7: αὐθάδης (overbearing, cf. 2 Peter 2:10), πάροινος (given to much wine, cf. μέθυσος [drunkard] in 1 Cor 5:11), πλήκτης (violent, also in 1 Tim 3:2), αἰσχροκερδής (pursuing dishonest gain); in Titus 3:3: ἀνόητοι (foolish, similar in Rom 1:31), ἀπειθεῖς (disobedient, cf. Rom 1:30 and 2 Tim 3:2), πλανώμενοι, στυγητοί, μισοῦντες ἀλλήλους (deceived, being hated, hating one another). These are no less than *thirty five sins*. If we also subtract the six sins, which have a single exact or approximate parallel in the other New Testament catalogues of vice—this applies four times to Romans 1:29ff—and the three sins, which occur repeatedly in the Pastoral Epistles, *twenty six sins* still remain. We may conclude that the lists of the Pastoral Epistles are much less bound to the *paradosis* than the catalogues in the rest of the New Testament, except for instance 2 Peter and Romans 1:29ff.

If we have now established that the teaching of "the ways" contained a list of sins, a large number of which we were able to determine with certainty or at least probability, and if it is established that the New Testament vice catalogues are several times placed alongside virtue catalogues, which have the same consistency as the vice catalogues, then we would have proved that the ways, apart from an enumeration of sins, contain an *enumeration of virtues*. The condition mentioned last is actually the case. The New Testament contains *eleven catalogues of virtues* (Gal 5:22ff; Col 3:12ff; Eph 4:2f; Phil 2:1f; 1 Tim 6:11; 2 Tim 2:22; Titus 1:8; 2:2; 3:1f; 1 Peter 3:8; 2 Peter 1:5ff). Their kinship, as we shall see, wholly corresponds to the kinship of the catalogues of vices. Only a few virtues occur singly. This happens more often in the Pastoral Epistles and in 2 Peter. Galatians 5:22ff and Colossians 3:12ff, where the catalogues of virtue follow catalogues of vice (1 Tim 6:11 and Titus 1:8), prove that the catalogues of virtues are the counterpart of the catalogues of vice. The enumeration of virtues preceding the enumeration of vices in Philippians 2:1 provides further proof. Since the number of the catalogues of virtue is significantly smaller than the number of catalogues of vice, which usually are also more extensive, we have to rely now on much less evidence.

The catalogue of vice in Colossians 3:5,8 has an equivalent catalogue of virtue in vv. 12ff. Since most of the words of the catalogue of vice certainly belonged to the *paradosis* we may expect a corresponding state of affairs in the enumeration of virtues. This expectation is not misleading. Σπλάγχνα οἰκτιρμοῦ (compassion) opens the list of virtues in Colossians 3:12. Philippians 2:1 instead offers σπλάγχνα καὶ οἰκτιρμοί (tenderness and compassion); and σπλάγχνα corresponds to εὔσπλαγχνοι (compassionate) in Ephesians 4:32 and 1 Peter 3:8. It is therefore *highly probable* that the *paradosis* mentioned cordiality in one of the forms before us. It is equally *probable* that the other virtues mentioned in Colossians 3:12 belong to the *paradosis*, namely χρηστότης (kindness; Eph 4:32; Gal 5:23); ταπεινοφροσύνη (humility; Eph 4:2; Phil 2:2; 1 Peter 3:8); πραΰτης (gentleness; Eph 4:2; Gal 5:23; Titus 3:2, also cf. 1 Tim 6:11) and μακροθυμία (patience; Eph 4:2; Gal 5:23). It is a reasonable assumption that the last four virtues formed a series in the *paradosis*, supported on the one side by Galatians 5:23, mentioning μακροθυμία, χρηστότης and further πραΰτης and on the other side by Ephesians 4:2, where ταπεινοφροσύνη, πραΰτης and μακροθυμία are in sequence.

Since it is fairly certain that the five virtues mentioned in Colossians 3:12 belonged to the *paradosis*, it is a reasonable assumption that the virtues listed further on in v. 13ff likewise belonged to it. This cannot be demonstrated for ἀνεχόμενοι ἀλλήλων καὶ χαριζόμενοι ἑαυτοῖς (bear with and forgive each other), which could be a paraphrase of a single word. Even though the similar expression in Ephesians 4:2 does not carry much weight, it seems somewhat probable, since it gains support from 1 Peter 3:8 where essentially the same thought is expressed, however differently it may be phrased, within a catalogue of virtues.

Moreover, we may note Colossians 3:14f, which mentions ἀγάπη, εἰρήνη, εὐχάριστος (love, peace, gratitude). Ephesians 4:2 and Galatians 5:22 show that ἀγάπη and εἰρήνη belonged to the *paradosis*, since these passages mention both virtues in one series with πραΰτης (gentleness) and χρηστότης (kindness) (cf. ταπεινοφροσύνη [humility]). Both virtues are next to each other in 2 Timothy 2:22; cf. moreover concerning ἀγάπη Philippians 2:2; 1 Timothy 6:11; Titus 2:2; 1 Peter 4:8; 2 Peter 1:7. But εἰρήνη probably ends the close contact to the *paradosis*; at least there is no parallel to εὐχάριστοι γίνεσθε (be thankful).

According to the virtues found in Colossians 3:12ff, all the virtues of the list in the letter to the Galatians belonged to the *paradosis*, except for χαρά, ἀγαθωσύνη, πίστις and ἐγκράτεια (joy, goodness, faithfulness, self-control). Of these words πίστις *very probably* belonged to the *paradosis*. Indeed, we do not find πίστις, which we find together with ὑπομονή (endurance) in the catalogues of the Pauline epistles, but we come across both words separated by ἀγάπη in 1 Timothy 6:11 and Titus 2:2. Both words also occur in the list of 2 Peter 1:5, which also contains ἐγκράτεια and ἀγάπη. With regard to πίστις we may also compare 2 Timothy 2:22. From the list of Galatians 5:22 only χαρά, ἀγαθωσύνη and ἐγκράτεια are left over. We can scarcely claim more than the possibility for their belonging to the *paradosis*. Concerning χαρά (joy) we may perhaps refer to Romans 14:17 where χαρά is mentioned with δικαιοσύνη and εἰρήνη (righteousness and peace) in one series as being at hand in the βασιλεία (kingdom). Ἀγαθωσύνη (goodness) is perhaps supported by Ephesians 5:9, where ἀγαθωσύνη, δικαιοσύνη and ἀλήθεια (truth) appear as fruit of the Spirit. However, ἐγκράτεια (self-control) *probably* belonged to the *paradosis*, since the word occurs again in Titus 1:8 and 2 Peter 1:6. The same is true for ὁμόφρων (to live in harmony) in 1 Peter 3:8, since the words in Ephesians 4:3 σπουδάζοντες τηρεῖν τὴν ἑνότητα τοῦ πνεύματος (make every effort to keep the unity of the Spirit), attached to several virtues of the *paradosis*, are in their sense equivalent to ὁμόφρων. The same, moreover, holds true for the expression τὸ ἓν φρονεῖν (to be like-minded), which appears in Philippians 2:2 in a section distinctly suggestive of the *paradosis*.

Δικαιοσύνη (righteousness) was *probably* also part of the *paradosis*. To support this assertion we may possibly quote Romans 14:17 and Ephesians 5:9, but certainly we may cite 1 Timothy 6:11 (where it appears alongside πίστις, ἀγάπη and πραϋπαθία [gentleness]); 2 Timothy 2:22 and Titus 1:8. According to Ephesians 5:9 ἀλήθεια (truth) may only claim the *possibility* of belonging to the *paradosis*. The same holds true for συμπαθεῖς and φιλάδελφοι (be sympathetic, love as brothers) mentioned in 1 Peter 3:8. For the latter word we may compare also 2 Peter 1:7 and 1 Thessalonians 4:9.

Surveying the results of our investigation of the catalogues of virtue we gather that *nine virtues very probably* belonged to the *paradosis* (εὔσπλαγχνος, χρηστότης, ταπεινοφροσύνη, πραΰτης, μακροθυμία, ἀγάπη, εἰρήνη, πίστις, ὑπομονή); for *four virtues* it is *probable* (forgiveness, δικαιοσύνη, ἐγκράτεια, ὁμόφρων); *perhaps probable* for *two* more (χαρά and ἀγαθωσύνη) and a *mere possibility* for *three* others (ἀλήθεια, συμπαθεῖς, φιλαδελφία).

The Pastoral Epistles contain four virtues which are otherwise not found in the New Testament but which are repeated within these writings, namely, φιλόξενος (hospitality) and σώφρων (self-control) in 1 Timothy 3:2 and Titus 1:8; ἄμαχος (not quarrelsome) and ἐπιεικής (gentle) in 1 Timothy 3:3 and Titus 3:2. We may add to this εὐσέβεια (godliness) in 1 Tim 6:11, which also occurs in 2 Peter 1:6. Furthermore, the Pastoral Epistles contain six virtues without any parallel, namely: φιλάγαθος (loving what is good) and ὅσιος (holy) in Titus 1:8; and ἀνεπίλημπτος (being above reproach), νηφάλαιος (temperate), κόσμιος (respectable) and διδακτικός (able to teach) in 1 Timothy 3:2. Two virtues found in 2 Peter 1:5 are without parallel: ἀρετή (goodness) and γνῶσις (knowledge).

CHAPTER EIGHT

Code and Context
A Few Reflections on the Parenesis of Col 3:6–4:1

Lars Hartman
(1987)

During the last decade or so, New Testament scholarly discussions have revealed a renewed interest in the so-called household codes, especially the two NT texts which deserve this designation, viz. Col 3:1-4:1 and Eph 5:22-6:9.[1] One reason is, of course, that the feminist movement has increased the embarrassment many exegetes have felt regarding the admonitions that wives be submissive.[2] Another is that new suggestions have been made in terms of background material, viz. the so-called household management traditions, and, as a matter of fact, these have also been used when it has come to grappling with the hermeneutic problems posed by the texts. In this paper some of these new insights will be combined with older suggestions

---

[1] Other texts referred to as household codes are: 1 Pet 2:18-3:7 (which does not deal with the whole household). 1 Tim 2:8-15; Titus 2:1-10; *Did* 4:9-11; *Barn* 19:5-7; 1 *Clem* 21:6-9; Pl *Phil*. 4:2-6:3 are no real household codes.

[2] E.g., D. L. Balch, "Early Christian Criticism of Patriarchal Authority: l Peter 2:11-3:12", *UnSemQuartRev* 39 (1984) 161-173.

concerning the possible role played by the Decalogue[3] in the context
of the Colossian household code. In addition, this will be carried out
with respect to the argument of Colossians. I find it natural to
dedicate this article to Professor Ellis, as it touches upon a field of
research on which he has done so much significant work, viz. the
investigation of the use of the OT in early Christian history and
traditions.[4]

It has been a widely spread opinion that the household code of
Col 3:18-4:1 is a textual unit that was formulated before Col was
written. Its style is different from that of the surrounding parenesis,
and if one should withdraw it, the text would flow smoothly all the
same. If, then, the passage is a loan, from where has it been
borrowed? Furthermore, what, if anything, does that tell us about the
history of the Early Church and about its relationship to the
surrounding world? Finally, how does the household code function
within the framework of the letter, and what is its function with
regard to the situation of the addressees?[5]

The questions of the preceding paragraph have received
different answers among NT scholars.[6] Thus, Martin Dibelius held

---

[3] Contemporary Jews counted the commandments of the Decalogue in such a
way that the one against making graven images became number two, and the
one on honoring one's parents number five, the last of the first table. In this
paper I will follow this way of counting. The Decalogue has been drawn into the
discussion of the household code by R. M. Grant, "The Decalogue in Early
Christianity", *HTR* 40 (1940) 1-17, and P. Stuhlmacher, "Christliche Verant-
wortung bei Paulus und seinen Schülern", *EvT* 28 (1968) 165-186, esp. 177-78.

[4] E.g., E. E. Ellis, *Paul's Use of the Old Testament*, Edinburgh, 1957; *id., Prophecy
and Hermeneutic in Early Christianity. New Testament Essays*. WUNT 18, Tübingen,
1978, Chaps. 9-17.

[5] One could use different terms for these two "functions". In another context
I have distinguished between a literary (or illocutionary) and a sociolinguistic
function (L. Hartman, "Survey of the Problem of Apocalyptic Genre", in
Apocalypticism in the Mediterranean World and the Near East, ed. by D. Hellholm,
Proceedings of the International Colloquium on Apocalypticism, Uppsala,
August 12-17, 1979, Tübingen, 1983, 329-343, § 3.3.1 and 3.3.2), but I here follow
the terminology of D. Hellholm, preferring "(text-) internal" and '(text-)-
external" (D. Hellholm, "The Problem of Apocalyptic Genre and the Apocalypse
of John", in *id., Dispersa Membra*, to be published in ConBNT, 3.3.2).

[6] For a discussion of the scholarly debate see J. E. Crouch, *The Origin and
Intention of the Colossian Haustafel*, FRLANT 109, Göttingen, 1972, chap. 1, and D.
L. Balch, *Let Wives be Submissive: The Domestic Code in 1 Peter*, SBL Monogr. Ser.
26, Chico, 1981, chap. 1.

(1913)[7] that behind the "Haustafeln" lay a "schema", which was originally Stoic and visible in the way such philosophers organized their discussions of what was "fitting" (*kathēkon*) "towards the gods, one's parents, one's brothers, one's country, and towards foreigners" (Epict. 2.17.31). He saw the Church's adoption of this pattern as a sign that it was on the way to abandoning the eschatological perspective which was thought to characterize its attitude from the beginning, and was adjusting itself to a life in this world.

Fifteen years later Karl Weidinger elaborated Dibelius' ideas, presenting more material from the philosophers as well as from Judaism.[8] "Hellenistic Judaism"[9] had also used the "schema", and he thought that it was possibly the milieu from which the Christians got it. But, in addition, the Christians assumed not only the "schema" but also the very texts themselves, at least in the case of the code of Col 3:18-4:1. They merely christianized the code by adding "in the Lord" at suitable places.

Dibelius' and Weidinger's ideas dominated the understanding of the household codes for several decades. In 1972, however, J. E. Crouch went through the material again.[10] He too assumed an "Hellenistic" origin of the codes, and thought that "Hellenistic Judaism" had had a decisive influence.[11] However, he criticized Dibelius and Weidinger for simplifying the problem of the role played by the eschatological expectations. Weidinger was also accused of being too quick to generalize, both in terms of the pre-Christian Stoic-Cynic *and* Jewish material, as well as when it came to the Christian codes.

Others have claimed that the household codes had a purely Christian origin. Thus, K. H. Rengstorf has derived them from an

---

7 M. Dibelius, *An die Kolosser, Epheser, an Philemon*, HNT 12, 3rd ed., ed. by H. Greeven, Tübingen, 1953, 48-50.

8 K. Weidinger, *Die Haustafeln. Ein Stück unchristlicher Paränese*, UNT 14, Leipzig, 1928.

9 Although I use this traditional expression (because the cited authors do so), the quotation marks are there to mark that I would rather replace it by "Greek speaking, largely non-Palestinian Judaism" or something similar.

10 Crouch, *Origin and Intention*.

11 E. Lohmeyer (*Die Briefe an die Philipper, an die Kolosser und an Philemon*, MeyerK 9, 9th ed. by W. Schmauch, Göttingen, 1953; the 8th ed., the first one written by Lohmeyer, appeared in 1930) also held the opinion that Col 3:18-4:1 was a pre-Colossian unit, but regarded it as being of purely Jewish origin. In so doing, he did not ask so much for the provenance of a "schema" as for the root system of the ideas.

early Christian interest in the *oikos*.[12] A partly similar opinion concerning the origin is held by David Schroeder.[13] He finds the roots of the form in OT apodictic law *and* in Stoic lists of the stations in life. But "the content is drawn from the OT, Judaic tradition, although with the addition of certain Greek (what is fitting) and Christian (*agapē*) concepts. The basic ethical conception of the NT codes—that without belonging to the world as such, one has responsibilities within the structure of society—takes us back to the teaching and example of Jesus himself."

The second half of the 1970's brought a new stage in research on the codes: instead of having parallels in the *kathēkon*-lists, the "stations" addressed in the codes, as well as some of the advice found in them, were seen as having clearer parallels in the philosophical treatises from Plato and Aristotle onwards, which dealt with household management, *oikonomia* or *oikonomos*.[14] Regarding the NT household codes in the light of this tradition led to new suggestions of what the Church was actually doing with its household codes. D. Lührmann saw therein a latent claim of the Christians that the Christian house was a model for society.[15] D. C. Balch concluded, having especially 1 Pet in mind, that "the code has an apologetic function in the historical context: the paraenesis is given in light of outside criticism", viz. from persons who "were alienated and threatened by some of their slaves and wives who had converted to the new, despised religion, so they were accusing the converts of impiety, immorality, and insubordination".[16] K. Müller

---

[12] K. H. Rengstorf, "Die neutestamentlichen Mahnungen an die Frau, sich dem Manne unterzuordnen", in *Verbum Dei manet in aeternum: Festschrift O. Schmitz*, ed. by W. Foerster, Witten, 1953, 131-145.

[13] D. Schroeder, "Lists, ethical", *IDBSup*, 1976, 546-547. His unpublished Hamburg dissertation from 1959 dealt with the household codes, their origin and their theological meaning. It has not been available to me.

[14] D. Lührmann, "Wo man nacht mehr Sklave oder Freier ist", *WortuDienst*, *NF* 13 (1975), 58-83; *id.*, "Neutestamentliche Haustafeln und antike Ökonomie", *NTS* 27 (1980/81) 83-97; K. Thraede, "Ärger mit der Freiheit", in *"Freunde in Christus werden . . ."*, ed. by G. Scharffenorth, K. Thraede, Berlin, 1977, 31-182; *id.*, "Zum historischen Hintergrund der 'Haustafeln' des NT", in *Pietas Festschrift für B. Kötting*, ed. by E. Dassmann, K. G. Frank—*JAC*, Erg. bd. 8, 1980, Munich, 1980, 359-368; Balch, *Wives Be Submissive*, after a Yale dissertation in 1974; K. Müller, "Die Haustafel des Kolosserbriefes und das antike Frauenthema", in *Die Frau im Urchristentum*, ed. by G. Dautzenberg, H. Merklein, K. Müller, QD 95, Freiburg, Basel, Vienna, 1983, 263-319, esp. 284-90.

[15] Lührmann, *NTS* 27 (1980/81) 86.

[16] Balch, *Wives Be Submissive*, 109.

seems to suggest something similar: the early Christians lived in a society, in which some people, including some women, questioned the age-old subordination system of the "house", whereas others wanted to hold on to or to reinforce the good old authoritative pattern. In such a situation "the oldest household code of the NT demonstrates . . . a highly, respectable early Christian decision in favor of a middle course of social morality".[17]

After this short review of some answers to the questions raised in the beginning of this paper,[18] let us turn to the text itself, first considering its context in the literary sense of the word.

As I see it, Col has a more hortatory character than one often assumes. This is seen not least from the fact that the author reverts to the second person when summoning the addressees.[19] T h e christologically loaded passages of 1:13-20 and 2:9-15 serve as bases for admonition; in 1:21-23 this is indicated indirectly, whereas 2:16-23 is directly addressed to the believers. To concentrate on the second instance, this part of the letter begins with 1:24-2:5. It functions as a *captatio benevolentiae* which is partly realized by tying bonds of affection between "Paul"[20] and the addressees. Then, an introductory exhortation follows in 2:6-8: "walk in him . . . as you were taught . . . See to it that nobody carries you away captive . . . according to the principles of the world (*ta stoicheia tou kosmou*), not according to Christ". This leads (*hoti*) directly into the Christological basis, 2:9-15, which is applied in the following admonition of 2:16-23: "thus (*oun*), nobody must judge you in terms of food or drink . . . If you died with Christ from the principles of the world, why do you allow rules to be laid on you: do not touch . . .". The whole section of 1:24-2:23 becomes the background against which positive ethical teaching is given in 3:1-4:6. In a sense 2:6-7 ("walk in him as you were taught") becomes specified in 3:1-4, and the life with Christ (3:1, 3) and the heavenly mind (3:2) are placed over against the human and this-worldly rules (2:8, 14, 16, 20-23) and the earthly mind (3:2), for which the "philosophers" stand.

---

17 Müller, "Die Haustafel," 290.

18 Müller's article contains a broader and slightly peppered review of the research. The strictly literary and form-critical questions have largely been left aside here. I deal with them in my contribution to the Festschrift to H. C. Kee, forthcoming.

19 See 1:9-12, 21-23, 2:4, 6-8, 10, 16, 18, 20.

20 I assume that the author is a member of Paul's school.

3:1-4 opens up the general christologically determined perspective for the ethics. Then, in 3:5-4:6 more particular instructions follow. Regarded in this way, the parenesis in 3:1-4:6 is not only a section added to the theological parts of the letter, but rather something that has been prepared for almost from the beginning of the letter (cf. "knowledge of his will", 1:9).

We need not discuss the details of how the instruction of 3:5-4:6 is construed,[21] but only state that 3:5-17 is largely made up of catalogues of vices and virtues with a tendency of grouping them by fives. 3:16 deals with worship, and 3:17 is often understood as a summarizing conclusion: "whatever you do in word and deed, do it all in the name of Lord Jesus, thanking God the Father through him". However, since the following household code starts without any connecting conjunction or particle, and because of the seven occurrences of "the Lord" in the code, 3:17 also becomes a bridge to the household code; indeed, it might very well be regarded as its introduction.[22]

As already mentioned, however, the code appears like an island in its context. The shift in style is one factor contributing to this effect, viz. the direct address, "You wives", etc., and the shape of the admonitions (address + imperative + motivation). Furthermore, it is tightly held together by its reference to the household.

After the household code, the style in 4:2 is once again more similar to that in 3:5-17, and these admonitions have a concluding character inasmuch as they contain several echoes from the preceding text. Such observations would seemingly confirm Lohmeyer's opinion (*ad loc.*) that "one could hardly surmise that there were a gap if this passage were blotted out".

---

[21] See, e.g. the literature referred to and the discussion in J. Gnilka, *Der Kolosserbrief*, HTKNT 10:1, Freiburg, Basel,Vienna, 1980, *ad loc*.

[22] As a matter of fact the three cases of *kai* introducing a main clause in vv 15-17 are a little strange (cf. W. Bujard, *Stilanalytische Untersuchungen zum Kolosserbrief als Beitrag zur Methodik von Sprachvergleichen*, SUNT 11, Göttingen, 1973, 42). Gnilka, *Kolosserbrief*, 198, concludes that they are to be explained through the assumption that "in 3:15-17 Einzelmahnungen zusammengestellt sind". It would, however, fit well with my suggestions below, if v 15 begins a re-interpretation of the Sabbath Commandment (sabbath—rest—peace). The idea that v 17 introduces the household instruction, which covers "everything" a man could be, is supported by, e.g., Seneca, *ep*. 94.1, in which he describes what is contained in a household management treatise: *eam partem philosophiae, quae dat propria cuique personae praecepta . . .* !

Of course one could assume, then, as does Lohmeyer, that there must have been something in the Colossians' situation that demanded the insertion of this text. This might very well be so, but that does not make it unnecessary to consider the possibility I mentioned at the outset, viz. that the Decalogue might have something to do with this parenetic section, the household code included.

As a matter of fact, the Decalogue is a structuring factor in several ethical catalogues.[23] Mark 7:21-22 is a Christian example: fornication, theft, murder, adultery, coveting, wickedness, deceit, licentiousness, evil eye, slander, pride, foolishness. The parallel text in Matt 15:19 brings the text even closer to the OT: murder, adultery, fornication, theft, false witness, slander. 1 Tim 1:8-10 is another NT instance:[24] "lawless and disobedient, ungodly and sinners, unholy and profane, murderers of fathers and murderers of mothers, manslayers, fornicators, sodomites, kidnappers, liars, perjurers . . ." There are echoes of the Decalogue in Jewish, non-Palestinian texts as well, e.g., Sib. Or. 4.24-39: "love the great god (in contrast to worshiping idols, 25-30), . . . no murder, . . . no dishonest gain, . . . no desire for another's spouse or for abuse of a male . . ." Similarly in the beginning of the ethical admonitions of Pseudo-Phocylides (3-21): "do not commit adultery, homosexuality, treachery, nor stain your hands with blood; do not become rich unjustly, . . . be content with what you have and abstain from what is another's, do not tell lies . . ., honor God foremost, and afterward your parents, . . . flee false witness . . . , do not commit perjury, . . . do not steal seeds . . . , give the laborer his pay".[25] In passing we may note that the order between the commandments is not always the same, and there are more examples of this than Mark 10:19.[26]

With the examples of the preceding paragraph in mind one is immediately prepared to endorse Gnilka's supposition in his

---

[23] K. Berger, *Die Gesetzesauslegung Jesu I*, Neukirchen, 1972, 272-73.

[24] See Grant, *HTR* 40 (1940) 7. Cf. A. Vögtle, *Die Tugend- und Lasterkataloge exegetisch, religions- und formgeschichtlich untersucht*, NTAbh 16, 4-5, Münster, 1936, 16; S. Wibbing, *Die Tugend- und Lasterkataloge im NT und ihre Traditionsgeschichte unter besonderer Berücksichtigung der Qumran-Texte*, BZNW 25, Berlin, 1959, 83.

[25] Berger, *Gesetzesauslegung Jesu*, 374, is not prepared to hear any echoes from the Decalogue here, but cf. M. Küchler, *Fruhjüdische Weisheitstraditionen*, OBO, 26, Freiburg, Göttingen, 1979, 277-79.

[26] Berger, *Gesetzesauslegung Jesu.*, 275-76.

commentary on Colossians[27] that the two vice catalogues of Col 3:5 and 8 are dependent on the Decalogue: "fornication, impurity, passion, evil desire, and covetousness, which is idolatry", and: "anger, wrath, malice, slander, foul talk". I would also add the beginning of v 9: "do not lie to (or, about) one another". Counting (with, e.g., Philo) the image-commandment as the second one, and taking hatred and murder as equal (Matt 5:21-22, 1 John 3:15), we see that numbers 2, 6, 7, 8, 9 and 10 of the Decalogue have counterparts in Col 3:5-9.[28] The application and interpretation of the commandments, visible in the lists of Col 3, have several parallels in Jewish texts.[29]

As a contrast, 3:10-4:1 presents the life of the New Man. The description of this New Man begins with the characteristic "neither Greek nor Jew". I find it natural to combine this detail with the abundant epithets applied to the addressees in the subsequent verse, "God's elect, holy and beloved". Commentators state that the author here transfers classical designations of God's people to the addressees.[30] However, in this context it is appropriate to remember that Israel's election and holiness was closely connected with the covenant and the Law (e.g. Exod 19:5-6; Lev 19; Deut 4:37-40), and that the covenant and the Divine Revelation were expressions of God's love for His people (e.g., Deut 4:37; 7:8). In Col 3, however, God's elect are those in the New Man, in whom there is neither Greek nor Jew. But, precisely as in the case of Israel, the election is bound up with duties, with "putting on" a particular sort of life.

Certainly the "put on" of 3:12 is the positive counterpart to the "put off" of 3:5. But one cannot put the virtues of vv 12-14 in a one-to-one contrast to the vices of 3:5-9, i.e., as precise positive instructions implied in the prohibitions as they have been rephrased and interpreted in the vice lists. Many Christians are used to reading the Decalogue in such a way, and may therefore be too ready to hear

---

[27] Gnilka, *Kolosserbrief*. 185.

[28] The *blasphēmia* of v 8 should hardly be taken as based on the commandment against taking the Name in vain.

[29] See Berger, *Gesetzesauslegung Jesu*, chap. 4. There are indications to the effect that the Decalogue had a central place in the synagogue worship in the times of the Early Church. That this position of the Decalogue changed is often assumed to have taken place because of the Christian usage of the Decalogue. See Grant, *HTR* 40 (1940).

[30] E.g., E. Larsson, *Christus als Vorbild*, ASNU 23, Lund, 1962, 210; E. Lohse, *Die Briefe an die Kolosser und an Philemon*, MeyerK 9:2, 14th ed. Göttingen, 1968, *ad loc.*; E. Schweizer, *Der Brief an die Kolosser*, EKKNT, Neukirchen-Vluyn, 1976, *ad loc.*

echoes from the Decalogue also behind the positive admonitions. Thus, e.g., Lutherans learn in Luther's classical small catechism that the commandment against false testimony means: "We should fear and love God, and so we should not tell lies about our neighbor, nor betray, slander, or defame him, but should apologize for him, speak well of him, and interpret charitably all that he does". In the Office of Instruction of the Episcopal Church we hear of the duties towards one's neighbor as brought forward by the tenth commandment: "Not to covet nor desire other men's goods; But to learn and labor truly to earn mine own living, And to do my duty in that state of life unto which it shall please God to call me".

When Philo comments on the Decalogue, there is not much of this sort of discovery of implicitly commanded virtues, but in the catalogue I just cited from Pseudo-Phocylides we come across a similar tendency to add a "but" to the prohibitions: "do not become rich unjustly, *but* live from honorable means, . . . do not tell lies, *but* always speak the truth" (5, 7) *(alla* and *de,* respectively).

In Col 3 the virtues are not, as we noted, directly related to the individual items of the vice lists, but nonetheless one could say that they counter the transgressions of the commandments concerning murder, stealing, false witness and covetousness as the author of Col has interpreted them. Like his master, Paul, and following Jesus, he also regards love as the all-embracing commandment (3:14; Matt 5:43-48; Mark 12:28-33; Rom 13:8-10, etc.).

So far we have traced nothing from the first five commandments (except for idolatry in 3:5), including the one concerning parents. Nor has the one on adultery, such as the author interpreted it been given any positive counterpart in 3:12-17. It seems to me that this lack is met in the household code of 3:18-4:1. But before delineating this let me point to the possibility that even the Sabbath commandment lies behind a piece of the parenesis in Col 3.

The author certainly has nothing but contempt for the "philosophers'" ceremonial rules concerning "a feast, a new moon or a sabbath" (2:16). But there are traces of Jewish speculations on the Sabbath and its deeper meaning, which, in my opinion, a writer who held the sort of cosmic wisdom-Christology we encounter in Col could use for an interpretation of the Sabbath commandment. Thus, Philo explains the meaning of "sabbath" as "rest" *(anapausis;* see *Abr* 28). He finds this very fitting, for number seven "is always free from factions and war and quarrelling and is of all numbers the most peaceful". Indeed, as a matter of fact, to real lovers of wisdom the whole of life is a feast, for they always strive for "a life free from war and peaceful" (*Spec. leg.* 2.45). Furthermore, to Philo, but even more to Aristobulos, the number seven is something like a basic principle to the All which becomes manifest in the celebration of the seventh day.[31] To a philosophically minded Christian interpreter of the Sabbath commandment this might become a point of departure for a reference to the "peace of Christ" with this followed by some advice that Christ's word should dwell among the addressees and that they should teach each other and praise God. The study and the teaching of the Scriptures are, as is well known, of central importance to Philo when he describes the Sabbath,[32] and to his fellow Jews as well. The picture Philo gives of prayers, singing, and instruction at the Sabbath worship of the Therapeuts[33] is not too distant from Col 3:16.[34]

Whether there be any intimations of the fourth commandment behind 3:15-16 or not, to anyone who has felt that the commandment concerning parents should not be left out of consideration, and that the one on adultery should also be addressed with positive admonitions, this feeling of something lacking would be satisfied in the household code, 3:18-4:1. But did anybody—author and/or reader—feel that lack and then regard 3:18-4:1 as complying with it?

It may be of some importance to an answer to that question that, e.g., Philo understood the fifth commandment as covering the laws which "deal with the relations of old to young, rulers to subjects, benefactors to benefited, slaves to masters" (*Decal.* 165).[35] He also saw parents and masters as, in some respects, being gods to the other members of the house (*Decal.* 107-120; *Spec. leg.* 2.225-27), which gives an extra echo to the references to "the Lord" in the household code: being obedient "pleases the Lord" (3:20), and the slaves are to serve as it were to the Lord (3:23). That is, if 3:20-4:1 somehow

---

[31]   M. Hengel, *Judaism and Hellenism I*, Philadelphia, 1974, 166-169.

[32]   *Decal.* 98, 100; *Spec. Leg.* 2.62; *Omn. Prob. Lib.* 82; cf. Euseb. *Praep. ev.* 8.7, 12-13.

[33]   *Vit. Cont.* 29, 75-80.

[34]   A scholar who is more fanciful than I might even be prepared to combine 3:17, about doing everything in the name of the Lord Jesus, with the commandment concerning God's name. I would be hesitant, though, and prefer seeing the verse as introducing the code, which covers "everything" one does as an individual; see note 22 above.

[35]   Similarly in *Spec. Leg.* 2.226-27. Cf. Crouch, *Origin and Intention*, 78-79, who criticizes Schroeder's thesis concerning the role of the Decalogue. Sib. Or 2.278, also includes servants who turn against their masters among those who transgress this commandment.

represents the fifth commandment, it does so in a way that was found in contemporary Judaism. Also in favor of a positive answer to my question, there is the fact that, when the author of Eph uses Col 3:20,[36] he finds it natural to insert an explicit quotation of the fifth commandment (Eph 6:2-3).[37]

Philo did not include the relationship between wife and husband in that which was covered by the fifth commandment. Nonetheless, it is undeniable that it provides the positive instruction that would give the other side of the coin also in the case of the adultery commandment. On the other hand we have to realize that the contents certainly have some parallels in the surrounding world, but not, as far as I know,[38] in connection with an explanation of the prohibition of adultery. Accordingly, we should either assume that our text represents an innovation in terms of Decalogue interpretation, or that the code derives its contents from reasons other than the author's wish to reinterpret and apply two commandments of the Decalogue.

It is possible that the alternatives are too harshly stated in the preceding paragraph. At least it may seem so, if we supplement our discussion of the contents with some literary and form-critical observations. There are good reasons to assume that the code is a pre-Colossian unit, or, rather, that it is written in accordance with traditional turns of phrase. Its coherence and the difference in style as compared to the context have been mentioned above, and its coherence is not only stylistic, but also caused by the thought pattern of the "house". Accordingly, I would suggest that the author does not draw upon a ready made development of the commandments about honoring parents and not committing adultery. Rather, when composing this parenesis with all its echoes of and interpretative applications of the Decalogue, he used this (partly pre-formulated?) code which was structured according to the role system of the "house". Thus, in the Col-context it came to fulfill the function of

---

36 Cf. H. Merklein, "Eph 4,1-5,20 als Rezeption von Kol 3,1-17 (zugleich ein Beitrag zur Problematik des Epheserbriefes)", in *Kontinuität und Einheit*, *Festschrift für Mussner*, Freiburg, 1981, 194-210.

37 Some modern authors are positive in finding the Decalogue in the background, see note 3, above.

38 Such a well informed author as Berger (*Gesetzesauslegung Jesu*) does not refer to any interpretation of that kind either.

applying parts of the Decalogue to God's elected and beloved people, in whom there was neither Greek nor Jew.[39]

I have argued above that the parenesis of 3:1-4:1 is not merely added to a "theological" part of the letter, but rather that Col as a whole has a more exhortatory character than is often realized. But the echoes of the Decalogue, of the Law in some sense of the word, is something also met with in Paul (Rom 13:8-10).[40] Our author had, however, not simply learned from his master that letters to Christian communities should have a parenesis. The phenomenon was not exclusively Pauline—in the NT 1 Pet, Jas and Heb follow a similar line. It is often held that most of the *material* that is parenetic in a form-critical sense has a non-Christian origin, viz. in Judaism and popular Philosophy.[41] Our deliberations above have not falsified that opinion. I would, however, suggest that the *practice* of admonishing one's addressees to hold on to the morals they had learnt is a tradition from Judaism. Thus, the Epistle of Baruch (2 *Bar* 78-86) is an example of a "letter" which should be read in the assemblies of the addressees (86), and in chapter 84 the author instructs them in different ways to keep faithfully to the Law. This invites us to conclude that the author of Col followed a convention not only when he concluded his letter with a parenesis, but also when he did so by using material that to such a large extent was interpretation and application of the Law, in this case, the Decalogue.[42]

It is now time to return to the questions I asked at the outset. Concerning the question of origin, it seems that we must reckon with a rather developed root-system behind both the household code of Col and the preceding parenesis. *Per se* the code and the other parenesis can have different roots. The tradition behind the preceding parenesis appears to have a Christian *Sitz* before its appearance in Col—the echoes of Jesus' teaching indicate this. But its interpretations of the Decalogue are ultimately inspired by Judaism. The list-form is widely used in Jewish as well as in other Hellenistic

---

[39] If Crouch *Origin and Intention*, 79, and Balch, *Wives Be Submissive*, 53, cite Schroeder's thesis correctly, the latter binds the code to the Decalogue in a way that is quite different from my approach.

[40] Cf. Stuhlmacher, *EvT* 28 (1968) 169-71.

[41] P. Vielhauer, *Geschichte der urchristlichen Literatur*, Berlin, New York, 1975, 53-55.

[42] See Stuhlmacher, *EvT* 28 (1968) 177-78.

circles.[43] On the one hand the household code is also to be related to the Decalogue, but indirectly, although its parallel in Eph explicitly quotes the fifth commandment in relation to a part of it. On the other hand, it regards people in their standard positions in society, i.e. in the "house". This thought pattern of the "house" organizes the code, but it is so general and natural in antiquity that one can hardly use it when asking more particularly for a milieu of origin. The manner of expression in the code reminds one of the so-called apodictic law, and indicates an OT-Jewish inspiration at the very bottom. But this does not necessarily mean that it was directly taken from there. On the contrary, the fact that the addressees have been "taught" (2:7) should indicate that the author makes use of traditions, though not necessarily very fixed ones, which were taught as being based on divine law and not human tradition (cf. 2:8, 22).

Does the presence of the "house" pattern tell us anything particular about the development of the Church, when seen generally? I doubt this—thinking in terms of the "house" was next to inevitable (cf. e.g., Matt 10:35)—and the connection with the Decalogue is only one more sign of the fact that in a way Gentile Christian churches were also Jewish-Christian.[44]

Most of that which has been said in the preceding paragraphs concerns the author's side of the letter's communication: his producing a text is allowed to testify about *his* ways of thinking and *his* background. But we should also ask for the function of the code and of its parenetic context within Col, and, as well, for their function in relationship to the addressees and their situation. As to the first question, I have already intimated an answer: the parenesis is there as a God-given contrast to the precepts advanced by this-worldly "philosophy", and it has been prepared for at least from 2:6 onwards (*peripateite*). The catalogues of vices and virtues in relation to one's fellowmen stand over against "humility", angelic service and visions (2:18, 23). The worship of 3:16 is different from the observance of feasts, new moon and sabbath (2:16), and the household code, in its

---

43 See E. Kamlah, *Die Form der katalogischen Paränese im NT*, WUNT 7, Tübingen, 1964, 2:III-IV.

44 H. Koester, "*Gnomai diaphoroi*. The Origin and Nature of Diversification in the History of Early Christianity", in *id*. and J. R. Robinson, *Trajectories through Early Christianity*, Philadelphia, 1971, 114-157, 115.

practical worldliness,[45] is quite different from "do not touch," etc., of 2:23.[46]

Scholars have suggested several solutions to the problem of the external function of the parenesis, and especially of the household code. I have mentioned some of them above. One such function is implied by the contrast to the "philosophical" rules I just pointed to. Are there also any attempts to temper some sort of emancipation on the part of women and slaves? There are no signs in the latter that the author was disturbed because the women of the Colossian community were caught up in the liberal tendencies of some circles. Also, if the sister church in Laodicea met in a house owned by a woman, Nympha, which is rather probable,[47] nothing in the text indicates that this circumstance called for any remarks. Thus, the Decalogue and "house" structures seem to be sufficient reasons for the wife-husband admonition, the contents of which seems to be what was rather normal in the sort of Jewish circles[48] that have been the original seedbed of both the Decalogue reinterpretation and the wisdom-Christology. But that which is said concerning slaves breaks the frames of style and proportion, as most commentators note. Already A. Deissmann assumed that this reflected the social structure of the church.[49] The situation of house slaves was not to be compared with slavery of more modern times,[50] but possibly the Christian view of masters and slaves as brethren in Christ can have caused problems.[51]

For the rest, even the circumstance that the whole parenesis seems to be making extensive use of traditional material can be

---

[45] Schweizer (*Brief an die Kolosser*) makes a lot of this "gute und nüchterne Weltlichkeit", 161.

[46] Of course I cannot pretend to know, any more than anyone else, what these rules of the "philosophy" actually aimed at.

[47] See the commentaries for a discussion of the MSS evidence and of the linguistic problem. I take 4:15 as saying "Nympha... in her house", regarding this to be the *lectio difficilior*.

[48] Philo, Josephus and Pseudo-Phocylides agree to a large extent in these matters of morality. See further Crouch, *Origin and Intention*, chaps. 5, 6.

[49] A. Deissmann, *Paul. A Study in Social and Religious History*, 2nd ed., London, 1926, 243.

[50] S. Scott Bartchy, *Mallon chrēsai: First Century Slavery and 1 Corinthians 7:21*, SBLDS 11, Missoula, 1973, chap. 2, and R. Gayer, *Die Stellung des Sklaven in der paulinischen Gemeinden und bei Paulus. Zugleich ein sozialgeschichtlich vergleichender Beitrag zur Wertung des Sklaven in der Antike*, Europ. Hochschulschr., 23:78, Bern, Frankfurt, 1976.

[51] See F. F. Bruce, *The Epistle to the Colossians, to Philemon, and to the Ephesians*, NICNT, Grand Rapids, 1984, *ad loc.*

regarded in two ways. On the one hand, being standard exhortations and having the Decalogue as a point of departure, the parenesis does not tell us very much about its particular external function. On the other hand, the very fact of its "standard" character might be a point: the "philosophy" seems to have claimed that the "standard" was not enough and that, instead, the perfect should stand in a good relationship also to other powers besides the Lord Jesus and hold to loftier and more particular rules than the standard ones. Against this the author has argued: the Lord Jesus was good enough, and so was the sort of life in him that they had learnt.

PART V

THE LOGIC OF PAULINE ETHICS
Indicative and Imperative

CHAPTER NINE

The Problem of Ethics in Paul[*]

Rudolf Bultmann
(1924)

In recent research on Paul, P. Wernle[1] pointed to the problem which emerges from Paul's statements which seem to be self-contradictory but appear side by side. Next to statements according to which the justified person is free from sin, no longer in the flesh but living in the Spirit, and has died to sin, are those statements which admonish the justified person to fight against sin (main references: Rom 6:1-7; 8:1-17; Gal 5:13-25; 1 Cor 6:9-11). The peculiarity of the problem becomes evident in that the different assertions - the indicatives and imperatives - are not only found in various passages of the letters, but rather are very closely tied together and form an antinomy,

---

[*] Translated by Christoph W. Stenschke.

[1] *Der Christ und die Sünde bei Paulus* [Freiburg im Breisgau: J.C.B. Mohr], 1897. [Material presented in parenthesis is not in the German original and is added for convenience according to the copies of the Universitätsbibliothek Gießen, the Fachbereichsbibliothek Evangelische Theologie in Marburg (Alte Aula) and Aberdeen's Queen Mother Library. The English rendering of Scripture is usually adapted from the NIV. The additional references given in section IV are intended to point the student to material not available everywhere.]

finding its paradoxical expression for instance in Galatians 5:25: εἰ ζῶμεν πνεύματι, πνεύματι καὶ στοιχῶμεν (Since we live by the Spirit, let us keep in step with the Spirit).

I.

It is a characteristic of all attempts to understand the problem[2] to take the *antinomy* as a *contradiction*, which may be explained by taking one side at a time by itself—the indicative as well as the imperative—and thus to explain it in a historical or psychological manner, tracing it back to special reasons and thereby understanding the contradiction as such historically and psychologically. It has not been considered whether we might rather be dealing here with a genuine antinomy, that is, with contradictory assertions which nevertheless belong together, developing from an undivided state of affairs and which therefore essentially belong together.

One is tempted to say that for Paul δικαιοσύνη (righteousness) means eschatological salvation (*Heilsgut*) and the δικαιωθείς (justified) is the new person of the era of salvation, for whom *this* world with its opportunities to act and to sin is no longer relevant. The indicatives therefore originate in Paul's eschatological consciousness. The imperatives would then be an inconsistency due to the fact, which does not fit well with an eschatological scheme, that δικαιοσύνη (righteousness), contrary to its intrinsic meaning, is ascribed to *the* person who still lives in the world. The imperatives are, on the other hand, necessary as a consequence of the notion of the will of a holy God, which is to determine a person's life in the world. Finally, they are necessary because of the practical occasions for paraenesis which the condition of the churches presented to Paul. With respect to the psychological understanding one may point to the eschatological tension in which Paul and the early Christian communities lived. We have in mind here the significance or the problems of the one justified living in this world which hardly became conscious to a person whose eyes were fixed on the consummation about to arrive shortly, a consummation which would

---

2 In addition to Wernle H. Windisch wrote a monograph on the topic: *Taufe und Sünde im ältesten Christentum bis auf Origenes [: Ein Beitrag zur altchristlichen Dogmengeschichte* (Tübingen: J.C.B. Mohr [P. Siebeck]), 1908]. Cf. in addition the numerous presentations of Pauline theology and of early Christian religion.

definitely devour all old conditions.[3] One may especially point to the conversion experience of Paul, whose radical break with the past makes it comprehensible that for him sin was swallowed up together with the old life. Finally, one may take into account the belief in sacraments, according to which the sinful quality of man is destroyed by baptism, and allow for a Christ-mysticism, in which the new life can be experienced as a present reality. All of this may indeed render the assertion that the justified is without sin to a large extent comprehensible. Of the material gathered above the first observation is not negotiable. It was not intended as a psychological explanation but simply as an objective interpretation, namely that δικαιοσύνη (righteousness) is the eschatological salvation.

However, this assertion is not justified by other considerations. In fact all of these suggestions are not satisfactory, as correct as they all are in a certain sense. They do not satisfy because the *meaning* of a theory is not comprehended simply by explaining its *origin*. They do not indicate what the sinless state of the Christian *means* for Paul. After all, it is clear that one misunderstands Paul if one interprets his statements historically and pschologically before having understood their sense. Proceeding in that fashion only leads to imputing a different sense to them than Paul intended. I would like to clarify my point by using the attempt of H. Weinel to give a psychological interpretation of the statements on sinlessness.[4] Weinel accounts for Paul's theory of sinlessness with reference to its foundation in the experience of God's grace. Having experienced God's grace an individual *cannot* but do the good; the good grows out of the one who is justified with the certainty of nature. The will of God is the good, namely, love. It is that which is man's very own and highest good. Moral life is for the justified only the necessary movement taken by the religiously filled inner life to become active in life.[5] The fact that the imperative must be interpreted as a relapse to legalistic religion[6] (*Gesetzesreligion*) surely raises suspicion, since it is apparent

---

3 Compared to this one may not emphasise too strongly that in Paul the perspective of the coming end also serves to motivate the moral appeal (e.g. Rom 13:11-14; 1 Thess 5:1-10). This usage, to be exact, contradicts the view that the eschatological tension serves to motivate the indicative and allows for the imperative to be forgotten. This inconsistency is acceptable.

4 *Biblische Theologie des Neuen Testaments [: Die Religion Jesu und des Urchristentums*, Grundriß der theologischen Wissenschaften III.2], 3. ed. [Tübingen: J.C.B. Mohr (P. Siebeck), 1921], pp. 316-21.

5 *Ibid.*, p. 370.

6 *Ibid.*, p. 322.

that for Paul imperative and indicative necessarily belong together (Rom 6, etc.; cf. the references given above). But it also is clear that Paul is not talking about the justified not being able to act differently. Rather, certain verses indicate that he clearly supposes that the justified can act differently (e.g., Rom 8:12: Gal 5:25). Above all it is clear that for Paul sinlessness does not consist in enthusiasm, the will and strength to accomplish the good. Rather, it is something negative, that is, freedom from the power of sin. Finally, for Paul the person who is justified exists in an eschatological dimension; the justified's existence is miraculous. He is not the person whose very own nature and highest aim can develop freely. Weinel thus has Paul say something completely different from what he is really saying. He does not take Paul's statements seriously, apparently because they seem to him to be absurd in their straightforward sense.

It appears to me that Wernle also offers further weight to the conviction that this way of interpretation is flawed, when he,[7] without detriment to psychological interpretation, bases the theory of sinlessness on the inner logic of the matter. After all, this is the intention when the theory of sinlessness is designated as "pure, unmasked insistence on doctrine." The theory is said to ensue from the doctrine of justification by faith: "If only faith saves and all believers are exempt from judgement, then the moral character of religion can only be preserved by postulating a fusion of justification and rebirth." Yet even this explanation is not possible because it presupposes that one could think of justification even though sin had not been abolished. But if justification were not primarily this liberation from sin, what meaning would it have for Paul? It can in no way be that justification concerns only the remission of sins committed prior to baptism, not having significance for the life of the justified following baptism. In that case its eschatological character— that justification is the ἔσχατον (last thing), the definitive event— would be misunderstood. Then indeed sinlessness would have to be declared merely a postulate so that now the imperative appears in direct contradiction to the indicative, so that next to the ethics of miracles there appears the ethics of the will.[8] It is exactly here that I perceive this interpretation's πρῶτον ψεῦδος (first falsehood), since Paul bases the imperative on the very *fact* of justification and *derives* the imperative from the indicative. *Because* the Christian is free from

---

7 *Der Christ und die Sünde bei Paulus*, p. 105.
8 *Ibid.*, p. 89.

sin through justification, he is now to fight against sin: εἰ ζῶμεν πνεύματι, πνεύματι καὶ στοιχῶμεν (Since we live by the Spirit, let us keep in step with the Spirit, Gal 5.25).

II.

If we want to comprehend this Pauline paradox, we have at the same time to draw attention to a second mistake of this manner of interpretation which has already been indicated. This mistake is also found in Wernle's description of the indicatives as an *ethic* of miracles. In truth, Paul's statements on the sinlessness of the justified do not deal with an ethic. All such attempts are unconsciously derived from a certain understanding of sin and of humanity, especially of justified humans, which is far from the understanding of Paul. Even if the latter appears absurd to us, nevertheless in the task of interpretation we have to take it seriously. For all such attempts at interpretation the sinlessness of man is only conceivable as an ethical capacity of man, as his psychological disposition; as the capacity, or rather the inclination to realise the good, to act perfectly. Only from this perspective can Paul's theory of sinlessness be described as "idealism striving heavenwards"[9] or "the formula of Paul's moral-idealistic optimism."[10] Only in this way does it become understandable why H.J. Holtzmann,[11] contrary to the statements of Paul, can speak of "the irreconcilable coexistence of a strictly supernatural mystical theory with an acute act of freeing from sin and an empirical-psychological conception in which sin's sudden destruction becomes a gradual vanishing." This also is the background for H. Lietzmann's more judicious opinion[12] that Paul must after all by himself have come to some kind of theory of development. This contradicts Paul's opinion that the δικαιοσύνη (righteousness) of the justified person consists of a δικαιοσύνη (ἐκ) θεοῦ (righteousness of God). Above all it contradicts Paul's view of the justified person, who completely stands on πίστις (faith). The

---

9   H.J. Holtzmann, *Lehrbuch der neutestamentlichen Theologie II*, [Sammlung theologischer Lehrbücher], 2. ed. [(Tübingen: J.C.B. Mohr [P. Siebeck], 1911)], II, p. 164.

10   H. Lietzmann [*Die Briefe des Apostels Paulus: Einführung in die Textgeschichte der Paulusbriefe. An die Römer*], Handbuch zum Neuen Testament 3.1, 2. ed. [Tübingen: J.C.B. Mohr (P. Siebeck), 1919], p. 66 on Rom 6:14.

11   *Lehrbuch der neutestamentlichen Theologie II*, pp. 166f.

12   *An die Römer*, p. 63 on Rom 6:4.

background of this conception, contrary to Paul's way of seeing man, is the understanding of man and his capacity to realise the good dominant in ancient as well as in modern rationalism and idealism. But it is clear that for Paul the notion of the good, whose idea determines action and which is to be realised through action, does not even exist. In consequence also his notion of the justified has nothing in common with that view of the ideal of humanity. This understanding has to reinterpret sinlessness as the ideal of humanity which has to be realised. However, for Paul righteousness, or rather, sinlessness, has an eschatological, miraculous character. It is the realised mode of existence of the justified. Although an imperative applies to this mode of existence, the command can by no means have the intention of realising this mode of existence. It is therefore a complete misunderstanding of the evidence, when Wernle, abandoning an earlier insight in his discussion of the book by Windisch, calls[13] sinlessness not a necessity but a possibility after conversion and affirms that the detailed indicatives are after all nothing but strengthened imperatives.

III.

Before attempting to understand the mode of existence of the justified according to Paul in a way that the imperative and also the whole paradox or antinomy becomes comprehensible, I would like to review another attempt to solve the problem in a different way. This attempt antedates the attempts referred to so far, but it far surpasses them in its depth of penetration into the problem. It is the view of F.C. Baur, which I will sketch according to his *Vorlesungen über neutestamentliche Theologie*.[14] Baur does not attempt to interpret the contradiction historically-psychologically by tracing back both of its sides to different motives. Instead, he tries to understand the contradiction as deriving from the very subject with which the doctrine of justification is concerned.[15]

According to Baur, justification is the absorption of a new principle into the will, namely the "principle of fulfilment of the law or of moral behaviour." If therefore Paul presents "the ethical

---

[13] In his review of the book by Windisch [cf. note 2], *Theologische Literatur-zeitung* 34, 1909: 588, [586-90].

[14] ed. F.F. Baur [Leipzig: Fues (L.W. Reisland)], 1864.

[15] *Ibid.*, pp. 174-82.

obligation concerning sin, namely, the obligation to die to sin as an actual death and thereby depicts it as a matter of inevitable necessity," the contradiction does not exist at all. By the indicative he describes the new principle which has been absorbed into the will. But we are dealing just with a principle of the will, which is as such characterised by the will. The believer really is δικαιωθείς (justified), because he is "in the πνεῦμα (spirit), as the principle working in him, he is actually and in truth placed in a relationship with God, which corresponds to the moral idea." The quantitative fulfilment of the law is now replaced by the qualitative; the disposition determines its value. Therefore, the person who is justified is in reality not the ἀσεβής (godless). The antithesis of πίστις (faith) and ἔργα (works) becomes a relative contrast, since already in Old Testament times ἔργα *could* have indeed emerged from a good disposition and on the other hand πίστις, as a living disposition, can naturally not be without ἔργα.

As appropriate as the formulation of the question is here, insofar as the antinomy is conceived as deriving from the essence of the matter, the answer is quite false when it is given in the sense of the idealistic conception of the nature of humanity. The clearer this answer is given, the clearer it becomes that here humanity is perceived in a completely different manner from Paul's perception, for whom man simply stands as a sinner before God and his justification does not lie in his disposition, his moral inclination. It is a failure to recognise the eschatological character of justification and that justification is God's miraculous act, his incomprehensible verdict. Here the second mistake, mentioned above,[16] is also present.

The study of the problem by A. Juncker follows similar lines.[17] It neither follows Baur dialectically nor is it apparently conscious of its consequences. Nevertheless I discuss it in this context with the others, trying to gradually gain through this critical approach the right perspective on the Pauline point of view. According to Juncker[18] justification is at the same time the moral renewal of man. The faith on which it rests is the decisive moral deed, which produces an immense number of other deeds, indeed a complete and uniform life. But if πίστις (faith) were indeed the decisive moral act (which is, after all, impossible according to Rom 10) the decision would indeed

---

16 [Cf. the beginning of section II.]
17 *Die Ethik des Apostels Paulus I* [(Halle a.S.: M. Niemeyer), 1904].
18 *Ibid.*, pp. 127 ff.

be handed over to humans; thus justification would rest on their act. Here humans are not radically conceived as sinners, since how could the *sinner* ever achieve πίστις, if this were the decisive act? It becomes evident from the exposition[19] that humans in Juncker's presentation factually redeem themselves. According to this exposition the human πνεῦμα (spirit) is akin to God and when a person acts in the strength of the divine πνεῦμα, he acts out of his own being, his "natural" predisposition. "God's Spirit weds the spirit of man and as the fruit of this intimate bond there is a completely new spiritual life."[20] All of this does not correspond at all to Paul's way of seeing man.

The much discussed issue,[21] whether Adam's fall can be traced back to a σάρξ (flesh), which was determined from the beginning and in its essence by ἀμαρτία (sin), or whether the σάρξ only became sinful flesh as a consequence of Adam's fall, thus whether— according to Juncker's expression—the connexion of σάρξ and ἀμαρτία is only of an empirical nature, having come into being within history, can serve to clarify the state of affairs. This controversial discussion is meaningless. It is without consequence for Paul's general view, with respect to which speculative thoughts he possibly might have had on this issue. For the Schoolmen as also for Luther the question of the *iustitia originalis* (original justice) was of fundamental significance, since through this issue the understanding of sin is determined. Is sin the privation of the *donum superadditum* (additional gift) or the *total corruptio* (corruption) of human nature? It is a matter of consequence for the understanding of redemption, whether is it somehow brought about by man or whether it totally rests on God's action. Paul does not consider the question of the original state of man in the light of this difficulty; for him the matter is simply thus: the man he considers is man determined by sin. Whether there once was a man (Adam) for whom this was not the case and for whom there were other possibilities of life, is—even if Paul should have pondered over this idea—a superfluous speculation, which asserts nothing for man as the object of justification. There is no other option for this man than the one of being a sinner. For this man a positive relationship with God does not exist in virtue of any natural endowment, but only in virtue of divine χάρις (grace). This emerges clearly from Paul's view of the

---

19 *Ibid.*, pp. 150 f.
20 *Ibid.*, p. 143.
21 *Ibid.*, pp. 42 ff.

significance of the Law in the history of salvation, since this significance really consists of bringing man to a position from which the impossibility of every other way to God, except for the way of χάρις, becomes evident (Rom 5:20f.; 7:7-25; Gal 3:19.22). There can therefore be no speculation when we are dealing with man, as he is and as he is justified.

Even Romans 7:14-25 should not deceive us in this matter, as if in this passage the ἔσω ἄνθρωπος (inner man) or the νοῦς (mind) designate a part of man not determined by sin. In verse 18: οἶδα γὰρ ὅτι οὐκ οἰκεῖ ἐν ἐμοί, τοῦτ᾽ ἔστιν ἐν τῇ σαρκί μου, ἀγαθόν (literally: But I know that there does not dwell in me, that is, in my flesh, anything good), the τοῦτ᾽ ἔστιν (that is) probably does not introduce an explanation, but rather a correction. Nevertheless the σάρξ and the ἔσω ἄνθρωπος are not two—in the same sense actual—powers in man; rather Paul wants to express as strongly as possible through inadequate dualistic terminology that man is *as a matter of fact* only determined by sin. The statements about the νοῦς and the ἔσω ἄνθρωπος express that sin is *sin*, not destiny or determination by nature, and that it is an inclusive part of man's being to be *claimed* by God. Romans 7:7ff. does not contain a confession of Paul or in general a description of the *psychical* state of unredeemed man, but a presentation of unredeemed man's objective existence, as it became visible from the perspective of redeemed man.[22] Thus one can paradoxically say: the ἔσω ἄνθρωπος is something which *is* not, in the sense in which σάρξ (flesh) and ἁμαρτία (sin) are, a reality for man.

IV.

Let us try now to understand the antinomy—the juxtaposition of indicative and imperative—as deriving from the very subject with which it is concerned. Or to put it in a different way: to understand the phenomenon of the δικαιωθείς (justified). It will bring greater clarity to take yet another detour, namely, to point to analogous phenomena, first of all with respect to a characteristic phenomenon in stoic ethics, a concept which is close to Bauer's view on this question.[23]

---

22 Cf. W. Heitmüller ["Die Bekehrung des Paulus"], *Zeitschrift für Theologie und Kirche* 27, 1917: 139f., [136-53].
23 [As presented by Bultmann in the first two paragraphs of section III.]

As Paul contrasts the ἁμαρτωλός (sinner) and the δίκαιος (righteous), so the φαῦλος (mean, bad) and the σοφός (wise), or rather the τέλειος (perfect, accomplished), are contrasted in the Stoa. It is indeed a radical contrast: whereas the φαῦλος has nothing of virtue, the τέλειος has all of it. Virtue is considered indivisible. The one who has *one* virtue consequently has all of it. There is no development, no transition from φαῦλος to τέλειος. It is well known that the stoicism of the intermediate period lessened this radicalism, insofar as it inserted the idea of προκόπτων (moral and intellectual progress[24]) between the notions of φαῦλος and τέλειος. The προκόπτων is the man moving towards τελειότης (completeness, perfection); he is neither φαῦλος nor τέλειος, or to express it better: he is both, yet in a way that his being is determined by the τελειότης. The τελειότης is therefore beyond the προκόπτων, and this position is the position of the idea; man's relation to it is a relation of infinite progress. Now apparently contradictory statements—indicatives and imperatives—can be made regarding the προκόπτων in the same sense as they characterise the existence of the δικαιωθείς (justified) in Baur's understanding.

The phenomenon of the προκόπτων apparently offers a formal analogy to the phenomenon of the δικαιωθείς in Paul, but it only is a formal analogy. However, it can open our eyes to the peculiarity of the Pauline perception. For (leaving other matters aside for the moment) the τελειότης does *not* correspond to δικαιοσύνη (righteousness), because the former describes a universal standard of human conduct, while the notion of δικαιοσύνη is not defined by the idea of a general norm of human conduct, but rather it characterises the position of the concrete, individual human being before God. The aim or rather the content of salvation, to be δίκαιος (righteous), does not mean that one has realised an ideal of human behaviour, but rather it means to be rid of one's whole concrete sin before God. The foundation of this view is a totally non-rational view of the being of man, which does not reckon with an idea of man, but with concrete, individual men.

But right from the outset we might also expect that essential analogies to Paul's view lie within the sphere of history of religions, and specifically in those instances where the believer intends to lay hold of salvation which is on the other side, which always is an ἔσχατον (last thing) in the present time. Thus we are speaking of

---

[24] [The English translations here follow H.G. Liddell, R. Scott, H.S. Jones, *A Greek-English Lexicon*, 9. ed. (Oxford: Clarendon, 1968).]

instances in which a difficulty arises from the fact of the continuance of earthly life and which thus corresponds in one way or another to the Pauline difficulty. For more than one reason the comparison with hellenistic mystery religions and hellenistic mysticism suggests itself for Paul, and indeed this analogy is able to bring us even closer to Paul's understanding.

The antithesis of those who are not born again and those who are born again corresponds in the hellenistic sphere—with which we are presently dealing—to the antithesis of the ἁμαρτωλός (sinner) and the δίκαιος. I may use this terminology for the sake of brevity because it suits the subject matter, even though its usage is limited. The condition of the born again is strangely contradictory because it is not what it *seems* to be, because its reality does not *appear*. This contradiction of the other-worldly nature of the born again and its empirical existence is for instance expressed in Hermetic writings:

ὁρῶν (ποτε) ἐν ἐμοὶ ἄπλαστον θέαν γεγενημένην ἐξ ἐλέου θεοῦ καὶ ἐμαυτὸν (δι)εξελήλυθα εἰς ἀθάνατον σῶμα, καί εἰμι νῦν οὐχ ὁ πρίν, ἀλλ᾽ ἐγεννήθην ἐν νῷ (τὸ πρᾶγμα τοῦτο οὐ διδάσκεται οὐδὲ τῷ πλαστῷ τούτῳ στοιχείῳ, δι᾽ οὗ (ὁρᾷς), ἔστιν ἰδεῖν.) καὶ διαμεμέλισταί μοι τὸ πρῶτον σύνθετον εἶδος. οὐκέτι κέχρωσμαι καὶ ἁφὴν ἔχω καὶ μέτρον, ἀλλότριος δὲ τούτων εἰμὶ νῦν. ὁρᾷς με, ὦ τέκνον, ὀφθαλμοῖς, ὅ τι δέ (εἰμι, οὐ) κατανοεῖς ἀτενίζων σώματι καὶ ὁράσει· οὐκ ὀφθαλμοῖς τούτοις θεωρῦμαι νῦν, ὦ τέκνον.[25]

([I have nothing to tell except this]: seeing within me an unfabricated vision that came from the mercy of God, I went out of myself into an immortal body, and now I am not what I was before. I have been born in mind. This thing cannot be taught, nor can it be seen through any elementary fabrication that we use here below. Therefore the initial form even of my own constitution is of no concern. Colour, touch or size I no longer have, I am a stranger to them. Now you see me with your eyes, my child, but by gazing with bodily sight you do

---

[25] *Corpus Hermeticum* [= Hermes Trismegistus, *Poimandres*] XIII.3, quoted according to R. Reitzenstein, *Poimandres[: Studien zur griechisch-ägyptischen frühchristlichen Literatur* (Leipzig: B.G. Teubner, 1904; repr. Darmstadt: Wissenschaftliche Buchgesellschaft, 1966)], p. 340.

<not> understand what <I am>; I am not seen with such eyes,
my child.[26])

This view is also the basis of the account in the apocryphal *Acts of
John* of the countenance of John.[27] Standing in front of his portrait the
apostle declares: "The picture resembles me, child, but is not like me,
only like the image of my body."[28] The true countenance of the
apostle would need to be painted with different colours: πίστις
(faith), γνῶσις (knowledge), etc., thus with the attributes which
constitute the other-worldly nature of the one born again.

The world beyond, with which we are dealing here, is not that
of an idea whose realisation lies in the future; the world beyond is
really present now. It is thought of as natural and substantive and
finds its characteristic expression in the consistently perceived idea of
a heavenly or pneumatic body. The relation of man to this life
beyond is that of participation. Something within him derives from
the world beyond, from the world of light, be it—depending which
mythological or cultic tradition determines the shape of thought—as
a particle of light which is from the beginning onwards and
originally sunk into matter, or be it due to a transformation or
infusion, brought about by sacrament or ecstasy. And this something
in man now constitutes the essential nature of the born again. But this
something has no substantial correlation with empirical man, his
action and his fate. This fundamental view finds expression in many
different forms, above all in statements that holy initiation or γνῶσις

---

26 [The English translation is taken from B.P. Copenhaver, *Hermetica: The Greek
Corpus Hermeticum and the Latin Asclepius in a new English translation, with notes
and introduction* (Cambridge: CUP, 1992), pp. 49-50. Also compare Copenhaver's
excellent notes, discussion and bibliographical references to the passage cited on
pp. 180-86; J. Büchli, *Der Poimandres: Ein paganisiertes Evangelium*, WUNT II.27
(Tübingen: J.C.B. Mohr (P. Siebeck, 1987, there survey of research pp. 1-7 (the
study only covers the first tractate); R. P. Festugière, *La Révélation d'Hermès
Trismégiste: IV Le Dieu Inconnu et la Gnose* (Paris: Lecoffre/ J. Gabalda, 1954), pp.
200-57: (Analyse de C.H. XIII, Les thèmes de la régénération) and *Hermetica . . . II:
Notes on the Corpus Hermeticum*, ed. W. Scott (Oxford: Clarendon, 1925), pp. 380-
81]

27 Chapters 26-29, [quote from c. 28].

28 [The English translation is taken from J.K. Elliot, *The Apocryphal New
Testament: A Collection of Apocryphal Christian Literature in an English Translation*
(Oxford: Clarendon, 1993), p. 314. A concise introduction to the work is there
provided on p. 303-11; cf. also K. Schäferdiek, "The Acts of John", *New Testament
Apocrypha II: Writings Relating to the Apostles, Apocalypses and Related Subjects*, ed.
W. Schneemelcher, R. McL. Wilson (Cambridge: J. Clarke, 1992), pp. 175-76 (152-
209)]

(knowledge) liberates from εἱμαρμένη (fate). Thus the initiate of Isis says:[29]

> Eat nunc (Fortuna) et summo furore saeviat et crudelitati suae materiam quaerat aliam, nam in eos, quorum sibi vitas in servitium deae nostrae maiestas vindicavit, non habet locum casus infestus ... videant irreligiosi, videant et errorem suum recognoscant : en ecce pristinis aerumnis Isidis magnae providentia gaudens Lucius de sua fortuna triumphat.

> (Let [Fortune] rage in all her fury and hunt some other object for her cruelty, for hostile chance has no opportunity against those whose lives the majesty of our goddess has emancipated into her own servitude. . . . Let the unbelievers see; let them see and recognise their errant ways. Behold! Lucius, set free from his tribulations of old and rejoicing in the providence of great Isis, triumphs over his Fortune.[30])

The same can be said of the γνῶσις (knowledge):[31]

> εὑρήσεις ὅτι ἀληθῶς πάντων ἐπικρατεῖ ὁ νοῦς, ἡ τοῦ θεοῦ ψυχή, καὶ εἱμαρμένης καὶ νόμου καὶ τῶν ἄλλων πάντων· καὶ οὐδὲν αὐτῷ ἀδύνατον, οὔτε εἱμαρμένης ὑπεράνω θεῖναι ψυχὴν ἀνθρωπίνην οὔτε ἀμελήσασαν, ὅπερ συμβαίνει, ὑπὸ τὴν εἱμαρμένην θεῖναι.

> (. . . you will find that mind, the soul of god, truly prevails over all, over fate and law and all else. And nothing is impossible for mind, neither setting a human soul above fate nor, if it happens that a soul is careless, setting it beneath fate.[32])

The hermetic teaching handed down to us by Zosimos is particularly characteristic of this:

---

29 Lucius Apuleius, *Metamorphoses* XI.15.

30 [The English translation is taken from Apuleius, *Metamorphoses Books VII-XI*, ed. and transl. J.A. Hanson, The Loeb Classical Library 453 (London: Harvard UP, 1989), p. 321. Cf. also the discussions of the passage in J.K. Krabbe, *The Metamorphoses of Apuleius*, American University Studies, Series XVII. Vol. 9 (New York, Bern: P. Lang, 1989), Index, p. 217]

31 *Corpus Hermeticum* XII.9.

32 [The English translation again is taken from B.P. Copenhaver, *Hermetica*, p. 45, discussion etc. on pp. 176-77 and *Hermetica . . . II*, p. 350.]

ὅτι οὐ δεῖ τὸν πνευματικὸν ἄνθρωπον τὸν ἐπιγνόντα ἑαυτὸν οὔτε
διὰ μαγείας κατορθοῦν τι, ἐὰν καὶ καλὸν νομίζηται, μήτε
βιάζεσθαι τὴν Ἀνάγκην, ἀλλ' ἐὰν ὡς ἔχει φύσεως καὶ κρίσεως.
πορεύεσθαι δὲ διὰ μόνου τοῦ ζητεῖν ἑαυτὸν καὶ θεὸν ἐπιγνόντα
κρατεῖν τὴν ἀκατονόμαστον τριάδα, καὶ ἐὰν τὴν εἱμαρμένην ὅ
θέλει ποιεῖν τῷ ἑαυτῆς πηλῷ, τουτέστι τῷ σώματι.[33]

(. . . because it is not right that a spiritual man who
understands himself either succeeds in anything through the
use of magic, even if it is thought to be something honourable
or should do force to necessity, but let things be as they are by
nature or the (course of) events. But he ought to live only to
seek for himself, to understand god and to conquer the
nameless triad and should allow destiny to do what it wants
to its own clay, that is to say the body.[34])

The concrete existence of man is so to speak no longer of
relevance. It is no longer of concern for the man who is born again,

---

[33] R. Reitzenstein, *Poimandres*, p. 103. R. Reitzenstein, *Die hellenistischen
Mysterienreligionen [nach ihren Grundgedanken und Wirkungen*, 3. ed. (Leipzig: B.G.
Teubner, 1927)], p. 301. [Discussion of the passage, pp. 300-02. Bultmann quotes
from the 2. ed., which was inaccessible to me, where it is on p. 152; he points to
further information there on pp. 151-56. The full Greek work of Zosimos
(Alchemista Panopolitanus) was edited by M. Berthelot, *Collection des anciens
Alchimistes grecs* (Paris: G. Steinheil, 1888), II, pp. 107-252, to whom Reitzenstein
refers. The quote comes from a treatise called *On Instruments and Furnaces:
Genuine Notes on the letter Omega* 4, (f. 190 r.) on p. 230, lines 2-8. This text of
Zosimos is also printed in *Hermetica . . . IV* (1936), ed. A.S Ferguson, pp. 104-112,
quote from pp. 105-06]. For gnostic material see G. Anrich, *Das antike
Mysterienwesen [in seinem Einfluß anf das Christentum* (Göttingen: Vandenhoeck &
Ruprecht, 1894)], pp. 90-92.

[34] [Translation C.S. I gratefully acknowledge the advice of Mr T.E.V. Pearce of
Aberdeen. I would like to add M. Berthelot's translation: ". . . que l'homme
spirituel, celui qui se connaît lui-même, ne réussit en rien par la magie, et ne
regarde pas comme convenable de violenter la nécessité. Mais il laisse aller (les
choses), telles qu'elles vont de nature et d'autorité. Il a pour seul object de se
chercher lui-même, de connaître Dieu, de dominer la triade innommable. Il laisse
la destinée faire ce qu'elle veut, en la laissant agir sur le limon terrestre, c'est-à-
dire sur le corps.", *Alchimistes grecs*, III, pp. 222-23. My translation differs by
taking the passive form of νομίζηται more seriously and not giving it an active
meaning, since there are no examples of active intention of the passive form in
LSJ, p. 1179. All of Zosimos' Greek writings are translated into French in
Berthelot's third volume, pp. 117-242. A French translation of the Corpus
Hermeticum was procured by A.-J. Festugière, *Corpus Hermeticum I-II*, Collection
des Universités de France: Association Guillaume Budé (Paris: Les Belles Lettres,
1945).]

the pneumatic. It is ignored. Not only libertinism but also asceticism can be the practical consequence. Thus the born again person is in essence not the concrete man, but is rather a certain something within him. The continuity of the born again person with the old man is torn to pieces and thus the born again has lost every trace of his own true character. The life beyond, which he can experience—for example in ecstasy—is the universal "life," just as in ecstasy all individual existence is wiped out. Here *forgiveness* of sin is out of the question, since forgiveness of sin is not something universal such as "life." Rather it would mean that the notion of the life beyond is determined by its reference to the concrete, individual person, whose sin is forgiven.

V.

Even though this already points to a dissimilarity to Paul, it is for the present moment still necessary to see the *extensive affinity between Paul and hellenistic mysticism*. It is not only that in Paul the content of salvation can also be designated as "life," which in itself might only imply an influence in terminology, but also that justification is for Paul established on a sacramental act, which is baptism. The πνεῦμα (spirit), which is bestowed through baptism, is for Paul also conceived of as a supernatural power, considered as having substance, which dwells as a certain something in man (cf. Rom 5:5; 8:11,16; 1 Cor 2:10-16). Furthermore, the σάρξ-πνεῦμα (flesh-spirit) view of Paul shows the character of metaphysical dualism, which is a characteristic of the hellenistic mystery religions. That is to say that σάρξ and πνεῦμα are conceived as powers having substance. This especially becomes evident in the teaching of the resurrection with its idea of the σῶμα πνευματικόν (spiritual body). 1 Corinthians 14 and 2 Corinthians 12:1-4 definitely (and probably also Rom 8:15, 26 and Gal 4:6) show that Paul is aquainted with the experience of the life beyond in ecstasy. It is clear that in Paul's case we must speak of a specifically mystical ecstasy, which has to be distinguished from prophetic ecstasy (naturally not as a psychical process but rather in its significance). For the prophet ecstasy is the means for his vocation (likewise in primitive religions for the shaman), that is to say in ecstasy God's word falls to his share which he is to proclaim, just as in primitive religions ecstasy is the means of attaining or enhancing magical power, for instance for the purpose of prediction. By contrast, for the mystic ecstasy is an end in itself. The words he hears in ecstasy are destined for him alone; for others they are ἄρρητα ῥήματα (inexpressible words), as Paul himself says (1 Cor 12:4). Finally, the ascetical motives, which derive from this dualism and from the mystical concept of the life beyond, are indisputably present in Paul. They are clearly seen in the motivation of the warning against fornication (1 Cor 6:12-20) as well as—in combination with other motives—in Paul's treatment of marriage in 1 Corinthians 7.

From these observations it now becomes possible to gain an understanding of that antinomy, namely the proximity of the indicative and imperative, which could claim to grasp the antinomy as deriving from the essence of the matter: other-worldly salvation is a present reality for the mystic, thus obviously indicatives can be used when speaking of the possession of salvation. To these the imperatives are not really incompatible, they rather demonstrate that the empirical, concrete man is to be erased. Should one wish to speak of a contradiction then it is situated in the basic conception of mystical piety.

With regard to this point of view it is not even necessary to become disturbed by the observation that Paul uses as characteristic designations for salvation the completely unmystical words δικαιοσύνη (righteousness) and δικαιωθῆναι (being justified) since they also appear occasionally in hellenistic mysticism[35] and perhaps are also in Paul occasionally conceived of mystically (Rom 6:7?; 8:30?; 1 Cor 1:30?; 6:11).[36] It is more problematic, however, that the onset of asceticism, which is the characteristic expression of that erasure of concrete man in mysticism, is so slightly developed in Paul. But even irrespective of that, this hypothetical construction cannot be maintained.

VI.

Now the fundamental difference of the Pauline view from analogous phenomena cannot be overlooked, and this difference has already been indicated. For Paul, justification, the deliverance from sin, is the nature of salvation situated beyond. This quality of lying beyond is neither the idea as it is in Stoicism, nor is it the life beyond of the

---

35 *Corpus Hermeticum* XIII.9.

36 Compare R. Reitzenstein, *Hellenistische Mysterienreligionen*, 2. ed., pp. 112-116. [3. ed, pp. 257-62.]

superior-nature as in hellenistic mysticism. Rather it has the character of coming to pass, of occurrence. It is established through God's action. It consists in God's verdict. That lines up with the fact that for Paul God is not a metaphysical substance which can be described by its attributes, as for instance described as φῶς, ζωή, ἀφθαρσία (light, life, imperishableness) in the hellenistic sphere. On the contrary God is the active will. When Paul proclaims the χάρις (grace) of God, he does not proclaim an attribute of God, which hitherto has not been recognized or appreciated. He does not present a new refined idea of God. On the contrary he speaks of God's new act of salvation. This means that for Paul the notion of the life beyond is determined by its reference to individual, concrete man. This is of course not intended in the sense of a modern individualism, since Paul is speaking exactly of mankind as a whole.[37] But exactly this thought of mankind is for Paul not determined by the idea of men generally. On the contrary, it is determined by the notion of individual, concrete men, *with whom God is dealing*; and only so far as God is *dealing* with men, one may (in Paul's sense) speak of God. Accordingly *man's relation to the life beyond* is neither the relation of infinite progress nor the relation of participation, but rather it is characterized by πίστις (faith). Πίστις is, however, man's obedience to God's act of salvation, renouncing any pretension to being capable of establishing the relationship with God on his own. It is the conviction that only through God's verdict is man considered justified.[38] Thus righteousness or sinlessness is—highly paradoxically—not a transformation of man's moral quality. It is neither something perceptible in man nor something he can experience in the sense of mysticism. Therefore it can only be believed.[39] Paul certainly knows ecstasy, but it is an exceptional

---

[37] Obviously without employing the abstract word "mankind."

[38] The various shades in the usage of the concept of πίστις are not relevant here. In my opinion they are mainly occasioned by Paul following the usage of hellenistic-Christian churches and of Christian propaganda.

[39] The old controversial issue, whether the δικαιωθείς is only *considered* righteous by God or whether he also *is* righteous, is to be dismissed. For Paul's understanding it is obvious that the man is righteous who is considered righteous by God. Cf. in particular Rom 5:19: ὥσπερ γὰρ διὰ τῆς παρακοῆς τοῦ ἑνὸς ἀνθρώπου ἁμαρτωλοὶ κατεστάθησαν οἱ πολλοί, οὕτως καὶ διὰ τῆς ὑπακοῆς τοῦ ἑνὸς δίκαιοι κατασταθήσονται οἱ πολλοί (For just as through the disobedience of the one man the many were made sinners, so also through the obedience of the one man the many will be made righteous). Just as sinners in Adam's sequence really *are* sinners, and not only are *considered* as such, so the δίκαιοι (righteous) *are* truly δίκαιοι. Also cf. 2 Cor 5:21. That controversial issue resulted only from an

charisma for Paul, not the normal Christian form of life (cf. 1 Cor 12-14).

We may, if we extend the lines of that which Paul directly affirms, even say: even sin is not something perceptible in empirical man, but it only exists inasmuch as man is seen from God's perspective. It is therefore not *identical* with moral shortcomings, as certain as sin might display itself in these. It only becomes perceptible the moment it is forgiven, that is, from the Christian viewpoint. This follows from the proper interpretation of Romans 7:7-25, which describes the condition of unredeemed man in the manner in which it is subsequently seen by redeemed man. It also follows from the fact that according to Paul the law thereby prepared mankind for χάρις (grace) in that it leads to sin. If man only has a positive relationship with God, when he knows God's χάρις, that is to say when he knows himself to be a sinner, then it follows that man can only understand himself in a real sense as a sinner before God when he knows of God's grace. Thus it will be in accordance with the fundamental notion of Paul's doctrine of justification to say that sin is not something empirically perceptible. The identity of justified and empirical man is *believed.*

Since it is concrete, empirical man (who from God's perspective is a sinner) who becomes justified, whose sin is forgiven, the relation of the justified to the life beyond does *not exist apart from or beside* his concrete conduct and destiny. He, the concrete man, who is the actor and the sufferer, is indeed the justified man, and his conduct and destiny have now acquired—viewed from God's perspective, the perspective of faith—a new sense. Here the dissimilarity from hellenistic mysticism becomes particularly evident. It is most prominent in the statements of 2 Corinthians 4:7-11. Not only is Paul's empirical fate of no importance; it serves the end: ἵνα καὶ ἡ ζωὴ τοῦ Ἰησοῦ ἐν τῷ σώματι ἡμῶν φανερωθῇ (so that the life of Jesus may be revealed in our mortal body, 2 Cor 4:11). To speak here of a Christ-*mysticism* seems to me to be entirely wrong. After all, it is this concrete fate itself, in which—for the perspective of faith—the "life of Jesus" beyond manifests itself, and not the *emotions* of the person suffering. That is precisely the case for the perspective of faith, in

---

idealistic interpretation of the δικαιοσύνη as the ethical constitution or attitude of man. I pointed out above that this is incorrect. In this ethical sense the δικαιωθείς obviously *is* not righteous, but in this sense he is not at all considered by God as righteous.

paradoxical revaluation, since experiences of whatever kind, which as such mediate powers beyond, are out of the question.

But the same viewpoint is also expressed in the statements which speak of the σῶμα (body) (and its members) as being in God's service (cf. Rom 6:12-19; 12:1; 1 Cor 6:19). These passages do not prove "that the apostle also considered the sensual-material organisation of man as fully accessible to pneumatic influence", and that therefore the connection between σάρξ and ἁμαρτία (flesh and sin) is only of empirical nature, as Juncker believes it to be.[40] Because all these passages have as their subject precisely the justified person, whose sinful life has been put to death, what they express can therefore only be said of the justified person. But these passages do prove that the justified is the entire concrete man and that his empirical existence, that is, his actions, are also influenced by justification. Thus the *continuity* of the old and the new man is not broken, as it is in hellenistic mysticism. The δικαιωθείς (justified man) is the concrete man, who bears the burden of his past, present and future, who is therefore also subject to the moral imperative. Thus this imperative does not become void, it only gains the new intention of *obedience* to God.

The moral activity of the new man can of course no longer carry the meaning of "works." That is to say, it can neither aspire to establish man's relation to the life beyond, nor aspire to realise righteousness, since this righteousness has already been realised. The moral activity can only carry the intention of obedience: the *entire* man understands himself as standing before God and, as far as he acts, he places himself at God's disposal (Rom 6:13: παραστήσατε ἑαυτοὺς τῷ θεῷ [offer yourselves to God]). But just as he does not witness in his fate special experiences and adventures, which *as such* could not also be witnessed by the unbeliever (only for faith they have a new meaning), so in his obedience nothing *extraordinary* is required of him, which would not also be required of others. For the believer the moral demand has *not* acquired a *new content* and his moral conduct is only distinguishable from the conduct of others in that it carries the character of obedience.[41] The demands placed on the justified person consist only of what is good, pleasing and perfect, what may be included among virtue and praiseworthy things

---

40 *Die Ethik des Paulus I*, p. 46.

41 Irrespective of the ascetic motives mentioned earlier. Here my concern is only with the fundamental notion.

(Rom 12:2; Phil 4:8). The moral commandments of the Old Testament carry the same weight as the catalogues of virtue and vice of the paraenetic tradition of hellenistic Judaism. Paul explicitly declares that one must say yes to the demands of the law (Rom 7:12,14) and that the conduct of the justified is the fulfilment of the law (Rom 13:8-10; Gal 5:14). Therefore, just as a new moral ideal cannot be derived from the δικαιοσύνη (righteousness) (or from faith), so one cannot claim, at least as a negative consequence, that the cessation of the ceremonial demands of the law follows from the δικαιοσύνη ἐκ πίστεως (righteousness by faith). From this righteousness it only follows that they are no longer to be fulfilled as "works." Paul pronounced from the viewpoint of πίστις concerning circumcision: οὐδὲν ἰσχύει, οὐδέν ἐστιν (it has no value, it means nothing) (Gal 5:6; 6:15; 1 Cor 7:19). That is to say, the ceremonial demands in themselves are irrelevant. Paul opposes them as "works." Once they are set aside as works, obviously they also have to fall in all areas, where they no longer are sensible as proceeding out of man's concrete situation, as demands that are aimed at him. Their cessation then does not follow from a specific moral ideal, binding for the justified, but rather follows simply from commonly accessible moral discernment.

But if it can be said of the justified that he places his σῶμα (body) at God's disposal, and that precisely this act has consequences for his moral conduct, must we then after all not conclude that the δικαιωθείς (justified) is distinct from the unbeliever in a commonly perceptible manner? Is not Paul after all also of the opinion that the life of believers is clearly set off against their former mode of life and against the mode of life of the pagan surroundings (cf. Rom 6:12-23; 1 Cor 6:9-11; Phil 2:15)? Above all does he not know of the πνεῦμα (spirit), with which the believer is endowed, as the power of a new moral mode of life (cf. Rom 8:4-14; Gal 5:16-25; etc.)? However, it would be a mistake to think that the peculiar character of the δικαιωθείς can be recognized by his moral behaviour. Because the deciding factor, the δικαιοσύνη (righteousness) accomplished only in God's verdict, cannot be perceived—except by the eyes of faith (just as also the existence of the unbeliever—as determined by sin—is only perceived by faith). No doubt the new mode of life *as such* obviously is commonly perceptible, as it also is self-evident that for the person whose activity truly occurs in obedience to God. The gravity of the moral demands as of God's law become alive in a new way and therefore the mode of life is indeed a new mode of life. But the decisive moment lies in the fact that all of man's moral perfection can be of no significance without this decisive verdict of God. Δικαιοσύνη rests only on this and never on the moral activity. Righteousness is therefore never commonly perceptible, since the moral mode of life as such could also be existent without it. Indeed under certain circumstances the heathen also do τὰ τοῦ νόμου (things required by the law) (Rom 2:14). Thus without the decisive divine verdict even the best moral mode of life would be of no significance. Thus it is not commonly perceptible whether or not this mode of life truly displays the character of obedience.

This insight may also be formulated to say that the believer never ceases to be ἀσεβής (wicked), and is always only justified as a ἀσεβής, even if we may not with certainty deduce this conclusion from Romans 4:5: τῷ δὲ μὴ ἐργαζομένῳ, πιστεύοντι δὲ ἐπὶ τὸν δικαιοῦντα τὸν ἀσεβῆ, λογίζεται ἡ πίστις αὐτοῦ εἰς δικαιοσύνην (to the man who does not work but trusts God who justifies the wicked, his faith is credited as righteousness). Of course we have to add that Paul never brought this thought to a conclusion. The terms πίστις and πιστεύειν (faith and believe) for Paul (due to the influence of the traditional terminology of mission) almost always retain something of the meaning of the first-time confession, of becoming a believer, even if this meaning of πίστις (πιστεύειν) entirely recedes in the antithesis to the ἔργα (ἐργάζεσθαι) (works, working). Since Paul expects the end of the present aeon to arrive soon, the life of the believer in this world for him never became a problem to the same extent as it was for Luther. Paul never mentions the fact that faith daily cancels sins. Neither does he speak of daily penitence and ever new forgiveness. However, even Wernle also says when he wishes to understand Paul's proclamation in its historical limitation as a missionary theology: "If Paul had carried out this view (namely, the doctrine of justification apart from works and by grace alone), his theology would have been infinitely closer to . . . reformed theology; for how can a man, who has estimated himself in such a way before God, ever cease to feel as a sinner in need of grace."[42] However, I do believe exactly this to be the most important task of interpretation, not to demonstrate how a particular concept is limited in its scope by the historical situation, but to develop the concept in its consequences

---

[42] *Der Christ und die Sünde bei Paulus*, p. 96.

and to thus make its peculiarity fully known.[43] But then it must be stated: If we take the notion seriously that man can only stand justified before God in virtue of χάρις (grace), then man also is *always* as ἀσεβής (a wicked one) a justified person; otherwise God's χάρις would indeed no longer have for him its meaning as χάρις.

If, however, the whole existence of the justified person is determined by χάρις, so also the imperative, addressed to him, must be determined likewise. Because being addressed by an imperative also belongs to the mode of existence of the justified. The believer can only understand this mode of existence as God's gift. Just as the moral demand—expressed by the imperative—is God's command for him, so the attitude of obedience—corresponding to that demand—is at the same time God's gift, brought about by the πνεῦμα (spirit), so that the demand does not lose its character as an imperative. Thus the paradox is fully understandable for faith: εἰ ζῶμεν πνεύματι, πνεύματι καὶ στοιχῶμεν (Since we live by the Spirit, let us keep in step with the Spirit, Gal 5:25).

---

[43] I am obviously not assuming to have grasped the whole of Paul as a historical figure with this attempt to understand a specific section of Paul's world of perception. My statements are not directed against W. Heitmüller's thesis "that in some respects Paul is not in the same way the father of the Reformation as he much more is the father of the old and medieval church" (*Luthers Stellung in der Religionsgeschichte des Christentums[: Rede zur 400 jährigen Reformationsfeier der Philipps-Universität*, Marburger akademische Reden 38 (Marburg: N.G. Elwert], 1917, p. 21). I only would like to emphasise "in some respects" and believe Luther's inner affinity to Paul to be much higher than it appears in Heitmüller's estimate. I also do not share the view, as far as I know first advocated by W. Wrede, that the doctrine of justification for Paul was only of apologetic-polemical significance in his practical work as a missionary. On the contrary I believe it to be in the very centre of his convictions. But here my only concern was to understand the meaning of this doctrine, for which it is indeed irrelevant, which practical circumstances occasioned Paul to develop these thoughts.

CHAPTER TEN

Being Precedes Act
Indicative and Imperative in Paul's Writing

Michael Parsons
(1988)

The relationship between the indicative and the imperative in Paul's writing is sometimes and understandably seen as the basic structure of his ethics.[1] By 'indicative' we have in mind the fact that the new life in Christ is a work of God; it finds its origin in the death and resurrection of the Lord and comes into being through the work of the Holy Spirit. The believer is thus a new creation; a member of Christ; a temple of the Holy Spirit; he is regenerated, and so on. By 'imperative' we mean that the apostle also indicates that the new life thus given is to be continually manifested and worked out by the Christian Believer. T. J. Keegan[2] suggests too much in expressing the

---

[1] See, for example, W. Dennison, 'Indicative and Imperative: The Basic Structure of Pauline Ethics' *CTJ* (1979), 1. 55-78, particularly 73; R. Bultmann, *Theology of the New Testament*, 1 (ET, London, 1955), 315-332; A. Verhey, *The Great Reversal: Ethics and the New Testament* (Grand Rapids, 1984), 104-106.

[2] T. J. Keegan, 'Paul's Dying/Rising Ethics in 1 Corinthians' in L. J. Daly (ed.) *Christian Biblical Ethics* (New York, 1984), 220-244, particularly 228.

relationship as 'a tension-producing opposition'; yet it is true that there is inherent in the relationship of the 'is' and 'ought' statements[3] a problem posed for readers of Pauline correspondence. To put this in the words of Stanley Hauerwas may usefully begin our discussion. He says:

> ... it is not clear ... how the 'indicatives' of the faith—God has done X and Y for you—provide the rationale or justify the imperatives: Do this X and Y. To put it concretely, there seems to be a problem about how the admonitions Paul delivers in Romans 12 follow from and/or are integral to the claim of justification in Romans 3.[4]

What follows is a brief attempt to outline the problem and to come to tentative conclusions which will, perhaps, be pointers to a clearer reading of Paul's letters and their ethical application. First the positions of Pauline scholars are distinguished—perhaps, rather artificially—as falling into three distinct categories: namely, that the indicatives and the imperatives are virtually not related; that they are so closely related as to be indistinguishable; and the middle position between these two extremes which holds that the indicatives and imperatives are very closely related yet that they maintain their distinctiveness. This will make clear the problem and show something of the marked divergence that recent attempts in this area have shown. Secondly, through an analysis of three individual examples (Rom 12:1-2; Phil 2:12-13; Gal 5:25) and a longer, sustained argument (1 Cor 6:12-20), the relationship between indicative and imperative in Paul's writing is shown to be, basically, that of the third position mentioned above. From this we can turn our attention to more specific conclusions that can be drawn from the study.

The virtual irrelation of indicative and imperative

C. H. Dodd is a principal and influential example of a New Testament scholar who seems to hold the indicative and the imperative of Pauline theology at arm's length from each other. This he does in an attempt to show that both are of equal importance, both

---

[3] J. C. Gagar, 'Functional Diversity in Paul's Use of End-Time Language' *JBL* (1970), 3. 325-337, distinguishes them in this way.
[4] S. Hauerwas, *The Peaceable Kingdom* (London, 1983), 92.

are essential to the apostle's thinking.[5] It is true that Dodd seeks to bring them into and to define a relationship between them, but in the attempt, I suggest, he actually divorces the two aspects of Paul's thought. The reason for this can best be discerned from a brief examination of his ideas on this point.

Dodd recognizes two distinct elements in the New Testament's understanding of Christianity: the religious element and the ethical. The former aspect denotes, amongst other things, faith, worship, communion with God, salvation and hope; the latter includes conduct, moral judgement, and the like. Dodd realizes the need to discover a relationship between 'religion' (which, broadly speaking, corresponds to 'indicative') and 'ethics' (imperative). He says, for example, 'it is impossible to understand either the ethical content of Christianity or its religious content unless we can in some measure hold these two together and understand them in their true, organic relations within a whole.'[6] Indicative and imperative *are* organically related, then. What does he make of this? How does he see the relationship? Surprisingly, perhaps, he seems effectively to drive a wedge between the two in his subsequent considerations of the problem. He speaks of them as two distinct 'parts': '. . . but the division between the two parts, though it is not absolute, is pretty well marked.'[7] How, then, is this 'well marked' division discernible in Paul's teaching and, perhaps more importantly, *why* is it there?

The division is seen, according to Dodd, very clearly in the division of the contents of Paul's letters. The epistles are 'divided into two main parts. The first part deals with specifically religious themes—deals with them, in the main, in the reflective manner which constitutes theology—and the second part consists mainly of ethical precepts and admonitions.'[8] For this idea he cites Romans, Galatians, Colossians and Ephesians as good examples, but insists that, by analogy, the other letters show the same tendency. This is supposed to be reflective of the earliest form of Christianity, which was two-fold: kerygma and didache.[9]

---

5 C. H. Dodd, *Gospel and Law* (Cambridge, 1963), 3-4.

6 *ibid*, 4. Later, he describes the relationship as the ethical teaching being 'embedded' in a context which consists of a report of historical facts and an explanation of their religious significance, 8.

7 *ibid*, 5.

8 *ibid*, 5.

9 *ibid*, 66. See 9-13; 66-57. This is discussed more fully in *The Apostolic Preaching and its Development* (London, 1936): lecture 1, 'The Primitive Preaching', 1-74; particularly 3-4, 17-18.

By the use of 'kerygma' Dodd means 'proclamation', 'public announcement' or 'declaration' (that is, preaching, gospel) whose content was the life and work of Jesus Christ, together with his resurrection from the dead; the aim of which was to speak to men of present confrontation with God, who had acted decisively in history. It also spoke to men of judgement to come. Those who then responded would be instructed in the ethical principles and obligations of the Christian life. Dodd adds that this is 'distinct from the proclamation', this is didache (that is, ethics, life, moral exhortations and instruction, teaching). His summary, again, tends to divide indicative and imperative in an irretrievable way: he states, '. . . first the kerygma, then didache'.[10] Though, at times, he insists that they *are* related, Dodd forces them apart. At best, kerygma is merely a corollary to the facts—not in any real way integral to them.

The reason for this unsatisfactory conclusion seems to be his view of the origin of the ethical elements in the apostle's writing. That is to say, he concludes on the basis of the recurrent presence of traditional ethical instructional material (catechesis) that Paul is simply following a partly stereotyped pattern of exhortation: 'It appears, then, that the ethical portions of the epistles are based upon an accepted pattern of teaching which goes back to a very early period indeed . . .'[11] This material is not necessarily to be conceived as Christian in origin: it may derive from the Graeco-Roman society in general, a society attempting to improve public morals. These ethical ideas were transformed, according to Dodd, by being brought into a context of Christian theology: principally with four concepts— Christian eschatology, the idea of the body of Christ, the imitation of Christ, and the primacy of love or charity. In other words, the basic building blocks are there in the society of Paul's day and are brought almost complete to a new relevance in Christian thought. No-one would argue that there is an absence of catechetical material in the New Testament, but Dodd's thesis has the effect of differentiating the imperative decisively from the indicative. Accordingly, the indicative and imperative are, and remain, quite separate.

---

10 *Gospel*, 10. Dodd defines 'kerygma' as that which God has done for men, and 'didache' as that which God expects of men. See 66ff. Also, see, *New Testament Studies* (Manchester, 1953), 83ff. Dodd here argues a clear distinction between 'living by the Spirit' and 'walking by the Spirit' which seems to closely correspond to the kerygma/didache distinction outlined elsewhere.

11 *Gospel*, 20.

This basic idea affected his exposition, of course. For example, on Gal 5:13 he states that 'Paul is clearly making a transition from the rather controversial theology of the earlier chapters to ethical instruction.' A similar comment accompanies the transition between Romans 11 and 12 where he says, 'outstanding theological problems have now been disposed of . . .', now Paul turns to ethical exhortation.[12]

Both the strength and the weakness of this position are obvious. Having distinguished so clearly between indicative and imperative, Dodd is able to give due weight and to attach equal importance to each. However, the weakness of such an idea is that it divorces the imperative from the indicative so much that it prevents Dodd from questioning a relationship between them in such a way as to come to any real or worthwhile conclusion. This is precisely Furnish's criticism of Dodd's work at this point.[13] Furnish sees the problem as 'Dodd's extraordinarily sharp distinction between doctrine and ethics . . .' Ultimately, then, Dodd's overemphasis on the distinction between the indicative and the imperative is unsatisfactory and unworkable as a true reflection of Paul's thought.

The fusion of indicative and imperative

A more widely held view of the relationship of indicative and imperative is that held, in different ways, by such scholars as Bultmann, Furnish and Ramsey, which posits such a close correlation between them that the two virtually become one; or at least two sides of the same coin.[14]

Bultmann certainly teaches that the indicative and the imperative structure is basic to Pauline thought and, indeed, this becomes his own chief interest [The Editor: see the previous chapter for Bultmann's main essay on the subject].[15]

For Bultmann there is seen to be an inner unity between indicative and imperative which is reflected in Love.[16] This concept

---

12 *ibid*, 16; *The Epistle of Paul to the Romans* (London, 1970), 197, respectively.

13 V. P. Furnish, *Theology and Ethics in Paul* (Nashville, 1968), 273.

14 One could add others to this list notably, perhaps, B. Häring, *Free and Faithful in Christ* (Slough, 1978), who holds a similar view, maintaining that the indicative *becomes* the imperative, (vol 1, 145-150; vol 2, 389, for example); P. Lehmann, *Ethics in a Christian Context* (London: SCM, 1963).

15 See Dennison, *CTJ* (1979) 55-78; Furnish, *op cit*, 262.

16 Bultmann, *Essays* (ET London, 1955), 112.

of unity is matched in the somewhat ambivalent way that Bultmann is able to speak of that relationship. On the one hand, he recognises that the imperative stems from the indicative.[17] The indicative is, in this sense, the Christian who is a new creature, and from this newness emerges ethical behaviour. 'Decision rests . . . in what at any given time I already am.'[18] On the other hand, it appears from Bultmann's theology that the reverse is also equally true. As Dennison puts it, 'For Bultmann the indicative can only be realised or laid hold of in the Christian's experience by the imperative, that is, man's daily existential decision to walk in the obedience of God by faith in the Christ-event.'[19] In this respect, then, Bultmann speaks of 'the love in which the new creation becomes a reality (Gal 5:6, 6:15)' and the eschatological event 'becoming real, so far as love is really present.'[20] For him, then, the indicative and imperative have become one in the moment of decision. It is this last phrase that is essential to our understanding of Bultmann's position. If we are to conclude that Bultmann's thesis at this point is fundamentally inadequate because it merges indicative and imperative too closely together indeed, it makes them one—then we need to see *why* this is so. The answer to this seems to lie in two directions: that is, first, his existentialist presuppositions and, second, his subsequent fear of legalism.

Bultmann seeks to effect a synthesis between Christianity and existentialism[21] which is bound to affect his view of the indicative/imperative relationship. Following Heidegger (particularly his work *Sein und Zeit)* Bultmann suggests that man truly exists only when he chooses his freedom in responsibility in the moment of decision, or at the decisive time *(Geschichte).* He thus locates meaning only in the present—denying that existence is a continuum at all.[22]

---

[17] E.g. Bultmann, *Theology* vol 1, 332. He cites Rom 6:14; 1 Cor 6:11, (*Theology*, 1. 315).

[18] See, for example, Bultmann, *This World and Beyond* (ET London, 1960), 71; *Essays*, 80.

[19] Dennison, *op cit*, 62.

[20] Bultmann, *Existence and Faith* (ET London, 1961), 145, 245; *Faith and Understanding* (ET London, 1969), 79, respectively (my emphasis).

[21] There is, of course, a great deal of literature on this point. See for example, H.-H. Schrey, 'The Consequences of Bultmann's Theology for Ethics' in C. W. Kegley (ed.) *The Theology of Rudolf Bultmann* (ET London, 1966), 183-200.

[22] R. C. Roberts, *Rudolf Bultmann's Theology: A Critical Interpretation* (Grand Rapids, 1976), 50, says, 'It is neither static, nor does it develop'—that is, it is the present moment which is the whole of its reality. He further explains this: '. . . a man is not in existential time, but rather becomes temporal in the moment of decision' (51).

It is clear from this that the structure assumes that the Christian existence cannot be termed 'an accomplished fact' and that, therefore, it would make nonsense of trying to separate the indicative from the imperative in the moment of decision. We can see that Bultmann's immanence philosophy has a controlling influence on his understanding at this juncture. However, it is an entirely inadequate starting point in theology. D. L. Baker indicates its inadequacy as 'a fundamental limitation of the existential method. By definition', he continues, 'its concern is with human existence and therefore only indirectly with God.'[23] Paul's ethical teaching rests on God's work accomplished historically by Christ and the subsequent status given to the believer—a point that escapes Bultmann's presuppositional stance.

The other reason for Bultmann's inadequate interpretation of Pauline ethics is his seeking to rid his theology from the danger of legalism and his consequent proposal for a radical obedience. The problem, as he discerns it, is that an ethical imperative could be learned and could become man's possession and security. He distinguishes, therefore, between 'formal authority/obedience' and 'radical authority/obedience'. The former is to be seen as a blind obedience to the commandment; for example, where man obeys simply because it is commanded. This, he argues, precludes man's complete obedience. The latter is a response to the demand of a concrete situation. Bultmann therefore rejects an articulated ethical system, believing that the command to love is not an ethical principle from which rules can be derived: 'I myself must at any given time perceive what it (love) demands at any given time.'[24] So, again, the indicative and the imperative must, on that basis, become virtually one in the moment of decision.

Roberts sees as positive Bultmann's fear of legalism as a motive in teaching radical obedience, but reasonably argues that it is not legalism merely to follow a rule. Legalism derives from motive and objective in following that rule.[25] Paul's writing itself is full of

---

23 D. L. Baker, *Two Testaments: One Bible* (Leicester, 1976), 175. Interestingly, R. Harrisville, 'Bultmann's Concept of the Transition from Inauthentic to Authentic Existence' in R. Harrisville/C. Braaten (eds) *Kerygma and Myth* (New York, 1962), 212, 228, argues that Bultmann's fault was not in *using* Existentialist philosophy, but in *misusing* it in his interpretation.

24 See, *Essays*, 79; also, 174-175. See *TNT* vol 1, 19; *History and Eschatology* (ET Edinburgh, 1957), 46; *Essays*, 155.

25 Roberts, *op cit*, 278. See also, 72, 74, 275.

regulations, instructions and injunctions, and these are clearly not seen as threats to human responsibility and obedience.[26] It remains the case, also, that Bultmann nowhere develops a satisfactory reason for their existence or an approach to their use.

Ultimately, then, Bultmann's position is dialectical and distinctively existential and sees less of the transforming effect of the historical, as well as the present, indicative in the believer's empirical life than Paul seems to assert.[27]

A more moderate position is taken by V. P. Furnish who reaches the conclusion that the indicative and imperative are one in that the former includes the latter without necessarily identifying them and saying that the one is the other.

In his work *Theology and Ethics in Paul*, Furnish analyses Romans to show that a clear-cut distinction between indicative and imperative such as is suggested by Dodd cannot, in fact, be sustained.[28] He states, more generally, 'Not only do the letters serve to reaffirm, defend, and clarify the preaching, but—as the apostle himself specifically says in 1 Thess 2:11-12 and 4:2—his original evangelizing activity already included exhortation, encouragement, and instruction.'[29] He bases his analysis on the assumption that Paul gives his theme in Rom 1:16-17: that is, that the whole of the letter is an explication of the gospel of righteousness from God, 'a righteousness that is by faith from first to last' (v. 17). This is seen to be worked out equally in the assertions of the first eleven chapters and the more obvious exhortations clustered from chapter 12 following. Therefore, he argues, rightly, that the objective of the final four chapters is the same—not different—to that of the first eleven. Furnish concludes, then, that 'Romans has, almost from the beginning, an hortatory aspect of which chs 12-15 are only, so to speak, the denouement . . .'[30]

Furnish further shows that an interpretation of the apostle's ethics dare not restrict itself to the so-called 'ethical sections' of his letters and goes on to question the division of letters into 'theological' and 'ethical' parts.[31] However, on this basis Furnish argues against

---

26   E.g. Rom 12:13-14; 1 Thess 4:1f; 5:12f; 2 Thess 3:6f.
27   See Furnish, *Theology and Ethics in Paul*, 138, 264. Also *TNT* vol 1, 338-339, 156.
28   Furnish, *Theology*, 106-111, 112-114.
29   *ibid*, 113.
30   *ibid*, 101.
31   *ibid*, 207, 110.

the distinction between 'kerygma' and 'didache'.[32] He does this along three lines. First, he claims that 'kerygma' is not a series of theological propositions: rather it is the event of preaching (1 Thess 2:13; Rom 9:6; 1 Cor 2:4) 'and God's coming to men in the preached word, not the verbal substance of that preaching.'[33] 'Kerygma', that is, is almost synonymous (in Paul's usage) with both 'gospel' and 'the word of God'. Secondly, he says that it is misleading to define 'didache' as merely moral instruction as opposed to theological propositions. By 'didache' the apostle intends preaching (Rom 6:17; 16:17; 1 Cor 14:6; 6:26). Thirdly, Furnish states that 'exhortation' can be used interchangeably with 'gospel'. Though Dodd assumes that paraclesis is synonymous with and designates 'moral instruction',[34] this is not, in fact, the case.

Furnish's own position, which is essentially opposite to that of Dodd, becomes clear. Though he states that 'from the gift arises the demand' and says that the earliest church's ethical teaching 'was founded upon' theological bases,[35] he suggests that it is not right to say that the imperative is 'based on' or 'proceeds out of' the indicative. In fact, grace is inclusive of obedience, and therefore he posits the idea of the unity of indicative/imperative: 'The Pauline imperative is not just the result of the indicative but *fully integral to it.*' This he calls 'the imperative indicative'.[36] Again, in a more recent work, Furnish draws the relationship by suggesting that love is 'a command inherent in the gift.'[37] It is because of this that Furnish rejects the notion of progress in Christian life. He says, 'If "progress" is to include the idea of increasing "achievement", then Paul allows no progress.' He bases this on the following reasoning: 'The idea of progressive achievement supposes that there is some programme of action which can ultimately be accomplished, such as full compliance with law or full correspondence to a pattern or example. But nothing of this sort exists for Paul.'[38] This is, of course, consistent with his

---

32 *ibid*, 106ff.

33 *ibid*, 107.

34 Dodd, *The Apostolic Preaching*, 8.

35 Furnish, *Theology and Ethics*, 156; *The Love Command in the New Testament* (London, 1973), 215, respectively.

36 Furnish, *Theology and Ethics*, 226, original emphasis (see also 137-138, 157, 207, 211, 225). Furnish cites Rom 5:1 as the classic instance: but also Rom 6:4; 7:4; 13:12; 14:8; 1 Cor 2:14; 6:11; 12:27; 2 Cor 6:16; 1 Thess 4:7.

37 *The Love Command*, 207. In this, as we have seen, Furnish basically agrees with Bultmann; cf. *TNT* vol 1, 270, 338-339; *Essays*, 112, etc.

38 *Theology and Ethics*, 239.

general idea of the imperative indicative. He insists that achievement is wholly given, not attained.

The force of this conclusion is that it does draw a close relationship between the indicative and the imperative; a relationship lacking, say, in Dodd's position outlined above. This is brought out most clearly in the following paragraph:

> Paul's preaching of love does not just stand alongside his emphasis on justification by faith but is vitally related to it. To believe in Christ means to belong to him, and to belong to him means to share in his death and in the power of his resurrection. Thereby one's whole life is radically reoriented from sin to righteousness . . .[39]

In this way it certainly appears to do justice to Paul's thinking. However, its inherent weakness is that in so fully combining the indicative and the imperative, Furnish virtually denies the possibility of genuine command and of the Christian pattern of conduct in Paul's thought.

Ramsey, in *Basic Christian Ethics*,[40] sets out an ethics in which the indicative and the imperative 'coinhere in Christ'. It is an ethic of liberty, claiming that the law is entirely finished by Christianity in its new 'obligation to love'.[41] Ramsey argues that in the first letter to the Corinthians Paul's position can be summarised as 'Love and do as you *then* please'.[42] In place of rules the apostle suggests self-regulation—not of a free and autonomous type and nature, but the self-regulation that is conditioned by the context of inter-relationship with others and their needs. Because of this, he argues that Paul's exhortations generally 'have authority only as love's directives, and hold in view the needs and "edification" or "building up of others"'.[43] Love becomes the crucial organizing feature of Pauline ethics:

> What should be done or not done in a particular instance, what is good or bad, right or wrong, what is better or worse

---

[39] *The Love Command*, 92. See, also, 103. At 109 he says '. . . the obligation "to love one another" inheres in what God has done, in the new life he has granted the believer in Christ' (emphasis original). See the appropriate passages in 2 Corinthians (New York, 1984).

[40] Ramsey, *Basic Christian Ethics* (London, 1950).

[41] *ibid*, 74-76, 89.

[42] *ibid*, 77 (original emphasis).

[43] *ibid*, 78; see 81, 88.

than something else, what are 'degrees of value'—these things in Christian ethics are not known in advance or derived from some preconceived code. They are derived backward by Christian love from what it apprehends to be the needs of others.[44]

This is summed up in the concept that obedience comes from gratitude to God.[45] This is shown in a diagram taken from *Basic Christian Ethics*, p. 129:

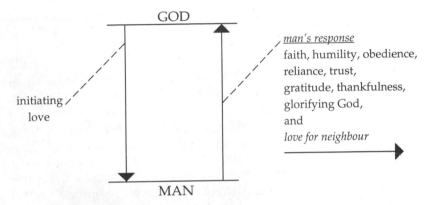

The right hand side list indicates how the Christian stands before God, and is summarised by the word 'love'. Love has a purely responsive character; responding, that is, to the initiative and the love of God. The Christian stands in the state of total liberty before God, living out the indicative of his own experience in response to the love of the Father.

It would not be correct to suggest that Ramsey posits a Christian ethics without rules or virtues yet it appears that he fuses indicative and imperative to such a degree that the latter is almost indistinguishable as the former is arguably put into an unPauline prominence in the relationship. Despite the fact that Ramsey speaks of rules it becomes clear that he subordinates them to 'agapé' and to the situation. He states, for instance: 'I also contend that it can be shown that a proper understanding of the moral life will be one in

---

44 *ibid*, 78-79 (original emphasis). Again, 89, 'Absolutely everything is commanded which Love requires'.

45 *ibid*, 78, 128. See also, Ramsey's essay, 'The Case of the Curious Exception' in G. H. Outka/P. Ramsey (eds) *Norm and Context in Christian Ethics*, 123, where he speaks of 'an ethic of gratitude'.

which Christians determine what we ought to do in very great measure by determining which rules of action are most love-embodying, but that there are also always situations in which we are to tell what we should do by getting clear about the facts of the situation and then asking what is the loving or the most loving thing to do in it. The latter may even be at work in every case of the creative casuistry of inprincipled love going into action.'[46] In other words, rules and imperative exhortations take a back seat: in practice, general norms and principles give the warrant for ethical action.[47]

One contributing factor to this ultimately inadequate position is, perhaps, that Ramsey, despite discussion on the matter, takes little account of the reality of sin in the believer. For him, sin is simply defined as 'the opposite of all that Christian love means' or as 'pride working through selfishness'.[48] Although, again, there is an element of truth in this, it is not good enough to suggest, as a consequence, that sin is no longer to be looked at as a particular 'infraction of a known moral law or series of such infractions'.[49] One wishes to agree with Ramsey that sinful man no longer images the will of God'[50] but seeks in vain to see how the will of God is given to man in any other way, according to Ramsey, than in the purely indicative, receptive and responsive state of a man loved by the Father. Again, we see that the indicative and the imperative merge and the latter loses its identity in the former.

A close relationship, incorporating a clear distinction between the indicative and the imperative

The two positions regarding the relationship between indicative and imperative that have so far been discussed show the extreme poles of thought: either the indicative and the imperative are so distinct from each other that the relationship is virtually not drawn at all; or, they

---

[46] *ibid*, 5.
[47] 'The Case', 73, 75. It is interesting to note that in his valuable work on abortion and euthanasia, *Ethics at the Edge of Life* (New Haven, 1980), Ramsey appeals, not so much to laws of any kind, but to concepts such as righteousness, faithfulness, loyalty, the awesome sanctity of life, the image of God, agapé, and the like. See also *Basic Christian Ethics*, 76.
[48] *Basic Christian Ethics*, 290, 291, respectively. 'Sin means anxious self-centredness or self-centred anxiety' (291).
[49] *ibid*, 285. See also 107, 284ff.
[50] *ibid*, 278.

co-exist in such a fusion that they become indistinct and are largely treated as one. However, the third approach in the area is that which posits the idea that the indicative and the imperative are closely related, but that they keep something of their own distinct existence in the apostle's thought.[51]

The imperatives are seen as based on the fact of a new nature and are therefore also a call to obedience to the one who has already established a relationship with the Christian; that is, the 'believer's every action is oriented on God's antecedent act in Christ'.[52] Ethical behaviour, then, is a consequence, not the cause, of the newness of the believer's being; it is an appropriation of what has already been assigned in the work of the Lord and of the Spirit. In Braaten's words: 'Being precedes act'.[53] On the other hand, Allen Verhey, for example, wishes to give an important priority to the indicative in Paul's thought, whilst keeping the relationship already suggested: 'The indicative mood has an important priority and finality in the process of the gospel, but the imperative is by no means merely an addendum to the indicative or even exactly an inference from the indicative.' He sees the concept of eschatology in Paul's writing to be decisive: 'The juxtaposition of indicative and imperative is possible . . . precisely because of the present co-existence of the old age and the age to come.'[54]

The interrelatedness of indicative and imperative is, of course, spoken of in various ways. Bornkamm, for instance, discusses what he terms the 'collocation' and 'conjunction' of the gospel and the summons, whilst Kümmel speaks of the conjoining and juxtaposition, 'a necessary, an indispensable antinomy'. Haarbeck, on the other hand, calls it 'the dialectic of indicative and imperative, gospel and law, gift and task . . .'[55] Nevertheless, these scholars rightly agree on the interrelation of indicative and imperative and

---

51 For example, see G. Bornkamm, *Paul* (ET London, 1971), 201-203; T. J. Deidun, *New Covenant Morality in Paul* (Rome, 1981), 78; Dennison, *CTJ* (1979), 73; L. Goppelt, *Theology of the New Testament* vol 2 (ET Grand Rapids, 1982), 136; W. G. Kümmel, *Theology of the New Testament* (ET London, 1980), 227; A. Lincoln, *Paradise Now and Not Yet* (Cambridge, 1981), 133; R. N. Longenecker, *Paul: Apostle of Liberty* (New York, 1984), 179.

52 Bornkamm, *Paul*, 201.

53 C. E. Braaten, *Eschatology and Ethics* (Minneapolis, 1974), 121.

54 A. Verhey, *The Great Reversal*, 104-105; see also 122.

55 Bornkamm, *Paul*, 202; Kümmel, *TNT*, 224, 227; Haarbeck, καινός *DNTT* 2. 673, respectively.

place them together, adjacently, rather than merging them into a one-sided unity or divorcing them entirely.

This interconnection is brought out in Paul's writing, for example, by the way in which he can make the same subject-matter at one point an indicative statement, at another a summons. In his letter to the Galatians he tells the recipients that they have all been clothed with Christ (3:27), whereas, later in the epistle to the Romans he exhorts the believers to clothe themselves with the Lord Jesus Christ rather than to continue gratifying the desires of their sinful nature (Rom 13:14). This phenomenon is more pronounced when it occurs in the same letter as it does in Galatians. On the one hand, the apostle encourages them to live by the Spirit (5:16), but on the other hand, he also makes the statement that they do, indeed, live by the Spirit and exhorts them, on this basis, to keep in step with him (5:25). Again, in Romans, Paul is emphatic that believers have already died to sin (6:2), yet a little later he wants them to consider that this is the case— '. . . count yourselves dead to sin, but alive to God in Christ Jesus' (6:11).

The close relationship between indicative and imperative is also seen in the way that Paul, for example, in Romans 6, combines assertion about 'the believer's new status in Christ with imperatives to encourage them to conform "the existing components"' of their lives 'in accordance with the new status'.[56] At verse 12 Paul uses language of exhortation in the form of inference to be drawn from what precedes: '. . . do not let sin reign in your mortal body so that you obey its evil desires.' The believer has been repeatedly declared to be dead to sin and alive to God through Christ (v. 2, 3, 6, 7, 8) and on the basis of that he is exhorted to live in a particular way. It must be said that the relationship between indicative and imperative is seen to be defined by that sort of inference: 'Because of X, therefore Y'.

Although this does not get us very much further in identifying and defining the relationship it is, at least, clear that indicative and imperative come together in equilibrium rather than in fusion. Bornkamm helpfully suggests this in the following words: 'The believer's actions derive from God's act, and the decisions taken by obedience from God's antecedent decision for the world in Christ. Thus the two come together in equilibrium: to live on the basis of *grace*, but to *live* on the basis of grace.'[57]

---

[56]   Moo, *Trinity Journal* (1982), 220.
[57]   Bornkamm, *Paul*, 202-203 (original emphasis).

The conclusion is both important and helpful, but we need to ask how the relationship can best be expressed. This question finds varying answers. For example, some scholars would summarise the relationship by the use of the phrase, 'Be what you are';[58] others write, 'Become what you are' or 'Let us become fully what we already are.'[59] Both of these ideas have an element of truth yet both seem inadequate to express Paul's thought. The former ('Be what you are') gives weight to a rather static concept; the latter gives more stress to the idea of growth and development which is inherent in Christian living as Paul sees it. One has to agree with Deidun, however, who finds these summary-expressions inadequate as they stand.[60] The reasons he puts are, first, that they make no mention of God's role in either the indicative or the imperative; and, second, that they detach the imperative from the indicative and thereby 'overlook precisely what is most characteristic of Pauline ethics: that what God demands, he also effects.'[61] Deidun's argument—basically, that Paul intends that his readers realise that the indicative itself (the power of the Spirit effecting what God demands) enters into the realization of the imperative—and his concluding summary-expression (Let God be God in the core of your liberty[62])—are worth considering as alternatives to the suggestions so far outlined.

Deidun's reasoning seems fundamentally sound. In a paragraph he delineates his thinking:

> The Christian imperative demands only free acceptance of a gift that is made independently of it. The Christian is *under obligation* not to resist the inward action of God's Spirit which already *impels* him to free obedience. He must 'abound' in holiness and love—that is, he must let God be God in the core of his liberty. This is the only formulation which, while doing full justice to the wonder of the indicative, gives full weight to the urgency of the imperative, and which respects both the sovereignty of God's action and the integrity of human freedom in the whole work of sanctification.[63]

---

58 E.g. Dennison, *CTJ* (1979), 72; G. Stählin, νῦν *TDNT* 4, 1121; A. C. Thiselton, 'Realised Eschatology at Corinth' *NTS* (1975), 517; etc.
59 Moule, *JTS* (1964), 14; Lincoln, *Paradise*, 51, respectively.
60 Deidun, *New Covenant Morality*, 241.
61 *ibid*, 241.
62 *ibid*, 243.
63 *ibid*, 243 (original emphasis).

There are some important aspects of Deidun's work which need bringing out. He maintains, for example, that self-understanding is the basis for exhortation in Paul's writing and that this must include an understanding of belonging to God in the new covenant and of the activity of the Holy Spirit to bring about both indicative and imperative. It is this last idea which needs brief elaboration. He states it in the following way: 'Christian imperative is simply the necessary effect of God's inward activity in as much as this demands the continuing "Yes" of human freedom.'[64] Therefore, the believer is not to become what he is, but to let God be what *he* is. Although there is germinal truth in this we seem to have moved back to the idea of fusing indicative and imperative, which we previously rejected as inadequate to convey Paul's thought. Indeed, Deidun expressly states this:

> Here indicative and imperative are cojoined: the Christian's 'new will', constantly flowing from the activity of the Spirit, is the divinely wrought indicative which *carries within itself* the Christian imperative. There can be nothing more 'indicative', and, at the same time, nothing more 'imperative', than the activity of the Spirit creating and sustaining my own personal instinct.[65]

Again, indicative and imperative appear to be one.

However, the merit of Deidun's conclusion is that he forcefully reminds us that the work of the Holy Spirit of God is integral to both indicative and imperative in Christian living; and that this does not preclude the believer's obligation to the concrete declarations of God's will contained in the apostle's injunctions.[66] Deidun's alternative, then, does some justice to the Pauline insistence that sanctification is of God; yet it is arguable whether he fully takes into account Paul's equal emphasis on man's role in this task.[67] Deidun's summary expression seems to underline this problem: 'Let God be God in the core of your liberty'. Perhaps a combination of emphases would give a balance more in line with apostolic usage. Would the exhortation: 'Work out your own salvation in Christ by the Spirit' be a more suitable and Pauline conclusion?

---

64 *ibid*, 82-83.
65 *ibid*, 79-80 (original emphasis).
66 See his section 'Paul's Directives', *ibid*, 175-183.
67 E.g. Phil 2: 12-13: an example to which we return below.

Examples of Paul's use of the imperative based on the indicative

Having briefly examined the relationship of indicative and imperative as it is presented in theology and having come to the conclusion that they are certainly and closely related yet distinct, we
now turn to analyse one or two examples from the writing of the
apostle Paul. The passages clearly reflect the idea outlined above:
they are Rom 12:1-2; Phil 2:12-13; Gal 5:25 and the longer exhortation
of 1 Cor 6:12-20.

Romans 12:1-2

Rom 12:1-2 is a passage that lends itself to analysis of indicative and
imperative. Here Paul exhorts his readers on the basis of God's
mercies to live in a particular way. The phrase 'by the mercies of
God' (RSV) is probably closer to Paul's intention than, for example,
'in view of God's mercies' as the New International Version
translates it. That is, on the ground of the indicatives already outlined
and argued, Paul requires 'a voluntary and enthusiastic response'[68]
to which he now urges them. Bowen seems to be far from the mark in
asserting here that 'because of God's mercy towards us, *we owe him a
duty.*'[69] This interpretation lacks something of the truth set out in
Ramsey's thinking, for example, which stressed an 'ethic of
gratitude': because of God's initiating love and grace we love him
and do his will.

However, it is clear that with Romans 12 a fresh and
concluding section of the epistle begins, as one writer puts it:

> . . . . with a transition from what has been predominantly
> theological exposition, conducted for the most part in general
> and somewhat impersonal terms, to parenesis marked by the
> first appearance in the epistle of Παρακαλῶ and Paul almost
> for the first time addresses his readers in the first person with
> apostolic authority.[70]

---

68 W. Hendriksen, *Romans* vol 2 (Edinburgh, 1981), 403.

69 R. Bowen, *A Guide to Romans* (London, 1984), 154 (my emphasis).

70 C. Evans, 'Romans 12: 1-2; The True Worship' in C. K. Barrett, et al (eds)
Dimensions de la Vie Chrétienne (Rome, 1979), 9. The whole essay (7-33) is worth
consideration. It is a useful examination of the language and ideas of the passage.

This transition needs to be examined in order to relate the admonitions of the apostle to the indicatives from which they spring.

Although Evans, for example, concludes that 12:1-2 does not play much part in determining the selection of the parenesis that follows[71] the question remains to be answered, 'With what does 12:1-2 connect, and to what does the οὖν refer?' Is it merely denoting a 'headline' for what follows, as some think, or is it better to see it as indicating inference with the force of 'Therefore', rather than merely as a transition-particle. The latter view seems most probable, particularly as it is supported by an appeal to the mercies of God, as Barrett points out.[72]

I suggest, then, that the opening words, 'Therefore, I urge you . . .' indicate, first, a connection with the foregoing teaching; and, secondly, that this is a conclusion to be drawn from the preceding verses. Cranfield sees it as indicating that what is going to be said follows from what has already been said, and concludes that Paul's ethics are theologically motivated.[73]

But, we might ask, what does Paul mean by 'the mercies of God'? Many commentators and scholars would see this as a reference to the whole of the epistle so far which has shown the action of the merciful God in salvation[74]—though it must be admitted that others do not. Evans, for example, says that to see the phrase as covering the whole of Romans 1-11 is to beg the question. The words ἔλεος and ἐλεεῖν are entirely absent from chapters 1-8.[75] Minear also argues against this. He sees chapters 12 and 13 as addressed to the self-assured Gentile Christians in Rome accustomed to scoff at the Jewish Christian—that group addressed previously in chapter 11, and, later, in chapter 14; the 'strong in faith', those who need to reject their earlier anti-Semitism and therefore to reject conformism to the age in which they live.[76] Wright, less radically, expresses dissatisfaction

---

[71] *ibid*, 33.

[72] C. K. Barrett, *A Commentary on the Epistle to the Romans* (London, 1973), 302ff.

[73] C. E. B. Cranfield, *Romans* vol 2 (Edinburgh, 1975), 596.

[74] *ibid*, 596. See also R. C. H. Lenski, *Interpretation of St. Paul's Epistle to the Romans* (Minnesota, 1961), 745; Bornkamm, *Paul*, 201; J. Murray, *The Epistle to the Romans* vol 2 (Grand Rapids, 1968), 110; H. E. Stoessel, 'Notes on Rom 12: 1-2. The Renewal of the Mind and Internalizing the Truth' *Interpretation* (1963), 162; Furnish, *Theology and Ethics in Paul*, 102; Bowen, *A Guide*, 154; etc.

[75] Evans, *Dimension*, 9.

[76] P. S. Minear, *The Obedience of Faith* (London, 1971), 82-84.

with the view—arguing that the phrase refers particularly to chapters 9-11 (though not necessarily excluding 18, thereby).[77]

Nevertheless, it is arguable that Paul had in mind the whole of the letter as the theological context of these exhortations which now cluster in the final chapters. Barrett expresses it in his summary:

> We have read of the universal sinfulness of mankind, and of the universal grace of God; of his infinite love in sending his Son to die for our sins, and of the free justification by faith alone which, in his mercy, he offers. We have read of the power of the Spirit of God to bring life out of death; of predestination, and God's eternal purpose for his creatures.

And, more succinctly, 'Because God is what he is, and has done what he has done, certain things follow; or rather ought to follow.'[78] Viard concurs and makes an interesting cross-reference to 11:35, which says, 'Who has ever given to God, that God should repay him?'[79]

Paul has shown previously God's character in his saving work—closely aligned to the idea of 'mercy': kindness (2:4), patience (9:22; 11:22), love (5:5; 8:35, 39) and grace (1:7; 3:24; 4:16; 5:2, 20, 21; 6:1, 14, 15, 17; 11:5, 6), for example, and, although the words οἰκτίρειν, ἔλεος and ἐλεεῖν are absent from chapters 1-10 the mercy of God is never far from Paul's mind. This is clear thematically as he outlines God's faithfulness to Jew and Gentile (chs. 1-3) and that despite their sin (e.g. 3:9, etc); justification by faith and life in Christ (chs. 4-7) and life by the Spirit (ch. 8). However, it is correct to say that 'mercy' is the particular keynote of chapters 9-11 (e.g. 9:15, 16, 18, 23; 10:12, 13, 20, 21; 11:22, 31, 32) as Paul reaches the climax of his teaching on the gospel of God's righteousness (1:17).[80] That, then, is the basis upon and by which the apostle motivates the believers to offer themselves to God—ethics thus rests upon the foundation of redemptive accomplishment: the imperative is grounded in indicative.

Paul urges those at Rome to offer or present their bodies 'as living sacrifices, holy and pleasing to God'. What does he mean? There seems no contextual reason for accepting Murray's inter-

---

77 N. T. Wright, *The Messiah and the People of God* (Oxford, 1980), 224.

78 C. K. Barrett, *Reading Through Romans* (Philadelphia, 1977), 65.

79 A. Viard, *Saint Paul Épitre aux Romains* (Paris, 1975), 256: 'Cet appel se fonde sur ce qui précède. Tout dépend de Dieu (cf. 11:35); et cela est surtout vrai du salut.'

80 Wright, *op cit*, 224.

pretation that by 'bodies' the apostle means their physical bodies only.[81] This does not fit well into vv. 3-8, nor 9-21, which exhort to attitude (vv. 3, 9-12, 15-16) as well as to action (vv. 6-8, 13, 17, 20, 21). Rather, it seems more likely that Paul indicates their whole beings,[82] or, perhaps, their whole beings in the concrete realities of life.[83] Evans suggests that if the singular θυσίαν ζῶσαν after σώματα may be pressed here; Paul is seen to be addressing his readers as a single community who are to offer themselves corporately as a single sacrifice.[84] This may, indeed, be the case—it would certainly seem to follow both from the words used and also from the context of Rom 12:3-8 (particularly) in which the apostle addresses the Roman Christians as the body of Christ to which each member belongs. However, the individuality in v. 3 has to be retained: Paul exhorts them 'For by the grace given me I say to every one of you . . .' (literally, 'to each one among you').

The apostle uses language of the sacrificial ritual, transforms and amplifies it[85] to urge believers to live lives pleasing to God who has been merciful to them. Deidun states it in these words: 'They must accomplish an act (παραστῆσαι—aorist) of radical self-detachment, whereby the totality of their existence is given over to God: this is their λατρείαν.'[86] That is, they are to consecrate themselves to God in a separation from 'the pattern of this world' and in orientation to God.

This, Paul says, is their 'spiritual worship'. The exact interpretation of this idea is notoriously difficult—a difficulty expressed in the variety of translations.[87] One of the problems with the phrase is that the word λογικός occurs only here in Paul's writing and in 1 Pet 2:2. Evans makes out a good case to suggest that the word requires the translation 'rational'. He does this by reference to its usage in Philo where the word is so often used as a necessary

---

[81] Murray, *Romans*, 110.

[82] Barrett, *Romans*, 231; Cranfield, *Romans*, 599; J. Calvin, *Romans* (ET Grand Rapids, 1979), 452; Hendriksen, *Romans*, 401; etc.

[83] F. J. Leenhardt, *The Epistle to the Romans* (ET London, 1961), 302; Lenski, *op cit*, 747. H. Ridderbos, *Paul: An Outline of his Theology* (London, 1977), 258-260, says that the parenesis is directed toward 'the new manhood.'

[84] Evans, *Dimensions*, 24-25.

[85] G. W. Forell, *The Christian Lifestyle* (Philadelphia, 1975), 5.

[86] Deidun, *New Covenant Morality*, 98.

[87] E.g. 'spiritual worship' (NIV, RSV); 'reasonable service' (AV); 'intelligent worship' (Phillips); 'the worship offered by mind and heart' (NEB); etc. Moffatt translates it '. . . that is your cult, a spiritual rite'.

adjective qualifying πνεῦμα; in which case it cannot mean 'spiritual'. His conclusion is that the Philonic usage, reflecting popular philosophy, shows that λογικός is employed frequently in the sense of 'rational': so much so that it suggests that this sole occurrence of the word in Paul should also be given that sense unless there is a strong reason to the contrary.[88] So λογικός probably points to the concept of the rational, in contrast to that which is automatic and mechanical: 'conscious, intelligent, consecrated devotion . . .'[89] This would certainly correlate with Paul's use of the word νοῦς in 12:2, which indicates renewed understanding, if this verse is seen as an explication of what the apostle states in v. 1.[90] The question to be answered, briefly, is 'To what does "rational" relate?' Is Paul speaking of worship that is of the mind and therefore 'rational'? Wright presents a good case for his conclusion that, as 'spiritual worship' is much too vague it should actually be paraphrased 'the worship to which our argument leads.'[91] This is a distinct possibility and one which ties together, as premise and consequence, the indicatives of chapters 1-11 ('the mercies of God') and the imperatives of chapter 12 and following.

However this particular idea is translated, the main point of inference from this connecting verse, and those that follow, is that which Calvin makes, '. . . this exhortation teaches us, that until men really apprehend how much they owe to the mercy of God, they will never with a right feeling worship him, nor be effectually stimulated to fear and obey him.'[92] That is, the imperative of Paul's thought is based upon the indicative (in this case, the mercy of God). The indicative and the imperative are, therefore, closely related but distinct in the apostle's writing at this point. The latter is an inference of the former.

Philippians 2:12-13

Phil 2:12-13 is important in the present context for two reasons: first, because it shows the indicative ('salvation') in a close juxtaposition

---

88 Evans, *Dimensions*, 19; see also 17-22 for a fuller discussion.

89 Murray, *Romans*, 112. (See Bowen, *A Guide*, 157).

90 The word ἀνακαίνωσις (in the phrase ἀνακαίνωσις τοῦ νοός) possibly Paul's own coinage, probably points to eschatological ideas here. The recreation of the mind is now taking place because of the coming of the new age.

91 Wright, *Messiah*, 224.

92 Calvin, *Romans*, 450.

with the imperative ('work out . . .') and, secondly, because it demonstrates that God's work is integral to both, not just to the indicative of redemption. This is the case in that the apostle, who earlier points out that the good work going on in the Philippian believers originated with God and will be carried on by him 'until the day of Christ Jesus' (Phil 1:6) and that they share in God's grace (1:7, 28),[93] also here in Phil 2:12-13 shows that God is at work in the believer's life of obedience (see also 3:12, 14).

Warren analyses the word translated 'work out' (κατερ-γάζεσθε).[94] He establishes that it occurs mostly in the writing of Paul (i.e. notably, several times in Rom 7: but also Rom 1:27; 2:9; 4:5; 5:3; 15:18; 1 Cor 5:3; 2 Cor 4:17; 5:5; 8:11; 11:11; 12:12; Eph 6:13—cf. James 1:13, 20; 1 Pet 4:3). The word is always transitive and always governs an object which is already in being and is normally rendered 'to work'. Based on this, he reaches the following two important conclusions. First, that the salvation mentioned in Phil 2:12 is 'here and now available or liable to be operated on or with, exercised drawn out, brought into action.' His second conclusion is that the believer, therefore, is not being exhorted to accomplish his salvation himself as this is already done for him in Christ.[95] Here, then, the apostle is admonishing the believer to finish, to carry to conclusion, to apply 'to its fullest consequences what is already given by God . . .'[96] Collange seems to have the point exactly: 'Ce qui est demandé c'est de "parachever", de "faire fructifier" . . . ce qui est déjà donné.'[97]

In this the relationship of indicative and imperative is clearly seen as one of dependence, closeness, yet distinction. But here the apostle takes it further and demonstrates, as it were, something of the role of God in the imperative: '. . . it is God who works in you to will and to act according to his good purpose.' The Spirit is part of the

---

[93] It is worth noting that J.-F. Collange, *L'Epître de Saint Paul aux Philippiens* (Neuchâtel, 1973), 97, sees v. 6-v. 11 as the salvation to which the apostle refers. This is certainly possible but not necessary for an understanding of v. 12-v. 13. The connection between v. 1-v. 11 (particularly v. 6-v. 11) with v. 12-v. 13 is rather that Paul wishes his readers to work out their salvation in the same attitude that Christ, too, was obedient to the Father.

[94] J. Warren, 'Work out your own salvation . . .' *EQ* (1944), 125-137.

[95] *ibid*, 128-129. See the confidence of the apostle in Phil 1:27 and 3:20, for example.

[96] J. J. Muller, *The Epistles of Paul to the Philippians and to Philemon* (Grand Rapids, 1976), 90.

[97] Collange, *Philippiens*, 97-98.

indicative state of those who belong to Christ. That is, the possession of God's Spirit is, for Paul (and for the rest of the New Testament) integral to the salvation given to believers; it is part of sonship (Gal 4:16), concomitant with belonging to Christ (Rom 8:9, 11). Paul sees the Spirit as the eschatological gift[98] with whom comes the power of the new age that has already broken into the old. The Holy Spirit is the link between 'the renewal which is taking place now in the inner man (2 Cor 4:16) and the consummation of the renewal in the heavenly body.'[99] The Holy Spirit, then, stands in closest possible relation to the ethical life of the believer: Rom 8 and Gal 5 make this abundantly clear, as does Paul's description of the Spirit's work as essentially that of sanctification (e.g. Rom 15:16; 2 Thess 2:13). It is within this general context that Paul speaks of God's working with the Philippians. It is, in fact, because he is at work that the Philippians are to 'work out' their salvation. Bornkamm is correct in affirming that 'the action is not divided up between God and man making two propositions supplementary to each other. Each proposition substantiates the other.' He concludes, 'Because God does everything you too have everything to do.'[100] Collange, on the other hand, is right to insist that it is God's work which motivates, energises and provokes man's activity.[101]

There seems good reason for accepting, along with Beare for example, that Paul's words in Phil 2:12-13, are directed to the corporate body, the church. However, this must not be pushed to the extent of losing sight of the individuality of each member (see, for example v. 4 'Each of you . . .').[102] The point is that, whether corporately or individually, they are to work out that which has already been given in Christ, namely, 'salvation'. The imperative is grounded upon and is the consequence of the indicative.

Galatians 5:25

Gal 5:25 has been termed the *locus classicus* for the indicative/imperative relationship.[103] Here the indicative and the imperative are placed in an emphatic (chiastic) relationship: εἰ ζῶμεν πνεύματι,

---

98 See Ridderbos, *Paul*, 66-67, 87.
99 Lincoln, *Paradise*, 67, 142.
100 Bornkamm, *Paul*, 202.
101 Collange, *Philippiens*, 99.
102 Beare, *Philippians*, 91. Collange, *Philippiens*, 97-99.
103 Deidun, *New Covenant Morality*, 241.

πνεύματι καὶ στοιχῶμεν. The apostle wishes to draw out a practical exhortation from the doctrine on which he has written: 'if the Spirit of God lives in us, let him govern our actions.'[104] Some would see this verse as simply the conclusion to the foregoing section (vv. 13-25);[105] others take it to be a programmatic statement for 5:25-6:10,[106] but it seems better, with Bonnard for example, to visualise the verse *both* as the conclusion of the preceding section and as a springboard for the new development.[107]

It must be emphasized that the apostle is speaking in v. 25, as throughout the chapter, of the Spirit of God, not of man's own spirit (renewed or otherwise). A most unsatisfactory conclusion is reached by Lenski on this subject. He insists that the word is to be interpreted as meaning the human spirit.[108] This runs contrary to the very point Paul makes—now, having received the Spirit (3:2b), they have a new power and ability to master the flesh: the believer is to take hold of that new possibility. Again, Bonnard makes this very clear. He asserts that 'the Spirit', here, denotes not merely an ideal, nor is it an impersonal force, but it is the action of Christ in both the believer and the church. Ridderbos makes a similar assertion:

> It is precisely the Spirit who is the great Inaugurator of the gift of the new aeon that has appeared with Christ; and consequently the contrast, so constitutive for Paul's preaching, between Spirit and flesh is not to be taken as a metaphysical or anthropological, but as a redemptive-historical contrast, namely as the two dominating principles of the two aeons marked off by the appearance of Christ.[109]

Briefly, then, three things in particular are worthy of notice for our discussion of indicative and imperative. First, it is important to realise that the first phrase, 'If we live by the Spirit', implies no uncertainty. Lightfoot makes a mistake in saying that Paul is here

---

104   J. Calvin, *Galatians* (Grand Rapids, 1979), 169.
105   This seems to be the conclusion of P. M.-J. Langrange, *Saint Paul Épitre aux Galates* (Paris, 1950), 153, for instance.
106   e.g. G. Ebeling, *The Truth of the Gospel* (ET Philadelphia, 1985, 259; J. Bligh, *Galatians: A Discussion of St. Paul's Epistle* (London, 1970), 480-481.
107   P. Bonnard, *L'Épitre de Saint Paul aux Galates* (Neuchâtel, 1972), 116.
108   Lenski, *Galatians* (Minnesota, 1961), 280. For a fuller discussion consult, e.g. D. Lull, *The Spirit in Galatia* (Chicago, 1980), 103-188.
109   Bonnard, *Galates*, 116; Ridderbos, *Paul*, 215, respectively. Ridderbos later speaks of the Spirit as 'the creating and renewing power of God . . . and the life principle of the congregation of the future'.

speaking of 'an ideal rather than an actual life: it denotes a state which the Galatians were put in the way of attaining rather than one which they had already attained.' Burton is closer to the mark when he interprets it to mean that the apostle assumes that they so live, but then incorrectly qualifies that remark by the phrase 'or intend to live by the Spirit'.[110] It must be stressed that the conditional clause supposes a present situation, it refers to a reality and is, therefore, not a matter of doubt, but rather a definite assumption. In this sense the New International Version is correct in translating the phrase 'Since we live by the Spirit . . .' This is the indicative state of the believers in Galatia.

Secondly, the whole point of the indicative is that Paul is reminding them that they do live by the Spirit; something which they had evidently forgotten (cf 3:3; 4:6). His exhortation to 'Live by the Spirit' (5:16) is a reminder of their true and present reality, their freedom in Christ; that the Spirit is the author of their new creation and new life (cf 6:15). It is important to notice that Paul is not exhorting them to do what they have not been doing; rather, he wants them to continue to 'keep in step with the Spirit' (literally, 'walk in rank with the Spirit'—virtually synonymous with 'live' and 'conduct yourself').

The chiastic shape of the verse shows clearly the relationship of indicative and imperative envisaged by the apostle. It emphasises equally the givenness and the responsibility of life and freedom which we saw above in connection with Phil 2:12-13. Life originates with the Spirit, he is its author: yet his is also the dynamic and the direction. In reality, then, God makes possible the life which he demands; that is, Paul 'justifies an imperative on the basis of an indicative'[111] as we have previously observed.

Thirdly, the indicative carries with it unavoidable responsibility. Having expressed their 'principal relation to the Spirit'[112] Paul then exhorts the Galatians to the activity which is required on the basis of the indicative. If the Spirit creates a new life-style (5:22-23) then it must be evident in the spiritual life of the believer. This is the moral corollary to the indicative statement that precedes it—their conduct should be evidently governed by the Spirit of God. That is,

---

110 J. B. Lightfoot, *The Epistle of St. Paul to the Galatians* (Grand Rapids, 1981), 214; E. de Witt Burton, *The Epistle to the Galatians* (Edinburgh, 1980), 322, respectively.
111 Ebeling, *The Truth*, 259.
112 Ridderbos, *Galatians*, 210.

the imperative action considered by this verse is, on the basis of the promissory future of 5:16 (οὐ μὴ τελέσητε—with the force of 'then you will not . . .'), assured by the work of the Holy Spirit in the believer. This parallels Paul's thinking in Phil 2:12-13, as we have already seen. Bruce sums it up: 'Here . . . we have the characteristic Pauline interplay between indicative and imperative; we live by the Spirit (granted); therefore let us keep in step with the Spirit.'[113]

1 Corinthians 6:12-20

So far in our study we have shown something of the relationship between indicative and imperative by analysing single texts, albeit in their own context. However, it is interesting and instructive now to turn to a passage in which two indicative ideas are seen to be the theological premise on which Paul exhorts his hearers to holiness in the area of sexuality. 1 Cor 6:12-20 shows very clearly that as it is the radical relationship that the Christian sustains to the Lord that is vital for the whole of life; so it is not merely an appeal to respectability alone, nor to human dignity, nor simply to 'natural morality', but it is the ethical significance of the status of the believer in relation to Christ (v. 15) and to the Spirit (v. 19) which is of utmost importance as the ground for exhortation.[114]

    Hurley,[115] rightly notices the recurrent sequence in this passage:

v. 12   quotations set out as assertion and then qualified by a retort opening with ὁ δέ

---

vv. 13-18a   *another slogan-retort sequence*
    1.   slogan, v. 13
    2.   retort employing τὸ δε', vv. 13-14
    3.   exposition of Paul's view beginning from a commonly held tenet introduced by οὐκ οἴδατε, v. 14-15
    4.   exhortation, v. 18

---

vv. 18b-20   *same pattern*

---

[113] Bruce, *op cit*, 257.
[114] See C. Wiéner, 'Notes sur 1 Cor 6:12-20' in V. Guénel (ed) *Le Corps et Le Corps du Christ dans la Première Épitre aux Corinthiens* (Paris, 1983), 93.
[115] J. B. Hurley, *Man and Woman in 1 Corinthians* (unpublished PhD thesis, Cambridge University, 1973), 113.

1.   slogan, v. 18b
2.   retort employing ὁ δε', v. 18c
3.   exposition of Paul's view introduced by οὐκ οἴδατε,
     vv. 19-20a
4.   exhortation, v. 20b

This is helpful to our present study. For our purposes it should be observed that the exhortations can be seen to be the negative and positive sides of the same coin: that is, 'Flee from sexual immorality' (18a) and 'Honour God with your body' (20b). We need to examine Paul's argument to see how and, perhaps more importantly, *why* he reaches these conclusions from the indicatives that he assumes.

There is general agreement that the quotations in v. 12 ('Everything is permissible for me' cf. 10:23) and in v. 13 ('Food for the stomach and the stomach for food'), which the apostle then qualifies, were in general use at Corinth. However, *the origin* of the former is less clear. It may have originated from the Gnostic group which was so troubling the young church, or with the apostle himself in his polemic against the legalism of Judaism. It may, therefore, be an idea that the Corinthians had grasped from Paul but had misinterpreted. It is perhaps likely though that the slogan initially came from the apostle in his preaching and exposition of the gospel and then used by the Gnostics at Corinth in a wrong way—for Paul seems, certainly to have given qualified agreement to the words themselves but not to the conclusion to which they had been forced.

It seems that the Corinthians largely undervalued or, perhaps, devalued the importance of the body both as a result of the philosophical influences in the church and, possibly, because of their over-enthusiastic anticipation of the resurrection which they interpreted as purely 'spiritual'. These ideas seem to underlie the whole section from 5:1 to 7:40; indeed they also inform the apostle's rigorous defence of the physical resurrection in ch 15. Hence in 6:12-20, Paul stresses that God, who raised Jesus from the dead[116] will also raise the Corinthians bodily. The body, he assures them, is meant 'for the Lord' (vv. 13-14).

The question needs to be answered: to what does 'body' (σῶμα) refer? This is vital to our understanding of the indicatives of the passage. There is no lack of support for the idea that 'body' here

---

[116] See 15:3-4; 12-34; with the argument of vv. 35f: 'How are the dead raised? With what kind of body will they come?'

indicates more than that which is physical, and that it actually refers to the whole person, 'myself'. Further, many would suggest that the word means the individual in relationship with the community and with Christ.[117] Orr and Walther, for example, suggest it from v. 16: 'Do you not know that he who unites himself with a prostitute is one with her in body?' To this they bring the idea that sexual intercourse is an act of the whole person:

> To become one flesh is the proper desire of those who incorporate their sex desires into a total relation of love and loyalty so that *they become one joint personality* and in their relationship express faith in God and love for each other. *This cannot be done in the isolated, commercialized action of prostitution.*[118]

With this statement, as it stands, one has to concur. But it is not what the apostle is actually stating in this passage. In fact, Paul deliberately singles out 'body' (as physical) precisely because the Corinthians were so devaluing the whole concept.

The believers, who thought nothing of their physical existence, had taken the guideline 'Everything is permissible for me' without any qualification. They had presumed, perhaps, that the body (as physical) had no permanent value because of its deterioration at death (see v. 14). From this they seem to have concluded that nothing done in the body had any moral value. Paul insists that this is not so. The body, taken in this sense, is essentially part of us as whole beings[119] and so in 'joining with' or 'uniting to' a prostitute physically (vv. 15-16) a man is inherently involved in the whole of his being (v. 18). Whether we understand the prostitute as involved in temple prostitution or not, Paul is clear that such union should not

---

[117] Barrett, *1 Corinthians*, 147, for whom 'body' is a neutral term representing the human self at the place of decision. See also, P. Jewett, *Paul's Anthropological Terms* (Leiden, 1971), 260. V. Guénel, 'Tableau des emplois de sôma dans la première lettre aux Corinthiens' in V. Guénel (ed.) *Le Corps*, 73; and J. Rouquette, '"Une Seul Corps." Nourriture et Sexualité dans la première épître aux Corinthiens' in *Le Corps*, 143; both emphasize the communal setting here and the relational understanding of the word.

[118] W. F. Orr and J. A. Walther, *1 Corinthians* (New York, 1976), 203 (my emphasis).

[119] This is the conclusion of, for example, R. H. Gundry, *Soma in Biblical Theology with Emphasis on Pauline Anthropology* (Cambridge, 1976), 51-80, particularly 79-80; and J. B. Hurley, *Man and Woman in Biblical Perspective* (Leicester, 1981), 149f and, idem, *Man and Woman in 1 Corinthians*, 89.

take place, and urges them to 'Flee from sexual immorality' on the one hand, and to honour God with their bodies, on the other.

First, Paul puts the exhortation negatively. They are to flee, or shun, that is, to take strong evasive action, in this area (φεύγετε τὴν πορνείαν). Secondly, the apostle seeks to indicate the positive. Although Conzelmann, for example, wishes to make the latter part of v. 20 refer generally and not to be restricted to the specific context of fornication and its avoidance[120] it seems clear that the apostle exhorts them to consider finally the honour which should be brought to the God who has bought them with a price (v. 20a). However, it should be noticed that Paul is very concerned with outsiders' opinions of the church, the gospel and, therefore, of God (5:1; 6:6; 6:20).

This, then, is the situation which Paul addresses. He exhorts the believers in Corinth to be sexually moral. What theological premises does he use in his argument? What indicatives form the base on which his imperatives stand? There are basically two foundational or organizational statements in the passage. We need to look briefly at them and to examine their relationship together and with the imperatives.

The first important indicative is found in v. 15: 'Do you not know that your bodies are members of Christ himself?' What does he indicate by the phrase 'members of Christ'? It must be suggested, firstly, that he has a real connection in mind; that is, it is not merely a figure, there is no thought here of mystical union.[121] The word 'unite' (vv. 16, 17) signifies 'to join together', 'to cling to', 'to enter into close relationship with'.[122] Some have inferred that Paul is speaking of the church, the body of Christ; others, of Christ personally.[123] But I would suggest that, *as they stand*, neither position is adequate; that is, the phrase *cannot* simply refer to the church because the contrast is a personal one—between being joined to Christ and united to a prostitute (vv. 16-17); and yet the idea does not indicate Christ personally, *alone*, for in the context of the letter union with Christ is

---

120 Conzelmann, 1 Corinthians, 113; cf. Barrett, 1 Corinthians, 152.

121 Conzelmann, 1 Corinthians, 111. 'Mystical union', that is, with any idea of absorption. As Conzelmann says, 'This is obvious at once from the counterpart—union with a prostitute' (see footnote 30).

122 On this and its implications see R. A. Batey, New Testament Nuptial Imagery (Leiden, 1971) 34ff.

123 Conzelmann, op cit, 111; Grosheide, 1 Corinthians, 148; Gundry, Paul's Anthropological Terms, 61, take the former view; whilst Fisher, 1 and 2 Corinthians, 217, adopts the latter.

union with his church also (cf. 12:12, for example). Notice the implication for ethics, however. Being united to Christ, it is utterly inconceivable that believers would join with prostitutes. They belong to him, they are his—both in spirit and in body (that is, wholly). They are members of Christ.

The second organizing indicative is closely related to this one. In v. 19 the apostle reminds them that they are, individually, temples of the Holy Spirit whom God has sent and that being such shows that they belong to God. Whether the idea of a price having been paid relates to a ransom concept[124] or to a rather crass, but striking, analogy with the price paid for a prostitute[125] the thrust of what Paul says is that the transaction is complete. If the Holy Spirit dwells within them they have no 'rights' of their own; the transfer of ownership has taken place and they now belong to the Lord. The exhortation then comes 'honour God with your body'. So the point of both indicatives is the fact that the believers in Corinth belong to the Lord, and in saying that, Paul stresses the fact that their bodies as much as their spirits are God's. Therefore, it does matter how the believer behaves physically.

Clearly, Paul searches for statements of truth concerning the status and condition of the believer which he considers will answer the question 'Why should/shouldn't I behave in such and such a way?' Having discovered two such reasons (indicatives)—that the believers are members of Christ and that each is indwelt by the Holy Spirit—he brings them to bear on the pastoral situation with which he is confronted.

Conclusions

A number of points can be made briefly in order to conclude our thinking on the relationship between the indicative and the imperative in Paul's Letters.

It must be stated that the indicative and the imperative are closely linked yet distinct aspects of the apostle's thought and writing. The connection is indissoluble—they cannot be separated. This position seems warranted by Pauline usage and also strongly

---

[124]   See 1 Cor 7:23; Gal 3:13; 4:5—Old Testament references, for example, would include Ex 6:6; 13:13; Ruth 4:4; Ps 103:4; Isa 43:1; etc. See Barrett, *1 Corinthians*, 152-153.

[125]   See Ruef, *1 Corinthians*, 51.

counters the possibilities of the fusion of the indicative and the imperative, on the one hand, and their virtual irrelation, on the other.

But, what of their relationship? In one way the indicative/imperative connection can be understood in terms of our actions flowing from our being ('Being precedes act'), but the matter is more complex than that.

The indicative speaks of that which has been accomplished by God in and through Christ—but does not denote simply the divine element as opposed to the human activity in fulfilling the imperative. We have noted that Paul's ethical admonition is directed to, and is determined by, the present redemptive historical situation. The new age that dawned with Christ's resurrection and the coming of the Holy Spirit determined that this should be so. The Spirit, himself, then, is the link between the indicative and the imperative of Christian reality and existence. He is at once an element of the former and a constituent part of the latter.

The imperative is grounded on the reality that has been given, appeals to it and is intended to bring it to full development (Phil 2:12-13). The moral behaviour of the believer is to reveal something of the character of the new life given by God. Therefore, the indicatives—past, present and eschatological—demand an application on the part of the recipients of Paul's correspondence: they are a motive force in the apostle's parenesis: a corrective factor to misbehaviour, and a sanction to right living before the Lord.

It is undoubtedly the indicative aspect of salvation as much as anything else which gives Paul his confidence in ethical exhortation—a confidence best summed up in his own words: 'Therefore, my dear brothers, stand firm. Let nothing move you. Always give yourselves fully to the work of the Lord, because you know that your labour in the Lord is not in vain' (1 Cor 15:58).

PART VI

THE FOUNDATIONS OF PAULINE ETHICS
Motivations, Norms and Criteria

CHAPTER ELEVEN

The Church in Everyday Life
Considerations of the Theological Basis of Ethics in the New Testament[*]

Eduard Lohse
(1980)

How did the everyday life of early Christianity emerge and develop? How did it receive its distinctive form? Which rules formed the behaviour of Christians in the family, at work and in society? On the basis of which assertions was a Christian ethic developed and how was this ethic given a theological basis in connection with sermons and teaching in the congregations?

The documents of the New Testament are occasional writings, which in every case refer to a particular situation of the early churches and take careful note of such situations. None of these writings can be compared with a philosophical treatise, which deals with a theme in a systematic manner and with an orderly train of thought. Therefore the passages which deal with specific questions of Christian life and conduct are from start to finish in answer to the

---

* Translated by George S. Rosner and Brian S. Rosner.

occasions which have led to the writing of a specific letter. As far as
the catechistic, didactic passages are concerned, many of them do not
show an immediate reference to a particular problem arising in any
particular church. But these nonetheless refer at least indirectly to the
life of the churches, because they reflect the didactic teaching of these
churches. In order to discover in what sense we may think about the
development and theological foundation of Christian ethics, we must
therefore pay attention to the context of early Christian sermons and
teaching.

I.

The New Testament writings consider the commandment of love to
have central meaning for the ethical orientation of the church. The
apostle Paul, whose letters are the oldest literary documents of early
Christianity, says in the letter to the Galatians that the whole Law
finds its fulfillment in one commandment: "Love your neighbour as
yourself" (Gal 5:14). With this assertion Paul obviously refers to
didactic tradition which is known to the church as an instruction for
correct behaviour. "He who loves his neighbour has fulfilled the
Law" (Rom 13:8). Thus the apostle writes with reference to
traditional, catechistic instruction to the church in Rome, and adds
that the various commandments—you shall not commit adultery,
you shall not kill, you shall not steal, you shall not covet—and all
other commandments are contained in one maxim: "Love your
neighbour as yourself" (Rom 13:9). Therefore love is the fulfillment of
the Law (Rom 13:10). In other words, only by unselfish love does one
fulfill what God by the gift of his holy, just and good commandment
wishes to find in the life of mankind as a possibility and realisation.
In love the path is trod which is higher than any other path. Love is
the path which leads further than any other path (1 Cor 12:31). Even
if a person achieves ever so much, if he manages to perform the
highest deeds, if he offers all his earthly goods, and even if he allows
his body to be burned, all this would be vain and useless without
love (1 Cor 13:1-3). Only love, which the apostle praises, will remain
longer than faith and hope. Faith will one day be changed to actual
sight and hope will someday be fulfilled; love, however, remains.
Therefore it is the greatest (1 Cor 13:13).

This emphasis on the love commandment is characteristic for
instructions given to all the churches and refers to the interpretation

which Jesus gave to the understanding of the divine commandment. The Gospel writers report that a rich young man asked Jesus the question, what one has to do in order to receive eternal life. Jesus answered by referring to the familiar commandments of God, "You shall not kill, you shall not give false witness, you shall not defraud, honour your father and your mother" (Mark 10:19; para.). These binding instructions of God-given laws do not require any defence: they are God's holy law which has been established and therefore require unconditional obedience. However, the will of God is only understood and fulfilled where there is not only obedience to this or that law, but where the whole life is sanctified. God's will is not divided into a large number of individual instructions, but rather it is valid and undivided with respect to all of life's concerns.

The same problem of recognising God's will and under-standing what a human being must do is framed in the following question which a scribe addressed to Jesus: which is the greatest commandment in God's law (Mk 12:28; para.)? By ever more closely reasoned casuistic considerations the scholastic discussions of that era had established a total of 613 commandments and prohibitions in which the divine will was unfolded. In this thicket of instructions and rules how could one decide what was the greatest commandment? According to the description of the gospel writers Mark and Matthew, Jesus himself gives the answer, but in the Gospel of Luke the question is returned to the scribe: "What is written in the Law? How do you read it?" (Luke 10:26). In response the scribe formulated the double commandment of love for God and one's neighbour as the sum of the Law and the Prophets.

That a scribe answers in this way is easy to understand from the background of the Jewish teaching of that era. A lot of thought was given in that era to the meaning of the love commandment. The Old Testament stresses on the one hand that man's love is due to the one and only God, but, on the other hand, it maintains that one must love one's neighbour as oneself (Deut 6:5; Lev 19:18). These two commandments were not connected in the Old Testament, but a link was established in Jewish tradition which again and again considered the question of the relationship of God's commandments to the lives and actions of human beings. Thus in the so called Testaments of the Twelve Patriarchs, a literature which received its form in hellenistic Jewry, it says: "love the Lord and your neighbour, take pity on the poor and the weak" (Test Iss 5:2; cf. 7:6), or "fear the Lord and love your neighbour" (Test Ben 3:3); or "Love the Lord throughout your life and love one another with a sincere heart" (Test Dan 5:3; cf. also Seb 5:1f.). Judaism in the days of Jesus was fully aware that the loving fear of God and the helpful deed which is due to one's neighbour belong together as an undivided obedience to God's will and command and constitute an indivisible unity.[1]

If the double love commandment was already known in ancient Judaism, where are we to look for the special foundation of ethics which Jesus emphasised? In Jesus' teaching the instruction to love one's neighbour becomes an absolute obligation through the determination of the question: Who is my neighbour? If according to the prevailing view in that era the neighbour was considered to be the person who belonged to the national community and who was a worshipper of the God of Israel, then Jesus acknowledges no restriction in the definition of one's neighbour. The parable of the good Samaritan moreover stresses that a stranger, who belonged to the hated Samaritans, lifted up the Jew who had been attacked by robbers, bound his wounds and took him to the nearest inn (Luke 10:29-37). However the tradition which linked the double love commandment with the parable of the good Samaritan is judged, either only established in church tradition[2] or already present in the preaching of Jesus,[3] there can be no doubt that Jesus does away with all man-made differences and places his listeners immediately under the exhortation and claim of the emerging kingdom of God. Because the kingdom of God is near there can be no casuistic relaxation of God's commandment, but rather it is as valid, undivided and pressing as the demand to render unto God what is God's. That command means to belong to Him completely and, correspondingly, therefore, to see in the person who suffers and needs help, in one's neighbour, the obligation to help.

In this way the love commandment receives an incomparable deepening, because it is considered anew from the perspective of its very roots. God lets his sun shine on evil people and on good people

---

[1] Cf. *G. Bornkamm*, Das Doppelgebot der Liebe, in: Geschichte und Glaube I, 1968, 37-45; *C. Burchard*, Das doppelte Liebesgebot in der frühen christlichen Überlieferung, in: Der Ruf Jesu und die Antwort der Gemeinde (Fs. J. Jeremias), 1970, 39-62; and concerning the presuppositions of religionsgeschichte *A. Nissen*, Gott und der Nächste in dantiken Judentum. Untersuchungen zum Doppelgebot der Liebe, 1974.

[2] For composition by the hand of the evangelist, who also formed the parable, see *G. Sellin*, Lukas als Gleichniserzähler: die Erzählung vom barmherzigen Samariter (Lk 10,25-37), ZNW 65, 1974, 166-189; 66, 1975, 19-60.

[3] So with most exegetes: *J. Jeremias*, Die Gleichnisse Jesu, 1970, 200-203.

and lets the rain fall on the just and on the unjust (Matt 5:45). If you therefore "only love those who love you, what is your reward? Do not even the tax collectors do the same?" (Matt 5:46). Indeed, such behaviour would not differ from sober considerations regarding purposeful and advantageous conduct, which was practised everywhere. For pious Jews, who endeavoured to learn the undivided will of God and to obey it, the rules of the Qumran community advise one "to love all which He (ie., God) has chosen and to hate all that he has rejected" (1 QS 1:3f). That is, "to love all the sons of light, each according to his lot in the council of God, but to hate all sons of darkness, each according to his guilt" (1 QS 1:9f.). Against this Jesus says: "love your enemies, do good to those who hate you; bless those who curse you; pray for those who illtreat you" (Luke 6:27f). In the Gospel of Matthew this commandment of loving one's enemies is stated in the form of an antithesis, which clearly reveals the decisive contradiction to the admonitions which are present in the rules of Qumran: "You have heard it said: You shall love your neighbour and hate your enemy. But I say to you; Love your enemies and pray for those who persecute you" (Matt 5:43f). This enlargement of the unconditionally binding commandment of love not only breaks every casuistic splitting of God's will, but also removes any boundary which divides human beings one from the other.[4]

There are in fact numerous comparable sayings in the Jewish interpretation of the Law in that era for the individual ethical instructions which are found in the tradition of the sayings of Jesus. Even the theme of a radicalisation of God's commandment, which must not be taken apart into a number of admonitions and definitions but rather is valid in an undivided way, is found in the teaching of the Qumran community.[5] Whereas there all teaching concentrates on the one law which Moses had taught and which all pious people must turn to, Jesus testifies to the limitless love of God, the love for one's neighbour, even for the enemy. Therefore, it is not the individual admonitions, for which the study of comparative religion can furnish ample parallel material, which give us the distinctive foundation of ethical instructions in Jesus' teaching. Rather, the foundation is the radicalisation of the love commandment, which Jesus extends to love for one's enemies. In the light of

---

4 Cf. *G. Bornkamm*, Jesus von Nazareth, 1974, 101-105: Das Liebesgebot.
5 Cf. *H. Braun*, Spätjüdisch-häretischer und frühchristlicher Radikalismus, 1969.

the in-breaking of the kingdom of God this love will clearly illuminate the signs of the incomprehensible mercy of God in the midst of this world.

The orientation of ethical admonition toward the commandment of love, as it is found in the early Christian teaching (in Paul's theology and in the preaching of Jesus) is especially clearly stated in the writings of John. These writings do not furnish concrete instructions for the conduct of Christians, but rather designate the commandment of love as the only commandment. "A new commandment—so speaks Christ according to John—I give to you, that you love one another, even as I have loved you, that you also love one another" (John 13:34). These words do not announce an ethical principle, according to which the life of the disciples should be lived. If these words were to be understood in this sense, then they would have to be separable from the person who spoke them, and could be described as a generally valid truth. But the new commandment is only established by pointing to the love which Jesus shows to those who belong to him. The one who turns to him experiences the love of his Lord, in which He humbles himself as a servant and stoops down to those which are His. In this way love is let loose, that is, the disciple of Jesus is freed from worry about himself and is able to worry about other people.[6] The love commandment is not called new because this commandment did not exist before Jesus and the foundation of his circle of disciples. Judaism of that era as well as the hellenistic world most definitely spoke of love, even if the concept of *agape* (love) which occupies a central position in the early Christian tradition, was used only rarely.[7] The love commandment is called new because it is fundamental to the community of disciples of Jesus and defines that community. Because Jesus loved his own unto the end, they are now united in love for one another (cf. John 15:12).

There is therefore no contradiction when the love commandment is described in the first letter of John as being the old commandment, since from the beginning it is God's will that human beings should meet one another in love (1 John 2:7). This love makes real and fundamental change in human community life possible. "God is love; and the one who remains in love, remains in God and God in him" (1 John 4:16). Even in this statement one does not talk of

---

6 Cf. *R. Bultmann*, Das Evangelium des Johannes, 1968, 403f.

7 Cf. *O. Wischmeyer*, Agape in der ausserchristlichen Antike, ZNW 69, 1978, 212-238.

a common truth, but of love which consists in the fact that "we did not love God, but that He loved us and sent His son as the atonement for our sins" (1 John 4:10). The power which flows from this deed of God shapes and molds the conduct of those who can say: "and so we know and believe the love God has for us" (1 John 4:16).[8]

II.

If the fundamental orientation of ethics may be seen in the love commandment, the concrete decision which has to be made in the life and conduct of Christians may certainly be derived from the teachings of ethical tradition, which have been taken over from popular philosophical discussion of that era or from the moral instruction of the synagogue. The earliest Christian churches entered a world in which everywhere there was a lively endeavour to recognise and realise proper ethical conduct. From the time of the teaching of Aristotle, the philosophical discipline described as ethics had achieved a solid place within the broad field of endeavour concerned with the determination of all human conduct. From then on one always had to deal in the various teaching traditions with the question of the behaviour of man in his world and in dealing with his fellow men. It is therefore easy to understand that Christian preaching referred to this ethical endeavour, and took up some of its instructions and handed them on as Christian instruction. Popular philosophical instruction, spread above all in the hellenistic world by Cynic-Stoic teachers, gave instructions for a life informed by reason and for conduct in accordance with these instructions, in the realm of individual conduct as well as in the realm of political decisions. All this proceeded from the assumption that the person who can discern the order of the cosmos will be able to derive hints from it regarding the orientation of man with respect to the harmony of nature. Man will then use the opportunities which are available in the world in a thoughtful and measured way. He will not allow himself to depend on things and experiences, but will rather maintain inner freedom which at all times allows him to recognise right conduct and action. These Stoic thoughts were linked in the hellenistic world with the Old Testament Jewish tradition, which discerned the will of the God

---

8 On the concept of love in the Johannine writings cf. M. *Lattke*, Einheit im Wort. Die spezifische Bedeutung von "agape", "agapan" und "filein" im Johannes-Evangelium, 1975.

of Israel from his commandments and from their interpretation. In the Synagogues one endeavoured to bring the biblical instruction into harmony with the well-known fundamentals of a philosophical ethic by emphasising that the thing that mattered was to lead a life which was in accordance with the divine will. In order to establish what would be regarded as righteous conduct and what would be avoided as erroneous conduct, lists of virtues were used, which should be zealously obeyed, and lists of vices, from which one should refrain. In this manner firmly formulated catalogues developed, which were discussed on various occasions and used in answer to concrete questions. In certain passages of the New Testament letters which are devoted to ethical questions, such virtue and vice catalogues are quoted repeatedly and used in the instruction of the churches.[9]

The popular philosophical instruction of the late classical period used a more detailed scheme, which dealt with duties and tasks in the various spheres of life. Through this a pattern of instructions emerged which showed how a pious man should worship the gods, serve the fatherland, behave in relation to parents, brothers and relatives, conduct his marriage and educate his children.[10] Hellenistic Judaism took over this form of moral teaching and used it with minor alterations in the teaching of the synagogue. Instead of worshipping the gods, obedience to the one God was spoken of, whose commandments were to be followed. These commands determine in detail what is to be done in marriage, in the education of children, in relation to friends and relatives, as well as in the treatment of slaves. The Christian churches which developed in many parts of the Mediterranean region through the rapid spread of the gospel found such instructions, which they mostly received from the hellenistic synagogues, to be a rich collection of material. This collection enabled one to discern what was generally proper and dutiful behaviour. In this way one concentrated on the immediate situation of life in which one found oneself among members of the family, slaves and masters, in order to develop according to the so called *Haustafeln* (household codes), instruction as to how every

---

[9] Cf. *A. Vögtle*, Die Tugend- und Lasterkataloge, 1936; *S. Wibbing*, Die Tugend- und Lasterkataloge im Neuen Testament, 1959; *E. Kamlah*, Die Form der katalogische Paränese im Neuen Testament, 1964.

[10] Cf. *K. Weidinger*, Die Haustafeln, 1928; *E. Lohse*, Die Briefe an die Kolosser und an Philemon, 1968, 220-223 (see for further literature); and *W. Schrage*, Zur Ethik der neutestamentlichen Haustafeln, NTS 21, 1974/75, 1-22.

Christian in his place should observe what is proper conduct before the Lord.

Formulas were developed and handed down not only for individual ethical conduct but also for the recognition of duties which are to be fulfilled in society and in ordering the state. That one had to regard the government of the state as an order established by God, that one had to show respect and to obey its rules, was impressed upon the citizens of hellenistic cities, and everyone followed this generally acknowledged rule. Those who held power in the state had the duty to collect taxes and charges in order to be able to carry out official tasks. They publicly praised those who had shown special merit and punished those who had disobeyed the laws. Therefore, the one who remained conscious of the task to further the common good as a conscientious citizen could live in peace and quiet and find positive recognition from the state authorities. The passage of the letter to the Romans, in which Paul deals with proper conduct with regard to state authorities (Rom 13:1-7), is wholly in accordance with this former tradition.[11] It does not add even one specifically Christian idea. Neither Christian faith nor love is mentioned here. The argument of the passage is rather concerned with pointing out the God given order and the duty of every person to follow his conscience. What was common service for everyone was also a duty for Christians, who live and conduct themselves in the world. But does the instruction given in this case have a specifically Christian reasoning?

The entire section of the letter to the Romans which is devoted to ethical questions is based on the demand that the believers should offer their bodies, and that means themselves in all their actions, as a living, holy sacrifice, pleasing to God, as their reasonable worship (Rom 12:1). The cultic terms which are mentioned here—holy, sacrifice, worship of God—are used in a sense which has left any cultic meaning far behind.[12] The distinction between holy and profane, which was recognised world-wide, is broken. Here, neither the temple nor a consecrated place is mentioned, but rather the fulness and breadth of human life, in which the task of individual

---

11 Cf. esp. *M. Dibelius,* Rom und die Christen im ersten Jahrhundert, in: Botschaft und Geschichte II, 1956, 177-228; and the commentaries on the passage, esp. *E. Käsemann,* An die Römer, 1974, 337-347, and *G. Bornkamm,* Paulus, 1973, 216-222.

12 Cf. *E. Käsemann,* Gottesdienst im Alltag der Welt, in: Exegetische Versuche und Besinnungen II, 1975, 198-204.

action is stressed. There is no such thing as holy territory which has a boundary and is distinguished as a place of devotion and sacrifice with special dignity. Rather, the whole world is the place where Christians perform their divine service in their everyday life. Therefore, Paul continues, they should not obey the form and force of their era, but should allow themselves to be formed by the renewal of their reasonable judgment, a renewal they are undergoing (Rom 12:2). The renewal of man, mentioned here by the apostle, refers to his power of reasoning, his ability to think critically and to judge. While Paul in another passage says of the heathen that their minds were depraved (Rom 1:28), here the renewed action of God in the life of man is spoken of, which relates to his considered and rightly balanced judgment. By the sober consideration of the world, as it is revealed to the Christian faith, the ability to weigh critically and to examine is awakened. In this way there is no programme with a specifically Christian teaching about society according to which the order of human community life should be framed. The ethical passages in Paul's letters rather refer uncritically back to Old Testament Jewish or Hellenistic-Stoic teaching in order to take over that which proves itself to be useful. How is this choice made? Critical examination of the extensive traditional material is organised according to the question of what constitutes God's will, that which is good, pleasing and perfect (Rom 12:2).

What is considered to be God's will is therefore in no way certain in a once and for all sense. Rather, the one renewed and able to judge, under the influence of the Spirit, must examine critically traditional ethical instructions in order to decide what is best (Phil 1:10). The proper procedure for this is mentioned by Paul when he states: "Whatever is true, whatever is noble, whatever is right, whatever is pure, whatever is lovely, whatever is admirable, think about these things" (Phil 4:8). The demand of the hour must be met afresh by critically considering what tradition has to offer by way of insight and advice. Every man who has experienced the liberating power of God's mercy, is challenged to don the weapons of righteousness and to fulfill the law of Christ in his conduct. Wherever Christ is acknowledged as Lord and where God-given renewal takes place, which encompasses the whole person, freedom and power to act in the world is given, which is led by a truly sensible judgement and by the inventive power of love.[13] Even if the words "ama, et fac

---

[13] Cf. G. *Sauter*, Was heisst "christologische Begründung" christlichen Handelns heute?, EvTh 35, 1975, 407-21.

quod vis," attributed to Augustine, which state that love is able to discern and judge what should be done in every situation contain some truth,[14] nevertheless there is still the definite need for a more specific description of right ethical conduct.[15] In this way, however, the separate instructions do not form a sum of legal claims which have to be obeyed. Rather they show what is valid in the light of rich human experience as an exemplary description of moral action. It is precisely in this way that in the letter of James passages of Old Testament Jewish wisdom tradition, passages from hellenistic popular philosophy and early Christian sayings are made into a small booklet of Christian morals.[16]

"So whatever you wish that men would do to you, do so to them in everything, for this sums up the law and the prophets" (Matt 7:12). These words of the sermon on the mount, which are called the golden rule, summarise in a few words traditional instruction which is orientated to the Scriptures of the Old Testament. It is styled so that the reasoning should be immediately clear. After all, how can one expect morally responsible conduct from other people, if one is not oneself prepared to meet them in the same way? In the old world there was the widespread so called silver rule, according to which one should not do that which one does not want to have done to oneself by others. There is, however, also a positive formulation in the Jewish-hellenistic letter of Aristeas: "If you . . . wish to experience the good, do the same to your subjects" (207). This instruction, the reasoning of which is clear, is very close to the words of the sermon on the mount. In any case it proves that the golden rule does not embody a fundamentally new insight, but rather expresses what is generally acknowledged to be prudent conduct.[17] These maxims and rules receive their Christian foundation only in connection with early Christian teaching and proclamation through which they serve as the description of the actions of love and worship which Christians have to perform in the daily life of the world.

---

14 Cf. W. *Schrage*, Die konkreten Einzelgebote in der paulinischen Paränese, 1961, 9.

15 So R. *Bultmann*, Theologie des Neuen Testaments, 1968, 570; cf. *Schrage*, op cit, 268.

16 Cf. E. *Lohse*, Glaube und Werke - zur Theologie des Jakobusbriefes, in: Die Einheit des Neuen Testaments, 1973, 285-306.

17 On the spread of this rule in the ancient world cf. A. *Dihle*, Die goldene Regel. Eine Ein führung in die Geschichte der antiken und frühchristlichen Vulgärethik, 1962.

III.

How then is Christian ethics to be developed? According to our findings, from the writings of the New Testament it is apparent that Christian ethics does not arise as a system of generally valid truths.[18] God's will is valid at any time and in any place. The obligating power of the love command is not subject to the option of only occasional compliance. That Christians have to do the right and just thing has been given to them as a constant direction on their way through life. However, that which has to be recognised as the good and right thing and has to be done, must in every instance be decided by careful questioning after the will of God and by careful examination of traditional teaching. We must question traditional sets of commandments (instructions for the conduct of a responsible person in the family and in society, teaching regarding a reasonable way of behaving in one's own life as well as life in communion with others) to find out in which way they depict what ought to be recognised as righteous deeds and how to realise these deeds in concrete experience. In this way it may very well be possible that an instruction which is today considered to be a definition of right conduct may tomorrow, because of changed conditions, be no longer valid.[19] When the apostle Paul speaks of the conduct of Christians vis-a-vis the state authorities, he is looking at settled conditions, which have appeared in the Roman Empire at long last after terrible wars, a situation regarded by people in the Mediterranean area as a blessing of peace. In this case, the power of the state endeavours to preserve rights and justice and to increase them. Paul does not see before him the case of a conflict, in which Christians have to resist because they should obey God rather than men. Or to give another example, the words of Jesus define marriage as a closed union for the whole of life; "What God has joined together, let man not separate"

---

[18] Cf. also *E. Jüngel*, Erwägungen zur Grundlegung evangelische Ethik im Anschluss an die Theologie des Paulus, in: Unterwegs zur Sache, 1972, 234-245. For a sketch of ethics in the New Testament see *G. Strecker*, Handlungsorientierter Glaube. Vorstudien zu einer Ethik des Neues Testaments, 1972; Strukturen einer neutestamentlichen Ethik, ZThK 75, 1978, 117-46; Ziele und Ergebnisse einer neutestamentlichen Ethik, NTS 25, 1978/79, 1-15; *H.-D. Wendland*, Ethik des Neuen Testaments, 1970; *J.T. Sanders*, Ethics in the New Testament, 1975.

[19] On this problem cf. *E. Schweizer*, Ethischer Pluralismus im Neuen Testament, EvTh 35, 1975, 397-401; and *W. Schrage*, Korreferat zu "Ethischer Pluralismus im Neuen Testament", ibid, 402-407.

(Mark 10:9; para.). The apostle Paul, referring explicitly to this word of the Lord (1 Cor 7:10), can nevertheless visualise cases where it is not possible to maintain a marriage, where the Christian must divorce his spouse: If then there is a marriage between a Christian and a non-christian, and if the non-christian is no longer willing to remain in the marriage, then one should not endeavour to keep the spouse, but rather divorce of the partner is permitted. "A believing man or woman is not bound in such circumstances" (1 Cor 7:15).[20] In this case the decision is not up to individual judgement, but rather the critical norm is the understanding of the peace to which God has called his own people. To phrase it in another way: Consideration for others, bound by conscience (1 Cor 8:7-13; 10:25-31) and by thought, decision and action influenced by love, determines the conduct of Christians. The love commandment is valid as the complete summation of God's will and is the fulfillment of the law. Therefore it does not act through a network of casuistic rules, but rather by its liberating and obligating power it determines all realms of the conduct of the life of Christians.

Ethical maxims which before, contemporaneous with and after Christ are found variously, seek to describe that which is to be considered as right. They have been devised to find as broad a consent as possible. They win this consent because of their clear power of conviction, which appeals to the understanding judgement of human beings. They have therefore to be formulated so that they may persuade not just the person who feels open to conviction because of his religion. Rather, they have to be appealing to everyone in the light of their firm exposition. After all, ethical consideration is directed to the person, who in various circumstances of life has the task of deciding what is the responsible thing to do. The phenomenon of ethics is what constitutes being human. Philosophical considerations do not create this phenomenon; they seek to understand it and to interpret it.

It is true that in present day philosophical discussion the ethical formulation of problems has occasionally been unduly pushed into the background. But there is today again, and rightly so, the demand that ethics must after all be considered "the essential, vital discipline", "about which philosophy has to think deeply."[21] In

---

20 Cf. *G. Bornkamm,* Ehescheidung und Wiederverheiratung im Neuen Testament, in: Glaube und Geschichte I (see fn. 1), 56-59.

21 *W. Schulz,* Philosophie in der veränderten Welt, 1974, 630.

distinction from an honourable tradition of the past, there is today the idea that ethics must be defined without metaphysics. This means that the endeavour to define a philosophical ethic must not refer to "abstract, metaphysical principles or articles of faith," but should only consider "what every clear thinking and rational person can consider to be true."[22] Thus the formation of general moral rules of conduct will succeed most convincingly "when a rationally controlled discussion regarding various principles of human conduct is possible."[23] Philosophical ethics tries in various ways to describe a generally binding fundamental norm for human fellowship or responsibility, which one human being has for the other.[24] By stipulating rational reasoning, it is intended that as many as possible human beings will find agreement, conduct their behaviour with reference to the ethic and act accordingly.

Since it is the task of theology to speak about that "which concerns the life of every human being" this task cannot be carried out independently of ethical concerns.[25] Theology must address thoughtfully and carefully the question of ethics because in the process of defining itself faith is concerned with both its content and obligations. Theology finds before it not only the questions posed by ethics but also a wide tradition of different answers. Theological consideration of ethics participates in this general endeavour to recognise and actualise the good. On the one hand, theology will consider critically the whole world of morals, to examine everything and then to retain the best, "only the best, and that means that which by God's grace is praised as the best."[26] Ethical maxims have a Christian character only when they are placed in the context of the frame of Christian proclamation.

Because the crucified and risen Christ is proclaimed as the Lord of all the world and of all realms of life, the ethical instruction of the church does not ask for this or that deed or performance, but rather addresses the whole person and summons him to follow Christ and

---

22 *G. Patzig*, Ethik ohne Metaphysik, 1971, 67.

23 Ibid, 66.

24 *W. Kamlah*, Philosophische Anthropologie. Sprachliche Grundlegung und Ethik, 1973.

25 *G. Ebeling*, Studium der Theologie. Eine enzyklopädische Orientierung, 1975, 146.

26 *K. Barth*, Christliche Ethik, in: Zwei Vorträge, TEH 3, 1946, 7.

place himself in the service of love.[27] In the whole body of theology, therefore, the general human phenomenon of ethics receives an essential deepening. Christian preaching addresses man as a sinner forgiven by God, who receives the meaning of his life not by his actions, but only through the mercy of God. To put it differently: Not through his works but only through the message of the gospel, which gives freedom to him for Christ's sake does a person gain a firm foundation for life. But this means that the intensification which ethics receives in connection with Christian proclamation does not consist in a multiplication of commandments and prohibitions, "but rather in a radical simplification into a single commandment of love, for which faith provides an outlet by including the believer in the love of God."[28]

Love, which seeks not its own, but rather the neighbour's advantage, orientates itself critically to the many traditions of ethical teaching. However, it is in no way set free from the responsibility to make this ethical teaching transparent for everybody by rational evidence and to aim for as broad a consent as possible. The specifically Christian foundation for the ethical instruction of the church and its members can however not be achieved by rational insight and cannot be accepted in this way. It is only realised by faith, which trusts in the saving power of the gospel.[29] Out of this grows the gratitude of Christians, who as members of the church live their daily lives and do not do their works for the sake of their own glory, but rather in order to praise God and to serve their fellow men.

---

[27] Cf. Schrage (fn. 14), 57; and Strecker, Strukturen (fn. 18), 137: "The distinctive of Christian ethics in the New Testament exists not in a new ethical programme, but rather in the christological dimension."

[28] *Ebeling*, op cit, 158. Cf. also G. Friedrich: "the Christian's actions are not prescribed by a dogma, but rather by love for the neighbour" (Die Verbindlichkeit neutestamentlicher Aussagen für das Handeln, Zeitwende 47, 1976, 237-48, here 248).

[29] Cf. Strecker, op cit, 144: "Christ expects man to let no one take away the responsibility for his actions, but rather to accept the risk of making an ethical decision."

CHAPTER TWELVE

How Paul Developed His Ethics

Motivations, Norms and Criteria of Pauline Ethics

Eckhard J. Schnabel
(1992)

The following discussion of motivations, norms and criteria of Pauline ethics proceeds on the basis of the following observations. First, while speaking of Paul's "ethics" we must be conscious of the fact that it is hardly possible to speak of "the ethics" of the Apostle Paul in the proper sense of the word[1]—if we define "ethics" as rational conception, systematic explication and methodical verification of human behavior. If we understand the term "ethics" in a more general sense as "evaluation, description and orientation of the human conduct of life",[2] we may well speak of "Pauline ethics": Paul reflected not only on questions of christology, salvation and salvation

---

[1] Victor P. Furnish, *Theology and Ethics in Paul* (Nashville: Abingdon 1968) 208-212.

[2] Trutz Rendtorff, "Ethik VII. Neuzeit", *Theologische Realenzyklopädie* 10 (1982) 481-517: 481.

history or ecclesiology, but also on the behavior of the believers in Jesus Christ.[3] If one intends to use an alternate term for "ethics", *paraklesis*[4] is to be preferred to the traditional term *paraenesis*.[5]

Second, the present study is not concerned to trace possible "developments" of ethical conceptions and perspectives between Paul's first and last letters. Rather, the focus is on the material content of Paul's ethics.

Third, I will not attempt to present the history of research, nor will I discuss different positions which have been held.[6] A few remarks at this point may suffice. The majority of non-evangelical theologians, at least on the continent, deny that Scripture teaches a "material ethics". They maintain that the New Testament approach to ethics implies a reduction of the will of God to the love commandment and an emphasis on Christian freedom; thus it can be summarized in Augustine's dictum *ama, et fac quod vis*.[7] This view of New Testament ethics is inadequate, however. It is a modern interpretation of Pauline or NT ethics along the lines of an "autonomous morality"[8] which owes more to the moral philosophy

---

[3] Cf. Wolfgang Schrage, *Ethik des Neuen Testaments* (Grundrisse zum Neuen Testament Band 4, Göttingen: Vandenhoeck & Ruprecht 1982) 13-14 with regard to the entire New Testament.

[4] Thus Anton Grabner-Haider, *Paraklese und Eschatologie bei Paulus* (Münster: Aschendorff 1968) 4; Rudolf Schnackenburg, *Die sittliche Botschaft des Neuen Testaments. Zweiter Band: Die urchristlichen Verkündiger* (HThK Supplementband II, Freiburg: Herder 1988) 8 with n. 2.

[5] Since Martin Dibelius *paraenesis* is a technical term referring to exhortations with a general moral content for a specific addressee; cf. Martin Dibelius, *Der Brief des Jakobus* (Kritisch-exegetischer Kommentar XV, (Göttingen: Vandenhoeck & Ruprecht 1984[6] = 1921) 16-18; cf. Johannes Thomas, *EWNT* 3 (1983) 5-6.

[6] Consult Furnish, *Theology*, 242-279; Rudolf Hasenstab, *Modelle paulinischer Ethik* (Tübinger Theologische Studien 11, Mainz: Grünewald 1977) 29-138.

[7] See the remarks in Wolfgang Schrage, "Zur formalethischen Deutung der paulinischen Paränese", *Zeitschrift für evangelische Ethik*, 4 (1960) 207-233: 207 who refers to Rudolf Bultmann, *Glauben und Verstehen* (Vol. 1, Tübingen: Mohr-Siebeck 1980[6]) 229ff, 234f. See also Furnish, *Theology* 233-237, 241; H. D. Wendland, *Ethik des Neuen Testaments* (Göttingen: Vandenhoeck & Ruprecht 1970) 59-63, 86f; Jack T. Sanders, *Ethics in the New Testament* (London: SCM 1975) 50-60; 64f; Eduard Lohse, "Kirche im Alltag: Erwägungen zur theologischen Begründung der Ethik im Neuen Testament", *Kirche* (FS G. Bornkamm, ed. D. Lührmann et al., Tübingen: Mohr-Siebeck 1980) 401-415: 401-406, 412-414 [The Editor: see the previous chapter in this volume].

[8] Cf. the Roman Catholic authors Anton Auer, *Autonome Moral und christlicher Glaube* (Düsseldorf: Patmos 1971); W. Korff, *Theologische Ethik* (Freiburg: Herder 1975); F. Böckle, *Fundamentalmoral* (München: Kösel 1977, 1991[5]) and the Protestants P. Richardson, *Paul's Ethic of Freedom*, 1979; Georg Strecker,

of Kant[9] and a one-sided interpretation of Luther[10] than an unbiased reading of Paul's letters.

Finally, it is not possible within the confines of the present study to present a systematic discussion of the sources, forms and the material content of Pauline ethics.[11] The following remarks presuppose the conviction that the ethics of the Apostle Paul can be grasped and described only in consideration of the theological foundations and impulses of his thought and his faith: God's action in Jesus Christ, the Risen One who is the Kyrios of the church, establishes, implies and inspires Christian behaviour.[12]

I shall attempt to develop the answer to the question how Paul arrives at ethical decisions and how he substantiates and motivates these decisions inductively by considering specific ethical questions as they are discussed by Paul. In order to obtain the broadest possible insight into the variety of motivations, norms and criteria of Pauline ethics it seems advisable to focus on a topic of Paul's exhortation to Gentile Christians which receives extensive treatment. The exhortation to overcome envy and strife and to pursue love and peace is such a subject.[13]

"Autonome Sittlichkeit und das Proprium der christlichen Ethik bei Paulus", *Theologische Literaturzeitung* 104 (1979) 865-872; Birger Gerhardsson, *The Ethos of the Bible* (Philadelphia: Fortress, 1981) 64-71.

9 Cf. Hasenstab, *Modelle*, 263f; L. Honnefelder, "Die ethische Rationalität der Neuzeit", *Handbuch der christlichen Ethik* (Vol. I, Freiburg/Gütersloh: Herder/Mohn 1978) 19-46: 34-36; Klaus Bockmühl, *Gesetz und Geist. Eine kritische Würdigung des Erbes protestantischer Ethik* (Gießen: Brunnen 1987) 522.

10 Cf. recently Bockmühl, *Gesetz und Geist*, 523ff.

11 Cf. Furnish, *Theology*, 1968; Sanders, *Ethics*, 1975; J. L. Houlden, *Ethics and the New Testament* (London: SCM 1979); Jean-François Collange, *De Jésus à Paul* (Genf: Labor et Fides 1980); Gerhardsson, *Ethos*, 1981; Schrage, *Ethik*, 1982; Siegfried Schulz, *Neutestamentliche Ethik* (Zürich: Theologischer Verlag 1987); Schnackenburg, *Sittliche Botschaft*, 1988.

12 Cf. Otto Merk, *Handeln aus Glauben: Die Motivierungen der paulinischen Ethik* (Marburger Theologische Studien 5, Marburg: Elwert 1968) 5: "The act of God as presupposition and substantiation of Christian being and doing" (heading of the first chapter; my translation). Similarly the heading of the first chapter in Schnackenburg, *Botschaft*, 14: "The foundation of Pauline morality: God's way of salvation in Jesus Christ" (my translation). Cf. Schrage, "Ethik IV. Neues Testament", *Theologische Realenzyklopädie* 10 (1982) 435f, 445f.

13 Schnackenburg, *Botschaft*, 63, regards this topic—besides the exhortation to holy living, the warning of immorality and greed and the exhortation to keep distance from the world and its enticements—as a central theme of the Gentile Christian *paraklesis* of the apostle, but does not elaborate beyond a brief descriptive sketch.

At first sight the subject "strife and peace" appears insignificant and not of greatest consequence for the present ethical discussion. However, at closer inspection the relevance of this topic becomes apparent, both with regard to ecclesiological questions and with regard to the praxis of church life. Of course the discussion of the role of women in society and in the church, or the question of Paul's view of slavery, or the issue of the Christians' attitude with regard to state authority appears more exciting and stimulating for a discussion of Paul's ethics. Still, the issue of why and how Christians should overcome discord and obtain peace is a more comprehensive and therefore a more basic ethical problem: church history, the present state of the church and the reality of Christian existence in the local churches may be taken as a proof.

I will discuss the relevant passages on the subject of "strife and peace" with the focus on the motivations, norms and criteria of orientation which Paul adduces or implies.[14] The form of a summary essay requires that exegetical decisions are presented as results; as regards the argumentative details one may consult the literature cited in the notes.

1. EXEGETICAL ANALYSIS

1. Gal 5.13-6.10. In his letter to the Christians in the Galatian churches Paul defends the truth of the gospel against the threat which the Jewish-Christian demands for observance of the (cultic) Torah presented. I follow those interpreters who regard 5.13ff as prophylactic argument concerning possible objections against his gospel, rather than as a discussion of actual conditions in the Galatian churches; the pericope is an integral part of the presentation of justification by faith in the earlier chapters of the letter and is thus to be regarded as a general exhortation.[15] Paul compares quarrels

---

[14] Wolfgang Schrage, "Ethik IV", *Theologische Realenzyklopädie* 10 (1982) 436 speaks of a "motivation level" and an "orientation level"; I suggest that one needs to add a "normative level"; cf. Eckhard J. Schnabel, *Law and Wisdom from Ben Sira to Paul: A Tradition Historical Enquiry into the Relation of Law, Wisdom, and Ethics* (WUNT 2/16, Tübingen: Mohr-Siebeck 1985) 299-342 passim.

[15] Cf. Franz Mußner, *Der Galaterbrief* (Herders Theologischer Kommentar zum Neuen Testament IX, Freiburg: Herder 1988⁵) 374; Hans-Dieter Betz, *Galatians* (Hermeneia, Philadelphia: Fortress 1979) 277; Udo Borse, *Der Brief an die Galater* (Regensburger Neues Testament, Regensburg: Pustet 1984) 20f, 189f; recently Joachim Rohde, *Der Brief des Paulus an die Galater* (Theologischer Hand-

between believers with the behaviour of wild animals which assault and devour each other in their fight for the prey (5.15). He urges the Christians to love each other (vv. 13-14) and to live by the Spirit (vv. 16-26). We note the following argumentative motifs in Paul's exhortation to proper ethical behaviour.

(a) The hyperbolic comparison of human behaviour with the atrocious aggressiveness of predaceous animals (5.15) implies the argument that human beings do not behave like animals who can destroy each other. Paul presupposes here the order of God's creation with the fundamental discrimination between man and animal as criterion of human, and particularly, Christian behaviour.

(b) The behaviour of animals fighting for the prey, attacking and destroying each other *(analiskō*, v. 15), should be regarded as ruled out since the result of such conduct is evident: self-destruction is unreasonable. The impact of the biting irony of v. 15 derives from man's power of judgment: human reason discerns the obvious consequences of such bestial aggressiveness and recognizes the self-laceration of animals as absurd and ridiculous.

(c) Comparisons of wrong behaviour with the conduct of wild animals are well-known motifs in Greek-Hellenistic literature.[16] Paul is not afraid to take up elements of contemporary pagan ethics. He presupposes evidently that Christians and non-Christians share important moral norms, in this case the discrimination between man and animal and the urge for self-preservation.

(d) Paul contrasts (*de*) the "beastly behaviour" which he denounces with brotherly love (vv. 13c, 14). He who loves his neighbour does not fight with him; the person who loves does not inflict wounds. The *agapē* of the believer has its roots in God's love and in the life of Christ: "It is no longer I who live, but Christ who lives in me; and the life I now live in the flesh I live by faith in the Son of God, who loved me and gave himself for me" (2.20). The love of the believer means self-sacrifice, becoming concrete in specific acts of commitment to others (*douleuete allēlois*, 5.13c). Love as service to others is concrete and specific, it is expressed in behaviour which is free from fighting each other. Such love is the result of faith (5.6) and

---

kommentar zum Neuen Testament 9, Berlin: Evangelische Verlagsanstalt 1989) 226f. Differently F. F. Bruce, *Commentary on Galatians* (NIGNTC, Grand Rapids 1982) 242.

16 Cf. Heinrich Schlier, *Der Brief an die Galater* (Kritisch-exegetischer Kommentar 7, Göttingen: Vandenhoeck & Ruprecht 1989[15]) 246 n. 1; Betz 277 n. 43 for references.

is part of the fruit of the Spirit (5.22). The *agapē* of the believers is thus
not a natural human capacity but a soteriological reality of life in the
Spirit. Paul grounds proper Christian behaviour in the reality of
Christ's rule.

(e) The *agapē* which the believers are exhorted to exhibit as
proper behaviour is a command of the law: "For the whole law is
fulfilled in one word, 'You shall love your neighbour as yourself'"
(5.14, quoting Lev 19.18). Paul cites a statement of the Old Testament
as norm of Christian behaviour. The formulation *ho pas nomos* does
not designate the sum total of the individual stipulations of the Torah
but, rather, the law which is in its entirety the expression of the will
of God.[17] And Paul does not argue for or imply a material reduction
of Torah to the love command:[18] the commandment to love,
designated as *heis logos* in the sense of the Jewish (rabbinic) *kᵉlal*, the
basic principle or "common denominator" of the Torah.[19] The
Christian believer who is "in Christ" and lives by the Spirit and
whose faith becomes effective in love (5.5-6) fulfills the law as a
whole by obeying the commandment to love. The Christian is not
absolved from fulfilling the Torah as the "law of Christ" (6.2), which
is however, for Gentile Christians, not a new way of salvation.[20] The
Torah has received a new controlling criterion as a result of the
atoning death of Jesus who is the Messiah and it has acquired new
contours as revelation of God's will: what has been accomplished in
the death of Christ once and for all and what has become possible
through association with that death—righteousness/justification,

---

[17] Cf. *BDF* §275.3; Betz, 275; Mußner, 370; Bruce, 241; Rohde, 229; also Hans
Hübner, *Law in Paul's Thought* (ET, Edinburgh: T. & T. Clark, 1984), 36ff.

[18] Contra Hübner, 38f, 76f; Heikko Räisänen, *Paul and the Law* (WUNT 29,
Tübingen: Mohr-Siebeck 1983) 26f. The *kᵉlal* is not a commandment, and *logos* in
v. 14 does not necessarily mean "commandment" either!

[19] Cf. Bruce, 241, following Hans-Joachim Schoeps, *Paul: The Theology of the
Apostle in the Light of Jewish Religious History* (Philadelphia: Westminster 1961)
208; also Ulrich Wilckens, *Der Brief an die Römer* (Evangelisch-Katholischer
Kommentar VI/3, Zürich/Neukirchen-Vluyn: Benziger/Neukirchener Verlag
1982) 68f, 70f with regard to Rom 13.8 and Gal 5.14.

[20] For this interpretation see Eberhard Jüngel, *Paulus und Jesus*
(Hermeneutische Untersuchungen zur Theologie 2, Tübingen: Mohr-Siebeck
1979⁵) 61; Andrea van Dülmen, *Die Theologie des Gesetzes bei Paulus* (Stuttgarter
Biblische Monographien 5, Stuttgart: Katholisches Bibelwerk 1968) 66-68; Ulrich
Wilckens, "Zur Entwicklung des paulinischen Gesetzesverständnisses", *New
Testament Studies* 28 (1982) 154-190: 175f; idem, *Römer*, 1:245; 3:71f; Betz, 166, 179,
229f; Schnabel, 277f; cf. Ferdinand Hahn, "Das Gesetzverständnis im Römer- und
Galaterbrief", *Zeitschrift für die neutestamentliche Wissenschaft* 76 (1976) 29-63: 57.

atonement of sin, does not have to be reacquired again and again by those who have been identified with Christ by faith. Consequently large parts of the Torah, particularly of the cultic Torah, have no further factual validity as normative will of God. But the Torah remains the revelation of God's will in its new relation to Jesus Christ.[21]

(f) Paul explains the exhortation to love each other and to abstain from egotistical fighting with reference to the Spirit: "So I say, live by the Spirit, and you will not gratify the desires of the sinful nature" (5.16, NIV). The Spirit of God enables the believers to do the will of God (v. 14). Those who live in the context of a new reality on account of their identification with Jesus Christ (2.19-20), a reality of true existence determined by God's Spirit (*zōmen pneumati*), can live in accordance with the Spirit (*pneumati stoichōmen*, 5.25). Paul's ethics is pneumatologically motivated.

(g) The introductory reference to the call to freedom (v. 13) which has been effected through Christ (v. 1) and the reference to the future inheritance of God's kingdom (v. 21) show that the fundamental and most comprehensive substantiation of Paul's ethic is God's salvational act in Jesus Christ. The *eleutheria* which has been given in and with Christ implies liberation from all other ways to salvation, liberation from sin as dominating power, liberation from the death sentence of the law—a liberty which is being demonstrated as real in the ability to serve one's neighbour.[22] The obedience of the Christian (*douleuete*, v. 13) is both the proof and the test of faith. The christological motivation of Christian behaviour is the foundational introductory statement at the beginning of Paul's *paraklesis* in Gal 5-6.

(h) Paul includes a catalogue of vice in order to warn the believers of specific acts of the godless sinner (5.19-21). A central place in the list is occupied by eight terms which are related to community life and which are linked with envy and discord:[23] enmity, strife, jealousy, anger, selfishness, dissension, party spirit, envy. The exhortation to proper behaviour implicit in the list concludes with the threat of exclusion from the future kingdom of

---

21 Cf. Wilckens, 3:71 who states that Christians hear in God's law the binding instruction for a life in righteousness: the fulfillment of God's law constitutes Christian righteousness as true righteousness.

22 Kurt Niederwimmer, *EDNT* 1 (1980) 431-34.

23 Mußner, 381 who assumes an *inclusio* formed by five initial (fornication, impurity, licentiousness, idolatry, sorcery) and two final terms (drunkenness, carousing).

God (v. 21b) and presupposes the conviction that adaptation and assimilation to the behaviour patterns of the world determined by sinful *sarx* are still possibilities for the Christian believer. He may be "entrapped" by some sin without having acted willfully (*prolēmphthē en*, 6.1). The locus of Christian ethics is determined, for Paul, by the salvation-historical time between the resurrection of Jesus Christ and his parousia. The simultaneous existence of the old "evil" aeon determined by the flesh and the newly inaugurated aeon of the new creation determined by the Spirit establishes the situation of the believer "between the ages". This salvation-historical tension explains why the indicative and the imperative appear side by side (*zōmen . . . stoichōmen*, 5.25).

(i) Both form and content of the catalogues of virtue and vice remind the reader of Greek-Hellenistic parallels[24] as well as of Jewish adaptations of such lists.[25] Paul did not simply borrow traditional lists of ethical values from such sources nor did he assimilate his message completely to the moral perspectives of other systems.[26] Scholars have repeatedly pointed out the differences between the meaning and function of traditional catalogues of virtue and vice in the Hellenistic or Jewish traditions and in Paul.[27] However, it cannot be denied that there are links both with regard to terminology and with regard to conceptual content. Paul appeals here and in similar passages[28] to a widespread recognition in conventional morality in the Mediterranean realm that there are phenomena of social life which are to be condemned and which must be shunned and other features which are to be praised and promoted.[29] Paul is not reluctant to take up contemporary moral criteria in the promulgation of Christian ethics.

---

[24] Cf. Siegfried Wibbing, *Die Tugend- und Lasterkataloge im Neuen Testament und ihre Traditionsgeschichte* (BZNW 25, Berlin: de Gruyter 1959); Ehrhard Kamlah, *Die Form der katalogischen Paränese im Neuen Testament* (Tübingen: Mohr-Siebeck 1964).

[25] Cf. Ps Sol 14.23-31; 4Macc 1.26-27; 2.15; TRub 3.3-6; TLev 17.11; TJud 16; 2Enoch 10.4-5; ApcBar 8.5; 13.4; 1QS 4.2-14; Philo SacrAbr 32.

[26] Thus James D. G. Dunn, *Romans* (Word Biblical Commentary 38, Dallas: Word 1988) 1:67 with regard to the catalogue of vice in Rom 1.29-31.

[27] Cf. Mußner, 329-395 with regard to 1QS 4; Wilckens, 1:112 in the context of his discussion of Rom 1.29.

[28] Catalogues of virtue: 2Cor 6.6; Gal 5.22-23; Phil 4.8; Eph 4.2-3,32; 5.9; Col 3.12; catalogues of vice: Rom 1.29-31; 13.13; 1Cor 5.10-11; 6.9-10; 2Cor 12.20-21; Gal 5.19-21; Eph 4.31; 5.3-5; Col 3.5,8. Cf. Mußner, 380 n. 33.

[29] Dunn, 1:67.

(j) Finally we notice that in order to substantiate his exhortations Paul refers to the future inheritance of God's kingdom (5.21), to the judgment of God over all who mock God by despising his Spirit and his fruit (6.7),[30] to the final judgment with the dual consequences of destruction and eternal life (6.8)[31] and to the rich harvest of God's blessing (6.9). The future hope of the Christians carries weight for their present conduct. The relation between sowing and reaping implies motivating power for the behaviour of the believer in the present aeon.[32] The indicative continues in the imperative as appeal to the responsibility of the individual not to become weary in doing good.[33] The eschatological reference of Paul's exhortation emphasizes the "Not yet" with regard to the present and influences and determines the behaviour of the Christians by pointing to the future as warning and as promise.

2. Rom 12-13. In order to make concrete what he has said earlier in chapters 6-8,[34] Paul begins his exhortation in Rom 12.1-15.13 with a general *paraklesis* in chap. 12-13. Part of his representation is the subject of overcoming envy and strife and seeking love and harmony.

(a) Starting in 12.3 Paul speaks of the conduct of the believers in the context of the organism of the church. He admonishes the members of the church to avoid anything which may break up the fellowship of the believers who have different gifts but form one body in Christ.[35] Nobody should "think of himself more highly than he ought to think". Rather, everyone should think of himself with sober judgment in accordance with the "measure of faith" given to him (v. 3b). Overestimation of one's own capacities leads to envy and discord. The criterion for proper self-assessment is indicated by *par' ho dei phronein*: the measure of his conviction which is set by God[36] (implying a theocentric norm for Christian behaviour), or reasonableness which has become possible as a result of the renewal of his *nous*

---

30 Mußner, 404f.
31 Cf. Schlier, 277; Mußner, 405; Rohde, 267.
32 Friedrich Hauck, *TWNT* 2:132f.
33 Alexander Sand, *EWNT* 2:359.
34 Wilckens, 3:2.
35 Peter Stuhlmacher, *Der Brief an die Römer* (Das Neue Testament Deutsch 6, Göttingen: Vandenhoeck & Ruprecht 1989) 172.
36 Walter Grundmann, *TWNT* 2:25 speaks with regard to Rom 12.3 of necessity grounded in the will of God; cf. Wiard Popkes, *EDNT* 1:279-80 who understands *dei* as a term implying in a more or less direct manner mostly a divine ruling (669). Also Wilckens, 3:11.

(v. 2). The second interpretation is to be preferred if Paul uses the seemingly traditional play on the word *pronein*[37] in order to allude to elements of general Greek ethics in which *sōphrosynē* was included among the cardinal virtues, defined as the skill to find and maintain the reasonable and sensible "golden mean" in the diverse situations of life.[38] If this interpretation is correct; Paul appeals to the reasonable mind of the believers as criterion of brotherly behaviour. We should note at this point that Paul had emphasized earlier that the *nous* of man which had become quite useless as a result of sin (1.28), incapable to reach beyond the knowledge of what is good while recognizing its own inefficiency (7.23),[39] has been drawn into the renewal of man through Christ.

(b) In 12.3c Paul mentions the "measure of faith" which God has given to each individual believer as the standard of proper behaviour. On closer inspection we notice two criteria: the apportioning action of God and *pistis* as the gospel of the atoning death of Jesus Christ and his resurrection which applies to all believers in the same manner and which has been given to them according to measure (*metron*), i.e. as norm and criterion for their behaviour.[40] Proper conduct in the church which makes harmonious living together as "body in Christ" (v. 5) possible is motivated theocentrically in the context of christocentric norms.

(c) Paul introduces his exhortation to self-effacing behaviour in the church for the sake of harmony with the sentence: "For by the grace given to me I bid every one among you" (12.3a). The verb *legō* signifies here, as in other passages, an imperative: it expresses Paul's consciousness of his apostolic call and mission.[41] As in 1.5, the term *charis* designates Paul's apostolic office which God by his grace and enabling call has given to him and which thus implies authority for the *panti tō onti en hymin*.[42] Paul evidently regards his apostolic instructions and injunctions as normative for the behaviour of the believers in the churches.

---

[37] *hyperphronein—sōphronein.*

[38] Wilckens, 3:11; Dunn, 2:721.

[39] Hans-Dieter Betz, "Das Problem der Grundlagen der paulinischen Ethik (Röm 12.1-2)", *Zeitschrift für Theologie und Kirche 85* (1988) 199-218: 214.

[40] Thus C. E. B. Cranfield, *The Epistle to the Romans* (International Critical Commentary, Edinburgh: T.&T. Clark 1979) 2:615f; Wilckens, 3:11f; Stuhlmacher, 172; pace Dunn, 2:721f.

[41] Hans Hübner, *EWNT* 2:856. Cf. the commentaries ad loc.

[42] Cf. Wilckens, 3:10; Dunn, 2:720.

(d) In 12.14 Paul admonishes the Christians not to respond to hostility with hostility: if this holds good with regard to persecuting enemies it applies even more so with regard to the brother and sister in the church. The background of the exhortation to bless those who persecute is the exhortation of Jesus in Mt 5.43-44; Lk 6.27-28[43] to which Paul alludes.[44] Paul does not explicitly designate the statement as a word of Jesus, perhaps because for him dominical sayings possessed a self-evident validity which is not dependent upon an external juridical quotation formula or upon literal correctness.[45]

(e) The exhortation in 12.3 is taken up again in v. 16: Paul calls upon the believers to "have a common mind", i.e. to "live in harmony with one another" (RSV, NIV). The admonition to abstain from haughtiness ("do not cherish proud thoughts", v. 16a) corresponds to the injunction "do not be wise in your own estimation" (v. 16d, RSV: "never be conceited"). Since Paul has brought together various motifs from the Jewish wisdom tradition we may assume that the exhortation of v. 16d was drawn from Prov 3.7 (cf. also Isa 5.21; Prov 26.5,12; 28.26) and that Paul expected his readers to recognize the allusion and thus acknowledge the scriptural force of the injunction.[46]

(f) The aim of the general *paraklesis* in Rom 12-13 is the lifelong commitment to the love command (13.8-10): those who love their neighbours will not hurt them (v. 10a). Paul grounds the love command in the stipulations of the Torah: the four commandments of the second half of the Decalogue which Paul quotes in v. 9a are only a selection ("and any other commandment", v. 9b). As those who have been loved by God respond to God's love by loving their "neighbours", they fulfill the law: love is that behaviour in which the law is being fulfilled.[47] Recent commentators recognize the

---

43 Cf. Ernst Käsemann, *An die Römer* (Handbuch zum Neuen Testament 8a, Tübingen: Mohr-Siebeck 1980⁴) 334; Wilckens, 3:22f; Stuhlmacher, 176.

44 Cf. Dunn, 2:744f for the relevant arguments. Cf. recently Michael B. Thompson, *Clothed with Christ: The Example and Teaching of Jesus in Romans 12.1-15.13* (JSNTSS 59, Sheffield: JSOT Press 1991) 90-109 who regards 12.14 as "an echo" and leaves the question open whether Paul *intended* the readers to recognize Jesus tradition.

45 Thus Schrage, *Ethik*, 201; idem, "Ethik IV", *Theologische Realenzyklopädie* 10 (1982) 448. For a recent discussion on criteria for evaluating allusions and echoes cf. Thompson, 30-36.

46 With Dunn, 2:747. Many commentators note the allusion to Prov 3.7.

47 Wilckens, 3:71.

significance of the implied "Christian reception of the Torah for the life of Christians".[48]

Paul includes the admonition to overcome discord and to strive for love and harmony not only in his general exhortation but also in his discussion of specific contexts linked to concrete situations. The following observations serve to elucidate the application of Paul's general exhortation to specific local church situations.

3. 1Thess 4.9-12. Paul does not consider it necessary, in view of their present conduct, to impress upon the believers in Thessalonica the commandment of brotherly love: they themselves have been "taught by God" (*autoi theodidaktoi*, v. 9).

(a) Paul evidently implies that the apostolic proclamation of the gospel conveys "being taught by God" (having been made effective by the Holy Spirit).[49] If this interpretation is correct, Paul's formulation in v. 9 claims divine authority for the apostolic *dicta*: he designates the apostolic instruction, including the ethical exhortation, as "God's teaching" without differentiating qualitatively between apostolic exhortation and divine will.

(b) Other scholars relate the phrase "taught by God" on the basis of Jer 31.33-34 to the efficacious work of the Holy Spirit.[50] If the Thessalonian believers recognized this reference, Paul's statement implies the pneumatological foundation and motivation of brotherly love as centre and principle of Christian ethics. The Spirit of God effects understanding and praxis of brotherly love both with regard to its scope ("all the brethren throughout Macedonia", v. 10a) and with regard to its necessity ([*ou*] *chreian echete*, v. 9).[51]

---

[48] Wilckens, 3:70 (my translation); he provides a concise statement of Paul's argumentation in Rom as "horizon of the thesis in 13.8-10"; cf. also Dunn, 2:781; Stuhlmacher, 187f.

[49] Thus Traugott Holtz, *Der erste Brief an die Thessalonicher* (Evangelisch-Katholischer Kommentar XIII, Zürich/Neukirchen-Vluyn: Benziger/Neukirchener Verlag 1986) 175.

[50] Cf. recently F. F. Bruce, *1 & 2 Thessalonians* (Word Biblical Commentary 45, Waco: Word 1982) 90; I. H. Marshall, *1 and 2 Thessalonians* (New Century Bible Commentary, London: Marshall, Morgan & Scott 1983) 115; Hans-Heinrich Schade, *Apokalyptische Christologie bei Paulus* (Göttingen Theologische Arbeiten 18, Göttingen: Vandenhoeck & Ruprecht 1984²) 149.

[51] Bruce, 90 alludes to the christological norm of love: "Love of one's neighbor was enjoined in the OT law (cf. Lev 19.18) and reaffirmed in the teaching of Jesus (Mark 12.31; cf. John 13.34 . . . where Jesus' love for his followers is the model for their love one for another)"; when the Christians are said to be divinely taught to love one another, "the reference may be both to the teaching of Jesus and to the

(c) If Paul thinks of the prophetic saying, Isa 54.13[52], where the sons of the new Jerusalem are said to be "taught by the Lord"[53], he may have drawn upon early Christian tradition;[54] according to John 6.45 Jesus quotes this passage and applies it to all those who hear his voice. The early church may have interpreted its life on the basis of Isa 54.13 as fulfillment of the prophet's promises for the people of God in the last days:[55] as members of the new covenant[56] they are "taught by God" in the new era of salvation. Paul does not proceed to unfold in specific and concrete terms what brotherly love as life in the new aeon entails for the Thessalonian believers; apart from hospitality and help for travellers one may think of caring for widows and the poor.

(d) The statement in 4.10b, "We exhort you, brethren, to do so more and more", expresses Paul's consciousness of his apostolic authority which he obviously links with God's authority. The conviction that the church is "taught by God" does not exclude the possibility, or necessity, of further exhortation by the apostle.

(e) The admonition in 4.11 shows that brotherly love is not to be confused with vague benevolence but implies "richtungskonstante Inhalte und Signaturen",[57] i.e. consistent substance and specific injunctions. Under the heading of brotherly love Paul insists on the obligation to work with one's own hands. In other words, the admonition that the believers must earn their own living is

---

inward action of the Spirit". The term *theodidaktoi* may then imply the deity of Christ (cf. T. I. Tambyah, *Expository Times* 44 [1932-33] 527-528).

52 Thus many commentators, cf. Ernest Best, *A Commentary on the First and Second Epistles to the Thessalonians* (Black's New Testament Commentaries, London: Black 1972) 172f; Bruce, 90; emphasized by Holtz, 174.

53 Jes 54.13 LXX: *kai pantas tous hyious sou didaktous theou.*

54 Cf. Holtz, 174.

55 Cf. Holtz, 174 with n. 160 who takes up the suggestion of Peder Johan Borgen, *Bread from Heaven* (NovT Suppl 10, Leiden: Brill 1965) 150 who argued that Is 54.13 is often quoted in the rabbinic tradition in order to show that God himself will teach the Torah in the age to come. See also PsSol 17.32 (*didaktos hypo theou* with regard to the kingly messiah); 1QH 7.10 ("Thou hast [established my mouth] in Thy Covenant").

56 Cf. Ethelbert Stauffer, *TDNT* 3:121, who refers to Is 54.13, Jer 31.34, Joh 6.45.

57 Schrage, *Ethik*, 207. He rightly rejects the opinion of Rudolf Bultmann who argued that the commandment to love never implies a specific content of behavior and that formulated positive stipulations contradict its character; cf. R. Bultmann, "Das christliche Gebot der Nächstenliebe", *Glauben und Verstehen* (Vol. I, Tübingen: Mohr-Siebeck 1980[6]) 229-244: 235; idem, *Theologie des Neuen Testaments* (Tübingen: Mohr-Siebeck 1984[9]) 570.

substantiated by the criterion of brotherly love. Love for the brother leads to a committed[58] way of life which does not burden the life of others with one's own life. The urge of one's own personal experience must not become the burden of the fellow believer but should rather help towards liberation from the brother's burdens.[59] Paul establishes his exhortation to work by referring to the independence of people: "so that you will be dependent on nobody" (v. 12b). Brotherly love not only requires that we help our "neighbour" but demands that we do not make ourselves a burden to others. We may assume that the believers in Thessalonica participated in the general shortage of goods: in this context the admonition that everybody must earn his own living in order to stay economically independent of the others was probably vital: the fellowship would destroy itself if its members disregarded the need to work.[60] Thus, apart from brotherly love as criterion of Christian behaviour we may have here an (indirect) ecclesiological motif of Pauline ethics.

(f) The reason for the unsettled lifestyle of certain believers who evidently meddled in the affairs of fellow Christians and who refused to earn their own living is probably linked with a consistently exaggerated expectation of the parousia.[61] As Paul corrects the one-sided eschatology of the Thessalonians[62] b y condemning idleness and by admonishing them to a life characterized by quiet order (in 4.15 he quotes a "word of the Lord" to substantiate his answer to the confusion in eschatological matters), the salvation-historical perspective of early Christian ethics becomes manifest. The parousia has not yet taken place, which means that the

---

58   V. 11a: *philotimeisthai* "to love or seek after honour, to be ambitious"; in Hellenistic Greek the meaning seems to have been weakened to "to engage, to seek something with all out effort"; cf. Holtz, 176 n. 173; G. H. R. Horsley, *Documents Illustrating Early Christianity* (Vol. 1, Macquarie University 1981) No. 48, 88. Thus in 1Thess 4.11a one's honour is not the criterion of behavior.

59   Thus correctly Holtz, 181, even though "liberation" is not mentioned in the context.

60   Holtz, 181. Marshall, 117 sees the exhortation as related to non-Christians: believers must not become a nuisance and a burden to other people.

61   Paul does not state the connection explicitly, but most commentators see the expectation of an imminent parousia implied; cf. the remarks on idleness in 4.11-12 and 5.14, which frame the eschatological section 4.13-5.11. Cf. Marshall, 117; Bruce, 91; pace Holtz, 178 who explains the Thessalonians' behaviour with their excitement over their newly found faith and the new fellowship with others.

62   4.13-5.11; cf. 2Thess 2.1-12; in 2Thess 3.6-12 Paul again discusses the problem of Christians neglecting work for earning their daily bread.

old order of the world has not been suspended yet: "The grip of the future cannot negate the creaturely maintenance of life in the present. The course of history still continues, we still need to live in accordance with it".[63]

(g) Paul points to the conventions of society as argument for the way of life on which he insists, conventions which show what it means to "live in a seemly manner" (euschēmonōs, v. 12; RSV: "command the respect of outsiders").[64] The Christian way of life corresponds, at least as regards order and work, to the accepted standards of the society in which Christians live. Christians meet the requirements which non-Christians expect from life. Paul thus presupposes that such standards of society correspond to God's orders.[65] The reason for Paul's admonition is surely not the aim that Christians should avoid any offence and thus discrimination and persecution but rather (perhaps primarily?) the missionary effectiveness of the church.[66]

4. 1Cor 1-4. In view of the situation in the Corinthian church Paul feels compelled to admonish the believers to live in harmony. The discussion on the opponents of Paul in Corinth and on the "parties" in the church continues.[67] Even though this discussion is highly relevant for Paul's argumentation and hence for his *paraklesis*, we will concentrate on a concise elucidation of the norms and the criteria of proper Christian behaviour as put forward or implied by Paul.

---

63 Holtz, 181 (my translation).

64 Marshall, 117; Holtz, 180.

65 Cf. Holtz, 180 who refers further to Rom 13.13; 2.14-15; Phil 4.8.

66 Cf. 1Pet 2.12; 1Cor 10.32; Mt 5.16 and similar Jewish statements; cf. David Daube, "Jewish Missionary Maxims in Paul", *Studia Theologica* 1 (1948) 158-164; W. C. van Unnik, "Die Rücksicht auf die Reaktion der Nicht-Christen als Motiv in der altchristlichen Paränese", *Sparsa Collecta* (Vol. II, NovT Suppl 30, Leiden: Brill 1980) 307-322; Merk, *Handeln*, 52; Holtz, 180f.

67 Cf. recently Gerhard Sellin, "Das 'Geheimnis' der Weisheit und das Rätsel der 'Christuspartei' (zu 1Kor 1-4)", *Zeitschrift für die neutestamentliche Wissenschaft* 73 (1982) 69-96 who assumes only a rivalry between a Pauline group and an Apollos party. The traditional assumption of four parties is maintained by Friedrich Lang, *Die Briefe an die Korinther* (Das Neue Testament Deutsch 7, Göttingen: Vandenhoeck & Ruprecht 1986) 23-26. Gordon Fee, *The First Epistle to the Corinthians* (New International Commentary on the New Testament, Grand Rapids: Eerdmans 1987) 4-15 emphasizes the common opposition of the Corinthian church against Paul, with tensions within the church along socio-economic lines. Cf. now the discussion in Wolfgang Schrage, *Der erste Brief an die Korinther* (Evangelisch-Katholischer Kommentar VII, Zürich/Neukirchen-Vluyn: Benziger/Neukirchener Verlag 1991) 1:46f, 142-152.

(a) In 1.10-13 Paul calls for harmony in speech (*to auto legēte*, v. 10b), in conviction (*to autos nous*, v. 10e) and in judgment (*hē autē gnōmē*, v. 10f). The motivation for the exhortation in v. 10 is fundamentally ecclesiological and christological. In the church of God (v. 2) all are "brothers" (v. 10a)[68] having God as their common father who granted them and continues to grant them grace and peace (v. 3). The phrase "by the name of our Lord Jesus Christ" in v. 10a indicates the ground of the exhortation: the lordship of Christ over the church, the authority of the Lord over those who belong to him.[69]

(b) In 1.13a the ecclesiological/christological foundation of the admonition to harmony is operative as well. The existence of parties in the church threatens the unity of the body of Christ: according to Paul Christ and the church belong intimately together (3.23). If other mediators of salvation are being interposed between Christ and the church, following Alexandrian Jewish (philonic) conceptions— particularly if *part* of the church continues to live more directly in dependence on Christ—the unity of the body of Christ is destroyed. Paul emphasizes against such tendencies (3.18-23): the church as a whole has a direct relationship with Christ and the apostles are functionally subordinated to the church (3.5).[70] Jesus Christ and the salvation granted by and through him establish the unity of the church which must not be divided or partitioned (*merizō*, 1.13).

(c) Paul condemns the discord in the church as an indication of a "wisdom" which is inadequate (chaps. 1-2). True "wisdom" which Paul holds to be compatible with the gospel is the mystery of God's plan of salvation whose content has been revealed in the crucifixion of the Lord of glory (1.17-31; 2.6-10).[71] We notice, again, that the most fundamental motivation of Paul's ethics is God's salvific action in Jesus Christ,[72] in the context of 1Cor 1-2 with emphasis on the atoning death of Christ on the cross.

(d) In 3.3-4 Paul establishes the necessity of harmony with a rational-philosophical argument: the Corinthians cannot be regarded as pneumatics since they quarrel—true pneumatics do not provoke divisions. "In the dualistic thought of Philo duality (disunion) is precisely a characteristic of the depreciated earthly, sarkic realm,

---

68 The first of 21 occurrences of the vocative *adelphoi* in 1Cor.
69 The phrase *dia tou onomatos tou kyriou* may refer to baptism, cf. v. 13.
70 Sellin, 93-95.
71 Sellin, 69,83.
72 Cf. Schrage, "Ethik IV", *Theologische Realenzyklopädie* 10 (1982) 446.

while unity is the characteristic of the spiritual realm. Thus Paul beats the pneumatics with their own weapons".[73]

(e) Concluding the appeal of 1.10-12 in 3.21-23, Paul gives salvation-historical and theological reasons for his exhortation that no one should boast of men. As a result of God's salvific revelation in Jesus Christ who is the wisdom of God, the mediator of creation and the Kyrios, the essentials of human existence—world, life, death, the present, the future (v. 22)—are put under Christ's jurisdiction. And therefore all those who live "in Christ" own these essentials as their free possession.[74] Questions concerning the apostles and the teachers of the church and questions regarding the world, life and death, the present and the future—and the answers which can be given and which may differ again and again—must not control the life of the believers in Corinth. These essentials do not "own" the believers: rather, they are the "possession" of the church. And further, God's complete unity as unity of father and son stands above all these essential realities (v. 23): the glory of God's activity in "all" has given all these things to the church, because God has become her God.[75] And because the one God of the church has given "all" to all believers, the utilization of God's gifts in party spirit is as uncalled for as discord and disharmony.

5. 1Cor 6.1-11. Paul rebukes the Corinthians since they allow internal disputes—probably over property or regarding an offence in a business transaction (*apostereō*, vv. 7-8)—to be decided by secular courts. He regards such behaviour as a serious faux pas.

(a) Paul calls on the church to settle the litigation of its members internally. The eschatological reasons given in vv. 2-3 do not really hold good at first sight: Paul says that "the saints" will judge the world and even the angels (at the final judgment) but does not explain what this fact means for his admonition that Christians should avoid secular jurisdiction (vv. 1, 6) and solve its legal problems in front of representatives of the church (v. 5). Paul's argument becomes clear if we take into consideration the Jewish attitude with regard to litigation. The synagogue referred its

---

73 Sellin, 82 (my translation), referring to Pythagorean numerical speculations.

74 Cf. Walter Grundmann, *TDNT* 9:550 who emphasizes the liberation from all powers and authorities through the commitment to Christ; cf. also Fee, 154.

75 Adolf Schlatter, *Paulus der Bote Jesu* (Stuttgart: Calwer 1962³) 141.

members to its own jurisdiction.[76] The Jews regarded the administration of justice not as a disposable matter but as a religious act where the judge dispensed justice by God's order and in submission to God's law. To refer jurisdiction to non-Jewish courts would be tantamount to a denial of the relevance, validity and authority of the law.[77] Paul designates non-Christian judges as *adikoi* (v. 1) and *apistoi* (v. 6): as he surely does not regard all pagan judges as "unjust" we may assume that the formulation of v. 1[78] is derived from Jewish terminology.[79] The adoption of Jewish terminology indicates at the same time that Paul takes over the material decision as well.[80] Paul does not give reasons for the behaviour which he demands; the order of God's law is the self-evident norm of Christian, even Gentile Christian, behaviour.[81]

(b) The rhetorical questions in 6.2 show poignantly the ecclesiological context of Paul's *paraklesis*. Paul rejects as intolerable an attitude which is an expression of contempt for the church, demonstrated by the willingness to settle legal disputes before pagan courts. If the saints judge the world, the church is responsible for judging lawsuits between its members. This responsibility implies a dignity (cf. *anaxioi*, v. 2c) which must not be disregarded. The nature of the church as the assembly of the saints implies the competence to settle legal matters[82] and to arrive at decisions—in general decisions concerning anything which belongs to everyday life (*kritēria biotika*, v. 4).[83]

(c) The context of 6.1-3 reflects the eschatological motivation of Paul's ethics. In comparison with the decisions in the final judgment,

---

[76] Josephus Ant 14,235 (10,17). Cf. E. Schürer, *The History of the Jewish People in the Age of Jesus Christ* (Revised English Edition, Vol. III.1, Edinburgh: T. & T. Clark 1986) 199f. Cf. Traugott Holtz, "Zur Frage der inhaltlichen Weisungen bei Paulus", *Theologische Literaturzeitung* 106 (1981) 385-400: 389f; see already Schlatter, 188; Erich Fascher, *Der erste Brief des Paulus an die Korinther* (Theologischer Handkommentar zum Neuen Testament 711, Berlin: Evangelische Verlagsanstalt 1988⁴) 169.

[77] Schlatter, 188f.

[78] In v. 9 the term *adikoi* is used in the sense of "the unjust".

[79] The term *adikoi* signifies with regard to the pagan judges people who do not know the divine law and who are thus in an "objective" sense "lawless", cf. Holtz, "Weisungen", 390.

[80] Holtz, 390; already Schlatter, 193, cf. Lang, 77.

[81] Thus with emphasis Holtz, "Weisungen", passim.

[82] The term *kritēria* vv. 2, 4 signifies "legal action"; cf. Wolfgang Schenk, *EDNT* 2:321; Horsley, *New Documents*, 4, 1987, No. 65, 157.

[83] Schlatter, 191.

everyday disputes are most insignificant trivialities *(elachistōn,* v. 2c). In view of this eschatological horizon Paul calls the very existence of legal actions between believers a "defeat" *(hobs hēttēma,* v. 7a). He reminds the wrongdoer of the irrevocable fact that the unjust (cf. the specific examples in the catalogue of vice in vv. 9b-10a) will have no part in the coming kingdom of God (vv. 9a, 10b).

(d) The plaintiff who has been wronged and who initiated the litigation is told that he will suffer defeat even if he wins the lawsuit (v. 7a).[84] He should be prepared to suffer wrong (from a brother) and to be defrauded (v. 7b). Paul gives no arguments for this exhortation which goes against the general sense of justice and against the established law (the following sentences in vv. 8-10 apply to the wrongdoer, not to the plaintiff). Paul probably presupposes that the Corinthian believers are aware of the grounds of this striking and uncommon request: specific injunctions of Jesus[85] such as Lk 6.27-28[86] (par Mt 5.43-44) and Mt 5.39-40[87] (par Lk 6.29-30) which Paul presupposes in Rom 12.9-21 and in 1Thess 5.15.[88]

(e) Paul excludes the possibility of Christians carrying their lawsuits before pagan authorities. But he allows for differing ways of Christian behaviour: the church may appoint arbitrators who will be responsible for settling disputes internally (vv. 1-6), or Christians may relinquish their rights (vv. 7-8). These options are not equally entitled to reflect ideal Christian behaviour: Paul prefers that believers relinquish their rights. But basically he allows the church latitude for her decision.[89]

(f) In conclusion Paul refers again and in more detail to the christological and pneumatological motivation of proper behaviour

---

84 Fascher, 171; Fee, 240f.

85 Rather than similar pagan philosophical or Jewish parallels (Fee, 241 n. 11 who gives no details, however). Cf. Ulrich Luz, *Das Evangelium nach Matthäus* (Evangelisch-Katholischer Kommentar I, Zürich/Neukirchen-Vluyn 1985) 1:294 who comments the differences between Mt 5.39-42 and such parallels: there is no motivation for non-violence, no tone of resignation, no optimistic calculation and no emphasis on the prudence of such demands.

86 Fee, 241 (179).

87 Fascher, 171.

88 W. D. Davies/D. C. Allison, *The Gospel According to Saint Matthew* (International Critical Commentary, Edinburgh: T. & T. Clark 1988) 543; Wilckens, *Römer,* 3:22f; Holtz, *Thessalonicher,* 255.

89 Schrage, *Ethik,* 183 who refers to Erich Dinkler, "Zum Problem der Ethik bei Paulus. Rechtsnahme und Rechtsverzicht (1Cor 6.1-11)", *Signum Crucis* (Tübingen: Mohr-Siebeck 1967 [1952]) 204-240.

in the church (v. 11). Jesus Christ and the Spirit of God effected regeneration, sanctification and justification in the lives of the believers which are the foundation and the enabling realities of holy living.

6. 1Cor 8-10 (cf. Rom 14-15).[90] Paul discusses the problem of dealing with meat sacrificed to idols in the context of disputes between "strong" and "weak" believers in the church.[91] Theologically Paul takes the side of the "strong" (cf. Rom 15.1) who have no scruples in eating such meat, but he declares his solidarity with the "weak". He grants the "weak" their differing decision in the matter and pleads for tolerance and fellowship. He calls the believers to welcome each other without trying to convert the other to one's own lifestyle and without despising his decision, but unreservedly with all due respect. Paul acknowledges the possibility of differing decisions with regard to the believers' *mandatum concretissimum*.[92]

(a) The basic motivation regarding the believer's individual behaviour is to be seen in the ecclesiological dimension of this situation which may threaten the unity of the church. Understanding without love leads to arrogant pomposity (*physioō*, 8.1b): the criterion for proper behaviour is brotherly love and the upbuilding of the church (*oikodomeō*, 8.1c). My behaviour and my freedom must not cause offence (*proskomma*) to the brother nor lead to his downfall (v. 9). This happens when he is induced to behaving in a way which he cannot justify before his conscience (vv. 10-11). Such inducement would be tantamount to sin against the brother and against Christ (v. 12). The criterion of right behaviour is the question whether my own decision precipitates my brother's fall (*skandalizō*, v. 13). The

---

[90] The problem between the "strong" and the "weak" which Paul discusses in Rom 14-15 is not exactly identical with the situation behind 1Cor 8-10, but the arguments which Paul adduces are similar; cf. Jürgen Becker, *Paulus. Der Apostel der Völker* (Tübingen: Mohr-Siebeck 1992²=1989) 363.

[91] Cf. the commentaries and monographs, e.g. recently Wendell L. Willis, *Idol Meat in Corinth: The Pauline Argument in 1 Corinthians 8 and 10* (SBLDS 68, Chico: Scholars 1985). Gordon Fee, "*eidolothyta* Once Again: An Interpretation of 1 Corinthians 8-10", *Biblica* 61 (1980) 172-197; idem, *Corinthians*, 357ff regards 1Cor 10.14-22 as reflecting the position of Paul: the basic problem is not idol meat which is sold on the market but "going to the temples"; for a critique of this view cf. John C. Brunt, "Love, Freedom and Moral Responsibility: The Contribution of 1 Cor 8-10 to an Understanding of Paul's Ethical Thinking", *SBL 1981 Seminar Papers* (ed. K. H. Richards, Chico: Scholars 1981) 19-33: 28-29 n. 7.

[92] Cf. Schrage, *Ethik*, 184.

motivation and purpose of my personal decision are not my own benefit but the well-being of the brother (*to tou heterou*, 10.24), the advantage of the many fellow-Christians (*symphoron . . . tōn pollōn*, 10.33) for the edification of the church.

(b) The salvation-historical horizon of the problem is seen in 8.6: here Paul mentions the criterion for deciding the question whether believers may eat sacrificial meat or not (because it renders unclean). The decisive criterion is the faith in God the Father and Creator of all things as faith in Jesus Christ who is Kyrios and to whom the believers owe their entire existence (*hēmeis di'autou*). In the new salvation-historical situation of the present, when Jesus Christ is Kyrios, food no longer decides man's status before God (v. 8) as it did in the old covenant. The logic of the theological problem is to be deduced from the "truth of the gospel", i.e. from the theo-logic of God's action in the atoning death of Jesus Christ.

(c) In view of the salvation-historical horizon of Christian existence Paul knows that whereas for the one who belongs to Jesus Christ everything is "permissible", not everything is beneficial (*ou panta sympherei*, 10.23). Thus Paul warns believers to beware of the manifold temptations (*peirasmos*) which continue to be a reality even in the new covenant which is determined by freedom (10.13).

(d) By exhorting the Corinthian believers not to cause offence to the brother (8.9, 13; cf. Rom 14.13, 21), which is the central admonition in the entire discussion, Paul evidently alludes to dominical sayings (Mk 9.42; Mt 18.6-7; Lk 17.1-2).[93] Even the theological point of view which Paul presents as the correct position—namely, that nothing is unclean by itself (8.8; 10.25-27; cf. Rom 14.14)—may be traced back to a saying of Jesus (Mk 7.15 par).[94]

(e) Another criterion for the behaviour of the believers is the order of creation. Paul assumes the existence of a norm for correct behaviour to which the Gentiles are subject despite their factual lapses. In 10.32 he formulates categorically: "Give no offence to Jews or to Greeks or to the church of God". Paul evidently thinks that it is possible to live among Jews and Greeks and among fellow-Christians in such a manner that nobody is turned off as a result of my

---

[93] Cf. Cranfield, 2:712; Dunn, 2:818 who refers to D. C. Allison, "The Pauline Epistles and the Synoptic Gospels: The Pattern of the Parallels", *New Testament Studies* 28 (1982) 1-32: 13-15. The transitive form of the verb *skandalizō*, which is used only rarely, occurs both in 1Cor 8.13 and in Mt 18.6.

[94] Cranfield, 2:712f; Dunn, 2:818f; Stuhlmacher, 20; Wilckens, 3:91 is uncertain concerning the possibility of a tradition-historical connection.

behaviour but becomes or remains receptive to Christ's call.[95] What is decisive here are not ethical norms of non-Christian society but rather the missionary motif to preserve the attractiveness of the gospel for outsiders. In the context of this motivation, generally accepted and expected ways of behaviour can well be criteria which help to decide how to behave in this or that situation.

(f) In 8.7-12 and 10.25-29 Paul refers to the conscience as criterion for the proper ethical decision. For Paul, *syneidēsis* is that tribunal in man which evaluates and makes conscious my own behaviour or (occasionally) the behaviour of others (2Cor 4.2; 5.11)—according to existing and acknowledged norms. The conscience reviews past actions, it may accompany the action itself and may influence the process of deciding between choices. The conscience does not itself make the ethical (or religious) decision but tests and reviews thoughts, words and deeds with regard to their correspondence with the acknowledged standard of what is binding and good.[96] In 1Cor 8 it is the *syneidēsis* of the "weak" which prevents them from eating meat sacrificed to idols: their behaviour in everyday life corresponds with their decision made on the basis of the normativity of (cultic) Torah or the normativity of their conversion "away from the idols" (1Thess 1.9). Paul does not discuss the question whether the theological presuppositions of the "weak" are correct or not, even though he leaves no doubt that he does not accept their position as valid: they are determined by custom (*synētheia*) and by defective knowledge (*gnōsis*, 8.7). Rather he discusses the behaviour of the "strong": their insistence on their *gnōsis* and *exousia* does not lead to the advancement of knowledge nor to the renewal of the *nous* but hurts the brother whose conscience condemns his assimilated behaviour which has not been grounded in his convictions. Thus the fellow-Christian is in acute danger. The "strong" must therefore give priority to respecting the tribunal of the conscience of the brother which judges according to primary norms, rather than insisting on a discussion of norms which is mainly linked with the *nous*.[97] At the same time the phrase *dia tēn syneidēsin* in 10.25, 27 describes the conscience as the authority "which calls man to take

---

[95] Schlatter, 306.

[96] Hans-Joachim Eckstein, *Der Begriff Syneidesis bei Paulus* (WUNT 2/10, Tübingen: Mohr-Siebeck 1983) 312.

[97] Cf. Eckstein, *255f*.

responsibility and which points the believer, through the correspondence of his accountability, to his responsibility before God".[98]

(g) The basic and decisive motivation of the believers' ethical decisions is again theocentric. "Do all to the glory of God" (10.31; cf. Rom 14.6-7). This statement negates at the same time the assumption that the possibility of ethical plurality may be related to all and everything: there is no neutral realm in which the Christian has been dismissed from his responsibility before God, not even in questions of eating or abstinence of certain food or in questions of celebrating or not celebrating certain days.[99]

7. Phil 1-2. An important theme of Paul's letter to the Christians in Philippi is the unity of the church and the integration of its members.[100] Paul asserts that the believers have love (*agapē*) but prays at the same time that it may continuously increase (1.9).

(a) The reference to love is not left abstract as "total demand" but made concrete:[101] the increase of love is to lead to insight (*epignōsis*) and practical understanding (*aisthēsis*, 1.9) of the will of God and its realization in practical conduct, as the members of God's new people are to live "pure and blameless" (1.10). An ever increasing love which leads to right conduct which is pleasing to God requires *epignōsis*: knowledge in the sense of intellectual insight into and existential acknowledgment of the will of God which becomes effective in the actual behaviour of the believer.[102] And love leading to right conduct requires *aisthēsis*, i.e. ethical discrimination, "that practical understanding which is keenly aware of the circumstances of an action".[103] The context of vv. 9-10 shows that Paul does not establish *agapē* as "norm" of the new life in contradistinction to the norm of the Torah in Judaism or to the norm of reason in Stoic philosophy:[104] love is regulated by the criteria of reasonable

---

98   Eckstein, 276 (my translation).

99   Schrage, *Ethik*, 184.

100   Cf. Becker, *Paulus*, 334. We cannot discuss here the literary unity of Phil; the integrity of the letter is defended by Gerald F. Hawthorne, *Philippians* (Word Biblical Commentary 43, Waco: Word 1983) xxix-xxxii; Peter T. O'Brien, *The Epistle to the Philippians* (NIGTC, Grand Rapids: Eerdmans 1991) 10-19.

101   Schrage, *Ethik*, 178.

102   Wolfgang Hackenberg, *EDNT* 2:25 on the basis of the meaning of "love" in the Old Testament tradition (note the 22 occurrences in Prov, of a total of 27 occurrences in the LXX).

103   O'Brien, 77; Gerhard Delling, *TDNT* 1 :187-88.

104   Contra Collange, 49.

knowledge and the rational ability to discriminate between right and wrong on the basis of past experience.[105]

(b) In 1.10 Paul describes the function of the *nous* with the term *dokimazein* which refers to the ability to examine and discriminate options of conduct.[106] The believers should be capable of examining and then deciding what is God's will in specific situations of everyday life and thus to know how they should behave in correspondence to the will of God. The object of the rational understanding of the believers is *ta diapheronta*: that which matters in the specific situation, which surpasses other things in being God's will.[107]

(c) In 1.9-11 Paul mentions several norms of Christian conduct: first, moral purity (*eilikrineia*, v. 9): consistent integrity which is not afraid of being examined in broad daylight;[108] second, moral inoffensiveness (*aproskopos*, v. 10): irreproachable conduct which is without blame before God and which does not cause downfall in the last judgment;[109] third, perfect[110] righteousness (*dikaiosyrē*, v. 11): that essential quality in man which makes him the person that he should be in his relation to God and to others,[111] which has been granted as a free gift of salvation in Jesus Christ and which is of enduring relevance before God (to his "glory and praise")—as concrete and specific conduct of the believer (*karpos*). The holy, righteous and good will of God continues to be the norm of life in the new covenant.

(d) In 1.10-11 Paul mentions fundamental motivations of Christian ethics: the last judgment as "day of Christ", righteousness which has been granted as a result of God's salvific action in Jesus Christ, the glorification of God in worship and the context of the church[112] as realm of insight into the will of God.

(e) After a review of past circumstances of his life (1.12-26) Paul resumes his effort to concretize the notion of love which was

---

[105]   Cf. Hawthorne, 27.

[106]   Ernst Käsemann, *An die Römer*, 318 with regard to Rom 12.2.

[107]   Walter Grundmann, *TWNT* 2:263; Lorenz Oberlinner, *EDNT* 1:315, O'Brien, 77.

[108]   Cf. Horst Goldstein, *EWNT* 1:949.

[109]   Cf. Gustav Stählin, *TDNT* 6:756.

[110]   Cf. the adjectival participle *peplērōmenoi*.

[111]   Karl Kertelge, *EDNT* 1:325-30.

[112]   Following Collange, 50, Hawthorne, 28 and others, one may interpret *aproskopos* in the transitive sense of carefully avoiding anything which may cause another to stumble; if the primary reference is to those within the church, the motivation of Christian behavior is linked to the ecclesiological context.

central in his prayer for the church. The community life of the church (*politeuesthai*, v. 27)[113] is carried out, as regards the outside world, in a context of conflict and struggle,[114] whereas the fellowship of the believers ought to be characterized by unanimity (1.27-30). The norm of church life (*axios*, v. 27a) is "the gospel of Christ", i.e. the proclamation of the gospel authorized by Christ who is its soteriological substance.[115]

(f) Paul substantiates the exhortation to unanimity, which he understands as unity in action, by referring to the presence of the Holy Spirit in which all believers share (1.27c)[116] as well as to the necessity (vv. 29-30) to defend the Christian faith against attacks and to spread the gospel to outsiders (v. 27). The unity effected by God's Spirit makes the common fight for the gospel possible: a fight in which the combatants do not try to distinguish themselves as individuals but stand together "as one man"[117] doing their utmost for attaining the common goal (*synathlountes*, v. 27). The unanimity of the church which has been established by God's salvific action in Jesus Christ and which is maintained in love is not destroyed in the conflict for the faith and in the suffering for Christ's sake (v. 29).

(g) After his summons to unanimity in fighting for the faith Paul admonishes the believers to maintain peace, love, humility and unselfishness (2.1-4). The unity of the church as a community of life is a unity of thinking and will (*to auto phronēte*),[118] of faith and action (*tēn autēn agapēn echontes*), of feeling (*sympsychos*)[119] and, again, of thought and purpose (*to hen phronountes*, v. 2). Of fundamental significance for the unity of the church is humility as modest self-assessment (*tapeinophrosynē*, v. 3b) which enables the Philippians to count others better than themselves independent of any social ranking.[120] The union granted by the Spirit is maintained in the

---

113 With Ulrich Hutter, *EDNT* 3:130 contra Hermann Strathmann, *TDNT* 6:534-35.

114 Cf. the terms *synathlountes* v. 27b, *antikeimenōn* v. 28a, *agōna* v. 30.

115 Cf. Georg Strecker, *EWNT* 2:181f.

116 1.27c *en heni pneumati*, cf. Collange, 74 who refers to Bonnard, Gnilka, Martin. Others interpret the phrase with regard to the human spirit in the sense of "with common purpose . . . having the same attitude or the same orientation of will" (O'Brien, 150 referring to Bultmann, Lohmeyer, Michaelis, Müller, Schweizer; cf. also Hawthorne 56f).

117 Alexander Sand, *EWNT* 3:1200; cf. NIV.

118 Cf. Georg Bertram, *TDNT* 9:232-34.

119 Cf. Horst Balz, *EDNT* 3:291.

120 Cf. Heinz Giesen, *EDNT* 3:333-34.

church if each believer marks down the perception of his own importance and seeks the advantage of his fellow believers.

(h) Paul goes on to define the necessary unity *ex negativo*: the union of the believers in the church of God does not allow for self-interest which is determined by egotism, selfish ambition and arrogant self-seeking (*eritheia*, 2.3a), nor does it allow for a boastful but empty thirst for glory where people are convinced of their own grandeur, competing with others for praise (*kenodoxia*, 2.3a).[121] Unity is possible where Christians do not look out for their own interests nor concentrate in selfish individualism on their personal affairs (2.4a). Selfishness, boastfulness and egotism damage and, finally, destroy the life of the church.

(i) The grounds for his appeal to maintain unity is, first, the apostolic proclamation and exhortation as well as to his own practice of kind-hearted and edifying encouragement and love (2.1a).[122] Secondly, Paul refers to the work of God's Spirit who effected the unity of the believers as well as to the mercy and compassion which God demonstrated and gave in Jesus Christ (v. 1b).[123] The christological motivation for the exhortation to unity appears again in 2.5ff: the thinking and the practical conduct of Christians are measured by Jesus Christ who determines as Kyrios the community life of the church.[124]

(j) In 4.2-3 Paul takes up a specific case where two women—Euodia and Syntyche, highly valued co-workers, had serious disagreements. Presupposing the authenticity of the context in 3.17-21, we may interpret Paul as establishing (*hōste*, 4.1a) his exhortation to reconciliation and unity by referring to the resurrection and parousia of Christ. The reference to the "book of life" (4.3d) provides eschatological grounds for the admonition.

I shall break off at this point. We could analyse further passages where Paul exhorts to overcome discord and to re-establish or maintain love and unity. The passages which we looked at are examples for the manner by which Paul substantiates and evaluates ethical decisions. The second part of my study will summarize and

---

[121]   Cf. Heinz Giesen, *EDNT* 2:281; Collange, 79.
[122]   Following Gustav Stählin, *TDNT* 5:820f.; Hawthorne, 65; differently O'Brien, 172 who interprets in the sense of Christ's love rather in terms of a reference to Paul's love for his Philippian readers.
[123]   Hawthorne, 66f.
[124]   Cf. Henning Paulsen, *EWNT* 3:1050.

present systematically the grounds and the criteria of ethical decision-making in the *paraklesis* of the apostle Paul.[125]

2. SYSTEMATIC CONCENTRATION

2.1   Theological Motivation

The fundamental motivations of Pauline ethics are substantially all related to God's salvific action in Jesus Christ and its consequences. This theological, or rather theocentric, foundation of Christian existence which Paul presents under a christological horizon is clearly expressed in several passages. Cf. 1Cor 6.20; 10.31; Rom 14.6-7.

(1) Christological motivation. The foundational motivation with reference to Jesus Christ comprises the past of his death and resurrection, the present of the salvation and lordship of Christ and the future of the parousia. Paul quite clearly reckons with the fact that the salvific atoning death of Jesus and his resurrection possess power and authority, not least with regard to the ethical dimension of Christian existence. Cf. 2Cor 5.14-15; Rom 6; 14.8-9; 15.30; Phil 2.5-11; Eph 5.25.

(2) Salvation-historical motivation. Christian ethics belongs to the time "between the ages" and takes into account the tension between the "already" and the "not yet". The salvation-historical basis of and reason for the dialectic of the indicative and the imperative i: (i) the dialectic correlation of the salvation which has already taken place in and with Jesus Christ and which is the "property" of the believer; and (ii) the salvation which will take place in the future judgment of the world and which will only then become the full and final inheritance of the believer. The old aeon has been brought to an end by Christ and yet has not been completely done away with in the present. The new aeon has already begun but has not attained yet universal fullness and perfection. Cf. Gal 5.19-21; 1Thess 5.21; 1Cor 7.5; 10.23; Rom 12.2.

(3) Pneumatological motivation. The Holy Spirit is the presence of Christ in the present life of those who believe in Christ. The gift of the Spirit is the fundamental power in the life of the believers who have of those who have been "born again" and as such

---

125   For the following see Schnabel, *Law and Wisdom*, 299-342.

determines and shapes Christian existence. The person and the conduct of the believer are being renewed by the Spirit. The Holy Spirit enables the Christian to do the will of God. Cf. Gal 5.13-16,22-25; Rom 8.3-4.

(4) Ecclesiological motivation. Paul's *paraklesis* is substantially related to the fellowship of the believers. The conduct of other churches, mutual responsibility of the believers and the edification of the (local) church are basic arguments for proper behaviour. Cf. 1Cor 8; 11.16; 12; Rom 12.16; 15.5; Phil 2.2; 4.2.

(5) Eschatological motivation. Paul holds that the hope of Christians regarding the future is relevant for their present behaviour. Allusion to the coming judgment warns the believers of false security and emphasizes the responsibility of the individual. The motif of reward is important as well. Cf. Gal 6.7-10; 1Thess 5.1ff; 1Cor 3.11-14; 4.5; 9.24-25; 2Cor 5.9-10; Rom 13.11ff; Phil 3.14.

2.2 *Normative Obligation*

Paul assumes binding norms in his explication and concretization of right Christian conduct. The presupposition and application of binding norms for the behaviour of the believers is implied in the use of terms such as *anankē, opheilein, dei,* and *kanōn.* Cf. Gal 6.16; 1Thess 4.1-2; 1Cor 11.10; Rom 13.5-8.

(1) The Torah. Paul holds that the Torah has been fulfilled in and through Jesus Christ and his atoning death on the cross. As *conditio et via salutis* the law has been nullified. As "law of Christ" it remains the revelation of God's effective will. Paul believes that the messianic era which has been inaugurated through Jesus Christ has not effected the abrogation of the Mosaic law but appointed a new qualification for the Torah. Since the death of the Messiah atoned for the sins of the world and opened up the way into the presence of God's salvation through identification with that death by faith, the Torah, i.e. its scope of application, is modified in the light of the death and the resurrection of Jesus Christ. An important pointer to the continued validity of the Hebrew Bible for Christian ethics is the fact that Paul takes over individual OT texts in an entirely natural matter that goes without saying. Cf. Gal 6.1; Rom 8.1-4; 1Cor 7.19; 5.13; 6.12-20; 2Cor 8.15; 9.9.

Paul never explains explicitly how and to what degree the Mosaic law has been affected and modified by the death and resurrection of Jesus Christ. It is evident, however, that at least the cultic stipulations of the law which regulate the atonement of sin have been affected, as well as the numerous ritual stipulations such as circumcision and the food laws which effect holiness and purity and which mark off the limits of the people of God: atonement, holiness, purity and membership in God's (eschatological) people are now acquired through affiliation with God's salvific action in the death and resurrection of Jesus Christ, i.e. by faith.

(2) The words of Jesus. For Paul, dominical sayings possess binding authority. Where the Lord has spoken, the discussion is over: the believers in the church know what they are meant to do. Cf. 1Cor 7.10; 9.14; 11.23-24; 1Thess 4.15.

(3) The injunctions of the apostles. Paul regards the apostolic exhortation as normative. Being an apostle of Jesus Christ he is conscious of the fact that he speaks in the name of Christ and in the name of God: God and Christ are the true authors of the apostolic proclamation and exhortation. Paul anticipates quite naturally that the believers of his churches will carry out his instructions. Similarly he can call on the Christians to emulate his example. Cf. 1Thess 2.13; 4.1; 2Cor 2.9; 1Cor 4.16-17; 11.1; Phil 4.9; 3.17.

(4) The orders of creation. Paul is convinced that God's salvific action in Jesus Christ makes the *cosmos* recognizable again as God's creation. On the one hand, the *cosmos* is still the realm of sinful man who has rebelled against God, a realm dominated by God's enemy: the *cosmos* thus cannot be the norm of Christian behaviour in an automatic and an unreflected manner. On the other hand, it is significant that the will of the creator is fulfilled by, through and in Jesus Christ: he is the manifestation of the wisdom of God, the mediator of creation and the new Adam. Thus the earth in its totality belongs to the "Lord", and consequently everything is clean for those who believe in Christ. Cf. 1Cor 8.6; 10.26; Rom 14.20; and Rom 2.14-15; 1Thess 4.12; 1Cor 10.32.

Thus there is a partial ethical consensus between Christian and non-Christian ethics. Norms of Christian conduct in the context of creation and in the context of pagan ethics are nature (with reference to God's original orders for creation and to historical orders such as custom and generally recognized traditions), orders of creation such as marriage, political authority and work as well as consideration for social conventions. Cf. Rom 1.26; 1Cor 11.13; 7; Rom 13.1-7; 1Thess 5.14; 2Thess 3.6-7; Rom 13.13; 1Cor 7.35; 13.5; 14.40.

2.3   *Concretising Orientation*

Paul holds that the individual believer is responsible for his specific conduct in everyday life. This responsibility implies two aspects: the believer is to live in correspondence to the binding norms of Christian ethics and he is to realize the "obedience of faith" in the concrete situations of everyday life. This realization of the will of God by the Christian believer is determined and guided by the following criteria.

(1) The Spirit of God. The Holy Spirit is not only the foundation and power of the life of the Christian believer but a guide into the "how" of right conduct as well. The power of the Spirit present in the believer overcomes the sinful tendencies of the flesh if and when the believer lets himself be guided by the Spirit. God's Spirit helps the believer to discern the will of God and to perceive proper behaviour in specific situations. The believer is thus able to realize God's claims in everyday life. Cf. Rom 8.4-5,9-13; Gal 5.16-17; Col 1.9-10.

(2) Love. The love of God which has been revealed in the sending of the Son is a soteriological reality which assumes central significance for the believer and his responsibility to realize God's will in the specific situations of his everyday routine (1Cor 13). Love is crucially important in the endeavor to master new situations. True love provides the believer with the capability to discern that which matters and helps him perceive how to behave in practical situations. Cf. 1Cor 7.4-5,36-38; 3.18; Phil 1.9-10.

(3) The existing orders. The position of the believers "in the Lord" implies a potential and effective reservation with regard to the orders of creation and society, particularly in the realm of human conventions: creation is fallen creation. However, Paul was prepared to take up elements of the contemporary non-Christian ethic. These traditional social orders and conventions are not *eo ipso* nor continuously identical with that which is appropriate "in the Lord". The process of critical examination and selection gives a new meaning to many traditional contemporary concepts and ways of behaviour and often transforms their substance: the phrase "in Christ" is not a mere formula! Cf. 1Thess 5.15; 1Cor 10.32; Rom 12.2.

(4) Reason. Paul occasionally refers the believers to their cognitive faculties when he talks about perceiving the will of God in the specific situations of everyday life. Human reason has become intrinsically useless as a result of sin. Nevertheless, Paul refers to reason as an instance in man which may distinguish between good

and evil. An important aspect of Paul's *paraklesis* is concerned with putting the Christian believer "in the right mind" (*nouthetein*), i.e. guiding him to proper insight into the right ways of conduct. The renewal of man in Christ and by God's Spirit embraces the *nous* as well. Cf. Rom 1.28; Col 2.18; Eph 4.17; Rom 7.21-23; 8.5; 12.2; 14.5; 15.14; 2Cor 10.5; Phil 1.9-10; 4.8-9.

(5) Conscience. Paul treats the conscience as that inner authority which examines and makes conscious the individual's behaviour or (occasionally) the behaviour of others on the basis of primary and generally acknowledged norms. The conscience is primarily related to the believer's consciousness of being guilty or blameless before God, i.e. to the judgment whether he has made the right decision and behaved properly. The conscience is guided by love for the brother and thus directed by faith. Cf. 1Cor 8.7-8; 10.25-27; 2Cor 5.10; Rom 14.10,23.

(6) Mission. Some passages imply the mission effectiveness of the church as motivation for right conduct. Cf. 1Thess 4.12; 1Cor 10.32; Phil 1.27; 1Tim 2.2.

As we attempt to understand the paradoxical relationship of binding norms and criteria which presuppose and require individual responsibility—law and Spirit, obedience and love, God's will and the freedom of the Christian—the correlation of law and wisdom of the biblical-Jewish tradition proves to be significant. The believer who is determined by God's salvific action in Jesus Christ is to live according to the demands of God's holy will. At the same time he lives as one who is called to the freedom of the children of God by the Spirit. Law and Spirit, commandment and love, obedience and responsibility are not contrasts which contradict each other. For Paul Christian ethics is neither legalistically motivated nor antinomistically executed nor situation-ethically privatized. God's salvific action in Jesus Christ grants believers the gifts of righteousness and holiness, the Spirit and love: believers reply with living according to God's command in the power of the Spirit and by the love of Christ, safeguarding their responsibility regarding the brother and the world, aiming at the glorification of God.

PART VII

THE RELEVANCE OF PAULINE ETHICS
All You Need is Love?

CHAPTER THIRTEEN

The Formal Ethical Interpretation of Pauline Paraenesis*

Wolfgang Schrage
(1960)

It is commonly denied that there is a biblical material-ethic.[1] Instead, nowadays Augustine's words "ama, et fac quod vis" (love and do whatever you wish) are gladly put forward as a valid expression of a supposed biblical witness. Many believe that the totality and fulness of New Testament moral demands may be reduced to the commandment to love, or may be concentrated therein so that all single commandments of a concrete content are superfluous. This reckoning of the love commandment as being absolute, thereby regarding it as the only ethical norm, makes impossible "every ethic

---

* Translated by George S. Rosner and Brian S. Rosner.
[1] Concepts such as ethics, material ethics, situational ethics, etc are not used here in a literal sense, since neither Paul nor any other New Testament author has developed a precise, systematic ethics.

which tries to give an answer to the question, what shall I do? It therefore absolves the individual of the need for an answer."[2] All that has to be done is summed up in love. Since love is the "only fundamental ground for behaviour," all lists of individual virtues are superfluous,[3] or even forbidden. The mere appearance of catalogues of virtues or vices can therefore be judged as a doubtful advocacy and symptom of moralism; love is thereby no longer the "ἐν καὶ πᾶν" (one and all) and the "general determination of the way of life . . . , which governs everything and knows no subordinate virtues."[4] Because a person knows what to expect from others, he also knows what he has to do himself and what he must not do, and therefore he has no need of further instructions.[5] The commandment to love advises someone what to do in the concrete situation vis-a-vis a concrete neighbour. In meeting his neighbour, the loving person simply knows how he has to develop his love with an ever new and different content.[6] But even when there is no situation-ethical nuance, it is emphasised that the New Testament leaves the concrete moral decisions principally to the conscience of the individual. Neither the apostle nor a third person, but only the individual himself has to decide how to realise the divine demand in concrete behaviour. This emphasises the independence or the "self-governance" of the individual,[7] or it stresses that all material demands are understood as a misunderstanding of human existence and its original relationship to the "you" (i.e., God).[8] An almost 'enthusiastic' understanding of the Spirit and his leading would produce similar results: "Where life moves in the Spirit, no more commandments have a place"; the Spirit himself points the way.[9] He is an "adequate ethical guide" so that the

---

[2] Cf. *R. Bultmann:* Glauben und Verstehen (Ges. Aufs.) I, 1954, pp. 234ff.

[3] *H. Preisker:* Das Ethos des Urchristentums, 1949, pp. 77 and 76; similarly *R. Liechtenhan:* Gottes Gebot im N.T., 1942, p. 87.

[4] *Preisker,* amongst other passages, p. 185; similarly *B.S. Easton,* Journal of Biblical Literature 51 (1932) p. 12.

[5] *Bultmann,* p. 38; cf. *E.H. Wahlstrom:* The New Life in Christ, 1950, p. 192.

[6] *R. Bultmann:* Glauben und Verstehen (Ges. Aufs.) II, 1952, pp. 18 and 70.

[7] *A. Juncker:* Die Ethik des Apostels Paulus I, II, 1904/19, I, p. 181 and 33; *H. Weinel* is of the opinion that Paul has demonstrated to his churches, "How one gives oneself moral laws" (Paulus, 1915, p. 95); Weinel himself indicates that here the concept of autonomy of Kant and Fichte has not been without its influence (pp. 93ff.).

[8] *Bultmann* I, op cit, pp. 229ff.

[9] *H. Lietzmann:* An die Römer (Hdb. z. N.T. 8), 1933, p. 71.

one who lives in the Spirit knows within himself what God's will is,[10] and carries "the norm within himself."[11] The Christian way of life understood as 'enthusiasm' can therefore "fly beyond" the individual commandments.[12]

There needs to be a closer examination of these matters to determine whether such a pushing back of and "flying beyond" the individual commandments is compatible with biblical ethics and, above all, with Paul's ethics.[13] It may be said plainly that the one-sided devaluation of all demands of a concrete nature needs to be corrected. Certainly there are many understandable reasons which have led to a devaluation of individual commandments: first of all, there is an endeavour to distance oneself quite clearly from all kinds of casuistry, which wishes to enmesh the new life in a narrow net of individual prescripts; then there is the "no" to all attempts to split and atomize the unity of the Christian way of life; further, there is the protest against all legalistic formalism, which is satisfied with a mere outwardly correct fulfillment of individual commandments and conceals the personal link with the Lord as well as the radical and total character of the obedience which is demanded; furthermore, there is the emphasis on the fallacy of rigidly shaping and regimenting the new life; and finally, there is the confrontation of Jewish and Catholic ethics and the influence of philosophical, and above all, idealistic ethics. We will not deal with these reasons or motives here. In any case they do not justify the exaggeratedly negative verdict on all concrete, individual commandments. Rather they call for a new consideration of the nature of biblical ethics, a new consideration which in any case wants biblical ethics to be more than a non-binding paradigmatic commentary regarding the commandment to love.

After all, a mere glance at one of Paul's letters or at a gospel makes it impossible to ignore the many individual commandments. Neither Jesus nor Paul has dispensed with stressing quite concrete single commandments and warnings next to the commandment to love. Because it cannot be argued that these commandments do not

---

10 L. *Marshall*: The Challenge of New Testament Ethics, 1950, pp. 220, 224ff.

11 *Liechtenhan*, op cit, p. 76.

12 *J. Weiss*: Das Urchristentum, 1917, p. 119.

13 Cf. the author's dissertation 'Die konkreten Einzelgebote in der Paränese des Apostels Paulus. Ein Beitrag zur biblischen Ethik' (Kiel 1959); the much abbreviated first chapter of the dissertation forms the foundation for this essay. The study will shortly be published by the Carl-Bertelsmann Foundation [Editor: It was published in 1961 at Gütersloh].

exist, the formal-ethical interpretation is open to some embarrass-ment. Indeed, the many attempts to explain away and to blunt the individual commandments, which undeniably exist, are based upon the existence of these more fundamental statements.

In the following there will be an analysis of the interpretation up to this point of the concrete individual commandments, as far as Pauline ethics is concerned.

ARE THE INDIVIDUAL COMMANDMENTS THE RESULT OF A PROCESS OF DE-ESCHATOLOGISATION?

The first attempt to explain Paul's concrete individual command-ments consists in the reference to the supposedly diminished or diminishing eschatological consciousness of the apostle. Here, the appearance of concrete pa*ænesis* is understood as a consequence of the delay of the parousia. This is supposed to have gradually forced Paul into a compromise with the reality of the world and its daily demands. *Dibelius* has in answer to the question of the creation of original Christian paræacus pointed to the eschatological belief of the original Christian churches, who were "organised for the passing of this world and not for living in the world."[14] Therefore, they had neither the inclination nor the ability to "undertake the ethical revewal of this world." Only as the years passed did the questions of daily life demand an answer in a Christian sense.[15] *Weidinger* builds upon this explanation, carrying it further. Dibelius recognised the absence of a specifically *Christian* paræacus in the early years of the church, and also reckoned with the use of secular paræacus traditions, but not with the absence of individual demands as such. On the other hand, Weidinger asserts that in the "glow of the Spirit which uprooted everything" there was no need for paræacus which dealt with the relevant individual problems. This state of affairs had, of course, to come to an end since "life with its relentless daily demands made it clear even to the Christians that they were still on earth and in the passage of time."[16] Therefore, the *Haustafel*

---

[14] *M. Dibelius:* Die Formgeschichte des Evangeliums, 1933, p.241; cf. also Geschichte der urchristl. Literatur II (Sammlung Göschen 935), 1926, p. 67.

[15] Der Brief des Jakobus (Krit.-exeg. Komm. über das N.T., 15. Abt.), 1959, p. 4.

[16] *K. Weidinger:* Die Haustafeln (Unters. z. N.T. 14), 1928, pp. 6ff., 8.

(household code) scheme was adopted, which constituted a "retreat" from the "hot breath of the first epoch."[17]

The explanation of *Dodd* is related to this view. He says that one could observe in Paul's letters a development from eschatological fever in the first letters to an ever stronger retreat from belief in the nearness of eschatological fulfillment in the letters Paul wrote from prison.[18] Dodd too uses this alleged development in order to explain the appearance of concrete ethics with Paul, in particular ethics which seems to reveal an appreciation of the "natural order," such as the state and marriage. Dodd says that the first letters show, apart from an impatient maintenance of the expectation of an imminent parousia, "a radical denial of the value of the present order" and that with "almost fanatical logic." With the alleged revision of eschatology, which he ascribes to Paul's "robust common sense," there is now a new valuation of the world and of the Christian relationship to it, "a recognition of natural human goodness, of the relative value of human institutions and the possibility of taking them up into the Christian life."[19]

These explanations, when first considered, seem to make a lot of sense, since the one who expects the end of the world at any moment naturally will not consider or have time for concrete ethics. Could a paraenesis, filled with content, only be developed and handed down at the moment when one reckoned with the continued existence of the world or at least thought of it lasting a long time? Was Paul therefore compelled to state concrete solutions for the conservation and shape of the life of the Christian in this world? When considered more closely, however, Weidinger's and Dodd's opinions prove to be in error.

To state that Paul's entire thought and action was characterised eschatologically is widely accepted today, since the fundamental basis of Paul's theology is beyond any doubt thoroughly eschatological. Without acknowledging this faith, that one is "at the end of time," at the beginning of the new world and at the edge of the time of salvation, not a single word of Paul can be rightly understood (cf. 1 Cor 10:11; 2 Cor 5:17). Compared with that, the question regarding the emphasis of this eschatological belief is of only lesser

---

17 *Weidinger*, op cit, p. 52.

18 C.H. *Dodd:* New Testament Studies 1953, pp. 109ff.; similarly Gospel and Law, 1951, pp. 28ff., and The Ethics of the Pauline Epistles (in: The Evolution of the Ethics, edited by *E.H. Sneath*), 1927, pp. 307ff., 305, 319.

19 *Dodd:* New Testament Studies, pp. 109ff., 118.

importance,[20] because what has already happened and what is happening are equally necessary and important. The one causes, establishes and challenges the other. Certainly, in the coming, death and resurrection of Jesus Christ the decisive, eschatological deed of salvation has already happened and the new aeon has arrived (cf. Gal 4:4; 1 Cor 15:20). This emphasis on the presence of salvation (cf. the eschatological νῦν "now," Rom 3:21: 5:11; 2 Cor 6:2) under the lordship of the present Christ has in no way led Paul to abandon the expectation of the future or to devalue it. If Christ is the turning point of the aeons, he is at the same time the one who is expected and who will come again soon (1 Thess 4:13ff; 1 Cor 16:27). If salvation of the new aeon is present, it is at the same time also in the future (Gal 5:5; 1 Cor 6:14; 2 Cor 4:14; etc.). The life of Christians also relates to the existence side by side of present and future salvation. Christians stand in the middle of this eschatological development in which the time of the old world passes and the new time of salvation arises. By Christ's death they have already been torn away from the power of the present evil aeon (Gal 1:4), transferred to the kingdom of Christ (Col 1:13) and already belong to the new creation (2 Cor 5:17). But Christians are and remain those who wait and hope (Rom 8:23; Phil 3:20f; 1 Thess 1:10). Even the new life is one that is hidden with Christ in God (Col 3:3), is covered with weakness (cf. 2 Cor 10:9f), attempted in "the flesh" and only saved in hope (Rom 8:24).

Both things, however, the eschatological qualification of the present as well as the clinging to the hope of fulfilment in the end, make it impossible to speak of a weakening of Paul's eschatological faith. "A progressive diminution of interest in eschatology"[21] is a pure construction. In any case, we find no evidence for such a movement in the letters preserved for us. In order to substantiate his thesis Dodd has to reinterpret eschatological statements in the earlier letters and, on the other hand, to spiritualise the eschatology in the later letters (eg. Phil 4:5) or to ignore it (eg. Rom 13:11ff). Rather, what is shown is that from the time of the first letters—after all, since

---

[20] Therefore Pauline ethics must not be confused with "provisional ethics", that is, with a concept which would be invalid without the expectation of the near end (as demonstrated by H. Greeven: Das Hauptproblem der Sozialethik in der neueren Stoa und im Urchristentum. Ntl. Forsch. III/4, 1935, p.106); according to *J. Héring* the passage in I Cor 7:30f has "great importance independent of the date of the parousia"; cf. also *0. Cullmann:* Christus und die Zeit, 1946, p. 188.

[21] *Dodd:* New Testament Studies, p. 54.

Paul's conversion about fifteen years had passed—the expectation of eschatological fulfilment remained alive in undiminished strength alongside the consciousness of the turning of the aeons in Christ. This expectation is not limited to an initial epoch. This means that the decisive assumption for the explanation of the concrete paraenesis due to the disappearance of the eschatological expectation is no longer tenable. If there is no such process of de-eschatologisation with Paul, one cannot make it responsible for the necessity or possibility of individual admonitions.

On the other hand, it can now be shown that next to the unchanged strong eschatological certainty of Paul's faith, there were right from the start concrete, individual warnings. Paul has not been the "herald of an imminent catastrophe" with a radical repudiation and devaluation of all present order in the sense of the apocalyptists, neither in the letters to the Thessalonians nor in 1 Corinthians.[22] Weidinger too constructs a situation for the early period which never existed, except for the 'enthusiastic' zealots against whom Paul fought. Where is the proof for the assertion that in "a glow of the Spirit which uprooted everything" one knew no need for paraenesis and at some point of time "disenchantment" replaced the "intoxication of the Spirit?"[23] Not the genuine Paul, but only a Paul falsified in an eccentric or gnostic way can be held responsible for misunderstandings in the sense of an enthusiasm which vaulted over the earthly existence and its order. The Corinthian example, for instance, makes this clear. Even the troubles in Thessalonica, caused by an overenthusiastic stressing of the eschatological expectation, which cannot be judged as an *inertia vulgaris* (common lethargy), but rather as a mistaken consequence of immediate expectation,[24] are sharply criticised by Paul (1 Thess 4:11ff.; 5:14; 2 Thess 3:6ff.). But even if the lassitude and laziness are not motivated eschatologically Paul's polemic yet proves that Weidinger and Dodd are mistaken. One should perhaps understand the laziness of the Thessalonians as

---

22 Against *Dodd:* New Testament Studies, pp. 110ff.
23 Thus *Weidinger*, op cit, pp. 7ff..
24 Thus *Dibelius* and *v. Dobschütz*; commenting on the passage in question; also *M. Goguel* (L'église primitive, 1947, p. 543); *H. v. Campenhausen* (Die Begründung kirchl. Entscheidungen beim Apostel Paulus, SAH 1957/2, p. 11 and in the Bertholet-Festschrift 1950, pp. 108ff.); *Preisker*, op cit, p. 188, and "Das Ethos der Arbeit im N.T.", 1936, pp. 3ff., 10ff., cf. also *C. Spicq:* Studia Theol. X, 1957, pp. 1ff.; finally, *W. Bienert:* Die Arbeit nach der Lehre der Bibel, 1954, p. 323: ". . . Greek disinclination to work, which has not yet been overcome" (cf. also pp. 370ff.).

a sign of missing eschatology rather than as misunderstood eschatology.[25] From the start Paul stood against the dangerous tendency of eschatological belief to strive toward "a kind of emancipation" which "abandons the every day life of the citizen too early by anticipating God's decisions."[26] The duty to work was already part of the missionary paraenesis in the letters to the Thessalonians,[27] which are influenced by a strong eschatological expectation. Eschatology and the duty to work stand side by side. Even 1 Corinthians 7, with its many individual rules regarding marriage which stand in immediate proximity to eschatological statements (vss. 29-31), proves that Paul is no eccentric, who, because of a pure expectation of the end, no longer takes seriously the manifold concrete problems of this world. Finally, Paul's position vis-a-vis the powers of the state does not speak for but rather against Weidinger. Weidinger regards Revelation 17 as being the only possible position regarding the Roman state at the time when the "hot breath of the first epoch" was in the air, whilst the more positive statement in Romans 13 could only be understood by him as "a retreat from the eschatological type of thinking."[28] But Paul neither denies the state nor its rights in Romans 13, nor should it be overlooked that he, side by side with this attitude, nevertheless holds onto the imminent expectation (vss. 11ff.; cf. esp. the ἐγγύτερον: "nearer"). Therefore the recent emphasis placed on the tight connection of eschatological faith and Christian obedience to the state is correct.[29] Certainly there is no *direct* relationship between the duty of obedience to the state of the Christian (vss. 1-7) and his knowledge of his standing in eschatological time. But Kümmel, too, who refers to

---

[25] *Bienert*, op cit, p. 372.

[26] *M. Dibelius:* An die Thessalonicher I, II (Hdb. z. N.T. 11), 1937, p. 54.

[27] *Dibelius*, op cit, pp. 54, 23.

[28] *Weidinger*, pp. 8ff.; similarly also *H. Wienel* (pp. 194ff., 198, and "Die Stellung des Urchristentums zum Staat", 1908) who believes that he cannot take Paul literally in Romans 13, since fundamentally Paul's relationship to the state must be described as being an attitude of indifference or contempt shown by a man who "ardently hopes for the passing away of this world" and therefore has an inner attitude of rejecting the state.

[29] *H. Schlier* (Zwischen den Zeiten, 10/1932, pp. 320, 327; printed again in: Die Zeit der Kirche. Exeget. Aufs. u. Vorträge, 1956, pp. 7, 13); *v. Campenhausen* (Bertholet-Festschrift, pp. 107ff.); *M. Dibelius* (Botschaftu. Geschichte II, 1956, p. 184); *H.D. Wendland* (in: Botschaft und Geschichte. Festgabe f. H. Schreiner, 1953, pp. 317ff., 326, fn. 19); *O. Cullmann* (Der Staat im N.T., 1956, pp. 40,42); *Preisker* (Das Ethos des Urchristentums, pp. 86ff.); on the other hand *O. Kuss* (Theologie und Glaube, 45/1955, pp. 331ff.).

this relationship, recommends the "consideration of the text in a larger context," instead of, for instance, deriving from the text itself the missing reservation for the duty to obey in Romans 13.[30] Furthermore, verses 11-13 themselves claim to be related to all the preceding admonitions.[31] Therefore, the placement of Romans 13:1-7 into the frame of eschatology (vss. 11-13) is here to be approved as well. Again there can be no talk of the retreat of eschatology here.

The same applies regarding the opinion that we are here dealing with an "adaptation to the 'world'" and that Paul, for the sake of daily life and its every day problems, had to move away from the alleged "exaggerated ideal." Weidinger's view creates the impression that the reception of daily demands was an emergency solution and that the church, more or less unwillingly and against its better judgement, had been forced into a "compromise" between final expectation and concrete daily needs by the superior might of "realities."[32] But even Romans 13 is to be subordinated to Romans 12:1-2 and therefore it is definitely not a compromise or adjustment to the world. Romans 12:1-2 makes it crystal clear that paraenesis is not to be considered an indication that the church began to accommodate itself to the world. Rather, to the contrary, the church was the expression and the effect of the fact that in Christ a *new* world had commenced, which now also wants to determine the concrete life of Christians. If the concrete duties of daily life have "irresistibly pressed forward," then that happened very soon after the creation of the churches and not only after the eschatological hopes waned. The letters to the Thessalonians written a few weeks after Paul's departure show this with their concrete admonitions and directions. In part, Paul only has to remind the Thessalonians of these instructions. In all of the Pauline writings the eschatological assertion stands alongside of ethical assertions. That this was so from the start is proven by the παραγγελίαι (directions: 1 Thess 4:2), παραδόσεις (traditions: 1 Cor 11:2; 2 Thess 2:15) and ὁδοί (ways: 1 Cor 4:17). These directions were given to the churches probably already during their evangelisation. The catalogues of virtues and vices in the missionary preaching probably already illustrated the ethical

---

30 W.G. *Kümmel* (Theol. Rundschau, 1948/49, pp. 137ff.).

31 Cf. below and fn. 39.

32 Weidinger, op cit, pp. 8ff., 10ff.; also according to Dodd (Gospel and Law, pp. 31ff.) it is only "under the impact of facts" that eschatology decreases and therefore there are "new moral possibilities," and "workaday precepts."

demands (cf. Gal 5:21: καθὼς προεῖπον; "how I have already said").[33] This finally proves the fact that Paul already took over some older paraenetic traditions (eg. words of the Lord) from the primitive church.[34] Due to the coming end the world certainly becomes a mere temporary thing, but the knowledge of this has not led Paul to eccentric excesses. Rather, in the midst of this temporary state he has held fast to God's creation and demand of holiness.

The existence side by side of eschatological and ethical assertions may be made even more clear,[35] because Paul was in no way satisfied just to place these two concepts side by side. The relationship of eschatology and ethics can be defined neither in the sense of two epochs of time, one after the other, nor as the tension between two concepts existing at the same time. Romans 13 already suggested that eschatology is the *foundation* of moral conduct. As we have seen, one should assume from the start that, like all of Paul's proclamations, his ethics is to be qualified eschatologically. The awareness of living in the last days will not leave even the concrete actions untouched since eschatology is, after all, not an appendix to the last chapter of Paul's dogma, but rather a "fundamental structure which determines the whole faith and all the actions of the Christians . . . from the beginning to the end."[36] This assumption is confirmed everywhere. The conduct of the Christian is shaped and motivated through the eschatological deed of salvation which happened in Christ and in baptism as well as through the view of the eschatological future. Both poles of eschatology are here also of decisive meaning. For a start one should point above all to the end time gift of the *Pneuma* (Spirit), which is given to the Christian

---

[33] A. *Vögtle:* Die Tugend- und Lasterkataloge im N.T. (Ntl. Abhandl. XVI, 4-5), 1936, pp. 18ff.

[34] Cf. *Dibelius* re. 1 Thess 4:1 and "Die Formgeschichte des Evangeliums", pp. 239ff.

[35] Concerning the relationship of eschatology and ethics refer especially to H.D. *Wendland* (Neue Kirchl. Zeitschr., 41/1930, pp. 757ff.; The Ecumenical Review, 5/1953, pp. 364ff.; Die Kirche in der Modernen Gesellschaft, 1955, pp. 37ff); *H.H. Rex* (Das ethische Problem in der eschatologischen Existenz bei Paulus, Diss. Tübingen, 1954, pp. 9ff., 89ff.); *M. S. Enslin* (The Ethics of Paul, 1930, pp. 199ff., 302); *R. Schnackenburg* (Die sittl. Botschaft des N.T., 1954, pp. 127ff.); *v. Campenhausen* (Bertholet-Festschrift, pp. 107ff.); *H. Rolston* (The Social Message of the Apostle Paul, 1942, pp. 32ff.); *A.N. Wilder* (Kerygma, Eschatology and Social Ethics; in The Background of the New Testament and its Eschatology. In Honour of C.H. Dodd, 1956, pp. 522ff.); *Preisker* (Das Ethos des Urchristentums, pp. 24ff., 39ff., 168ff.).

[36] *Wendland*, Neue kirchl. Zeitschr., 1930, p. 794 (cf. p. 800).

through baptism and has to be recognised as the fundamental power and the fundamental principle of the new life of obedience.[37] The shaping of Pauline ethics by the eschatological future quite clearly reveals the manifold promises of reward. But it is also seen in many passages in which Paul unmistakably speaks of judgement according to works, even and emphatically for the Christian (2 Cor 5:10, etc.), since the Christian too will be held accountable for all his or her actions and deeds.[38]

A good example of this is found in Romans 13:11-14: if Romans 12:1-2 is the heading of the two paraenetic chapters 12 and 13, here we find the so-called corresponding conclusion.[39] The whole paraenesis is a warning related to the eschatological *kairos* and to the pressing nearness of the "day," and the just περιπατεῖν (conduct) is one that is shaped by a knowing expectation of the coming day. It is the conduct of the "children of light and of the day" (1 Thess 5:5), who have nothing to do any more with night and darkness (cf. the [ἄρα] οὖν; "therefore" in Rom 13:12 and 1 Thess 5:6). The view of the future goal also determines the present in quite concrete action, which is demonstrated by the relationship of the τοῦτο (this) in verse 11 to all the preceding admonitions. But even in verses 11-14 Paul in no way limits himself by demanding quite generally a ὡς ἐν ἡμέρᾳ εὐσχημόνως περιπατεῖν (honorable conduct, as it should be during the day); the thing to do is to put on Christ (vs. 14) as well as to take up quite concretely and in detail the "weapons of light" and to abandon the "works of darkness," which Paul lists in verse 13. Both belong

---

37 Cf. *R. Bultmann* (Theologie des N.T., 1958, pp. 159, 164, 338ff.); Enslin, op cit (pp. 118ff., 297); *Marshall* (p. 230); *Wahlstrom*, op cit, (pp. 111ff.); *J. Kooy* (Die Paränese van den Apostel Paulus, 1926, pp. 64ff.); H.D. Wendland (Theol. Lit. Ztg., 77/1952, pp. 462ff.); *L. Dewar* (An Outline of New Testament Ethics, 1949, pp. 99ff.); *E. Schweizer* (Theol. Wörterbuch, VI/S. 425ff.); *L. Nieder* (Die Motive der relig.-sittl. Paränese in den paulinischen Gemeindebriefen; Münch. Theol. Stud., I/13, 1956, pp. 128ff.).

38 Cf. *Wendland*: NKZ, 1930, pp. 763ff.; *H. Braun*: Gerichtsgedanke u. Rechtfertigungslehre bei Paulus (Unters. z. N.T. 19), 1930; *F. V. Filson*: St. Paul's Conception of Recompense (Unters. z. N.T. 21), 1931; *W. Joest*: Gesetz und Freiheit. Das Problem des Tertius usus legis bei Luther u. die N.T. Paränese. 1956, pp. 165ff.; *C. Haufe*: Die sittliche Rechtfertigunglehre bei Paulus, 1957, pp. 31ff.; *G. Bornkamm*: Der Lohngedanke im N.T., in: Studien zu Antike u. Urchristentum, Ges. Aufs., Bd. II, 1959, pp. 69 ff.

39 Cf. *0. Michel*: the τοῦτο (this) must therefore refer to the whole of the preceding paragraph 12:1-13:10 and should be amplified by an imperative or indicative ποιεῖτε (does) (*F. Blass, A. Debrunner*: Grammatik des ntl. Griechisch, 1954, 480, 5; also *Nieder*, p. 34; *Michel* and *Lagrange* z. St.).

together: not only an old and a new man corresponding to the old and the new aeon, but also old-evil and new-good deeds (cf. Col 3:9: ὁ παλαιὸς ἄνθρωπος σὺν ταῖς πράξεσιν αὐτου; "the old man with all his deeds"). All that belongs to night and darkness has to be abandoned. Whether or not this happens is shown by whether certain definite evil works like orgy and drunkenness, sexual transgression and lack of self-control, strife and jealousy (vs. 13) still play a role in the life of the Christian or not. Taking part in the coming kingdom presupposes breaking with certain sins (1 Cor 6:9f; Gal 5:19-21), sins which attract the wrath of God (Rom 2:8ff.; Col 3:6).

Apart from the eschatological motivation of Christian conduct the question should be asked here whether eschatology apart from the power of motivation also has a regulating power for the concrete life of the Christian. In other words, whether it determines only the "that" or also the substance of the "what" of action. *Bultmann* asserted at one time that eschatology declares only the pathos and the moment, but not the content of the demand (eg. forgoing property and marriage).[40] *Von Dobschütz* too denies that Pauline ethics is "effected as to content" by eschatology and that eschatology is more than "an urgent motive" in the paraenesis.[41] The καὶ τοῦτο (and this) in Romans 13:11, which may be considered to be an intensification, does indeed encourage one to find an additional and increasing motivation of the preceding paraenesis ("considering" . . . "and this all the more because" . . .). The knowledge of the nearness of the "day" without a doubt sharpens the urgency of the warning. Furthermore, it is clear that the warning against orgies, drunkenness, fornication, dissolute living and similar things is not a specifically eschatological, not even a specifically Christian warning, but points to the fact that eschatological ethics does not in itself mean an ethic with extraordinary content demanded beyond normal standards (cf. 1 Cor 7:17ff.).

But this is only one side of the matter, as is shown above all by 1 Corinthians 7. First, there are verses 29-31. The eschatological character of these verses is clear: the *kairos* is compressed (vs. 29), the

---

[40] R. *Bultmann*, Zeitschr. f. Theol. u. Kirche, 27/1917, pp. 76ff.; in ZNW, 23/1924, p. 124, therefore considers Romans 13:11-14 and I Thess 5:1-10, where the view to the End serves to "motivate the moral appeal," as virtually "inconsequential," since the eschatological tension otherwise definitely motivates the indicative, but allows us to forget the imperative. In this view Bultmann is close to Weidinger and Dodd.

[41] E. *v. Dobschütz:* Die Thessalonicherbriefe (KEK, 19. Abt., 1909, pp. 214ff.).

world is hurrying to its end, and is already passing away (παράγει; "passes away"; present tense! vs. 31). In view of this situation of the temporary character of all things the conduct of Christians with respect to the things of this world can be only one of the ὡς μή (as those who are not . . .). That is, a last critical reservation, a last inner freedom and distance, determine their relationship to marriage and family, profession and state, joy and sorrow, goods and values of this world.[42] This new relationship to the world in its inner freedom[43] is now a wholly ethical relationship, especially because it does not derive from apocalyptic fever fleeing the world. More specifically, it implies and draws out of itself quite concrete rules of conduct. It is good not to stress too strongly the "inner" character of Christian independence from the world, in order not to lose the view which shows that this freedom will manifest itself quite concretely and "externally" in an *opus oboedientiae externum* (external deed of obedience; Luther). It is true that the early rules designated by ὡς μή are most paradoxical: οἱ ἔχοντες γυναῖκας ὡς μὴ ἔχοντες ("those who have wives are as though they had none"). Paul too stresses in 1 Corinthians 7:17ff.: "Let everyone lead the life which the Lord has assigned to him, and in which God has called him." Not even the slave shall change his standing even if the opportunity occurred (1 Cor 7:21).[44] The message that these orders and realities shall end works itself out in concrete everyday reality with its orders and

---

42 R. *Bultmann:* Theologie des N.T.s, pp. 186, 353.

43 Despite all the relationship, this does not signify the Stoic *ataraxis* with its contempt of all feelings (cf. Rom 12:15); the ἀνέχου καὶ ἀπέχου (remain relaxed and keep away) is not a Pauline solution, and ἀπάθεια, ἀταραξία and ἐποχή (indifference, lack of passion and aloofness) are not Paul's words. Only he who overlooks this (according to J. *Weiss,* op cit, p. 460 and *Dewar,* op cit, p. 157; *Enslin,* op cit, p. 189, *Preisker,* op cit, p. 174) can experience the paradox of the Christian relationship to the world in 1 Cor 7:29-31 as a contradiction to Col 3:19 (correct according to *Héring* and *Kümmel;* commenting on the passage in question; *Rex,* op cit, p. 89; *Schnackenburg,* op cit, p. 150).

44 As the whole context teaches (cf. vss. 17, 20, 24), the μᾶλλον χρῆσαι (but rather use) not to be completed by τῇ ἐλευθερίᾳ (the liberty), but rather by τῇ δουλείᾳ (the slavery) (cf. the literature called χράομαι in W. Bauer's Wörterbuch; besides H. *Schlier* (Theol. Wörterbuch II, p. 498), *Greeven* (pp. 50ff.), J. *Leipoldt* (Der soziale Gedanke in der altchristl. Kirche, 1952, p. 123); with a different view however, K.H. *Rengstorf* (Theol. Wörterbuch II, p. 274), *Bienert* (p. 338); recently, quite a different opinion held by G. *Kehnscherper* (Die Stellung der Bibel u. der alten christl. Kirche zur Sklaverei, 1957), who is of the opinion that an original message of liberation of the slaves had been turned into an eschatological spiritual consolation (pp. 85ff.).

obligations—as paradoxical as this may sound. But this does not mean that the life of the Christian should continue in the ways and norms which hitherto prevailed (cf. Rom 12:1-2). Even if Paul does not value endeavours to alter and reform the social, sociological, legal and commercial circumstances and conditions, one should not in any way conclude that he represents conservatism or patriarchalism which sanctions all existing order as being holy or in God's will. How could there be something definite or absolute in a world that was passing away? Nor can one conclude that Paul teaches only uncritical, humble obedience and restricted himself to a reconciled, peaceful side-by-side existence of eschatological faith and concrete conduct in life. If the new conduct of the Christian takes place within certain given "structures" (in the home, profession, state, etc), then the conduct within these structures is influenced in a concrete way by eschatology, not only in pathos and intensity, but also in the manner and mode, in the content.

The position regarding marriage and celibacy in 1 Corinthians 7 makes this quite clear. Even here the eschatological viewpoint which calls for a break is shown in a certain dialectic, because for Paul marriage is neither the normal state nor a duty, nor however a necessary evil or even something inferior.[45] Because of its charismatic character celibacy can certainly not become an ethical commandment of a generally applicable nature (1 Cor 7:7). On the other hand, the position regarding celibacy—and this is a highly concrete issue!—has changed decisively in contrast to Judaism where marriage is regarded as a divine commandment.[46] On account of the ἀνάγκη (distress)[47] of the End Times it is now better not to marry (1 Cor 7:26).

---

[45] The latter has been asserted by G. Delling (Paulus' Stellung zu Frau und Ehe, 1931, p. 67); H. Preisker (Christentum u. Ehe in den ersten drei Jahrhunderten, 1927, p. 127); J. Leipoldt (Die Frau in der antiken Welt und im Urchristentum, 1955, p. 180); correctly: O. Michel (Theol. Stud. u. Krit., 1933, pp. 221ff.); H. Greeven, op cit (pp. 136ff.); F. Büchsel (Theol. Blätter, 1942, pp. 119ff.); B. Reicke (Nov. Test., 1956, pp. 24ff.).

[46] See evidence cited by Strack-Billerbeck II, pp. 372f.; even the Stoa recognised the duty to marry (proofs by Greeven, pp. 119, 134 and Enslin, p. 31).

[47] Διὰ τὴν ἐνεστῶσαν ἀνάγκην (for the sake of the present tribulation) means not only "a time or the menace of persecution" (contra J. J. v. Allmen: Maris et femmes d'après S. Paul, 1951, p. 15) or "Les difficultés actuelles des fidèles—peu nombreux au sein d'une grande ville corrumpue, exposés sans doute comme adhérents d'une religion nouvelle et partant non licite aux enquêtes policères" (contra Ph.-H. Menoud, Revue de Theologie et de Philosophie, 1951, 24) or also the tension between the demands of the coming aeon and the life in this kosmos

But this shows that the freedom of the ὡς μή now also gains an outward form. Marriage is not the last thing, but the penultimate thing, which passes away with the σχῆμα (form, substance) of this world. This critical reserve with respect to marriage does not derive from ascetic-dualistic motives or as a contempt or fight against an inferior carnality. Rather, it is determined by the nearness of the End. Even the temporary abstention from sexual intercourse for the sake of prayer (1 Cor 7:5), the admonition to stay together in mixed marriages (1 Cor 7:12ff.), the agreement for separation through divorce of the unbelieving partner and to accept separation for the sake of the Lord as a reason for divorce (1 Cor 7:15ff.), show in concrete points that marriage was for Paul something penultimate. Above all, in the *charisma* (gift) of celibacy and in the call for a total devotion to Christ (1 Cor. 7:32ff.) it is shown that the limit of marriage is not only temporal but at the same time it is also not essential. Eschatology appears already now in the midst of this world. It works through the concrete life of the Christian and thereby does not leave the structure of the world untouched (cf. also 1 Cor 6:1ff.).

However one may finally decide, whether the eschatology of Pauline ethics only motivates or also shapes (regarding content), it is in any case clear that one has to understand the existence side by side of eschatological and ethical assertions not as a compromise, but as a substantial expression of the issue itself. The necessary analysis of the concrete reality of this world cannot be understood at all without the certainty of the coming of the new world. It is precisely this new world which Paul wants to make concrete by his individual admonitions in the many circumstances of life and every day reality of Christians.

ARE THE INDIVIDUAL COMMANDMENTS A COMPROMISE BETWEEN THE IDEAL AND REALITY?

A further explanation (which is in a certain way related to the thesis we have just discussed) claims to have found a different kind of compromise in Paul in order to make understandable the concrete admonitions of the apostle. If there it was a compromise with the so called "reality" occasioned by history, a relaxation of eschatological

---

(contra Grundmann, ThWNT I, pp. 394ff., and Nieder, op cit, p. 56), but rather the tribulation of the eschatological time.

tension, here it is a compromise of a more fundamental kind: the compromise between the ideal and reality, between theory and practice. This attempted explanation values the duality of Paul's assertions, which we usually describe as the relationship of the indicative and the imperative.[48] This duality is here understood not as an essentially necessary antinomy, but as an "existence side by side of the ideal and reality, of religious-enthusiastic notion and empirical-realistic perception."[49] The imperative in this view is a corrective against the "heavenward idealism" of the optimistic Paul. This imperative is brought about by rough reality and by bitter experiences or it is a corrective out of pedagogical considerations. The consequence is the "hiatus between theory and reality."[50] This understanding of the indicative and the imperative naturally also has consequences for the interpretation of the *concrete* imperative. This applies above all for the interpretations which are one-sidedly oriented to the indicative. These consider every imperative as being inappropriate for the matter discussed or even as a regression to Jewish observance of the Law. If there are no commandments and no obedience in the ideal of the new life, understood as "moral enthusiasm", but rather only the soul joyfully agreeing with God's will,[51] then a correct appreciation of concrete demands can hardly arise. After all, if the Christian is no longer able to do anything other than the good because the good grows out of him "with the security of what is natural,"[52] he is equally by nature able to know the what and the how of what has to be done, even if Paul now and then is forced to compromise.

The information which we receive from *Juncker* regarding the concrete commandments also corresponds to this alleged

---

[48] Cf. *R. Bultmann*: Zeitschr. f. d. ntl. Wissenschaft, 23/1924, 123ff.; *H. Windisch*, pp. 265ff.; *G. Bornkamm*: Das Ende des Gesetzes, 1958, pp. 34ff.; *W. Mundle*: Zeitschr. f. systemat. Theol., 4/1927, pp. 456ff.; *W. Gutbrod*: Die paulinische Anthropologie, 1934, pp. 205ff.; *E. Dinkle*: Zeitschr. f. Theol. u. Kirche, 49/1952, pp. 167ff.; *A. Kirchgässner*, op cit, pp. 3ff. (more literature quoted there), pp. 147ff.

[49] *J. Weiss* re. 1 Cor 3:1ff. (Der erste Korintherbrief, Krit.-Exeg. Komm. über das N.T., 5. Abt., 1925, p. 71), in similar manner in: Das Urchristentum, p. 400; cf. also *A. Jülicher* re. Rom 6:1ff.; *H. Lietzmann* re. Gal 5:25; *H. Windisch*: Taufe und Sünde im ältesten Christentum, 1908, pp. 98ff.; *A. Wikenhauser*: Die Christusmystik des Apostels Paulus, 1956, p. 101.

[50] *H. J. Holtzmann*: Lehrbuch der ntl. Theologie, Bd. II, 1911, p. 169, cf. 166ff.

[51] *J. Weiss*: Das Urchristentum, p. 400.

[52] *H. Weinel*: Biblische Theologie, 1928, pp. 256ff., and 1921, p. 322.

compromise. Strictly speaking, according to the specific Pauline ideal, Christians are "lifted above every outward statute and norm" because they possess "in the Spirit the infallible norm for the knowledge of that which is God's will for them." But Paul has to place this "principal-ideal" point of view alongside the "empirical" point of view here as well. The factual condition of the churches forces him to do so. Their gnosis is "often in the first instance an implied gnosis" which lacks the "more accurate development and shape, lucidity and depth."[53] The discrepancy between the ideal and reality can be observed not only with respect to the *fulfillment* of the divine will, but also with regard to the question regarding its *discernment* and the necessity of concrete commandments. Strictly speaking, the Christian needs "no special orientation" but the "imperfect reality" recommends reaching back towards "proven remedies" (eg. the catalogues), even in the case of those who were converted long ago.[54]

We need no longer adopt a position regarding the understanding of the relationship of the indicative and the imperative which is based on such an interpretation. This has been demonstrated several times with great detail. The indicative concerning and expressing the new life is, after all, not an ideal to be realised, but rather has a miraculous eschatological character. It represents not an empirical-analytical verdict but rather a verdict of faith. It does not however exclude the imperative, but includes it. The indicative lays a foundation for the imperative; the imperative comes out of the indicative. The relationship of the ideal and reality cannot be considered a factual interpretation of the indicative-imperative relationship. This definition does not throw light on our problem. Even here Paul is not an idealist, who in an audacious flight of thought at first develops an "ideal theory"[55] and then, in practice, takes away more and more items because hard reality does not correspond to his ideal. Furthermore, we know far too little regarding the degree to which the Pauline churches corresponded to the alleged ideal of Paul, because the available sources do not for the most part provide detailed accounts of the more or less obedient response to the apostolic exhortations. The specific questions regarding the interpretation of Pauline demands with which we are

---

53 *A. Juncker*, op cit, I, pp. 179ff.

54 *A. Juncker*, op cit, II, p. 98; similarly also *J. Weiss:* Das Urchristentum, p. 449; *K. Benz:* Die Ethik des Apostels Paulus, 1912, pp. 80ff., 91.

55 *Windisch:* Taufe und Sünde im ältesten Christentum, p. 123.

dealing here are those that ask whether the Pauline "ideal" is really one that deals with a conduct completely free of individual commandments and instructions and whether individual exhortations should be considered a compromise between the ideal and reality. Only a more exhaustive investigation can answer these questions. We shall raise an important objection against the abovementioned attempt at clarification in the following paragraphs because there is a decisive connection between the following interpretation and the interpretation listed above: strictly speaking, individual exhortations should not be necessary.

ARE THE INDIVIDUAL COMMANDMENTS ONLY VALID AND NECESSARY TEMPORARILY, BUT IN THE LONG RUN SUPERFLUOUS?

The point of view that individual exhortations are really superfluous is the fundamental conviction of the explanation now to be discussed and of the one outlined above. The difference is only found in the consideration that it is more strongly felt here that the compromise between that which ought to be and that which unfortunately, de facto still is, will only be of a temporary nature. With the passage of time the ideal of self-determination of the individual with the corresponding abandonment of all concrete instructions will prevail, and then all individual commandments will also be superfluous in practice. Here, therefore, the appearance of concrete exhortations is judged in quite the opposite way than the way employed by those who attempt an explanation expressed in the first section. Whilst there the individual exhortations only became necessary with the passage of time, here they become superfluous with the passage of time and are considered necessary and valid only for the first passing phase as an aid at the very start of things. If there the eschatologically determined time of the beginning was without individual commandments, here the period following the time of the beginning shall be an epoch without individual commandments.

The condition of the young missionary churches is most often made responsible for the exhortations which are necessary temporarily. The young churches, which manifested side by side free love and sexual abstinence, the eating of sacrificial meat and the abstention from eating such meat, still required an energetic guiding will. They could not yet be turned over to "their conscience forthwith," but needed a lot of laws because "a new moral sense had to develop slowly by a transformation of the old sense."[56] God's will should really not first of all be demanded by moral commandments, but should be fulfilled by the power of the Spirit. Unfortunately, however, the condition or the "emergency" of the young missionary churches is such that they still require "the teaching," which "spells out individually what should be done, and above all, what should not be done."[57] Specifically ("logically": *Enslin*; "essentially and in principle": *Wahlstrom*), the exhortations are unnecessary even at the early period, but many Christians are still νήπιοι (babies: 1 Cor 3:1), so that prescriptions, rules and examples were, after all, necessary.[58] By himself the Spirit as an "adequate ethical guide" makes all concrete instructions superfluous, but because of the experience of the huge gap between the ideal and reality Paul cannot as yet rely on the Christians to realise the ethical consequences in detail by themselves.[59] After the churches have existed for a longer period of time the spiritually childish diseases of immature churches will certainly disappear and the essential superfluity of all concrete individual commandments will sooner or later be realised in practice.

The first thing which one would have to expect when dealing with temporary, essentially superfluous exhortations of the apostle would be certain assertions which thrust toward such moral independence, which emphasise the time limits of the apostolic admonitions or note the unfortunate necessity of such admonitions which still exist. In fact, though, we hear nothing of such wishes or complaints from the apostle. Although again and again reproachful and disapproving sounds are heard, these reproaches and complaints refer to factual defects, but not to the necessity of admonitions as such. The two things are certainly not the same, since admonitions are not necessarily based on defects (cf. below!). Even a brief consideration of the nature of early Christian admonitions reveals on the other hand that the thesis of the preliminary nature and superfluity is in error. Early Christian admonitions are basically shaped for repetition and memory, for ever new application and actualisation. One cannot therefore acquire them once and for all, but

---

56 *H. Weinel:* Paulus p. 185; cf. also in the above-mentioned quotations from Juncker the temporal restrictions: "for the time being."

57 *M. Dibelius - W.G. Kümmel:* Paulus (Sammlung Göschen 1160) 1951, pp. 84ff.

58 *Enslin,* op cit, pp. 118f.; *Wahlstrom,* op cit, pp. 156, 158; cf. also *A. Alexander: The Ethics of Paul,* 1910, p. 117.

59 *Marshall,* op cit, pp. 219ff.

they must be heard in their substance again and again and one must take them to heart. They are in this way *ethica viatorum* (the ethical path),[60] destined for those who are still on their way and have not yet reached the goal. This state of travelling remains a steady qualification for every Christian existence which cannot be outstripped (cf. Phil 3:12ff.).

Yet there are dangers along the way. One can only speak of the temporary and superfluous nature of Christian admonitions and commandments by overlooking or underestimating the seriousness of the temptation and threat facing even the Christian. Paul certainly knew that in spite of the radical nature of the break between the past and the present (Col 1:21ff.; 3:7ff.; 1 Cor 6:11) and the *Totaliter aliter* (total difference) of the "newness of life" (Rom 6:4; 7:6; 2 Cor 5:17), the Christian is, nonetheless, not spared menace and temptation (1 Cor 10:12; Gal 6:1). The Christian too, and especially the Christian who yet lives "in the flesh" (Gal 2:20; 2 Cor 10:3) or lives "in a mortal body" (Rom 6:12), is always exposed to the danger of falling and of apostasy. The Christian is also in the territory of battle (Gal 5:17) and is called to battle (cf. the frequently used images of battle in 2 Cor 10:3ff.; 1 Thess 5:8). If the battle because of baptism can now be waged in the sign of Christ's victory, nevertheless it is still present or has even been intensified. *Sarx* (flesh), *kosmos* (world) and *Diabolos* (devil) have not yet ceased to exist despite the lordship of Christ and have therefore not lost their threatening power for the Christian once and for all.[61] Since there is no immunity against these powers of temptation the church requires warning and admonition not to live "according to the flesh" (Rom 8:12ff.) and to beware the tempter (1 Cor 7:5; 2 Cor 2:11).[62] For this reason the apostolic admonitions are not primarily directed to sinners, apostates or those who were left behind but rather to the "saints" (cf. the introductory parts of the letters, and to the *pneumatics* ("the spiritual"; Gal 6:1). Because their being Christians is totally at stake, the content of the demands refers in no way only to trivialities or the rest of heathen conduct not yet abandoned, but rather clearly to the central issue (Rom 13:14; 6:1ff.; Gal 5:25). The fact that the Christian is threatened has to be

---

[60] *Th. Preiss:* La vie en Christ, 1951, p. 66.

[61] Cf. *Kirchgässner*, op cit, pp. 53ff.

[62] Cf. also 2 Cor 11:3; according to Kümmel Paul emphasises by the reference to the myth "the danger of apostasy and thereby the apostolic duty to preserve the church from wrong paths" (z. St.).

considered next to the hiddenness of the new life (Col 3:3; 2 Cor 5:7)[63] as the main reason for the necessity of continued admonitions.

Of course the question of the necessity of the imperative has been almost exclusively discussed *formally*, at least as far as the imperative itself was touched upon by it. The same observation applies also to quite concrete individual commandments. That is, the baptised person does not just have to be continually admonished and challenged to the *reditus ad baptismus* (return to baptism), but must also ever again be confronted with quite concrete individual commandments and admonitions. 1 Corinthians 10, for instance, shows that Paul does not in any way confine himself to the general admonition of verse 12: "he who thinks that he stands, let him take heed that he does not fall!", but he makes it concrete in a "typological" interpretation of the stories of the fathers with a warning against *porneia* (v. 8) among other matters.[64] Especially those who have been baptised like the fathers and have partaken of spiritual drink and food (vss. 2-4), especially those for whom the end of time is approaching, require this νουθεσία (reprimand) (v. 11). It is especially said to the Christians that fornicators and the like will not inherit the kingdom of God (1 Cor 6:9). More weighty and striking than the obviously concrete character of the apostolic paraenesis (cf. also 1 Cor 7; 1 Thess 4; Rom 13) is of course the fact that Paul gives many admonitions and prescriptions which with all their concreteness must be counted according to their content to be fundamental commandments of moral conduct and should be for Christians—as one may emphasise here—a matter of self-evident understanding, because they have been known to the churches for a long time. One may not explain these fundamental rules, which are encountered everywhere, for instance the prohibition of *porneia*, as merely being of a psychological-historical nature, by pointing to "entrenched sinful customs," to the difficult position of the recently baptised "in the midst of the most developed and ruthless life of

---

63 Cf. *G. Bornkamm*, op cit, pp. 45ff.; *E. Schweizer*, Ev. Theol., 1947, pp. 347ff.; *Kooy*, op cit, pp. 99, 103ff.

64 Even here in viewing the Old Testament connection between fornication and idolatry one can probably come to no alternative decision regard the meaning of the term *porneia*. Even in the fundamental text in Num 25 the indecent intercourse with Moabite women is meant as well as the participation in cultic sacrifices; cf. also the intimate connection of both in the catalogues of vices, above all 1 Cor 6:9, but also 1 Cor 5:11; Gal 5:19f.; Col 3:5ff. In any case, the first issue appears to be more strongly stressed (cf. intercourse with a prostitute, 1 Cor 6:12ff.).

commerce, luxury and usury" and similar conditions.⁶⁵ It is self-evident that such moments of practical experience cannot be excluded but Paul saw the danger to the Christian life more radically and therefore he saw the necessity of warnings more deeply and founded on principle. This very fact, namely that Paul did not press on past the supposed self-evidence and original basis of Christian morality, or passed on to teaching those who were morally advanced or even discontinued his relevant admonitions, speaks against the thesis of the gradual superfluity of concrete admonitions. Paul does not feel vexed by having to instruct the churches again and again, and in this way the admonitions which he directs to the churches after missionary enterprise of only three weeks (1 Thess) do not differ in their character from those which he directs to churches after a labour lasting one and a half years (1 Cor). A few more examples will underscore this further.

In 2 Thessalonians 3:10 Paul refers to his oral παραγγέλλειν (command) and emphasises to the church again that the one who will not work also should not eat. In this passage the imperfect tense probably indicates that this oral παραγγέλλειν had already been given. Nevertheless, Paul therefore considers it necessary to repeat a rule which was already known to the church from his oral instruction. That is, he repeats a command which was of a most concrete and "self-evident" nature (cf. also 2 Thess 3:6). More important, because it was not caused by an acute defect in the church, is 1 Thessalonians 4:1ff.,11. Here, too, Paul refers to his earlier commandments, which are known to the church already from the missionary paraenesis (eg. the catalogues: cf. above!). The apostolic letters therefore in no way bring only new unknown moral instructions with demands involving new content (eg. 1 Cor 7). Rather, they ever reinforce anew that which has been known for a long time, which the church does not only already know (cf. the frequent "do you not know"), but which the church already does (1 Thess 4:1,10; 5:11; 2 Thess 3:4). This shows in a most striking and special way that the idea of the individual admonitions becoming superfluous with the progressive maturity of the Christians is not tenable. The church must be urged again and again to act the right way. Philippians 3:1 shows that Paul does not mind repeating himself in his written admonitions. He does not shy away from

---

65   Thus Vögtle, op cit, pp. 26ff.

"writing the same thing" (cf. also Phil 3:18).[66] 1 Corinthians 4:17 belongs here in this same connection, where Paul mentions the mission of Timothy, whose task it was to admonish the Corinthians and to remind them of the "ways," that is, of the specific and traditional moral rules and instructions.[67] Such an *anamnesis* (reminder) again presupposes that the church knows these "ways." It is not superfluous, but rather imperative to call them to remembrance anew and to actualise them. In 1 Corinthians 7:1ff., where Paul replies to the questions of the church, there is no word of reproof for the fact that the Corinthians still need such an apostolic instruction and are unable to arrive at an answer by themselves. This is all the more obvious because Paul can, after all, look back on an activity of one and a half years in Corinth. The shaming fault does not lie in the fact that the church does not understand sufficiently well to find its own "ways," but rather in the fact that it does not walk in the "ways" which had been known for a long time. That this is not always the reason and cause of apostolic admonitions is evident in 1 Thessalonians 4:1,10; 5:11; and 2 Thessalonians 3:4. Even for the church, which is filled with goodness, with all understanding and is itself able to admonish its members, the apostle's paraenesis is not superfluous. Paul "reminds" even this church (Rom 15:14ff.). This action is described here as "inculcation of the catechistic tradition."[68]

There still remains 1 Corinthians 3:1ff., which is used by some of the authors mentioned above as a proof that although the admonitions are in themselves superfluous, they are *still* necessary for the νήπιοι (immature). Here Paul contrasts the σαρκινοί (fleshly/carnal) or the νήπιοι (immature) with the πνευματικοί (spiritual). He wants to rebuke the *pneumatic* (spiritual) people using the paradox that they do not allow themselves to be influenced by the *pneuma*. The rebuke therefore refers to the *unpneumatic* life. But he does not rebuke them for the necessity to warn against such a life. Nothing suggests that the pneumatic no longer needed any admonitions and that the "milk" in the paraenesis, which was still

---

[66] The manifold warning of which Paul speaks here, happened "at the foundation, but also later, by letter" (*W. Michaelis*, commenting on the passage in question).

[67] Cf. *Dibelius* (Die Formgeschichte des Evangeliums, p. 240); *H. Greeven* (ZNW, 1952/53, p. 20); *v. Campenhausen* (Die Begründung kirchl. Entscheidungen beim Apostel Paulus, p. 14, Anm. 21); *W. Michaelis* (Theol. Wörterbuch V, p. 92, Anm. 169).

[68] *Michel*, commenting on the passage in question.

required, existed only for the immature and unripe Christians. It is also not indicated when Paul considers the defects in chapters 5 and 6, and alludes to a "moral inferiority."[69] The fact that 1 Corinthians 3:1ff. does not wish to criticise the pneumatics for needing admonitions is also shown in Galatians 6:1 where Paul addresses his admonitions especially to pneumatics[70] and draws their attention to the fact of how great the danger of a fall still is for them.

The examples quoted therefore show that the appearance of concrete paraenesis cannot be explained by pointing to its alleged temporary nature and essential superfluity. Since Paul neither belittles sin nor the openness to temptation of Christians, he admonishes the church again and again. If he criticizes anything, it is sin and not the necessity of his admonitions. Anyway, the few examples have already shown that the indispensable admonitions are not limited to an imperative lacking in colour and form, which is bare of all contours and concreteness. As one can today no more understand the imperative as a process of rejudaisation and obedience to the Law, one should also refrain from calling the necessity of concrete individual admonitions mere casuistry. Growth and maturing of the Christian are, it is true, demanded, but it does not consist in an ever growing independence from the apostolic commandments, but rather in ever more faithful observance of them. The necessary progress of the Christian is firstly and above all a progress along the path already taken and in the direction pointed out by the apostolic commandments (1 Thess 4:1).[71] It does not consist in leaving the apostolic commandments behind, as if the admonitions were only valid for the newly converted, or those who had relapsed or had been left behind. Everything which one could say about the claim of the apostolic commands to be binding and their capacity to be taught and passed on, the activity of teachers and similar problems points in the same direction. The reference to the alleged temporary character and superfluity of the individual apostolic admonitions is after all a weak argument. It cannot relativise the necessity and validity of the Pauline admonitions.

---

[69] Thus *Hering*; also similarly *Allo* and *Bousset*; in this connection Paul only points to the schisms.

[70] *A. Oepke* rightly rejects an "ironic tone"; on the other hand, *H. Lietzmann*, commenting on the passage in question.

[71] Correctly, *Ch. Masson* and *J. A. Frame*, commenting on the passage in question.

ARE THE INDIVIDUAL COMMANDMENTS EXCLUSIVELY CONCRETE AND ONLY APPLICABLE TO CERTAIN SITUATIONS?

The interpretations hitherto discussed understood the concrete individual admonitions either as a compromise or as a provisional arrangement, whereby the admonition or its concrete form was felt to be really unsuitable for Paul's concern. In a further explanation the historic reality which up to now had been depicted as injuring and perverting Paul's "ideal"—either in the shape of "realities" imposed from the outside or in the shape of factual transitional events in the young missionary churches—has been almost too strongly emphasised. If the concrete apostolic commandments had been viewed until now more as an emergency or temporary solution, they are now looked at as being principally and exclusively concrete and effective, as related wholly to a historic situation happening but once and limited to this situation.[72] *Cullmann* is perhaps an example of one who holds to such an understanding of Pauline ethics. Just as the instructions of Jesus are only concrete examples and can be only understood and substantiated as arising out of the concrete situation, according to Cullmann one should in the case of Paul take the "paradigmatic character" seriously and acknowledge that here too there are "no general ethical demands," but "always only concrete instructions for concrete cases."[73] Even according to *Jentsch*, Paul "always [writes] concretely,"[74] and according to *Vischer*, the commandments of the New Testament "are all addressed to a particular situation."[75] *Greeven* asserts something similar regarding the statements of the New Testament concerning marriage: these are "always instructions 'here and now', they refer to concrete situations."[76] The examples could easily be multiplied, especially out

---

[72] Of course, the more systematic questions, which deal with the problems of epoch limitations, transferability and practical application of Paul's ethics in our time, cannot be discussed here. Cf. "Die Autorität der Bibel zur Welt", edited by A. *Richardson* and W. *Schweitzer*; "Der Weg der Bibel zur Welt", edited by the Studienabbtg. des Ökum. Rates d. Kirchen. 1948; E. *Wolf:* Libertas christiana. Grundsätzl. Erwägungen zur Frage nach der bibl. Autorität für die soz. u. pol. Botschaft der Kirchen heute (Theol. Existenz heute, NF 18, 1949).

[73] 0. *Cullmann:* Christus und die Zeit, pp. 202ff.

[74] W. *Jentsch:* Urchristliches Erziehungsdenken, 1951, p. 257, Anm. 7.

[75] L. *Vischer:* Die Auslegungsgeschichte von 1. Kor. 6,1-11, 1955, p. 5.

[76] H. *Greeven:* Die Weisungen der Bibel über das rechte Verhältnis von Mann und Frau, 1954, p. 16.

of the realm of systematic theology. Here we shall only mention *K. Barth*, who is also of the opinion that God's command in the New Testament confronts us "in the form of many historically *particular* and *one-time-only* concrete orders, prohibitions and instructions."[77]

There can be no doubt that many Pauline admonitions and instructions were caused by actual questions, problems and dangers confronting the church and are aimed at such concrete situations. They share this concrete-actual cause and character with the letters, in which they are embedded, and the two together thereby reflect the historic character of revelation generally. All Pauline letters are *real* letters. That is, they are occasional letters at a certain time and hour addressed to a certain people with a wealth of allusions and relationships to concrete conditions of the churches as well as conditions of the apostle. They can only be understood properly by steadily noticing their close relationship to the presumed situations. This observation of the relationship to situations is also indispensable for the correct comprehension of Pauline paraenesis, because here, too, partially quite specific needs, defects or dangers have to be presupposed. Whether Paul argues against gnostic libertines or ascetics, or admonishes anxious weaklings, judaizers sticking to the Law or enthusiastic visionaries, is not only of "merely historical" interest, but is of eminent meaning for the understanding of Paul's intentions in general. The actual character of apostolic admonitions which refer to certain situations is shown particularly clearly in 1 Corinthians, where Paul definitely takes a stand regarding the church's questions (περὶ δέ ["as regards/now concerning"]: 1 Cor 7:1,25; 8:1; 12:1; 16:1)[78] and maybe even quotes the contents of the questions. Even his comments regarding the events mentioned in chapters 5 and 6 refer to actual defects in the church. But other questions as well, which we cannot explicitly specify, would have been addressed by the churches to Paul either orally or in writing, or Paul himself was forced to address them. Thus it is certain that the question of slavery, which was "in the horizon of Jesus not yet as acute" only became a problem at the time of the earliest Christian writings and was mentioned when the mission proceeded beyond

---

[77] *K. Barth:* Kirchl. Dogmatik, III/4 (1951), pp. 11ff.

[78] Some exegetes link the περὶ δέ in 1 Thess 4:9,13; 5:1 to a letter of the Thessalonians (*Frame* and *Masson* z. St.; ; *Faw* in Journal of Biblical Literature, 1952, pp. 217ff.); Bradley understands the περὶ δέ as the introduction of a paraenetical topos (Journal of Biblical Literature, 1953, pp. 244ff.).

the borders of Palestine.[79] Something similar applies to the enlargement of the prohibition against divorce to the woman (1 Cor 7:10ff.), which has the Roman divorce practice as a presupposition and an aim. Similarly, Paul's fight against laziness became necessary not in the Palestinian world but only in the hellenistic world with its avoidance of work and its contempt for work.[80] Furthermore, the lack of any admonition directed to the government authorities may certainly be traced to the sociological structure of the early churches, because the rulers due to the prevailing conditions were in a different class and the church mostly consisted of the lower or petit-bourgeois classes of the population (cf. 1 Cor 1:26ff.; 2 Cor 8:2; also the frequent names of slaves in the introductory greetings). It should also be noticed that Paul in some instances addresses his admonitions to certain individuals or groups of persons within the churches or also recommends proper conduct with regard to individuals (cf. Phil 4:2; Col 4:17; 2 Cor 2:5ff.; 2 Thess 3:12). The most personal admonitions are found, as is well known, in the only "private letter" available to us, which is addressed by the apostle to Philemon, a letter which we can quote wholly as a proof.

All this says that manifold personal, political, social, economic, judicial and other assumptions and occasions have not only provoked the moral decisions of Paul and his church, but have also had a considerable influence on them. The historical reference and aim do not allow us to understand the apostolic instructions simply as unrelated to time and as moral truths independent of all historical conditions and coincidences which Paul taught stereotypically in all the churches. His admonitions are not without exception addressed for all people in all places and for all times, but rather in part they are entirely unique and cannot be repeated. This reference to the situation is not only in accordance with the Pauline admonition but is also useful for the conduct demanded of the Christian. It stands therefore in sharp contrast to the conduct of the stoics, who strive to keep themselves out of the situation according to the individual-ethical foundation and the ideal of the *ataraxy*.[81] Christian behaviour,

---

[79] *H. Greeven:* Das Hauptproblem der Sozialethik in der neueren Stoa und im Urchristentum, pp. 47ff.

[80] Cf. *Bienert,* op cit, p. 322.

[81] The stoical wise man lives "to a certain degree in an unhistorical, unworldly way, by turning away from all encounters, by locking himself away from every fate"; therefore his decision is never a concrete one, but rather "paradoxically always ever the same decision for the unimportance of the moment" (*R.*

on the other hand, will always be realised in the nearest relationship to the historical neighbour and will succeed in the realisation of the demands of the hour (cf. the many appeals to the *nous* [mind], wisdom and discernment of the Christian and the demand for the δοκιμάζειν ["examination"] of the divine will) and in coping with the unique, historical situations and their demands (cf. Col 4:5; Gal. 6:10 and the possibly original text of D#, G, 5, it, Ambst in Rom 12:11).

If it is thus rather easy to achieve agreement regarding the actual cause and concrete emphasis of many apostolic letters and admonitions, it is also necessary, with the same degree of emphasis, to draw attention to some reservations regarding excessive emphasis and against declaring this state of affairs to be absolute. These reservations have a fundamental nature and are valid without any consideration of the present state of research regarding the relevant introductory questions. Even apart from the fact that we will not proceed further in the case of introductory questions past more or less assured hypotheses, it is necessary to ask whether the historical background and impetus is really necessary for our understanding regarding all admonitions, and above all, whether the assertions made above (cf. "always only concrete instructions for concrete cases") make for a generalisation of undoubted factual situations. Can one really say that the Pauline statements can be understood "always only in connection with the recipients of the letters,"[82] or is this assertion going too far in the face of Pauline paraenesis?

Despite their strictly epistolary character the apostolic letters are in no way *purely* occasional writings, but rather they are intended, partly right from the start, for the reading and information of further circles of readers and for the circulation and exchange with other churches (cf. Gal 1:2; Col 4:15ff.). This seems to suggest that the essence and content of such letters was intended from the start to be for this form of publication and should not be understood exclusively as resulting from the special situation of a single church receiving the letter. The well known "inserts" make clear that the special situation of the letters does not explain everything (1 Cor 13; Phil 2:5ff.; etc[83]). These inserts were not formed for the correspondence in an *ad hoc*

Bultmann: Das Urchristentum im Rahmen der antiken Religionen, 1949, pp. 158, 162).

[82] Thus *Marxsen:* Theol. Existenz heute, NF 59, 1957, p. 18; cf. pp. 19, 44.

[83] Cf. *M. Dibelius:* Geschichte der Urchristl. Literatur II, p. 12; Wendland: Die hellen.-röm. Kultur / Die urchristl. Literaturformen (Hdb. z. N.T. I, 2-3) 1912, p. 349.

fashion, but were formed beforehand by Paul or the church, even if through their present context they may in part receive a special interpretation. If the Pauline letters are not dogmatic-ethical writings without reference to time, they are not products of chance with "to and fro momentary emotions" either, which have been thrown together "under one hundred different impressions"[84] or—expressed less psychologically than situation-ethically—they are not *only* instruction and advice on particular problems then of moment."[85] Certainly, they show references and allusions to the situation of those addressed. They are therefore not a witness without an aim. However, again we find quite general passages, which refer to no actual situation or take no notice of it. This is valid especially for the letter to the Romans, which with all its regard for the Roman situation "reaches beyond the incidental condition of the Roman church."[86] Paul responds here more succinctly only to a single concrete question of the Roman church (Rom 14-15). But the other Pauline letters rise up "often enough above the actual situation to a generally applicable validity in the form of a sermon.[87]"[88]

This applies to an even greater degree to the apostolic paraenesis. Next to the admonitions referring to actual situations there are found sufficient admonitions and commandments which have no reference to a special situation or motive. Thus the entire paraenetic block of Romans 12-13 has no reference to a special situation. That means that in contrast to Romans 14-15 this block deals with generally applicable rules and instructions for Christian conduct in the church and in the world. Something similar may be said of 1 Thessalonians 4 and Colossians 3. Here too we have to assume instead of an actual motive, more probably a prophylactic motive (see below). Especially the paraenetic passages mostly appearing at the ending of the letters with a style different from the other parts of the letter (mostly single sayings loosely arranged one after the other or speech passages without a discernible disposition)

---

[84]   Contra *A. Deissmann:* Licht von Osten, 1923, p. 205.

[85]   Contra *Enslin,* op cit, p. 192.

[86]   *G. Schrenk:* Studien zu. Paulus, 1954, p. 85, cf. pp. 81ff.; others call the Letter to the Romans even a "teaching script"; thus *Dibelius,* II, pp. 23ff.; *P. Wendland,* p. 351; *A. Nygren,* Theol. Lit. Ztg. 77/1952, p. 592.

[87]   *Dibelius,* II, p. 9.

[88]   That they are doing it in the language and the concepts of their era should be clearly stated in order to avoid misunderstandings. Here we are interested in the clear reference to the situation and the clear aim of Paul's letters, not in the historic form of dress of their message.

do not allow us to recognise a direct reference to the situation of the letter. These apostolic admonitions and rules are not formulated for "certain churches or concrete cases, but for the general needs of earliest Christendom. They do not have *actual* but rather *usable* meaning."[89] This is also confirmed by the fact we have already mentioned, that the Pauline admonitions and commandments are by no means only the result of already existing defects or transgressions (cf. 1 Thess 4:1).

Furthermore, it may be shown that Paul frequently goes on from actual admonitions and uses them as a reference point for other admonitions which are not connected with the acute motive. Thus he follows a situation-relevant admonition to make allowances for the "weak" in the Roman church (Rom 14:1-6) in a complete passage (vss. 7-9) by an assertion of a general nature which "places individual conduct into the systematic principles of Christian existence."[90] Romans 15:1ff. makes it quite clear that Paul is no longer talking about the special case of the weak people in Rome, but generally has his eye on the relationship of the strong and the weak which throws fundamental light on the specific case in question. These examples can easily be multiplied (cf. 1 Cor 8-10; 2 Cor 8-9; 1 Cor 5).

Furthermore, one must distinguish the cause of the letters from the admonitions contained in them. If the letter to the Colossians is, for example, a letter warning of the acute danger of Jewish-gnostic false teaching, the same cannot be said of the *Haustafel* contained in the letter (Col 3:18-4:1), because the assumption of an actual motive for writing is in the case of the *Haustafeln* far less likely than the consideration of a traditional topos of paraenesis known to early Christendom, even if this topos could certainly be altered if the need arose.[91] The catalogues of virtues and vices, too, are recounted in the churches addressed without special relevant connections. Even if 1 Corinthians and the letter to the Galatians were caused by certain definite dangers and defects, there is no use trying to understand the catalogues of vices mentioned in them by linking them to a special

---

[89] M. *Dibelius:* Die Formgeschichte des Evangeliums, p. 239.

[90] 0. *Michel* (commenting on the passage in question) at the same time it becomes clear that Paul does not only progress from actual admonitions to those not caused by specific situations, but that he considers even the concrete situations from a point of view which is *above* the situation; further examples for this idea may easily be provided.

[91] Cf. *Weidinger*, op cit, and M. *Dibelius - H. Greeven:* Exkurs zu Kol 4,1 (An die Kolosser, Epheser, an Philemon, Hdb. z. N.T., 12, 1953, pp. 48ff.).

situation of the churches addressed. Vögtle's work has not been able to give a basic cause for the actual motives, relative situations and *ad hoc* formulations of the catalógues. It has been rightly argued that, for instance, the items of Galatians 5:20 which referred to splits and divisions, should really not have been absent in 1 Corinthians, if Paul formulated the catalogues listed there while he was really thinking of the special conditions in Corinth.[92] The method does not allow us to link individual points in the rest of the letter with the catalogues in order to postulate in this way the concrete relationship to those addressed. Even individual concepts which agree with the situation of the letters may be more or less accidental and stereotypical. It is obvious that Paul considered "the whole situation of the early church," but it is hardly possible to prove the "taking into consideration of concrete situations of individual churches."[93]

Thus it is impossible to presuppose in all admonitions an actual need or to claim to discover special circumstances or defects in the individual churches. Not everything has been written as a result of a certain cause[94] or for concrete cases. This fact confirms that the admonitions are addressed to people who are spiritually threatened and are therefore not devised for those who have already fallen and are acute sinners. This means that the assertion that Pauline ethics consists always only of directions for "concrete cases" is untenable. Certainly much is related to concrete cases but not all apostolic instructions have a concrete-actual cause. The fault lies in the overemphasis and exclusivity of the assertion. That even the other part of that assertion, namely that all admonitions are "always only concrete instructions" is false, we mention only on the margin, since indisputably the Pauline letters contain, next to concrete instructions, also quite general unconcrete paraenesis, as is shown clearly by the paraenetic final chapters of the letters (cf. further Rom 6; Phil. 4:8ff.; 2

---

[92] Cf. *W. Bauer*, Theol. Lit. Ztg., 1937, p. 233, and *Enslin*, p. 162.

[93] Contra *Vögtle*, op cit, pp. 28ff.

[94] It is known that the failure to pay attention to this fact has led to strange misinterpretation of such texts, which are, after all, not formulated ad hoc and are not addressed to concrete situations in the churches (see eg. *Weidinger*, op cit, p. 3). One must however consider that the reception of paraenetic traditions does not carry a verdict regarding the situation of the church, since the reception may be due to an acute need. Weidinger does not differentiate enough here. The above-mentioned assertions do not however lose any weight; it is only that here there has to be a case by case decision.

Cor 1; 1 Cor 15:58; etc).[95] Even *Bultmann*, who again and again strongly asserted the "character of address" of Christian proclamation and paraenesis, points to the fact that some Pauline imperatives, for instance, Romans 12:21 and Philippians 4:8, are to be valid as "general truths" and that this general statement should be "said and heard as an address" in concrete situations.[96] But we shall not expand any further on this line of thought here.

It is more important that with Paul there are found actual-situation-related as well as general admonitions and, above all, that both kinds of instruction do not exclude a concrete character. We should consider the fact that even concrete instructions do not have to relate to certain one-time situations, and that even admonitions, which do not refer to an actual situation may nevertheless be concrete. Here we must further differentiate more sharply than *Dibelius, Weidinger, Bradley* and *Andrews*. One may therefore not, as usually happens, mistake the actual for the concrete or simply identify both as being the same thing. The authors mentioned[97] distinguish, as we have said, two types of Pauline admonitions, but relate the concrete commandments exclusively to those parts of the letters in which Paul deals with actual problems or questions of the churches, whilst the general admonitions are looked at as being only suitable generally, fundamentally and for 'every' situation. But this method confuses the cause and content of the admonitions. Not everything that is caused by an actual situation is therefore automatically also concrete, but above all, not everything that is concrete is caused by an actual situation and is referring to historically unique situations.

The last part of the assertion made above is of great significance. We have already referred to the catalogues and *Haustafeln*. It is true that Paul writes both without a special cause, and yet both are concrete. Apart from 1 Thessalonians 4:3-6, Romans 13:1-

---

[95] It is interesting to find that some exegetes come to an opposite verdict regarding the character of Paul's paraenesis: *C.H. Dodd* (The Ethics of the N.T., in: Moral Principles of Action, ed. by *R.N. Anshen*, 1952, p. 553): ". . . usually broad and general rather than specific"; *F.C. Grant* (An Introduction to N.T. Thought, 1950, p. 323): ". . . principles more than . . . details of application"; *Sanday-Headlam* (quoted by *Rolston*, op cit, p. 38): "great broad generalities ... not minute regulations."

[96] *R. Bultmann*, Zeitschr. f. Theol. u. Kirche, 54/1957, pp. 247, 249.

[97] *M. Dibelius* (Die Formgeschichte des Evangeliums, pp. 239ff.); *Weidinger*, op cit (pp. 3f., 9, 12, 75ff.); *D. G. Bradley* (Journal of Biblical Literature, 72/1953, p. 239); *M. E. Andrews* (The Genesis of the Ethical Teaching of Paul, 1931, p. 7).

7 is a good example, since here the concrete admonitions especially are dealt with fundamentally and do not furnish a relationship to concrete conditions in the Roman church. An actual causation or emphasis, which may point to zealous irritability, revolutionary tendencies or eccentric enthusiasm in the Roman church,[98] can be discerned just as little as the contours of a certain state or even a certain form of a state, even if Paul initially thought of the Roman authorities. Rather, the statements are valid in principle for all situations (cf. πᾶσα ψυχή, "everyone"; αἱ δὲ οὖσαι, "however those who overcome"; προσκαρτεροῦντες, "steadfastly considered" . . .[99]). It may be true that even in Rome, as generally in early Christendom there was "the same danger of an apocalyptic-eccentric unease and irritability,"[100] but the admonition in Romans 13 itself is not caused by actual circumstances, but is one of principle and at the most thought of prophylactically regarding such dangers. Bornhäuser's opinion, "that Paul gave quite concrete instructions to the small church in Rome, considering their situation, how they should behave vis-a-vis the temporal powers under which the church found itself" (Bornhäuser translates: "Everyone *of you* should subordinate himself to those who *there in your Rome* are in charge of you") has already been justly rejected by Schlier, even if this was done with regard to a different viewpoint. The "definite relationship to the church in Rome" in Romans 12-13 is definitely no more than questionable.[101]

---

[98] Thus *0. Michel*, commenting on the passage in question; *Liechtenhan*, op cit, p. 112; *Nieder*, p. 94; *Schrenk*, Theol. Wörterbuch II, p. 443; *H. Clavier* (The Duty and the Right of Resistance according to the Bible and to the Church, 1956, pp. 52, 56; *K. Bornhäuser* (Christentum u. Wissenschaft 7/1931, p. 203); *F. Keienburg* (Die Geschichte des Auslegung von Röm. 13,1-7, 1956, pp. 17ff.); more cautiously *0. Cullmann* (Der Staat im N.T., 1956, p. 42). The opinion of *T. Gaugusch* leads one completely astray (Theol. und Glaube, 26/1934, p. 530). He explains that the omission of suggestions which were meant to deal with the special circumstances of a rebellious Judeo-Christian section of the Roman Church were due to Paul omitting them "due to respect for his ethnic group."

[99] In this connection it appears to be hardly accidental that Paul uses φέρειν instead of φορεῖν, which according to *W. Bauer* means "always carrying, carrying for a long period of time, being used to carry it" (therefore not only temporarily or just for a period of time).

[100] *v. Campenhausen* in the Bertholet-Festschrift, p. 112.

[101] Contra *Bornhäuser* (Christentum und Wissenschaft, 7/1931, pp. 201ff.); correct apart from Schlier (Zwischen den Zeiten, 1932, p. 321, fn. 5, once more printed in: Die Zeit der Kirche, 1956, p. 8 fn. 5) also *F. Hauck* (Christentum und Wissenschaft, 3/1927, p. 144.), *Preisker*, (p. 85); *K. Pieper* (Urkirche und Staat, 1935, p. 38), *A. Schlatter* (Gottes Gerechtigkeit, 1952, p. 350); cf. now also *E. Käsemann*, Zeitschr. f. Theol. u. Kirche, 1959, p. 318.

That there are concrete admonitions which have no actual cause is also underlined by the fact that the validity of the concrete commandments cannot unconditionally be limited regarding the day and hour of being written and heard for the first time. This is shown by the many admonitions with ἐάν and εἰ ("when or if"), in which a certain prophylactic quality is also expressed.[102] They are, we may say, admonitions regarding eventualities: when a certain event or case happens, then they are valid and should be obeyed. An example is 1 Corinthians 7:36ff., where Paul even mentions several conditions: If a betrothed man thinks that he is not acting honestly and is a mature man, he should marry his betrothed; but he who is true to his heart and is not in any sexual condition of compulsion, and who has power over his will, does well not to marry her.[103] In this instance the iterative character of the conditional sentences also shows that by no means all apostolic admonitions are related to once-only and unrepeatable situations. Because the admonitions address the churches with ἐάν with the subjunctive, the "that which is expected under certain circumstances, from the given general or concrete standpoint in the present,"[104] they show this tendency, but even the admonitions with εἰ point in the same direction. Käsemann has shown that in the New Testament there are found casuistic sentences of holy law, which are introduced by εἴ τις, or with equal meaning by ἐάν τις or ὅς δ' ἄν ("in case of"). These sentences close with an announcement of punishment (Pauline examples: 1 Cor 3:17; 14:37ff.; 16:22; Gal 1:9). It is characteristic that Paul includes such casuistic sentences in his parænetic warnings, even if this is done in an altered form: 2 Corinthians 9:6; Romans 2:12.[105] It can hardly be denied that there are in all this, especially in the conditional warnings mentioned, the beginnings of an ethical casuistic system. Paul has quite frequently been condemned for this. Even the manifold warnings, which are to protect the church from coming dangers or to save them from possible wrong conduct, are not conceived actually, but prophylactically. Furthermore, this prophylactic character is in accordance with the essence of all parænesis and is used as a literary

---

[102] Cf. 1 Cor 7:9ff.,13,15,28,36ff.,39ff.; 10:27ff.; 11:6,15ff.; Rom 13:4; 14:15,23; Col 3:13; 2 Thess 3:10; etc.

[103] Cf. *G. Kümmel* regarding this interpretation of the passage: Verlobung und Heirat bei Paulus (1. Kor. 7,36-38), in Ntl. Studien f. R. Bultmann, 1954, pp. 275ff.

[104] *Blass-Debrunner*, 371, 4.

[105] *E. Käsemann:* New Testament Studies 1, 1954/55, pp. 248ff.

fiction even for collections of paraenetic content.[106] The Pauline admonitions are therefore not related to situations through and through, least of all the fixed parenetic passages (catalogues, *Haustafeln*, topoi).

But even where one will assume that Paul is addressing a concrete situation and that there is a specific cause, the claim of the relevant instructions is not necessarily applicable only once, but is repeatable. For instance, it would be absurd to be of the opinion that the prohibition of *porneia*, which was caused by an acute case in the Corinthian church (1 Cor 5), was referring only to the relevant case of fornication, and had validity only for this one case. The ever recurring warnings show this clearly.[107] Furthermore, Paul himself repeatedly points out that he is teaching concrete individual admontions also πανταχοῦ ἐν πάσῃ ἐκκλησίᾳ ("everywhere in every church"; 1 Cor 4:17; cf. 1 Cor 11:16; 14:33ff.; 7:17). Concrete admonitions, whether they are caused by an acute condition or not, are in any case not so "concrete" that they exclude repetition and ever new obedience. We must distinguish not only the cause and the content but also the cause and the claim of the admonitions.

---

[106] For example, Pseudo-Isokrates does not give his advice to Demonikos because they are already applicable for the present situation of the person addressed, but rather that in the future "he may fetch this advice as from a treasure chamber" (M. Dibelius: Geschichte der urchristl. Literatur II, p. 65); cf. also the fictitious-prophylactic warning against false teachers in the New Testament letters and above all Ignatius ad Trall 8:1; ad Magn 11; ad Smyrn 4:1.

[107] Even if 1 Cor 6:12ff. only considered an actual case of dealing with Hieroduloi of Aphrodite, which is considered possible by *Nieder* (p. 49), the motives and norms which thereby became apparent would not in any way "suffer a loss of their common validity" (contra *Nieder*, p. 49).

CHAPTER FOURTEEN

New Testament Social Ethics for Today

Richard N. Longenecker
(1984)

AN INITIAL DILEMMA: To Whom Shall We Go?

Christians generally have accepted the New Testament as their guide
for faith and life. But Christians vary widely in their beliefs as to how
the New Testament should be used in moral theory and practice.
Often we are like the disciples of old who cried out in their
confusion: "Lord, to whom shall we go?" (John 6:68). Most
Christians, in fact, come up short at the very beginning of their
attempt to think and act "Christianly" in areas of social morality,
unable to decide how the New Testament should guide them in
doing so. And being thwarted here, they become catatonic ethically.
It is therefore necessary to look at various ways in which the New
Testament has been understood as a guide to Christian morality, then
to highlight certain basic features of a biblical ethic that say
something about how we should resolve our hermeneutical dilemma,
and, finally, to propose a working solution as to how the New
Testament should be used in moral theory and practice.

A. FOUR WAYS OF USING THE NEW TESTAMENT

Broadly speaking, there are four ways in which Christians use the New Testament in ethical decision-making and practice. Each has its own advocates, who generally are so enamored with their own approach that they identify it alone as worthy of the name "Christian." Yet each position needs to be set out and evaluated so that we might be better able to make a proper start in our ethical thought and action.

The first of these positions is that which takes the New Testament as a book of laws or a summation of codes for human conduct. It argues that God has given prescriptive laws in the form of commandments and ordinances, which can be found in both the Old and the New Testaments. If people want to know what they should do, the laws of God stand objectively before them in written form, and they have only to refer to them. This was the ethical approach of Rabbinic Judaism, which came to systematic expression in the Halakic codifications of the Mishnah, the Tosephta, the Palestinian and Babylonian Gemaras, the "Sayings" collections of individual ancient rabbis, Rashi's commentary on the Talmud, and Maimonides' 613 commandments. It is also the attitude of many fervent Christians today, whether they focus narrowly on the teachings of Jesus or on the letters of Paul, take into account the entire New Testament, or include the broader spectrum of both Old and New Testaments.

The truth of such a position lies in the fact that the words of Jesus and the statements of the New Testament writers are given with prescriptive force and do not come to us as tactical suggestions. Jesus reaffirmed such Old Testament commands as those having to do with loving God (cf. Mark 12:29-30, par.; quoting Deut. 6:4-5), loving our neighbors (cf. Mark 12:31, par.; quoting Lev. 19:18), honoring our parents (cf. Mark 7:10; Matt. 15:4; quoting Exod. 20:12; 21:17), and the indissolubility of marriage (cf. Mark 10:7-8; Matt. 19:5; quoting Gen. 2:24). Matthew's Gospel, in fact, portrays Jesus as in some sense a new Lawgiver (especially chapters 5-7), and John's Gospel presents him as speaking of his teachings as commandments and as commending obedience to his words (cf. 13:34; 14:15, 21; 15:10, 12). Throughout the New Testament, as also in the Old Testament, the divine will is set forth as that which is objective to all human calculations and normative for every human activity. In the later Pauline and Petrine epistles, in fact, the Christian religion is depicted in terms of a new law (cf. the use of "commandment" in 1 Tim. 6:14 and 2 Pet. 2:21).

Yet the Gospels also proclaim Jesus as being much more than a Moses *redivivus*, and the New Testament presents the Christian life as much more than regulated behavior. Indeed, to take the New Testament as a law book seriously misconstrues the nature of the Christian gospel—both as to what it proclaims and as to what it calls for by way of response. The problems with such a use of the New Testament for ethical theory and practice boil down to two: (1) such an approach does not create moral beings, but only controls the worst features of non-moral behavior; and (2) laws require an accompanying body of oral or written interpretations to explicate and apply them in new situations. Sadly, history reveals that where an accompanying authoritative tradition comes into play in order to relate Scripture as a set of laws to the contemporary situation, all too often the tradition takes precedence over Scripture—as witness, for example, rabbinic codifications, Roman Catholic ecclesiastical law, and the many Protestant cultic expressions of the Christian faith.

In matters of personal morality where the biblical commands to love and honor are taken seriously, a law-book approach to the New Testament may work out fairly well, particularly when a person internalizes love and honor and develops new attitudes. But a law-book approach apart from some accompanying body of tradition (whether written or oral) seldom has much to say about social ethics, simply because circumstances change so rapidly that codified laws are soon outdated. Jesus, for example, said nothing specific about life in a geriatrics ward, or about collective bargaining, or about genocide. And those who take the New Testament as an ethical law-book find that they too have very little to say as Christians about such matters.

A second way of using the New Testament for ethical guidance is that which places all of the emphasis on the universal principles which can be found to underlie the New Testament accounts. Here the particular statements and practices of the New Testament are not considered binding, but the principles behind them are. It was Adolf Harnack's *What is Christianity?* originally given as a series of non-technical lectures in Berlin during the winter of 1899-1900 under the title "Das Wesen des Christentums," that popularized this approach. For Harnack, the difference between the Jewish law-book approach to religion and Jesus' approach was this:

They thought of God as a despot guarding the ceremonial observances in his household; he breathed in the presence of God. They saw him only in his law, which they had converted into a labyrinth of dark defiles, blind alleys and secret passages; he saw and felt him everywhere. They were in possession of a thousand of his commandments, and thought therefore that they knew him; he had one only, and knew him by it. They had made this religion into an earthly trade, and there was nothing more detestable; he proclaimed the living God and the soul's nobility.[1]

Jesus' message, as Harnack saw it, can be summed up under three headings: (1) the kingdom of God and its coming; (2) God the Father and the infinite value of the human soul; and (3) the higher righteousness and the commandment of love. In the final analysis, however, these three emphases, as Harnack understood them, coalesced into something of a Christ-inspired religious humanism, for "ultimately the kingdom is nothing but the treasure which the soul possesses in the eternal and merciful God. It needs only a few touches to develop this thought into everything that, taking Jesus' sayings as its groundwork, Christendom has known and striven to maintain as hope, faith and love."[2]

Such a focus on the underlying principles of the New Testament—and, in fact, on the Bible as a whole—provides a means for appreciating how biblical norms can be applied to changing situations, both in the areas of personal morality and social morality. For while the Bible reflects various laws suited for different and differing situations, behind those laws are principles which have remained fixed because they are universal in nature. It is therefore the task of the interpreter, so this view maintains, to look beneath the rules and regulations having to do with particular problems in order to discern the universal principles which gave rise to such legislation, and, after discovering them, to apply those same principles to the issues of the present day.

The problems with such an approach, however, are numerous—though their intensity varies considerably depending on the skill and sensitivity of individual interpreters. Two major problems in particular tend to recur: (1) in the search for universal principles it is all too easy to turn biblical theology into philosophy,

---

[1] Harnack, *What is Christianity?* trans. J. R. Wilkinson (London: Williams & Norgate, 1901), pp. 50-51.

[2] Harnack, *What is Christianity?* p. 77.

with Jesus Christ heard only as an echo of Socrates; and (2) Christian ethics often becomes a subcategory of natural law, with the moral imperative of life rooted in man himself and human reason viewed as the main guide for moral judgments.

A third way of using the New Testament in ethical decision-making is that which places all the stress on God's free and sovereign encounter through his Spirit with a person as he or she reads Scripture, and the ethical direction given for the particular moment in such an encounter. Indeed, Scripture as a record of God's past encounters and the Spirit as the agent of such encounters can never be separated, for God has chosen to meet men and women and to reveal his will to them through the Scriptures. Yet neither the Old nor the New Testament, it is asserted, gives us a descriptive ethic in the form of either laws or principles. What the Christian finds in reading the Scriptures is that there he or she is met by the sovereign God who himself defines the "good" for that particular moment and places on the obedient heart an imperative for action.

Emil Brunner was one of the most illustrious modern advocates of this position, and his *The Divine Imperative* is devoted to laying the theological basis for such a view, and "thinking through the concrete problems of particular spheres of life" in light of this approach. In the chapter called "The Definition of Christian Ethic," Brunner sets forth this position concisely:

> Whatever can be defined in accordance with a principle—whether it be the principle of pleasure or the principle of duty—is legalistic. . . . The Christian moralist and the extreme individualist are at one in their emphatic rejection of legalistic conduct; they join hands, as it were, in face of the whole host of legalistic moralists; they are convinced that conduct which is regulated by abstract principles can never be good. . . . There is no Good save obedient behaviour, save the obedient will. But this obedience is rendered not to a law or a principle which can be known beforehand, but only to the free, sovereign will of God. The Good consists in always doing what God wills at any particular moment.[3]

Later, in discussing "The Divine Command as Gift and Demand," Brunner insists that "in a Christian ethic we are not dealing with 'counsels' nor with exhortations, nor with 'values'," but rather "we

---

3 Brunner, *The Divine Imperative*, trans. O. Wyon (London: Lutterworth, 1937), pp. 82-83.

are confronted by a Command which must be taken in dead earnest."[4] It is true, Brunner acknowledges, that the New Testament represents its authors as frequently exhorting their readers. But here he sees a major difference between the Old and the New Testament, for in the Old Testament it is commands, not exhortations, that are given. And he goes on to insist,

> The form of the exhortation is simply intended to remind us of the ground on which the Divine claim is based; that is, that every believer can indeed know the will of God for himself, through his faith in Christ. The apostolic exhortation implies that the believer is no longer a minor, and it sweeps away all legalistic heteronomy. Not even an Apostle can tell you what you ought to do; God Himself is the only One who can tell you this. There is to be no intermediary between ourselves and the Divine will. God wishes to deal with us "personally," not through any medium.[5]

Historically, of course, such an emphasis on God's sovereign encounter and his personal direction of life came like a breath of fresh air amid the often arid formulations and withering regulations of Christian theology, whether liberal or conservative. It seemed to free the Christian for authentic ethical living before God in both the personal and the societal areas of life. Yet many today have backed off from an exclusive acceptance of such a position, believing that in its renunciation of propositional revelation it makes Christian theology too subjective, and in its disavowal of laws and principles it makes Christian ethics too individualistic. Today there is a widespread appreciation of the need for God by his Spirit to encounter individuals through the Scriptures for there to be authentic Christian conversion, authentic Christian theology, and authentic Christian life. But there is also a widespread hesitancy to deny to the Bible any intrinsic authority in favor of only an instrumental authority and to exclude all external criteria as factors in the direction of life.

The fourth way of using the New Testament in ethical decision-making and practice arises largely out of the third approach, and shares with it an opposition to prescriptive laws and principles. It differs, however, from the third in laying primary emphasis on the individual's response to whatever situations are confronted. Several variations of this approach have been proposed, but all of them can

---

4   Brunner, *The Divine Imperative*, p. 118.
5   Brunner, *The Divine Imperative*, p. 118.

be described by the term "contextualism," or "situation ethics." What this view argues is that rather than looking to laws or principles, which is the essence of legalism—or even to an encounter with God as providing the ethical criteria, for that is much too subjective—Christians can determine what should be done in any particular case simply by getting the facts of the situation clearly in view, and then asking themselves, What is the loving thing to do in this case? Such an approach, of course, does not entirely rule out the prescriptive, for it accepts love as the one great principle for life. Yet it insists that "the law of love" allows no predefinition for action in any given circumstance, but must be reapplied separately and moment by moment in every situation faced. Nor are all biblical exhortations set aside by a situation ethic. They are, however, treated as tactical suggestions rather than prescriptive norms—that is, as cautionary advice indicating how matters usually work out, but advice which should be set aside whenever the principle of love in the situation requires it. The major question in every ethical exigency, therefore, is simply this: What single act or set of actions will prove most love-embodying and love-fulfilling in the present situation?

Perhaps the best example of a contextual approach is Paul Lehmann's *Ethics in a Christian Context*, which argues for "a *koinonia* ethic" and defines that ethic as one that "*is concerned with relations and functions, not with principles and precepts.*"[6] Joseph Sittler's *The Structure of Christian Ethics* is of the same type, though more flamboyant. In discussing the Sermon on the Mount, for example, Sittler argues for an ethic like that of Jesus which "cracks all rabbinical patterns, transcends every statuary solidification of duty, breaks out of all systematic schematizations of the good—and out of the living, perceptive, restorative passion of faith enfolds in its embrace the fluctuant, incalculable, novel emergents of human life."[7] And this approach was popularized by Joseph Fletcher in his *Situation Ethics: The New Morality*.[8]

Certainly situation ethics has much to say in the area of social morality—though it is often less vocal with regard to personal morality. To do the loving thing in each situation of life is highly

---

6 Lehmann, *Ethics in a Christian Context* (New York: Harper & Row, 1963), p. 124 (italics his).

7 Sittler, *The Structure of Christian Ethics* (Baton Rouge: Louisiana State University Press, 1958), p. 48.

8 Fletcher, *Situation Ethics: The New Morality* (Philadelphia: Westminster Press, 1966).

laudatory. But while love must always motivate and condition every human action if such actions are to be truly ethical, love as the sole criterion for ethical decision-making is highly suspect. Like the classical utilitarian principles of "the greatest happiness" and "the greatest good," love as a moral criterion is an easily adjustable norm. When set in a theological context, it may carry a fairly standard meaning because of its association with other concepts. When defined within a humanistic or naturalistic framework, however, it signals other sets of ideas and other meanings. During the sixties and early seventies, the ethics of contextualism appeared to many to be eminently Christian. But there has been a decided retreat from situation ethics of late simply because of its refusal to allow any predefinitions for the nature and content of love, and its blithe optimism that individuals, given only encouragement, will usually act lovingly when they understand the various facets, ramifications, and implications of the particular situation—an optimism that utterly disregards human egoism, stupidity, and cruelty, as repeatedly testified to by history and personal experience.

We began this section by speaking of a hermeneutical dilemma set up in the minds of many by four competing models of how to use the New Testament in ethical decision making and practice. Then we laid out, in brief, the substance of these four approaches. It must be said, however, that not everyone who speaks of laws in the Bible is an Orthodox Jew, a Roman Catholic, or a Protestant Fundamentalist. Nor is everyone who stresses ethical principles a classical liberal; nor everyone who speaks of a Christ-encounter an existentialist; nor everyone who gives attention to the particular situation a contextualist. It may be that each of these approaches is more wrong in what it denies than in what it proposes, and that each in its own way is setting forth a necessary aspect of truth for a Christian ethic— some, admittedly, more than others, but each to some degree highlighting an aspect of truth that is minimized or neglected by others. But that can be determined only as we move beyond mere description to evaluation, which we undertake next.

B. SOME BASIC BIBLICAL PERSPECTIVES

Every process of evaluation requires the acceptance of a stance from which to view the data and weigh the evidence. Without such a stance, the rendering of value judgments and the integration of knowledge would be impossible. Various stances, of course, have been and are being advocated for interpreting the data of life, with each requiring both theoretical and experiential testing. As Christians we affirm that the Bible is the touchstone for faith and life, and we believe that it is only on the basis of the perspectives provided by the Bible that we can make adequate sense out of the data of life and be led to think and act aright before God. It is therefore necessary for us to remind ourselves here of some of the basic biblical perspectives in the area of ethics, with the hope that they will shed some light on how to resolve our initial hermeneutical dilemma. Then we will be in a position to propose a way of understanding the various statements and practices of the New Testament that relate to our subject of social morality.

Basic to the ethical teaching of the Bible is the insistence that the final measure for human conduct is not to be derived from individuals but stems from the nature of God, from the quality of his love for mankind, and from the character of his redemptive activity. "Be holy because I, the Lord your God, am holy" (Lev. 19:2; cf. 11:44-15; 20:7; 1 Pet. 1:16) is a typical ethical maxim that spans both testaments. Likewise, the depiction of God's love as expressed in his mighty acts on behalf of his people (cf. Exod. 20:2; Pss. 105, 106), in his personal relations with his people (cf. Isa. 54:5-8; Hos. 1-14; Heb. 12:5-12), and pre-eminently in sending his Son for our redemption (cf. John 3:16; 1 John 4:9-10) is the basis for the injunction, "Dear friends, since God so loved us, we also ought to love one another" (1 John 4:11). Throughout the Bible, in fact, the pattern for social morality among God's people is what God in his great love has done for humankind, and all appeals to an ethical life are based on that. There are no depictions of the merits of particular cases; no analyses of the intrinsic worth of certain actions; no sociological surveys laying out a consensus of opinion that should be followed. Rather, the Bible portrays in bold and gripping terms what God has done for man and urges a response of like quality directed both to God and to one's fellows.

A corollary to this first perspective is a second: that the moral teaching of the Bible is always presented in closest relation to the Bible's message as a whole, which means that ethics for a Christian can never be considered either some autonomous entity or a trivial matter. Atheistic and naturalistic systems of thought view morality as wholly autonomous, independent of divine sanctions and supportable only because of social desirability or some intrinsic value. The mystery religions of the Greek world tended to trivialize ethics in their disparagement of the material world and their stress on salvation as being for the soul alone. The Bible, however, always joins theology and ethics, and always insists that the one cannot exist without the other—which is why the oral tradition of Judaism emphasized Halakah (that is, "how to walk" or "conduct one's life"), and why some of the most profound Christological statements of the New Testament are set in the midst of ethical exhortations (for example, Phil. 2:6-11; 1 Tim. 3:16).

Yet, thirdly, just because they are of the nature of a response to a holy and loving God, biblical ethics reflect a different value system than do those ethical systems which spring only from social needs. Aristotle's virtues of justice, temperance, fortitude, and prudence in his *Ethics* and *Politics*, for example, were qualities valuable for improving social and civic life. They were means to an end to accomplish a thoroughly this-worldly purpose. The New Testament, however, strikes deeper when it speaks of "love, joy, peace, patience, kindness, goodness, faithfulness, gentleness and self-control" (Gal. 5:12-23; cf. Matt. 5:3-10, 21-48)—virtues which relate more to the quality of the person than to the efficiency of what he or she does, and certainly virtues which are not always viewed as practical or necessary for the welfare of society or the state. Some of the ethical tenets of the New Testament, of course, are merely transpositions into another key of virtues that were traditionally esteemed. Modesty as heightened by Jesus into self-denial is an example, as is alms-giving heightened into sacrificial generosity. Others take on a new meaning when set in a Christian context, as does the simple virtue of neighborliness: "Anyone who gives you a cup of water *in my name because you belong to Christ* will certainly not lose his reward" (Mark 9:41; italics mine). Yet should all such virtues reside in a person, one thing more, according to the Bible, is needful: for pride itself—even pride in these virtues—to be abandoned. For, as J. L. Houlden points out, "where God has shown himself generous to the point of the cross, man is called upon to imitate him and to adopt a new scale of values."[9]

A fourth matter to note when considering basic biblical perspectives is that the New Testament proclaims a message of freedom from codes of law—that is, freedom not only from the delusion that status before God can be gained by keeping his laws ("legalism") but also from the requirement to express relationship

---

[9]   Houlden, *Ethics and the New Testament* (New York: Oxford, 1977), p. 18.

with God in prescribed ways ("nomism").[10] The prophets of the Old Covenant had much to say against legalism, but they never attempted to set aside the Mosaic law as the proper vehicle for the expression of Israel's faith. Life lived under Torah characterized the best of Old Testament piety, and it continues to epitomize the nobler expressions of Judaism today. The New Testament, however, rather than laying out detailed codes of conduct for various situations, speaks of the Christian life as being a life of responsible freedom "in Christ." "If the Son sets you free," said Jesus, "you will be free indeed" (John 8:36). "Now that faith has come," insisted Paul, "we are no longer under the supervision of the law" (Gal. 3:25). In fact, as Paul wrote later, God "canceled the written code, with its regulations, that was against us and that stood opposed to us; he took it away, nailing it to the cross (Col. 2:14). Christians, therefore, have ceased to regard their relationship with God in terms of law at all, either as a means of attaining that relationship or as an expression of it. They know God personally in Christ, and therefore agree with Martin Luther that he who tries to mix faith and works either for attaining righteousness or as the necessary expression of righteousness is (paraphrasing one of Aesop's fables) like "the dog who runs along a stream with a piece of meat in his mouth, and, deceived by the reflection of the meat in the water, opens his mouth to snap at it and so loses both the meat and the reflection."[11]

Still, and fifth in our enumeration of biblical perspectives, Christian freedom is not antinomianism. While the New Testament does not lay out any set of rules for the guidance of conduct, it does set before the Christian an ethical task that is presented as obligatory. In the main, this task is presented in terms of following Jesus' example and teachings, which are given to set a standard for conduct pleasing to God, to indicate the direction in which Christian morality should be moving, and to signal the quality of action to be expressed. As a standard, the example and teaching of Jesus "help towards an intelligent and realistic act of 'repentance', because they offer an objective standard of judgment upon our conduct, so that we know precisely where we stand in the sight of God, and are in a position to accept His judgment upon us and thereby partake of His

---

[10] Cf. my "The Pedagogical Nature of the Law in Galatians 3:19-4:7," *Journal of the Evangelical Theological Society*, 25 (1982), 53-61.

[11] "The Freedom of the Christian," *Luther's Works*, vol. 31, ed. H. T. Lehmann (St. Louis: Concordia, 1957), 356.

forgiveness."[12] As indicating direction and quality, "they are intended to offer positive moral guidance for action, to those who have, in the words of the gospels, received the Kingdom of God."[13] Thus Paul speaks expressly of "the law of Christ" in Galatians 6:2, where he says that in bearing one another's burdens his converts are fulfilling "the law of Christ" (*ton nomon tou Christou*), and in 1 Corinthians 9:21, where he refers to himself as not being lawless in his freedom but being "under Christ's law" (*ennomos Christou*; literally, "in-lawed to Christ"). And so the New Testament writers habitually reflect the teachings of Jesus in their ethical exhortations (cf. Rom. 12-14; 1 Thess. 4:1-12; James passim) and appeal to the example of Jesus as the pattern for Christian living (cf. Phil. 2:5-11; 1 Pet. 4:1).

Two further matters, however, need to be highlighted here, lest Christian ethics be thought of as only a discipline of following Jesus' example and teachings. The first of these (and sixth in our listing of biblical perspectives) is that which Paul puts to the fore in discussing the issues at Corinth and that which distinguishes Christian ethics from all forms of legalism and Stoicism: immediate and personal direction by God through his Holy Spirit (cf. 1 Cor. 2:10-16). Paul identifies this feature of Christian living as "the mind of Christ" (*nous Christou*), meaning by that that Christ's example and teachings become operative in the lives of Christians by means of the activity of the Holy Spirit. Throughout the New Testament the Christian life is presented as being dependent for both its inauguration and its continuance on God's Spirit, who in his ministry confronts men and women with the living Christ, brings them into personal fellowship with God through Christ, and sustains them in all aspects of their new life in Christ. Thus Christians are said to live their lives "in the new way of the Spirit, and not in the old way of the written code" (Rom. 7:6), and Christian ministry is portrayed as being "not of the letter but of the Spirit" (2 Cor. 3:6). This is the realization that caused Paul to speak of the Christian as a "spiritual man" (1 Cor. 2:15; 3:1) and of the Christian life as a "fellowship with the Spirit" (Phil. 2:1) as well as a "fellowship with his Son Jesus Christ" (1 Cor. 1:9).

Finally, it is necessary to remind ourselves that ethics in the Bible are always set in relational contexts. Israel had been brought

---

[12] C. H. Dodd, *Gospel and Law* (Cambridge: Cambridge University Press, 1951), p. 64.
[13] Dodd, *Gospel and Law*, p. 64.

into covenant relationship with God, and Jewish life was to be lived in response to that relationship and with the interests of the community always in view. Christians have also been brought into covenant relationship with God through Christ, and our lives are likewise to be lived in response to that relationship and with the interests of the corporate Body of Christ always in view. So morality according to the Bible is not something either received in isolation or expressed in isolation. Rather, it is that which proclaims by its every endeavor an existing relationship with God and which works itself out always with the particular circumstances of people in view. In that sense, therefore, biblical ethics may legitimately be called contextual or situational ethics—though perhaps, as some would insist, only after considerable disinfecting and rebaptizing of those terms for more appropriate use.

C. TOWARD A RESOLUTION OF THE DILEMMA

Do these perspectives shed any light on our hermeneutical dilemma of how the New Testament should be used in moral decision-making and practice? Some may feel compelled to answer such a question differently. But if the seven biblical perspectives listed above have been expressed anywhere near correctly, both as to substance and as to emphasis, I believe that they shed a great deal of light on our question and go far to resolving our dilemma.

On the basis of these seven points, we must say, in the first place, that the ethical statements of the New Testament are to be taken with prescriptive and obligatory force, and not just as tactical suggestions which may or may not be heeded by Christians. That is the truth of the position which takes the New Testament as a book of laws for ethical conduct—though to express this truth in the way in which that first position does seriously distorts the true nature of Christian morality. Second, the ethical statements of the New Testament are given not as detailed codes of conduct but as principles or precepts which seek primarily to set a standard for the kind of life pleasing to God, to indicate the direction in which we ought to be moving, and to signal the quality of life our actions ought to be expressing. That is the truth of the position which wants to abstract universal principles from the various ethical statements and actions of the New Testament—though, again, to state this truth in a way which turns theology into philosophy and special revelation into natural law seriously distorts Christian morality.

Third, for there to be an ethic that in any sense can be called Christian, there must be the direct action of the Holy Spirit in the Christian's life and in the particular circumstances confronted. Indeed, not only does the Spirit regenerate; he also gives guidance as to how the principles of Christ should be applied in given situations and empowers the Christian to put these directives into effect. That is the truth of the position which places all of the emphasis on God's direct encounter with a person through his Spirit. And, fourth, for any action to be truly Christian, it must be expressive of a relationship with God through Christ and must work itself out with attention to the specific situations it encounters, always motivated and conditioned by love for God and love for one's fellows. That is the element of truth in any contextual system of ethics.

How, then, should we resolve our hermeneutical dilemma regarding the use of the New Testament in ethical theory and practice? Without attempting to be too eclectic, yet recognizing elements of truth in each of the four proposed models on the basis of the biblical perspectives enumerated above, we should probably define New Testament ethics as follows: prescriptive principles stemming from the heart of the gospel (usually embodied in the example and teachings of Jesus), which are meant to be applied to specific situations by the direction and enablement of the Holy Spirit, being always motivated and conditioned by love. Such a definition is important to provide a hermeneutical beginning.

CONCLUSION

Seven Questions for Paul's Ethics
1 Thessalonians 4:1-12 as a Case Study

Brian S. Rosner

In chapters 1-3 of 1 Thessalonians Paul expresses his continuing concern for the Thessalonian Christians and offers an explanation for not returning to the church. 1 Thessalonians 4:1-12 is an ethical exhortation which, introduced by the inferential conjunction οὖν, "therefore," presents the encouragement and instruction Paul would have liked to have delivered in person. The section consists of a general exhortation to ethical progress (4:1-2), a call to sexual holiness (4:3-8) and instructions concerning brotherly love and the quiet life (4:9-12). Raymond F. Collins describes these verses as "the most ancient documented example of early Christian moral parenesis."[1] This assumes, of course, that Galatians was written on Paul's third missionary journey, after the Thessalonian letters. Whether or not an earlier date for Galatians is preferable, there is no doubt that 1

---

[1] Collins, *Studies on the First Letter to the Thessalonians* (Leuven: Leuven University Press, 1984), p. 300.

Thessalonians 4:1-12 represents a choice and early sample of Paul's ethics.

We shall not here engage in a verse by verse exegesis.[2] Our purpose is rather to demonstrate the value of the seven questions around which this book is based for understanding Paul's ethics. Thus we shall enquire concerning the origin, context, social dimension, shape, logic, foundations and relevance of Paul's instructions in these twelve verses.[3] The aim is not to provide exhaustive answers (the authors of the essays would not of course agree on these) but merely to demonstrate that each question represents a valid and fruitful perspective. In other words, this concluding essay attempts to show that the fourteen essays in this book are not merely a loose anthology, nor just a chronicle of a century of research; together they provide a coherent agenda of ways of research into Paul's ethics.

I. Origin

That Paul's ethics in 1 Thessalonians 4:1-12 arises from a Biblical/Jewish milieu is clear from certain terms and motifs in the passage and from the main exhortations. George P. Carras[4] has pointed to several features which indicate the Jewish character of Paul's instructions: (1) the use of παραλαμβάνω, "I learn," in vss. 1-2 recalls the Hebrew קבל, a rabbinic technical term for the transmission of tradition, especially moral instruction; (2) the call to walk, περιπατέω, which occurs twice in the opening verses, reflects the common rabbinic use of הלך to denote proper conduct (cf. *halakah*,

---

2　For this see *inter alia* the excellent commentaries of E. Best, A Commentary on the First and Second Epistles to the Thessalonians (London: Black, 1972); I. Howard Marshall (Grand Rapids: Eerdmans/London: Marshall, Morgan & Scott, 1983) *NCB*; Traugott Holtz (Zürich: Benziger, 1986) *EKK*; and Charles A. Wanamaker (Grand Rapids: Eerdmans/Exeter: Paternoster, 1990) *NIGTC*.

3　Four of the essays in this book concentrated on one passage, but only from a single perspective; Winter, ch. 4, on the context of 1 Cor 6:1-8; Theissen ch. 5, on the social dimension of 1 Cor 8-10; Harris, ch. 6, on the social dimension of 1 Cor 5; and Hartman, ch. 8, primarily on the shape of Col 3.

4　Carras, "Jewish Ethics and Gentile Converts: Remarks on 1 Thes 4,3-8", in *The Thessalonian Correspondence*. Edited by Raymond F. Collins (Leuven: Leuven University Press, 1990), pp. 306-7. Carras concludes, p. 314, that the teaching of the passage "is what one would expect of a person writing from a Jewish point of view influenced and informed by the diaspora synagogue around the first century."

Jewish teaching on conduct according to the Law); (3) correct behaviour is set in contrast to that of the "heathen who do not know God" (4:4), a motif which has ample Jewish precedence (eg. Wis 13-14);[5] and (4) the notion of God's will as a source of guidance is a major motif in early Jewish writings. We may add to this list (5) the use of "brother" (4:6,10) to refer to members of the community was common amongst Jews of Paul's day (see 1 and 2 Macc and many rabbinic texts; cf. Exod 2:11; Deut 3:18);[6] (6) the desire to make a good impression on those outside of the community, one's heathen neighbours, which appears in 4:12, is a concern which Paul almost certainly inherited from Biblical and Jewish sources;[7] (7) the sanctification motif (4:3-4,7) is a Biblical one with a long history;[8] (8) 4:6 may be an allusion to Psalm 94:1; (9) 4:8 may find an antecedent in 1 Samuel 8:7 (there are also parallels in the gospels; eg. Luke 10:6); and (10) Θεοδίδακτος, "taught by God," recalls Isaiah 54:13.[9]

The main exhortations of the passage also appear to have a Biblical/Jewish origin. In 4:3b-6a Paul issues a call to sexual holiness and the refusal to greedily cheat one's brother.[10] Not only are both unchastity and greed prominant vices in Paul's Bible, Eckhard Reinmuth has shown that the two frequently appear in tandem in early Jewish moral teaching which built upon the Biblical witness.[11] The call to an even greater abundance of brotherly love in 4:9-10 is an

---

[5] Marshall, *1 and 2 Thessalonians*, p. 110, points out that "The language is drawn from the OT (Ps. 79:6; Jer. 10:25)."

[6] "Brother" was also used in pagan cults and clubs.

[7] Cf. Exod 32:12,15; Num 14:15-16; Deut 9:25-29; 1 Kings 20:28, etc; on its development in intertestamental Jewish writings see W.C. van Unnik, "Die Rücksicht auf die Reaktion der Nicht-Christen als Motiv in der altchristlichen Paränese". In *Judentum, Urchristentum, Kirche: Festschrift für Joachim Jeremias*. Edited by W. Eltester BZNW 26. Berlin: Töpelmann, 1964. pp. 221-34. Rom 2:24, which contains a kindred thought, quotes Isa 52:5 (cf. Ezek 36:20) in support.

[8] Cf. Wanamaker, *1 and 2 Thessalonians*, p. 150: "Paul understood God to be the holy God of the OT who was set apart from every form of sin and impurity and demanded similar holiness from the [ie. His] people."

[9] See Wanamaker, *1 and 2 Thessalonians*, p. 160.

[10] Whether 4:6 refers to business dealings or is a euphemism for sexual misconduct does not detract from the point we are making. See the commentators.

[11] Reinmuth, *Geist und Gesetz: Studien zu Voraussetzungen und Inhalt der paulinischen Paränese*. TA XLIV (Berlin: Evangelische Verlagsanstalt, 1985). He cites a wide range of texts including Ps-Phoc, T. 12. Patr., Sib. Or., Men-Phil, 1 Enoch, Syr-Men, Ps-Herac, CD; eg., T. Jud. 18:2: "Guard yourselves therefore, my children, against sexual immorality and love of money."

instruction that ultimately finds its roots in Leviticus 19:18, "you shall love your neighbour as yourself" (cf. Rom 13:9; Gal 5:14).

II. Context

In the introductory essay we noted that included in this question are both institutions and conditions, which Paul's instructions presuppose, and Græco-Roman ethics, with which we may compare Paul's instructions. We shall sketch the latter for 1 Thessalonians 4:1-12, although the former would also be a profitable avenue of research (eg. one could look at gentile attitudes to labour, which typically were not positive, in relation to 4:11-12).

As you might expect, when placed in the context of first century moral exhortation, certain aspects of Paul's instructions appear more distinctive than others. Wayne A. Meeks describes the reminder in 4:2 of instruction previously given (cf. "as you know" in 1;5 2:2,5,11; 3:4) and the fact that Paul's exhortations in ch. 4 follow reference in the first part of the letter to the friendly relations between writers and recipients to be "typical of pagan exhortation."[12] It is common in paraenetic letters of Paul's day to assume the readers are living as they should and to encourage them to make further progress, which is what we have in 4:1,9-10.[13] Furthermore, even some of the moral directions of the passage are, according to Meeks, "commonplaces in philosophical speeches and letters of the time."[14] These include "a quiet life," "minding one's own business," monogamy, sexual purity and special affection towards brothers. Indeed, the stress on the solidarity of the community of Christians (4:9-10) was something with which even a Plutarch would have identified, since he wrote a treatise "On the love of brothers." These same words are a heading for 1 Thessalonians 4:9-12 in some Bibles.[15]

All this is not to say that Paul's instructions were unremarkable. The apostle used conventions, but not without his own special twist and his own specific purpose. The friendly relations of the opening chapters focus not on shared experiences

---

[12] Meeks, *The Moral World of the First Christians* (Philadelphia: The Westminster Press, 1986), p. 126.

[13] See Stanley K. Stowers, *Letter Writing in Greco-Roman Antiquity* (Philadelphia: Westminster, 1986), p. 103.

[14] Meeks, *Moral World*, p. 127.

[15] Meeks, *Moral World*, p. 129.

between individuals but on the Thessalonians' conversion (1:9-10) and involve the whole community. Plutarch's advice concerned blood relatives whereas the family Paul had in mind had spiritual ties. Above all, Paul's ethics are distinctly more theocentric than Græco-Roman ethics. The notion of pleasing God in 4:1, which in the light of 1:9 is equivalent to serving God as a slave pleases a master, was, according to Meeks, "a familiar concept in the religions of the ancient Near East and in the Bible, but rare in Greek or Roman religious sentiment."[16] As Bruce C. Johanson notes: "that which particularly distinguished even the more elevated Hellenistic philosophical thought on ethical standards from Jewish and Christian thought was that Jews and Christians began with God."[17] We see this in our passage in the references to God's authority (4:3,8) and calling (4:7) and in the threat of judgement from God (4:6b). In A.J. Malherbe's words, "Paul is concerned with the sanctified rather than the rational life."[18]

III. Social Dimension

In commenting on 1 Thessalonians 4:1-12 Wanamaker states:

> The social function of this material is twofold: it helps to define the boundaries of the community (that is, what it means to be a Christian) over against the dominant pagan society, while at the same time it helps to develop what Meeks (*First Urban Christians*, 100) describes as "internal cohesion" within the community.[19]

Several terms and elements in the passage reveal its social dimension.

Paul's "brother" language signals the kind of "deep resocialization"[20] that was typical of his missionary strategy. In portraying the community as a family those members with no previous contact became aware of how to behave towards one another and cohesion within an otherwise diverse community became an important goal. The exhortation in verse 6, however it is

---

16 Meeks, *Moral World*, p. 128.

17 Johanson, *To All the Brethren; A Text-Linguistic and Rhetorical Approach to 1 Thessalonians* (Stockholm: Almqvist & Wiksell, 1987), p. 114.

18 Malherbe, "Exhortation in First Thessalonians," *NovTest* 25 (1983): 150-51.

19 Wanamaker, *1 and 2 Thessalonians*, p. 147.

20 Meeks, *Moral World*, p. 129.

understood (fraud in business or adultery), was especially important to protect this sense of kinship in the community. The sort of behaviour prohibited there would seriously disrupt harmony within any group. The instructions of 4:11-12 suggest that Paul was aware of the danger that some might take advantage of the generosity of the new community. As well as advocating intimacy and sharing, Paul is concerned that familial love not be exploited. Paul's churches were in no way to be self-absorbed. This can be seen in 4:10 where he commends their concern for believers in the whole of Macedonia. Such a linking together of the various churches for mutual support was a cardinal feature of his work as a missionary and, to use the modern term, church planter (cf. 1 Cor 16:1,19; 2 Cor 1:1; Gal 1:2).

The language of holiness and the call to abstain from sexual immorality as an expression of God's will constituted in practice a call to break with the readers' pagan past. As such it operated as a group boundary, defining what it meant to belong to the newly formed group. This is made explicit in the reference to the negative model of "the gentiles who do not know God." Meeks has noted that "similar language had helped Jews of Diaspora synagogues maintain their sense of uniqueness in a pagan world."[21]

Finally, Paul hoped in 4:12 that the church would gain the respect of outsiders, perhaps, we could conjecture, in part to soften the blow of any wave of persecution that might arise in the future.

With the aid of models and insights from the social sciences many of these observations could be taken further. It suffices to say at this stage that the social dimension of Paul's ethics ought not to be ignored. As Malherbe has correctly observed: "Rather than simply organize a church [in Thessalonica], Paul founded, shaped and nurtured a community."[22]

IV. Shape

Eduard Lohse believes that in 1 Thessalonians 4:-112 "we find a collection of traditional material" which was part of "the common

---

[21] Meeks, *Moral World*, p. 128. Cf. Carras, p. 314: "the application of Jewish ethics to Gentile converts served a social function. It helped to distinguish these converts from the morals of their non-Christian contemporaries in a similar way that Jewish ethics marked out Jews from pagans."

[22] Malherbe, *Paul and the Thessalonians* (Philadelphia: Fortress Press, 1987), p. 1.

stock of early Christian tradition."[23] Wolfgang Schrage agrees. He claims that Paul "incorporates [material] in the parenetic chapters of his epistles" that is "pre-Pauline" (1 Thess 4:1ff; Rom 12:12ff; Gal 5:16ff are cited as prime examples). Schrage points out that "a comparison of Rom. 12:10ff with 1 Pet. 3:8ff, for example, shows clearly that both drew on a common tradition."[24] The essays by Seeberg and Hartman (chs. 7 and 8) supply more evidence for the assertion that in giving moral instruction Paul adopted and applied both Biblical/Jewish and early Christian moral teaching. In the specific case of 1 Thessalonians 4:1-12 it is difficult to go beyond this general point. We do not find here catalogues or a code, nor any trace of or pointer to Seeberg's early catechism.

V. Logic

1 Thessalonians 4:1-12 is not one of the key passages of Paul's ethics for investigating the interrelation of the indicative and the imperative. It does not display the baffling yet compelling logic of 1 Corinthians 5:7, Galatians 5:1 or 5:25. Neither does it unpack with the same clear-cut gift-demand structure as does Romans 6. Perceiving the mix of indicative and imperative here is not as straightforward as recognising the mood of the verbs, as in 1 Corinthians 6:12-20. In fact 1 Thessalonians 4:1-12 is not even mentioned in Bultmann's or Parson's essays on the logic of Paul's ethics in section V of this book. However, if the passage can truly claim to be a representative sample one would expect the so-called heart of Paul's ethics to be evident.

It is true that we do not find the logic of 'become what you already are' in our passage. Nonetheless, the softer and less specific version of the same notion, identity informs and motivates behaviour, is a basic assumption. As Wanamaker states, Paul offers the Thessalonians a powerful argument for his injunction to sexual holiness "by linking the morality he had taught them to their very identity as Christians."[25] Verse 5 makes this clear. By contrasting the conduct he expects from the Thessalonians "with the [behaviour of the] heathen who do not know God," Paul stresses the separation of

---

23 Lohse, *Theological Ethics of the New Testament* (Minneapolis: Fortress Press, ET, 1988), p. 146.

24 Schrage, *The Ethics of the New Testament* (Edinburgh: T. & T. Clark, ET, 1988), p. 132.

25 Wanamaker, *1 and 2 Thessalonians*, p. 150.

Christians from their pagan neighbours. Since Paul also differentiates the new community from the Jews (cf. 2:14-16), they must therefore be a new group of people. Who are they? They are those who have come to know God (4:5; to reverse the description of the gentiles), those who have been called by God to salvation, the purpose of which is sanctification (4:7). Not only so but they are, Paul informs them, people whose manner of life pleases God (4:1) and who, having been taught by God, love all of God's people throughout Macedonia (4:9-10). All of this information, which concerns their status as Christian believers, is strictly speaking unnecessary for the delivery of the moral exhortations. It is not, however, empty flattery or unrelated and unnecessary window dressing. In Paul's case, these indicatives, to use the traditional terminology, which are developed in other parts of the letter (eg. ch. 1), are the positive warrant for all of the moral imperatives in 4:1-12.

VI. Foundations

Paul exhorts the Thessalonian Christians to God-pleasing conduct, sexual holiness, brotherly love and the quiet life. To understand the resources he draws on in presenting these instructions we shall follow Schnabel's lead (ch. 12; see esp. section 2, systematic concentration, for a summary) and discuss briefly motivations, norms and criteria.

What is to motivate obedience to Paul's moral admonitions? All five motivations listed by Schnabel are in fact evident in our short passage. The christological motivation appears in verse one: the Thessalonians are exhorted "in the Lord Jesus" (4:1), which means that Paul's commands carry the authority of the Lord.[26] The thought that the Thessalonians know God (4:5), having been called by God to salvation (4:7), reveals the salvation-historical motivation. The enabling power of the Holy Spirit (4:8) sets forth the pneumatological motivation. The ecclesiological motivation is present in 4:9-10, where Paul's paraenesis is related to the wider fellowship of believers. Finally, in alluding to coming judgement we have in 4:6 the

---

26 The phrase "through the Lord Jesus" in v. 2 can be understood in several ways. Marshall, *1 and 2 Thessalonians*, p. 106, however, is right when he insists that: "however we take the phrase the point is clearly that the commands [Paul gives] are to be thought of as the commands of Jesus to his church and Paul is merely his agent in passing them on to his readers."

eschatological motivation. It is typical of Paul to bolster his commands with many and varied motivations to obedience.

How has Paul arrived at the ethical admonitions? What binding norms are assumed by his instructions? Unfortunately there are only a few hints with regard to the answers to these questions in our passage. In discussing the origin of Paul's instruction (Section I) we discovered a dependence upon Biblical and Jewish sources, which would point, to recall Schnabel's words, to "the continuing validity of the Hebrew Bible for Christian ethics." The influence of the words of Jesus cannot be ruled out, say for instance with respect to brotherly love, but it is not explicit (as such influence is, for example, in 4:15). What is clear is the fact that the injunctions of the apostle himself are normative. This is implied throughout the passage (Paul is the one who instructs, beseeches, urges, gives instuctions, tells, and warns) and it is given explicit indication in verse eight ("whoever disregards this [command], disregards not man but God"; cf. 2:13). The consensus between Christian and non-Christian ethics, which Schnabel calls "the orders of creation," is apparent in the instructions of 4:11-12 regarding work and financial independence. Such counsel is simply wise behaviour which will "command the respect of outsiders."

By what criteria is the realisation of the behaviour Paul enjoins to be guided in everyday life? Out of Schnabel's list of six items, three may be noted as relevant here: God's will is realised in concrete behaviour with the help of the Holy Spirit, with an eye to love and to the missionary effectiveness of the church. In context, the Holy Spirit leads the believer to holiness and not to uncleanness (4:7-8), love teaches the believer not to wrong one's brother (4:6,9-10) and the concern for the reputation of the church before outsiders forbids irresponsible behaviour with respect to work (4:11-12).

VII. Relevance

There are several indications that Paul's instructions in 4:1-12 have general and abiding validity. The two most striking are the appeal to "the will of God" (4:3) and the claim that the real author of the instructions is God himself (4:8). When confronted by moral decisions Paul does not abandon believers to their intuitions or emotions. There is no evidence here that he advocates a substantially open situation-ethics. It is true that there are points in Paul's letters where he leaves matters to the conscience of the individual. Sexual immorality and the obligation to love do not, however, fall into the category of such neutral matters.

To some extent answering the six questions we have already covered is prerequisite to a full and informed answer to this the most important question, that of relevance. Having ascertained the origin, context, social dimension, shape, logic and foundations of Paul's instructions we are in a position to affirm, appreciate and appropriate their relevance. Nothing emerged in our previous discussions to limit the instructions to a particular situation, group or time. Furthermore, the teaching was found to be built upon the revelation of the Jewish Scriptures, the Old Testament, and inextricably linked to Christian identity (to recall our answers to the questions of origin and logic respectively). Paul calls us, no less than he did the Thessalonians, to God-pleasing conduct, which consists in sexual holiness, familial love and the quiet life.

Suggestions for Further Study

1. Take a portion of Paul's practical teaching (eg. 1 Cor 8-10; Rom 12-15) and assess to what extent it derives from the Scriptures and Jewish sources. Respond to the comments of Harnack and Holtz (chs. 1 and 2) on the same passage.

2. What is Paul's attitude to the Law of Moses? In what sense does it have continuing validity for him? Be sure to consider both what he says about it (both "negative" [Rom 4:15; 5:20; 7:5,8-11,13; 10:4; 2 Cor 3:6; Gal 3:23-25; etc] and "positive" comments [1 Cor 4:6; 9:10; 10:6,11; 14:34; Rom 7:12; etc]) and what he does with it.

3. Trace the development and use of an Old Testament moral theme (eg., greed, theft, slander) or passage (eg., the Decalogue or a part thereof; Lev 18-20) through the intertestamental Jewish literature and in Paul's letters.

4. Make a comparison of some aspect of Paul's moral teaching (eg., sexual immorality, work, leisure) with the moral philosophy of his day.

5. Study Paul's teaching on slavery not against the background of nineteenth century slavery in the western world, but with relevant first century Græco-Roman social conditions in mind.

6. To what extent do distinctions of social class among early Christians help explain the moral problems that arose in the churches Paul addressed?

7. Does sociological analysis of Pauline churches and moral teaching play down theological factors?

8. How do the practical portions of Romans, Ephesians or Galatians relate to the overall argument and purpose of the letter which they bring to a close?

9. How do Paul's lists of virtues and vices relate to the argument of the letters in which they appear? Are the items in the lists conditioned by the circumstances of the letter?

10. Make a study of Paul's exhortations on a particular issue (eg. sexual immorality, boasting, idolatry) and seek to discover their foundations (motivations, norms and criteria), that is, the resources Paul used to arrive at them.

11. "All you need is love": Is this statement a fair summary of Paul's ethical teaching?

12. What matters does Paul leave to the conscience of the individual?

13. To what extent do specific situations in the the churches give rise to Paul's moral admonitions? Give examples of instructions which are clearly situation-related and those which have a more prophylactic function. What evidence is there that Paul addresses concrete situations from a point of view which is above the situation?

14. What role does the renewal of the mind (Rom 12:2) play in Paul's attempts to transform the behaviour of the Christian? Does the mind matter?

15. What are the central themes of Paul's paraenesis?

16. Study a passage in Paul's ethics from all seven angles (as we did in the concluding essay with 1 Thess 4:1-12).

Index of Pauline References

Index of Modern Authors